AF692361

INDIA'S INDUSTRIAL POLICY
A REASSESSMENT

INDIA'S INDUSTRIAL POLICY A REASSESSMENT

Growth, Employment, and Gender Justice in Tamil Nadu

PADMINI SWAMINATHAN

PRIMUS BOOKS

50 years

mids Madras Institute of Development Studies

PRIMUS BOOKS
An imprint of Ratna Sagar P. Ltd.
Virat Bhavan
Mukherjee Nagar Commercial Complex
Delhi 110 009

Offices at
CHENNAI LUCKNOW
AGRA AHMEDABAD BENGALURU BHOPAL COIMBATORE
DEHRADUN GUWAHATI HYDERABAD JAIPUR JALANDHAR
KANPUR KOCHI KOLKATA MUMBAI
PATNA RANCHI VARANASI

© *Madras Institute of Development Studies 2026*

All rights reserved. No part of this publication may be reproduced, stored in a retrieval system or transmitted, in any form or by any means, without the prior permission in writing from Primus Books, or as expressly permitted by law, by licence, or under terms agreed with the appropriate reproduction rights organization. Enquiries concerning reproduction outside the scope of the above should be sent to Primus Books at the address above.

First published 2026

ISBN: 978-93-7033-649-0 (hardback)
ISBN: 978-93-7033-148-8 (POD)

Published by Primus Books

Lasertypeset by AG Infographics
aginfographic@gmail.com

This book is meant for educational and learning purposes. The author(s) of the book has/have taken all reasonable care to ensure that the contents of the book do not violate any existing copyright or other intellectual property rights of any person in any manner whatsoever. In the event the author(s) has/have been unable to track any source and if any copyright has been inadvertently infringed, please notify the publisher in writing for corrective action.

Contents

Tables

Acknowledgements

It seemed like a tall order when a former colleague and close friend, Professor M. Vijayabaskar, called me over phone and persuaded me to consider putting together my published papers on 'Industry' towards MIDS' Golden Jubilee. This was immediately followed by a formal letter from another long-time colleague, Professor A.R. Venkatachalapathy, general editor-in-charge of MIDS publications, detailing the outline for the book but leaving it to me to decide how I wanted to structure and order my papers, thematically or chronologically. My acceptance to work on the book led the then officiating Director of MIDS, Professor L. Venkatachalam to formalize the proposal and sign the agreement with the publisher, Primus Books. I am extremely grateful to all three of them for getting in touch with me long after I had retired from MIDS. The fact that this team considered my papers still worthy of being brought together, goaded me to think deeply and critically examine my own writings for their relevance for the present generation of scholars. The introductory chapter, that has ordered the papers thematically, is an outcome of this exercise. Whether I have succeeded in this endeavour to contextualize the papers to highlight their continuing relevance, only time will tell.

The book would not have seen the light of day but for the meticulous work carried out behind the scenes by the Publications Department of MIDS. Be it making available copies of papers which I could not locate, keying-in papers afresh, proofreading, liaising with publishers, and/or getting permission from journal editors (where some of these papers had been published earlier), M.R. Prasanna (Publication Officer) and A. Arivazhagan (Publication Assistant) provided such efficient service that at no point did I feel any deficiency in the logistical support that I needed to work on the book. Prasanna, as the contact person between the publisher, MIDS and me, was ever ready to receive calls and clarify doubts, making the whole experience a smooth one.

I am equally grateful to Dr Prasun Chatterjee, Deputy Head of Primus Books, for agreeing to bring out this publication—a decision that most commissioning heads would not take unless they are sure of its relevance and worth. Ms Jyotika Mansata, Associate Editor at Primus Books, oversaw the thankless editorial tasks. MIDS and I remain indebted to Primus Books.

My sincere thanks to Professor M. Suresh Babu, who took over as Director of MIDS, from the officiating Director, Professor Venkatachalam, for the seamless manner in which the processes involved in getting this publication out has been facilitated. This journey has been both an honour and a humbling experience.

PADMINI SWAMINATHAN

Introduction

The Context

In no other realm of public affairs were the differences between British and Indian perspectives as wide, indeed as fundamentally irreconcilable, as in economic philosophy and financial and industrial policy. To begin with, the British allowed mercantilism to be their guide; after 1813, free trade became the standard viewpoint. Mercantilism protected British manufacturing and shipping from Indian competition and this principally served British interests. After British cotton manufacturing became the most efficient in the world, protective policies were no longer necessary and, through free trade, inflicted a devastating influence on Indian manufacturing. By way of recompense, later, the British sought to improve the economy of India through programmes of capital investment, agricultural technology, and public works but these were never notably successful.[1]

The justification for the misappropriation of India's meagre revenue resources were summed up tersely by a War Office memorandum that categorically stated: 'India is a dependency of the British Crown...the principles of fair dealings enunciated by Lord Kitchner might be applicable to two independent states in alliance with each other; they are inapplicable to a dependency

[1] P. Swaminathan, *Evolution of Industrial Policy in the Madras Presidency: 1900–1947*, Working Paper no. 105, Chennai: Madras Institute of Development Studies, 1991, p. 1.

inhabited by alien races, our hold over which is not based on the general goodwill of those disunited races'.[2] Curzon admitted before the Lords 'that Indian fiscal policy is settled and decided not at all in Calcutta but in Manchester; not in Indian interest but English.'[3]

The beginning of the twentieth century saw the rise of a nation-wide agitation for economic self-sufficiency—the Swadeshi Movement—with renewed and vociferous demands for fiscal reform, especially tariff protection for indigenous industries and discriminating intervention in favour of Indian industries.

In the Madras Presidency, however, the closing stages of the nineteenth century and the dawn of the twentieth century saw vigorous attempts at stimulating industrial activity in the province thanks to the ambitious, pioneering, and never-say-die personality of Alfred Chatterton, an engineer by profession who was appointed Superintendent of the School of Arts in Madras in 1897. It was proposed that he should devote himself to the restoration, organization, and development of indigenous trades and industries, especially metal works, which appeared most likely to prove successful. It was also decided that he would reorganize existing industrial schools and establish new ones, thereby combining industrial development and technical education for upgrading labour skills and improving quality of products to make the latter exportable.

In 1900, the Secretary of State had no objection to the working of pioneer industries by the government on a commercial scale provided that as soon as their success was assured, they were handed over to private enterprise. Thus began a more direct intervention by the government

[2] Ibid., pp. 1–2.
[3] Ibid., p. 2.

in certain spheres of industrial activity in the province without the aid of any formally laid-out plan specifying physical and/or financial targets.

The attempt in this book is to bring together writings written over a considerable period that begin by tracing the rudimentary evolution of an industrial policy in erstwhile Madras Presidency followed by papers that examine specific aspects of the growth and development of industry in Tamil Nadu in the post-Independence period. Besides, aspects germane and integral to achieve growth and development, namely, human resource development in terms of education and skill development, including the role that gender has played in such development, are also covered. We elaborate below on the rationale and relevance of our attempt to reflect on past writings to highlight the significance of an industrial policy from a political economy perspective for meaningful growth and development apart from introducing readers to the specific papers covered.

Themes Covered in the Book

The Beginnings of an Industry Policy in Colonial Tamil Nadu: Provincial vs Imperial

In 'State Intervention in Industry: A Case Study of the Madras Presidency', published in the *Indian Economic and Social History Review* in 1992, we discussed the attempts made by the provincial government of the Madras Presidency to foster some form of economic development through a demonstration of the commercial success of certain lines of business pioneered under state patronage, and through its concern for, and insistence on, developing industrial education in the state. This initiative on the part of the provincial government brought it into sharp conflict with the European mercantile community of the country in general and of the province in particular, who perceived this initiative as a threat to their own interests. Additionally, this case study highlights the fact that when a provincial government attempted to depart from the accepted imperial norm of a passive role of 'night watchman',[4] howsoever small the effort and miniscule the impact, the attempt was soon aborted and the provincial government reprimanded for daring to address the imperial authority to reconsider its decision.

In 'Prison as Factory: A Study of Jail Manufactures in the Madras Presidency,' published in *Studies in History* in 1995, we highlighted an aspect of colonial state intervention that evoked considerable opposition among commercial groups in the Madras Presidency and elsewhere; this was related to the establishment of industries in jails, utilizing jail labour. The issue was seen as the state competing with private enterprise; and, with the introduction of power machinery in some jails, the cry was raised that the state was no longer competing against private enterprise with convict labour, but with 'means of production which greatly enhanced the output' of the jails.[5] Manufacturing was considered to be the exclusive preserve of private enterprise; it was ostensibly sought to be premised on the principle of *laissez-faire* but in fact was rooted in imperial self-interest.

While there was acceptance later, following protests from locals, of the need for the state to intervene positively to promote industrialization, the colonial state was reluctant to translate intentions into fruitful action even when industry was declared a provincial subject. This was discernible in the inadequate fiscal/financial autonomy provided to the provinces. What also comes out clearly from a reading of the colonial documents is

[4] Ibid., p. 480.
[5] Ibid., p. 77.

the inability of the state then (as of now) to involve the private sector/indigenous entrepreneurs in the process of planning for industrial development even after realizing that the successful implementation of any plan would require the active collaboration of the private sector, an argument forcefully enunciated thus by Danik Rodrik:[6]

> (T)he task of industrial policy is as much about eliciting information from the private sector on significant externalities and their remedies as it is about implementing appropriate policies. The right model for industrial policy is not that of an autonomous [government] applying Pigovian taxes or subsidies but of strategic collaboration between the private sector and the government with the aim of uncovering where the most significant obstacles to restructuring lie and what type of interventions are most likely to remove them.[7]

While the colonial government's agenda was never about making India an economic power house, the papers discussing the attempts at economic development through industrialization in post-Independence India, with Tamil Nadu as case, illustrate in no uncertain terms the abject lack of coherence in the different components that were put together as constituting an industrial policy.

Post-Independence Attempts at Industrialization: Some Illustrations

In a paper titled 'The (Un)Making of a (Non) Competitive Economy', published in the journal *Productivity* in 1993, we argued that ideology rather than theory

[6] Dani Rodrik, 'Industrial Policy for the Twenty-First Century', Draft Working Paper prepared for UNIDO, September 2004, see https://drodrik.scholar.harvard.edu/files/dani-rodrik/files/industrial-policy-twenty-first-century.pdf, accessed 30 December 2024.

[7] Ibid., p. 3.

informed (and continues to inform) much of government intervention in industrialization in late industrializing countries, including India. The sub-optimal performance of the Indian industrial sector, when say, compared to South Korea or Taiwan, was attributed to inefficient governments and poor governance mechanisms that actively promoted rent seeking, thereby concluding that government failures were always worse than market failures, even when same or similar sets of policies had successfully catapulted the economies of South Korea and Taiwan to the realm of industrially advanced nations.

Further, in the same paper we have discussed how the theme of 'state capacity' as an important factor in policy choice and outcomes has been singled out by several economists[8] who have studied late industrializing economies attempting to 'catch up' with advanced industrial economies. India and Brazil have been contrasted with the East Asian Tigers to illustrate that unlike the former, the East Asian states not only had higher levels of administrative capacity but also exercised greater selectivity in the tasks that they undertook. More important, the combination of a 'carrot and stick' policy enabled the East Asian economies to weed out free-riding entrepreneurs during their import substitution period in particular, a policy tool that the Indian state had instituted but failed to secure accountability in its implementation.

Our study of Tamil Nadu's TVS business group published in the *Economic and Political Weekly* in 1988, demonstrates how the then technology policy to modernize the country's manufacturing capability and enhance the exportability of products produced failed the

[8] Peter Evans, 'The State as Problem and Solution: Embedded Autonomy and Structural Change', in *The Politics of Economic Adjustment*, ed. Stephen Haggard and Robert R. Kaufman, New Jersey: Princeton University Press, 1992.

economy but benefited industrialists. While continuous and systematic import of technology enabled the group to dominate the market for automotive ancillaries and components, vertical integration characterizing the organization of the group helped to further perpetuate this dominance. The liberalization of licensing policy since the late 1980s (and fast tracked in the 1990s) enabled the group to expand its hold over the market. Further, the liberal imports of technology substituted for local R&D confirming what several macro studies[9] on technology have pointed out, namely that the import of technology in India has been a substitute rather than an input to Indian R&D, and the failure to adapt, innovate, and diffuse already imported technology has resulted in high cost of production and drainage of resources; worse, assimilation of technology being pseudo in character, technological dependence was, and, is real.

A joint paper[10] on the knitwear cluster of Tiruppur in Tamil Nadu highlights an important aspect of the broader theme of 'Forms of Business Organization', namely 'industrial clusters', that has till today received very little policy attention. Examining in detail how from humble beginnings, Tiruppur became a visible presence in the international knitwear market, the study reveals the significance of social embeddedness of the

[9] K.K. Subrahmanian, 'Collaboration Agreements and their Impact on Assimilation and Diffusion of Know-how and Outgo of Resources', in *Science and Technology Policy in the 1980s and Beyond*, ed. M. Gibbons, P. Gummett, and B Udgonkar, UK: Longman, 1984, pp. 246–69; Mohanan Pillai, 'Technology Transfer, Adaptation and Assimilation', *The Economic and Political Weekly*, vol. XIV, no. 47, 24 November 1979, pp. 121–6.

[10] P. Swaminathan and J. Jeyaranjan, 'The Knitwear Cluster at Tiruppur: An Indian Industrial District in the Making?', in *Economy and Organization: Indian Institutions under the Neo-Liberal Regime*, ed. Amiya Kumar Bagchi, New Delhi: Sage, 1999, pp. 94–121.

community that defines its internal structure and strength and which has enabled it to prosper despite poor physical and financial infrastructure and with very low levels of support from public authorities. Given that industrial clusters specializing in different products are strewn around the country, the insights from this paper have important lessons for our attempts to craft an industrial policy that addresses, among other things, the present government's pet theme—*atmanirbhar*—as well as the government's attempts to rejuvenate the Micro, Small, and Medium Enterprises (MSME) sectors.

The 2000s have seen a proliferation of studies on clusters across the globe and in India as well. Among the more recent is a set of studies published in a book[11] that discusses the theme of industrialization for employment and growth in India based on small firm clusters. Among the important takeaways from the studies, relevant for our argument, and echoing some of the themes already covered in our papers mentioned above, include the following important point emphasized by the editor in his introduction:

> The well-performing clusters are those that have benefited from considerable state support, a close working relationship between entrepreneurs, local industry associations, and the state- and district-level promotional agencies... To reindustrialize for employment generation, and to meet the national goals of Make in India, it is imperative to reimagine the industrial policy in its nitty-gritty. It has to be national in scope and, local, context-specific in its implementation,

[11] R. Nagaraj, Introduction to *Industrialization for Employment and Growth in India: Lessons from Small Firm Clusters and Beyond*, ed. R. Nagaraj, New Delhi: Cambridge University Press, 2021, pp. 1–23.

and flexible and agile. Local public goods for facilitating production and their movement to highways, railheads or ports need to get special attention.[12]

While the joint paper on Tiruppur mentioned above concentrated mainly on capturing the dynamics of production organization within Tiruppur, there was no engagement whatsoever with 'environmental' issues that had begun to surface consequent to indiscriminate emphasis on increasing output and foreign exchange earnings through exports. Between 2005 and 2012, as a member of the committee appointed by the High Court of Madras to examine and suggest measures to resolve the pollution of the Noyyal River (flowing through Tiruppur) caused by indiscriminate discharge of effluents largely by the dyeing and bleaching units in the town, I had occasion to study the nature of the environmental issues that had become increasingly visible. A paper titled 'Regulating Industrialization Through Public Action and Legal Intervention: Interpreting an Ongoing Experiment in Tamil Nadu,' published in 2014 discusses in detail the efforts made to address the problem of industrial pollution as also the key challenges that continue to plague the region.

An important learning that no industrial policy as yet has been able to tackle is the reluctance of end-users of products (in this case knitwear garments), based largely in the global North, to share the costs of such industrialization. Going back to the different ways in which buyers and consumers (located largely in the Global North) have eschewed any responsibility for why environmental standards are what they are in producer countries (even while demanding adherence to ethical standards of production), we admit that our entire effort

[12] Ibid., pp. 19–20.

as a committee, to contain the pollution problem caused by the expanding garment cluster in Tiruppur, at no point addressed the buyers in particular as a constituency mainly responsible for the environmental damage by their acts of omission or commission. While attempts were made (howsoever inadequate) to estimate the different kinds of local losses, the remedial measures suggested by the committee neither mentioned the need to negotiate higher value realization from global brands that reflected the cost of production, nor did it include ways and means by which the Indian state could have been compelled to highlight, at various international fora, the link between Tiruppur-like situations and unsustainable consumption patterns emanating largely from the Global North, resulting in unsustainable and environmentally damaging patterns of global value chain production in supplier countries located largely in the Global South.

Subsequently, in a book entitled *Reverse Subsidies in Global Monopsony Capitalism: Gender, Labour and Environmental Injustice in Garment Value Chains*,[13] the attempt was precisely to bring this aspect to the fore, namely, one that would

> involve a redistribution of value along the chain… How we can move forward to establish a market economy system in which prices would cover the costs of production of labour power and environmental services is a question of political economy, a matter of analysing how the required coalition of forces to bring about such a change can be established'.[14]

[13] Dev Nathan et al., *Reverse Subsidies in Global Monopsony Capitalism: Gender, Labour, and Environmental Injustice in Garment Value Chains*, New Delhi: Cambridge University Press, 2022.

[14] Ibid., p. 236.

Industrial Growth, Employment and Education: The Missing Link

The theme of the linkage between economic development (in our case through industrialization) and human development is captured in the papers that discuss the interface (or the lack of it) between education and employment, and in the gendering of such development. We explicate below the theme in some detail based on the papers included in this book.

In 'Technical Education and Industrial Development in the Madras Presidency: Illusions of a Policy in the Making', published in the *Economic and Political Weekly* in 1992, we have traced historically the rudimentary efforts that were made to impart some sort of 'technical' education with a special focus on the classes of people involved in occupations (such as aluminium, leather, weaving) that were hitherto being conducted in a 'primitive' manner for want of access to state-of-the-art technology as well as lack of knowledge and opportunities that improved quality of products could fetch at the national and global markets. During the colonial period there was much discussion about: (i) what should be the interface between industrial expansion and concomitant investment in technical education; (ii) whether technical education should be under control of the industries department or under the department of education; (iii) how to make 'technical' education 'more practical' and/or how much of 'practical education' was to be introduced into 'technical' instruction, and (iv) how deep and how far should the state involve itself in such questions.

Post-independent India is characterized by a growing disjuncture between employment and education. In the paper on 'Making Sense of Vocational Educational

Policies: A Comparative Assessment', published in the *Indian Journal of Labour Economics* in 2005, we not only demonstrate how successive governments in independent India have come nowhere close to matching the alacrity with which the colonial government in the Madras Presidency attempted to address the issue, but also contrast the Indian industrial performance with that of the High-Performing Asian Economies (HPAEs), to highlight the nature and intensity of investment that these HPAEs have made for developing core competencies among their workers, post their school education. While each HPAE has followed a route suitable to it, the bottom line is the recognition that, howsoever difficult, states need to constantly engage with the challenge of matching education with employment and more important, of maintaining the relevance of this match. Economies such as India, even now faced with growing imbalance between the output of the school system and the absorptive capacity of their labour markets for such types of educated personnel, are still engaged in attempting to reform the contents of education without questioning their development strategies or development goals.

In a subsequent paper on the same theme, 'Education and Skill Development in the Context of Declining Rate of Formal Employment Generation: Issues for Discussion', published in the *Indian Journal of Labour Economics* in 2008, we recapitulate and carry forward the theme of the disjuncture between education and employment but with a focus on the sub-optimal performance of bodies such as the All-India Council for Technical Education (AICTE) that were created and are in charge of the status of technical education in the country, including monitoring the performance of institutions that come under its purview. This same paper includes a discussion of a

World Bank study that has, among other things, looked at the quality of teaching and relevance of the curriculum taught in vocational institutes. An important observation made by the World Bank which is of considerable significance to our theme of a coherent and relevant industrial policy is the need to involve employers at every stage of the process—be it standard setting, curriculum design, and performance evaluation of students within a framework agreed upon by government as facilitator and industry as implementer. Equally significant is the stipulation made in the AICTE Act that it shall be the duty of the AICTE to promote schemes for technical education of women, the handicapped, and weaker sections of society. The committee that reviewed the functioning of the AICTE was constrained to observe that no special schemes had been put in place by the AICTE either for women students or for the handicapped. The review committee, for its part, merely suggested that disaggregated data be collected in each discipline, that studies to ascertain problems faced by women students, the handicapped and the marginalized be conducted and that women students be provided with accommodation in all institutions.

Our paper on 'Patriarchy and Class: An Approach to a Study of Women's Education in the Madras Presidency' examines a range of issues surrounding the efforts to impart formal education to girls. While some of the more contentious issues relating to, for example, access to education for all sections of the population, provision of basic educational infrastructure, recruitment of more women teachers and the like stand resolved to a large extent, several others continue to remain intractable even today, militating against women's struggle towards equality. To highlight a couple of these unresolved issues:

two different sets of exercises were conducted by the present author using Census data of 1991 and 2001 with a specific focus on capturing the direction of the movement of education and work participation rates for the female gender across location and social group.[15] In the first exercise, using Census data 1991, an analysis was conducted to gauge how the female population had fared against their male counterparts in an otherwise 'socially and economically developed' state such as Tamil Nadu. The juxtaposing of employment and education data brought forth interesting but disturbing patterns. While at one level the disparity among genders (females per 1000 males) increased significantly when disparity was computed for different levels of literacy, what data also corroborated was the fact that districts with high levels of adolescent girls in employment were also the ones where significant proportions of adolescent girls were 'not attending schools'. These trends signify poor levels of formal education among the female workforce in Tamil Nadu. In addition, data also revealed that the proportion of women workforce returned as illiterate was not only significant when compared to men, but that, unlike in the case of men workers, women not in employment (as per Census definition) were more educated than those in employment.

In 2001, using data from the Census and from that provided by the Central Statistical Organization we tried to comprehend 'change' during the 1990s both

[15] Padmini Swaminathan, 'Literacy and Levels of Formal Education of the Indian Population: A National Report Card', Zakir Husain Second Memorial Lecture, National Council of Educational Research and Training, New Delhi, January 2009; Padmini Swaminathan, 'Outside the Realm of Protective Labour Legislation: Saga of Unpaid Labour in India', *Economic and Political Weekly*, vol. XLIV, no. 44, 31 October 2009, pp. 80–7.

at the all-India and Tamil Nadu levels. The analysis of the literacy levels of the 'worker' population for 2001 revealed a disturbing contrast between male and female workers. While almost 71 per cent of the *male workers* were literate (in contrast to 63 per cent literacy among males in the population in general); only 36 per cent *female workers* were literate (against 45 per cent literacy among females in the population in general). What we concluded was that, while 'development' may have increased the work participation rate for females, it had not translated into a greater proportion of *literate* women becoming workers as had happened in the case of males. What was equally of concern was that, the above national picture of relatively greater illiteracy among female workers population was repeated in socially and economically developed states such as Tamil Nadu as well.[16]

Kalaiyarasan's[17] critical examination of the NSSO-PLFS data for 2020–1 reveals the current paradox relating to female workforce in Tamil Nadu. To quote the author in some detail:

> A woman in Tamil Nadu is likely to be educated, to find work in a modern sector of the economy. But she is also likely to be paid far lower than men for the same work, and, experience segregation in the workplace... Modern sectors in Tamil Nadu employ a larger proportion of women workers compared to most states—58% compared to 39% for Gujarat and Maharashtra and the all-India average of 37%. This sectoral shift from agriculture for women workers in Tamil Nadu is significant given the larger national trend towards feminisation within

[16] Swaminathan, 'Outside the Realm of Protective Labour Legislation'.

[17] A. Kalaiyarasan, 'A Gender Paradox in Tamil Nadu', *The Hindu*, Chennai, 31 July 2023, p. 9.

agriculture... This achievement...doesn't always guarantee inclusion since they suffer from wage discrimination... The gender earning gap ratio (ratio of women's earnings to men's earnings) in Tamil Nadu is among the highest in the country... What explains this earning gap? It cannot be the typical 'human capital' differences since the literacy gap in the state is much lower as compared to many other states. It could be partly an outcome of occupational segregation as only 12% of women are in white collar jobs while a substantial number of them are concentrated in semi-skilled or un-skilled jobs.[18]

In Part IV, we carry forward the discussion on the nature of women's employment to highlight not just the theme of gender injustice—a consequence of the specific paradigm of development path chosen—but more important, to emphasize how women's 'paid and unpaid labour' subsidizes the cost of industrial development of the country. While economists in charge of planning for industrialization recognize the significance of women's labour, policies to address special concerns of women labour continue to fall severely short of addressing these concerns.

Economic Development: Why Gender Matters

An abiding project of feminists across space and time has been to constantly study how gender 'takes on social import, how it varies in its salience and consequence and how it operates to produce and maintain power and inequality in social life'.[19] The Gender Mainstreaming (GM) project that emerged in the 1990s building on the empowerment discourse of the 1980s, was defined

[18] Ibid., p. 9.

[19] Jane L. Parpart, 'Exploring the Transformative Potential of Gender Mainstreaming in International Development Institutions', *Journal of International Development*, vol. 26, no. 3, April 2014, p. 384.

by the United Nations as the integration of gender into the 'design, implementation, monitoring and evaluation of policies and programmes in all political, economic and societal spheres'.[20] It was built on the assumption that transforming unequal and unjust power relations is doable; that it 'simply required GM to be everyone's responsibility, everyone's job'.[21]

Within a short time, the operationalization of the GM transformative agenda has demonstrated the pervasive nature of resistance to the project and to the instability of the concept itself. Drawing on feminist theory and critical development analysis, Parpart[22] describes how, notwithstanding the wide acceptance of the notions (and policies based on such notions) of gender equality and women's empowerment, the same is constantly subverted; that gender has become a synonym for women and girls, *and GM a promise of inclusion, rather than transformation* (emphasis ours).[23]

Feminist scholars dealing with the themes of transformation of the state in industrial countries of the West, particularly OECD countries, have sketched the trajectory that states in these countries have followed to address the issue of gender inequality, the outcomes of

[20] Economic and Social Council (ECOSOC), 1997, Chap. IV, see https://www.un.org/esa/documents/ecosoc/docs/1997/e1997-64.htm, quoted in Parpart, 'Exploring the Transformative Potential of Gender Mainstreaming in International Development Institutions', p. 384.

[21] United Nations Development Program (UNDP), 2002, see https://www.undp.org/sites/g/files/zskgke326/files/publications/iar2002-complete.pdf, quoted in Parpart, 'Exploring the Transformative Potential of Gender Mainstreaming in International Development Institutions', p. 384.

[22] Parpart, 'Exploring the Transformative Potential of Gender Mainstreaming in International Development Institutions'.

[23] Ibid., p. 389.

which have, in turn, led to change in state structures.[24] This trajectory traces the manner in these societies have moved from a male-breadwinner model to adult-worker model family to dual-earnership models—all of which is premised on women being part of the labour force. Feminist examination of these models has revealed the persistence of gender inequalities despite large numbers of women being part of the labour force. One set of mainstream policy makers have explained this persistence in terms of 'incomplete revolution' in women's roles necessitating therefore more attention in three areas (education, employment, and entrepreneurship); another set has emphasized social investment in response to the 'inability of traditional economic and social policy frameworks to address changing demographic trends, including population ageing and declining birth rates in most OECD countries, high unemployment, child poverty and the intergenerational transmission of poverty and disadvantage'.[25]

Turning to the Indian subcontinent, we observe that in the various otherwise seminal reports of commissions and committees aimed at documenting the status of women in India constituted by the Government of India (GOI), we find that 'integration into existing development processes' takes precedence over 'transformation' of the existing order of society. Thus, for example, the understanding that addressing issues pertaining to provision of 'drinking water, energy and environment' constitute important

[24] Julia S. O'Connor, 'The State and Gender Equality: From Patriarchal to Women Friendly State', in *The Oxford Handbook of Transformations of the State*, ed. Stephan Leibfried et al., Oxford: Oxford University Press, 2015, Chapter 25, pp. 482–98; Jane Jenson, 'Lost in Translation: The Social Investment Perspective and Gender Equality', *Social Politics: International Studies in Gender, State and Society*, vol. 16, no. 4, December 2009, pp. 446–83; for example.

[25] O'Connor, 'The State and Gender Equality', p. 487.

attempts 'to reduce *women's drudgery* considerably' (emphasis ours)[26] has come to stay; it is not simply reiterated plan after plan and only in plan documents; but has found its way into documents of officially constituted committees and commissions presided over and consisting of women activists with long years of engagement with the women's movement in India.

The dilemma that such phrasing of the important issue of basic infrastructure poses for feminists is the proverbial Hobson's 'choice' embedded in the phraseology itself: choose between 'practical' gender needs or forgo 'practical needs' and wait for 'strategic' gender needs to materialize. Given the particular manner in which economic development has/is taking place in the country since the dawn of Independence, where citizens cannot demand basic services as a right, there is no scope as yet for some of the 'practical' gender needs being translated, even if gradually, into 'strategic' gender needs. Hence, even the most vocal and radical of feminists find themselves acquiescing, under these circumstances, to go along with the demand for provision of sufficient investment in basic infrastructure even if the latter is seen as addressing 'women's issues' and not that of the household. Given a 'male model of work', the partial/poor quality services provided by the state and the almost static traditional role of men, has meant very little change in the quality of rural women's lives in particular, with the result that women are forced simply to do more and accept double/triple shifts.

In our paper titled, 'Outside the Realm of Protective Legislation: The Saga of Unpaid Labour in India',

[26] Government of India, *Shramshakti: Report of the National Commission on Self-Employed Women and Women in the Informal Sector*, New Delhi: Department of Women and Child Development, Ministry of Human Resource Development, 1988, p. 274.

published in the *Economic and Political Weekly* in 2009, we trace 'the trajectory of simultaneous exclusion and (peripheral) inclusion of women by going back to some of the seminal documents that were the outcomes of officially constituted commissions and committees. These documents not only engaged with the broad theme of exclusion/inclusion extensively and holistically, but also strongly recommended, among other things, the enactment of new laws, modification and expansion of coverage of existing laws, and stringent implementation of all laws in the spirit of enhancing the status of the marginalized (women included) from non-citizens or second-class citizens to full citizenship. An avowed purpose of this exercise was to comprehend what accounts for the continued denial of 'worker' status to large numbers of women, whose presence as 'informally employed' and as 'unpaid family workers' is otherwise recognized. Through a critical reading of these documents, we revisited some of the arguments and recommendations of these bodies.[27]

In the paper titled 'The Formal Creation of Informality, and Therefore, Gender Injustice: Illustrations from India's Social Sector', published in *The Indian Journal of Labour Economics* in 2015, we critique the 'smart economics' approach of the GOI 'that makes women work for development, rather than development enabling women to procure 'decent' employment. As illustrations of these attempts, we critically engaged with: (a) the Accredited Social Health Activist (ASHA) programmes by juxtaposing official-speak on the subject with studies that examine its functioning on the ground; (b) a critical reading of the institution of para-teachers; and (c) studies that have assessed not just conditions but also the position of *anganwadi*, paid domestic, and mid-day meal workers as

[27] Ibid, p. 80.

part of the larger developmental efforts of the State. This exercise enabled us to discuss the gendered consequences of the nature of 'doing development through gender'.[28]

In the Working Paper 'Employment and Maternity Protection: Understanding Poor Coverage of Beneficial Legislation through Content Analysis of Some Judgments', published by the Madras Institute of Development Studies in 2010, not only does the Indian State come out as a poor employer, but even the few cases that we have dealt with relating to the operation of the Maternity Benefit Act, 1961, revealed how and why the coverage of the Act even in the organized sector remains abysmal. Hence, while struggles for extending the coverage of the Act to establishments and women workers outside the purview of the Act needs to be strengthened, equally important is the need to unravel ways and means by which organized sector women workers get excluded from provisions of such beneficial legislation.

By Way of Conclusion

By now, it should be clear to readers of this book that the need to confront our development paradigm (currently characterized as jobless growth) and its inability to generate formal employment, particularly for the rising educated youth, is long overdue. What is also evident is that merely increasing the base of formally provided vocational education/skill training is by itself not sufficient without the material base being expanded simultaneously to absorb the products of higher education.

The continued anxiety of the nation to be globally relevant in the economic field, necessitates an industrial policy that addresses the theme of how to improve 'state

[28] Ibid., p. 23.

capacity' and intervene meaningfully such that economic development is premised on, and augments human development—a theme flagged since the colonial times to the present and captured by our papers mentioned above. Equally, we could not agree more with Danik Rodrik[29] when he states that:

> (I)t is not the lack of trained scientists and engineers, absence of R & D labs or inadequate protection of intellectual property that restricts the innovations that are needed to restructure low-income economies. Innovation is undercut instead by lack of demand from its potential users in the real economy – the entrepreneurs. And the demand for innovation is low in turn because entrepreneurs perceive new activities to be of low profitability... When we put ourselves in the shoes of an entrepreneur engaged in cost discovery, we immediately see the key problem: this is an activity that has great social value and yet is very poorly remunerated. If the entrepreneur fails in his venture, he bears the full cost of his failure. If he is successful, he has to share the value of his discovery with other producers who can follow his example and flock into the new activity... The trick for the government is not to pick winners, but to know when it has a loser.

In sum, economic development through manufacturing needs an industrial policy with the state at the centre to coordinate investment and production decisions; hence, the question that as yet remains unresearched: Is the sub-optimal performance of the Indian economy a manifestation of poor 'state capacity' to achieve necessary coordination for the greater good? Or, is it a manifestation of a type of coordination that serves particular interests to the detriment of the larger population?

[29] Rodrik, 'Industrial Policy for the Twenty-First Century'.

PART I

The Beginnings of an Industry Policy in Colonial Tamil Nadu

Provincial vs Imperial

CHAPTER 1

State Intervention in Industrialization

A Case Study of the Madras Presidency

At the macro level, the role of the colonial state in the economic development of the country has generated a fair amount of literature. Defenders of the British Raj emphasize the benevolent impact of colonial rule on the Indian economy, namely the growth of the modern sector, the development of factory industries, the expansion of commerce, and the inheritance of some basic prerequisites for development—rudimentary

*This is part of an ICSSR-funded study, 'Growth of the Corporate Sector in the Madras Presidency'. I am extremely grateful to: The Commissioner, Research Officer and staff of the Tamil Nadu Archives, Madras for their cooperation and help during the collection of material, R. Sumathi who assisted me in data collection, S. Ambirajan, C.T. Kurien, S. Neelakantan, M.S.S. Pandian, Nirmal Sengupta, Nasir Tyabji and an anonymous referee for comments and suggestions on an earlier draft of this paper. T. Maheswari and C. Narasimhan who patiently typed several drafts. Needless to add I alone am responsible for the remaining errors of omission and commission.

Previously published in the *Indian Economic and Social History Review*, and as an MIDS Working Paper no. 99, 1991.

education, Western technology, the concept of law, and the foundations of a civil service, irrigation, and railways. Critics on the other hand have emphasized not only the quantitative insignificance of these growth phenomena and their limited impact on the rest of the economy, but, more importantly, raised the issue of the character and origin of the specific features of underdevelopment in colonial economies like India—features which continue to inhibit growth.[1] The debates also recognize the limited value of all-India generalizations (given wide regional variations) and the need to capture the process by which the fact of colonial rule frustrated the potentialities for growth, particularly in the field of industrialization.

This chapter aims at exploring at the regional level, in a concrete manner, the attempts made by the provincial government of the Madras Presidency (largely on the initiative of one of its officials, Alfred Chatterton)[2] to

[1] For a general introduction to the debate, see, for example (a) Sabyasachi Bhattacharya 'Laissez-faire in India', *The Indian Economic and Social History Review (IESHR)*, vol. II, no. 1, January 1965, pp. 1–22; *IESHR*, vol. V, no. 1, March 1968, especially the articles by Morris D. Morris, Bipan Chandra and T. Raychaudhuri.

Note: All G[overnment] O[rders] refer to those issued by the Madras Government and now maintained at the Tamil Nadu Archives, unless otherwise specified.

[2] According to a biographical sketch provided in K.D. Bhargava, ed., *Selections from Educational Records*, vol. IV (Technical Education in India, 1886–1907), New Delhi: Government of India for the National Archives of India, 1968. Sir Alfred Chatterton was born in 1866, educated at Finsbury Technical College, and Central Institution, South Kensington, before joining the Indian Educational Service in 1888. He was Professor of Engineering, Madras, from 1888 to 1900; Director of Industries, Madras, 1908; Director of Industries and Commerce in Mysore, 1912; Member of the Indian Industrial Commission, 1916–18; Controller of

foster some form of economic development through a demonstration of the commercial success of certain lines of business pioneered under state patronage, and through its concern for developing industrial education in the state. This initiative on the part of the provincial government brought it into sharp conflict with the European mercantile community of the country in general and of the province in particular, who saw in the action of the state, a threat to their own interests. The analysis of the tension created between the provincial government and the mercantile community over state pioneering/promotion of industries brings into sharp relief not only the differing perceptions (over the role of the state) between officials and businessman (both British) *within* a province, but also the difference in perception *between* a provincial government and the imperial authority. The debate at the national level on the issue of what Gerschenkron calls the ideologies of delayed industrializations,[3] has effectively brought out the link between the doctrine of *laissez-faire* and *imperialism*.[4] This case study at the regional level highlights, in addition, the fact that when a provincial government attempted to depart from the accepted imperial norm of a passive role of 'night watchman',[5] howsoever small the effort and miniscule the impact, the attempt was soon

Indian Munitions Board 1917; and Industrial Adviser to the Tata Industrial Bank, Bombay.

[3] A. Gerschenkron, *Economic Backwardness in Historical Perspective: A Book of Essays*, Cambridge, MA: Belknap Press of Harvard University Press, 1962, Chapter I.

[4] In this context see Bhattacharya, 'Laissez-faire in India'.

[5] Term used by Morris D. Morris in 'Towards a Reinterpretation of Nineteenth Century Indian Economic History', *IESHR*, vol. V, no. 1, March 1968.

aborted and the provincial government reprimanded for daring to address the imperial authority to reconsider its decision.

Chatterton strongly asserted that India had to recognize that there was no short-cut to industrial well-being, that state action in some form or other was necessary. In the absence of a central coordinated effort, and, given that private enterprise in the Madras Presidency was very weak, state intervention was legitimately called for and undertaken. He came down heavily on the Chambers of Commerce who had attacked the provincial government's pioneering of new industries as being unsound in principle and uncalled for. Chatterton however felt that, 'the arguments adduced might be justly applied to countries where private enterprise is active, but in Madras they savour somewhat of a dog-in-the-manger policy that is not consonant with British traditions in the East'.[6]

Chatterton spelt out the line of policy which he felt, the state in general and the Madras government in particular should adopt if the two were serious about taking active measures to better fit the artisan of the country to meet the stress of Western competition. In a Memorandum on the Encouragement of Indigenous Industries in India[7] he pointed out that in Madras alone, upwards of Rs.2 crore worth of piece-goods were being imported annually and it therefore seemed to him a much more hopeful matter to try and regain the local market in cotton fabrics than to attempt to create new markets in distant countries. He also felt that an enormous

[6] A. Chatterton, 'Industrial Evolution in India', *The Hindu*, Madras, 1912, p. 368.

[7] Chatterton's Memorandum recorded in Educational G.O. no. 40, 24 January 1901.

impetus would be given to local industries if the GOI were to issue orders that the public works in this country were to be carried out with locally manufactured stores wherever it was possible to do so. While no great industry could be established on these lines, a certain amount of success would encourage further efforts and such simple beginnings would ultimately lead to larger results than could be obtained by adoption from the outset of the huge scale of working in iron which prevailed in Western countries. His chief idea was to try and make in Madras the articles which were then imported and he was certain that with the attainment of some measure of success in this direction private enterprise would take the matter up and would do the needful in the way of export trade. While the expenditure of a few lakh rupees would not revive the Indian industries that were suffering from competition with the West, a judicious spending of the same, in Chatterton's opinion, would serve to bring out the latent skill and capacity of the people in those branches of handicraft that had become hereditary occupations in the most rigid sense.

Chatterton's true character and the motive for the missionary zeal with which he went about organizing his tasks are revealed in his following statement:

> The welfare of Great Britain is intimately bound up with the prosperity of its great Indian Empire, and to put the matter on no higher ground than that of purely selfish considerations, it is of vital importance to the expansion of our trade with India that industries should be developed out there, that labour should be properly trained and efficiently employed so that the low standard of living that now prevails may be gradually raised.[8]

[8] Chatterton, *Industrial Evolution in India*, p. 369.

For convenience of analysis, the rest of this chapter is divided into separate sections, each dealing with a specific activity, which was either initiated, developed and/or in which Chatterton had a major role to play. This segmentation enables discussion of the individual and peculiar problems of each of the activities, the depth of Chatterton's understanding of the problems and his reaction to each, the degree of state intervention, and concomitantly the degree of controversy surrounding each (given the strong opposition of the European mercantile community to what was termed state-sponsored industrial activity). We have dealt with the development of the aluminium, chrome-tanning, and handloom weaving industries. These by no means exhaust the entire gamut of activities undertaken by Chatterton and/or by the provincial government.[9] However, precisely because the latter was able to successfully demonstrate in these areas how state intervention could benefit the local population, the controversy that such intervention generated was the maximum—and hence our focus on these industries. The final section highlights the controversy at the national level leading to the eventual closure of the industrial department of the Madras Presidency. The period covered in the chapter spans two and a half decades (1890–1915) roughly from the time of Chatterton's active involvement in the industrial activity of the province up to the loaning of his services to the Mysore Government and the setting

[9] For a general idea of the range of activities undertaken by the government (in most of which Chatterton had a large say) see 'Memorandum on the Department of Industries in the Madras Presidency', Appendix J, *Indian Industrial Commission, 1916–18*, Main Report, Calcutta, 1918, pp. 402–24.

up of the Indian Industrial Commission. We begin with a brief note on Chatterton's official position and on the creation and closure of the Department of Industries in the Presidency.[10]

Establishment of the Department of Industries

In December 1897, the Superintendent of the School of Arts in Madras fell ill, and Chatterton, who was then Professor of Engineering at the Engineering College, was placed in charge of the school. In 1899, the Provincial Government applied to the Secretary of State for permission to employ Chatterton for a term of three years for furthering the progress of technical and industrial education in the Madras Presidency. This was sanctioned in February 1900. During this period, Chatterton's major preoccupation was with the aluminium industry along with experiments in handloom weaving, oil engines, and centrifugal pumps for lift irrigation and chrome tanning. Chatterton went on leave in 1904 and on his return was again placed on special duty for the purpose of exploiting and developing technical trades and industries in the Presidency.

In order to convert Chatterton's appointment to a more permanent one, and also organize his development activity on a stable and orderly basis, a scheme was submitted to the Government of India in 1905 for the further advancement of the industrial development of the Presidency.[11] To that end it was proposed to create a department which would make a survey of existing industries and would investigate the possibility of

[10] What follows has been summarized from ibid.

[11] Ibid.

creating new ones. There were no proposals to work industries experimentally on a commercial scale, but merely to initiate experiments which might assist private enterprise to take up fresh industrial undertakings. It was also proposed to establish a bureau where the best available advice on industrial methods could be obtained.

By this time Lord Morley had become the Secretary of State for India and he did not view the general principles underlying the scheme with much favour. He regarded with scepticism the prospect of attaining satisfactory results from the direction of state effort towards the creation of industries, and he doubted whether the lack of industrial energy and progress in the Madras Presidency might not be, due to economic causes, beyond the reach of state endeavour. However, by way of experiment, he sanctioned the creation of the new department and the appointment of Chatterton as the Director of Industrial and Technical Enquiries for a term of five years. Thus, the Department of Industries came into existence in August 1906.[12]

In September 1908, an industrial conference was held in Ootacamund, a hill station in the Presidency, which was attended among others, by the European mercantile community. The latter, in a minute of dissent, recorded their displeasure at the government's active involvement in the creation and promotion of new industries in the State. The resolutions passed at the conference were sent to Lord Morley for approval. Lord Morley, however, differed fundamentally from the views expressed at the conference as contained in the resolutions, and, in his despatch dated 29 July 1910, he, among other things, negatived the proposal to establish a Department of

[12] Ibid.

Industries. He, however, sanctioned the appointment of a Superintendent of Industrial Education working under the Director of Public Instruction, as also the recruitment of dyeing, weaving, and leather experts, but on the condition that they should be employed for instructional purposes only. As a result of these orders, the Department of Industries (which on the recommendation of the conference had been put on a more or less permanent footing with Chatterton as Director, in anticipation of sanction), was abolished and Chatterton was placed under the control of the Education Department as Superintendent of Industrial Education. In July 1912, his services were requisitioned by the Mysore Durbar, a neighbouring Princely State after which he did not return to the Madras Presidency in any official capacity.

The Aluminium Industry

The first reference to aluminium in Madras[13] that appeared in the records was in 1891 when Chatterton approached the government for help in the utilization of water power in

[13] The material on the aluminium industry has been put together with the help of the following sources:

a) Revenue Department G.O. nos. 1626–7, 1 May 1899.
b) Revenue Department G.O. no. 563, 11 March 1901.
c) Educational Department G.O. no. 200, 10 May 1900.
d) Educational Department G.O. no. 675, 20 December 1900.
e) Educational Department G.O. no. 40, 24 January 1901.
f) Educational Department G.O. no. 330, 17 June 1901.
g) Educational Department G.O. nos. 522–523, 16 September 1901.
h) Educational Department G.O. nos. 167+8, 24 March 1902.
i) 'Memorandum on the Department of Industries in the Madras Presidency', pp. 406–8.

the manufacture of aluminium. His proposals were placed before the Secretary of State who appointed a committee of experts to report on them. The committee's report was published and the matter left to private enterprise. During his furlough in 1896, Chatterton consulted the offices of the British Aluminium Corporation who informed him that commercial success in the manufacture of aluminium depended on the existence of a large local market for the metal. Initially at his own expense, and later with the help of a small grant[14] from the provincial government, Chatterton began his experiments which subsequently became an integral part of the work of the School of Arts. Copper-smiths and bell-metal founders were employed; indigenous ways of working were initially adopted with changes being introduced very slowly and at convenient opportunities. From the outset, there was a good demand from the military authorities and from Europeans for aluminium vessels, and, by establishing agents and subsidiary workshops at various places, the Indian demand was also stimulated.

Some of Chatterton's observations on the declining state of the Indian metal industries, the helplessness of the Indian artisan class in the face of imports, and on the role he perceived the School of Arts could play in arresting this phenomenon, to some extent, are indeed revealing. They display not just his concern for the growing misery of the mass of the population; his approach towards a solution, which had the object of encouraging private enterprise through first strengthening the hands of the subject population in order to be able to deal effectively with foreign competition, differed diametrically from the general imperialist attitude of non-intervention so as

[14] Amounting to Rs.3,800.

not 'to take the bread out of the mouths of workers in England and France'.[15]

Chatterton observed that the metal-workers of southern India were a skillful lot of men, but they had been slowly pushed to one side for want of technical assistance by the productions of metal factories of western India where drawn and spun work were turned out. He felt that by his intervention he had been able to arrest the decline of the industry and place the hand metal workers of Madras on a better footing than they had ever before enjoyed.

> ...The most important conclusion that this aluminium venture has demonstrated is this, that if government through industrial schools want to raise the status of the Indian artisan they must be prepared to work them on a sufficiently large scale to be able to supply any equipment or machinery that experience may show is desirable and to be able to give the men employed in them practical training in every branch of the trade.[16]

The work and the fair amount of success achieved by the Aluminium Department of the School of Arts brought forth protests from all over the country, including the company that Chatterton helped to set up, namely the Indian Aluminium Company.[17] The secretary of the Punjab Trades Association in north India, in a letter to the Chief

[15] See Notes connected with Educational G.O. no. 523, 16 September 1901.

[16] A. Chatterton, 'Memorandum on the Encouragement of Indigenous Industries in India', in Educational G.O. no. 40, 24 January 1901.

[17] See Chatterton's letter to the Director of Public Instruction dated 17 July 1901, no. A1/1639, wherein he has given an account of the formation of the Indian Aluminium Company in the growth of which he had, had a major hand—Educational G.O. nos. 522–3, 16 September 1901.

Secretary to the Madras government, accused the Madras School of Arts of having injuriously entered into direct competition with private enterprise.

> However laudable the object for which the department was started may appear at first eight, it assumes a different aspect when, instead of fostering private enterprise, it injuriously enters into competition with it....it appears to the Committee that the object for which the department was started has been attained and that sales to consumers among the outside public ought to be discouraged the work of the school being restricted to teaching only.[18]

Eardley Norton, Chairman, Indian Aluminium Company (Ltd.), while acknowledging and appreciating the work done by Chatterton for the aluminium industry in general and the Indian Aluminium Company in particular, nevertheless took the credit for saving the industry from foreign competition. The company also protested against the proposal of the GOI to establish additional institutions similar to the School of Arts in Madras as being exceedingly detrimental to the interests of the Indian Aluminium Company and of others engaged in metal-working industries and as being opposed to the declared policy of government of non-interference with private enterprise.[19]

Chatterton, however, was convinced of the correctness and usefulness of the approach he had undertaken. He emphasized the need to maintain an efficient industrial school for which a certain minimum outturn was

[18] Letter from C.O. Ardwise, Secretary, Punjab Trades Association, to the Chief Secretary to the Government of Madras, dated Simla, 28 June 1901—Educational G.O. nos. 522–3, 16 September 1901.

[19] Letter from Eardley Norton to the Secretary to the Government of India, Finance and Commerce Department, dated 30 November 1901—Educational G.O. nos. 167–8, 24 March 1902.

necessary, which 'amount must be done and placed on the market for sale'[20] to keep up a high practical standard of efficiency as an industrial school. Tracing the origins of his venture to the aluminium industry, Chatterton stated that after preliminary experiments he had brought the matter to the notice of every firm in Madras but one and all, except M/s Best and Co., had declined to have anything to do with the business. However, after the School of Arts had commenced the movement, the Madras Aluminium Factory, the Indian Aluminium Company, and M/s Murugesa Buther and Co. had followed on exactly the same lines, testifying to what Chatterton considered a sound procedure adopted by him in his attempt to build up the indigenous industries of the Presidency.[21]

To the charge that the aluminium industry had been developed at the expense of the brass and other metal workers, Chatterton pointed out that if the manufacture of aluminium goods had not been started in India, there is unquestionable evidence that they would have been imported from Germany and other countries. As an example, he pointed out that thousands of German water bottles were brought into India, but the school had succeeded in manufacturing by hand in Madras a more serviceable water bottle and completely stopped the importation of the foreign article.

Being merely an officer-in-charge of the Aluminium Department of the School of Arts, Chatterton obviously could not take a decision on the demand for cessation of manufacturing activities in the School of Arts given by the Punjab Trades Association and others; he,

[20] Letter from Chatterton to the Director of Public Instruction dated 17 July 1901, Educational G.O. nos. 522–3, 16 September 1901.

[21] Ibid.

nevertheless, gave a vehement justification for the need and continuance for such work at the School of Arts.

> The Aluminium department of the School of Arts is an experiment in industrial education on lines which I think are suited to the country. I started work in a perfectly fresh field; it has been so far successful, and I think it would be a great pity not to allow the experiment to be carried right through. It is the first time any assistance on a scale commensurate with the necessities of the situation has ever been rendered to Indian artisans, and it seems to me desirable that the principles on which the aluminium business has been developed should have a fair trial.[22]

In 1903, it was decided by the imperial government that the time had arrived when private enterprise could be left to carry on the business unaided. Accordingly, in September 1903, the Indian Aluminium Company took over the Aluminium Department of the School of Arts, purchasing all the tools, plant, and stock after valuation. The memorandum on the Department of Industries submitted to the Indian Industrial Commission, however, acknowledged the contribution made by the Madras School of Arts to the establishment of the aluminium industry in the country. One indicator of the fact that the industry was of some dimension was revealed by the increasing imports of aluminium into India.[23]

[22] Letter from Chatterton to the Director of Public Instruction dated Madras 31 July 1901, A 1/881— Educational G.O. nos. 522–3, 16 September 1901.

[23] Aluminium was not made in India and the then existing industry extended only to the manufacture of aluminium vessels. Imports of aluminium into India increased from 890 cwt (1904–5) to 14,849 cwt in 1915–16. *Memorandum on the Department of Industries in the Madras Presidency*, Home (Education) G.O. no. 141, 7 February 1917.

The Chrome-Leather Tanning Industry

Chatterton's major contribution in the field of tanning and working on leather in the Madras Presidency[24] was a comprehensive monograph which traced the historical growth of the industry, the communities that dominated the industry, the process of tanning, and the inputs that went into it, the leather goods that were manufactured and prospects of the trade—and a lengthy article on chrome tanning detailing the advantages and emphasizing the need to introduce chrome tanning in the Madras Presidency in order to arrest the decay of the industry. Chatterton repeatedly stressed the need to direct attention to the manufacture of goods for the local market.

The question of intervention by government in the Madras tanning industry was taken up in January 1903 when the Chamber of Commerce was consulted as to the causes that had led to the decline of the industry

[24] Sources for this section include:

a) A. Chatterton, *A Monograph on Tanning and Working in Leather in the Madras Presidency*, Madras: Printed by the Superintendent, Government Press, 1904.
b) A. Chatterton, *Agricultural and Industrial Problems in India*, Madras: G.A. Natesan and Co., n.d., pp. 103–19.
c) A. Chatterton, *Industrial Evolution in India*, Madras: Hindu Office, 1912, Chapter VII on Chrome Tanning, pp. 163–202.
d) Educational Department G.O. no. 434, 12 September 1903.
e) Revenue Department G.O. nos. 650-51, 22 May 1906.
f) Revenue Department G.O. no. 820, 22 August 1906.
g) Notes to Revenue Department G.O. no. 641, 8 March 1909.
h) Revenue Department G.O. no. 1160. 1160, 30 April 1909 (confidential).
i) Revenue Department G.O. nos. 2392-93, 30 August 1909.
j) Revenue Department G.O. nos. 2768-70, 8 October 1909.
k) Revenue Department G.O. no. 3346, 4 December 1909.
l) Revenue Department G.O. no. 3322, 2 December 1909.

in Madras and as to whether the government could do anything to assist the industry. The Chamber ascribed the decline to a natural reaction of overproduction in the previous years and opined that the industry would revive in the natural course without interference by the government. The Chamber also felt that chrome tanning was not feasible in Madras owing to climatic difficulties.

Chatterton, however, was convinced that chrome tanning had to be introduced in India if the industry was not to disappear altogether.[25] He classified the difficulties in the successful establishment of an export trade in chrome leather from India under three heads:[26]

Want of Capital

Chrome tanning with the accompanying leather dressing shops required a large amount of machinery and apparently could only be successfully worked on an extremely large scale. Chatterton knew that, given the dubious prospects

[25] Chatterton, in his *Monograph on Tanning*, drew attention to the change that had come over the leather trade throughout the world owing to the introduction of chrome tanning. According to him, the production of vegetable leather was a long and tedious operation, which, when carried out in the most perfect manner possible required from a year to eighteen months. Chrome tanning was a more rapid process and even the thickest hide seldom required more than a week for complete conversion into leather. Further the leather exported from India had hitherto been sent away in an unfinished condition and the dressing of the skins or the currying of the hides was completed in the importing countries. With chrome tanning it was found necessary to proceed with the finishing processes immediately after the material was taken from the tanning bath. This was because chrome leather once dried can never be properly wetted again. See Chatterton, *Industrial Evolution in India*, pp. 167–8.

[26] Chatterton, *Monograph on Tanning*, p. 206.

of success in the industry and the deplorable condition under which the industry was then being carried on in the country, it was quite hopeless to expect capital to be forthcoming for investment in the industry.

Want of Skilled Labour

Chatterton observed that only the lowest castes did manual work in a tannery and even, they as a rule, only took it up after failing to obtain employment elsewhere. Any improvement would mean the installation of machines for certain kinds of work and the employment of skilled labour, which would in turn mean the education and training of the existing labour or the supply of labour from other sources, both of which were not feasible propositions in the short term.

Climatic Conditions

The hot climate was cited as a deterrent but Chatterton felt that the evidence offered in this case was by no means conclusive and felt that the failure to turn out a marketable article was more due to defects in finishing rather than anything being wrong in the process of tanning itself.

Chatterton devoted his time and energy to one class of leather goods which were in very large demand namely, *kavalais* or buckets for lifting water from wells. According to his estimate, the Presidency used not less than a million hides every year for this article alone. Though the buckets were made of well-tanned leather, constant immersion in water and exposure to a hot sun caused them to deteriorate very rapidly, causing the *ryots* a lot of inconvenience. The introduction of chrome-tanned leather for these buckets promised to be a great improvement and offered extremely considerable prospects of commercial success.

Chatterton then approached the government for a small grant[27] to defray the cost of a series of experiments on tanning hides with chromic oxide. Chatterton's experiments placed beyond any reasonable doubt the fact that chrome leather could be manufactured in Madras and that it was well-adapted to the needs of the country. From the making of *kavalais*, the industry diversified to the making of boots and shoes; in the process, the business attracted considerable attention among the local tanners with the number of applications for admission to work in the tanning department rising considerably. Chatterton attributed the initial failure of those people who attempted to start chrome-tanning units of their own to the inadequate appreciation of the fact that chrome tanning was a chemical industry and required the possession of requisite scientific knowledge. He was convinced that before any very large business in this leather could be secured it would be necessary, first of all, to train a sufficient number of local chemists to carry on practical work in the tanneries and at the same time to bring the products of the latter prominently before the agricultural population.

The demand for water buckets was not great at first, and hence the diversification into the manufacture of boots, shoes, and sandals, partly in order to popularize the use of chrome leather and partly to dispose of the leather cuttings not utilizable in the making of water buckets. The increasing scale of these operations necessitated the removal of the department from the School of Arts, and in March 1908, the department moved over to a tannery

[27] Amounting to Rs.2,000.

of its own at Sembiam near Madras.[28] Chatterton's work in connection with chrome leather was not confined to merely promoting its use. Students from all parts of the country were admitted to the Government Tannery where they were given training and instructions in the processes carried on in it. Encouragement was also given to the starting of private chrome tanneries under the management of men trained in the Government Tannery.

The commercial side of the venture began to attract a lot of attention, with protests being registered by not just the members of the European business community in Madras but also from outside the province, namely the Upper India Chamber of Commerce. C.B. Simpson of the Madras Chamber of Commerce, in his note to the government, wanted the Madras government to confine their efforts to research and experimental work (such as could be carried on in a laboratory) and to technical training. 'I think', he added 'the same attention devoted to the improvement in the quality of cattle which would benefit the quality of the hide would prove a much more valuable asset to the country as a whole and to the tanning industry in particular'.[29] Another member of the Madras Chamber of Commerce, A.J. Yorke's contention was that private tanners could be trusted to prove the success of chrome tanning without Chatterton playing around with tax-payers' money to useful end.[30] The loudest and longest protests came from G.A. Chambers of M/s Chambers and Company, who had

---

[28] 'Memorandum on the Department of Industries', *Industrial Conference Papers*, Madras: Superintendent, Government Press, 1908, p. 409.

[29] Note dated 8 September 1908 by C.B. Simpson, *Industrial Conference Papers*, p. 185.

[30] Note dated 14 September 1908 by A.J. Yorke on Industrial Development, *Industrial Conference Papers*, p. 195.

been engaged in the leather export trade of the Presidency for over twenty-five years. In his letter to the Governor of Madras, Chambers emphatically stated:

I view with decidedly antagonistic feelings the growth of the output of the government tannery which is already a disturbing element in the trade.... I have a great admiration for Mr. Chatterton's energy and enterprise but nevertheless I am very strongly of opinion that as a government institution the establishment of such a commercial undertaking as the government tannery is a mistake.[31]

Giving details of his business, he admitted that five years back he had started work in chrome tanning in Madras but suspended the same for a time in order to develop the more remunerative export branch of his business. A few paragraphs later, however, he accused the government tannery of selling at prices which did not make it sufficiently profitable for him to take up the business of chrome tanning seriously.[32] The Upper India Chamber of Commerce protested against a circular issued by Chatterton to the commanders of regiments, inviting their attention to the advantages of chrome leather for marching boots. Three factors formed the basis of the complaint:

1. The issue of the circular.
2. Competition of chrome leather with the bark tanning industry.
3. Competition of boots and shoes made by the chrome tanning department with chrome leather boots made by the Kanpur firm.

[31] Letter from G.A. Chambers, proprietor M/s Chambers & Co., Madras to the Governor of Madras, dated 19 September 1908. See Notes to Revenue G.O. no. 641, 8 March 1909.

[32] Ibid.

The Upper India Chamber of Commerce also queried as to whether the chrome leather industry was not sufficiently well-established to be made over to private enterprise.[33]

Chatterton's replies to each of the above protestors, substantiated with facts and very often backed by supportive arguments from his superiors, exposed very starkly the selfish motives of the European mercantile community in preserving intact their monopoly of the trade in the garb of saving private enterprise from state interference. In replying to the protests from the Madras Chamber of Commerce, Chatterton referred to the circumstances under which the government had started the chrome leather industry, namely, *after* the Chamber of Commerce had clearly stated that chrome tanning was not commercially feasible in Madras owing to climatic conditions. The process, according to the Chamber, had already been tried in Madras by a thoroughly experienced tanner brought over from England for the purpose but was found to be impracticable. Further, the Chamber was not hopeful of finding an outlet for the product even if the chrome tanning process had succeeded. In the Chamber's opinion, therefore, no government assistance was necessary.

Deprecating the attitude of the Chamber of Commerce, Chatterton maintained that the latter had no idea beyond tanning skins for export.

> The tanners of Madras are mainly engaged in the export trade and care little or nothing for the internal trade, and I think I may fairly claim that it is entirely due to our efforts that the local demand for leather has received such meagre attention

[33] Protect contained in letter from the Government of India, Department of Commerce and Industry, no. 1498–11, dated 18 February 1909 to the Madras Government—Revenue G.O. no. 1160, 30 April 1909 (confidential).

as has recently been bestowed upon it; if government had not embarked upon the manufacture of chrome leather the condition of things would have been the same as they were five years ago.[34]

In his reply to the Upper India Chamber of Commerce, Chatterton justified the issuance of the circular to the Army commanders on the ground that the business was conducted on commercial principles and that the circular which invited a trial of chrome leather was only a modest effort to make known the merits of chrome leather. Chatterton admitted that to change from bark tanning to chrome tanning would be a costly business for the big tanneries in Kanpur who would naturally prefer to keep intact their practical monopoly and would therefore resist any attempt to divert the military orders in another direction: 'But that can scarcely be a sufficient reason for the troops of the Indian army being supplied with inferior boots if better ones can be obtained. The circular issued by this department simply invites a trial of chrome leather and offers to Commanding Officers an opportunity of testing its merits.'[35]

The threat to competition with private enterprises repeatedly alluded to by the Chambers of Commerce had no basis since the internal trade of leather in India amounted to many crores of rupees while the sales of the chrome leather made by the Department of Industries in Madras amounted to slightly over a lakh of rupees in 1908–9.

[34] Demi-official from Chatterton to A.G. Cardew, Secretary to Government, Revenue Department, dated 6 October 1908—Notes to Revenue G.O. no. 641, 8 March 1909.

[35] Letter from Chatterton to the Secretary to the Government, Revenue Department, dated 10 March 1909, no. 80–G; Revenue G.O. no. 1160, 30 April 1909 (confidential).

The value of boots and shoes turned out may [perhaps therefore] be taken roughly at one-fifth of the work of the department and considering the enormous demand for boots and shoes which must exist all over a continent like India the work of a department which turns out such articles to the value mentioned above can have very little effect, it is submitted, on the general trade.[36]

In 1905, when Chatterton had visited Cawnpore, he was told by the representatives of M/s Cooper Allen and the North West Tannery that there was no future for chrome leather in India; however, after the work and fair success of the chrome tanning department in south India, 'they had so far changed their opinion to put forward the proposition that the industry is now sufficiently well established to be made over to private enterprise'.[37] In Chatterton's opinion, which was endorsed by his superiors in the government, the time had not yet arrived to stop the experimental work in the government tannery or to hand the tannery over to private enterprise.

However, following the Secretary of State for India's despatch disallowing the setting up of a Department of Industries and/or the active promotion of industries in the province, the government had to withdraw from the venture; in the beginning of 1911 the government tannery was sold to the Rewah Durbar, a Princely State in central India.

The Memorandum on the Department of Industries submitted to the Indian Industrial Commission, however, recorded that 'the chrome leather industry is

[36] Letter from the Government of India, Department of Commerce and Industry no. 1498–11, dated 18 February 1909; Revenue G.O. no. 1160, 30 April 1909 (confidential).

[37] Letter from Chatterton to the Secretary to Government Revenue Department, dated 10 March 1909, no. 80-G.

now firmly established in India at any rate as regards certain class of leather, and there is no doubt that the Madras government helped materially to contribute towards this result'.[38]

Handloom Weaving

As in the case of the tanning industry, Chatterton's extensive writings in the field of handloom weaving[39] reveal the depth and range of his observations on a number of issues connected with the industry—the condition of the weavers, the influence of the climate of the locality where weaving was carried out, the problems associated with introducing an improved loom to suit the climate, and the indigenous varieties of cloth being used.

In 1901, Chatterton added an experimental weaving department to the School of Arts, Madras, with the object of improving the methods of handweaving in the south of India. In the Basel Mission weaving establishments of the west coast, the European handloom was employed with considerable success for a great variety of fabrics all of which, however, were of European style and mainly for European use. Chatterton's idea was to try the European loom or simple modifications of it for weaving indigenous varieties of cloth. The results of the

---

[38] See Appendix J to the *Report of the Indian Industrial Commission*, 1916–18 (Main Report, Calcutta, 1918).

[39] Sources for this section include:

a) Chatterton, *Industrial Evolution in India*, Chapter VIII.
b) Chatterton, *Agricultural and Industrial Problems in India*, pp. 120–9.
c) Revenue Department G.O. no. 1088, 6 November 1905.
d) Revenue Department G.O. no. 863–4, 12 April 1907.
e) Revenue Department G.O. no. 961, 24 April 1907.
f) Educational Department G.O. no. 406, 11 May 1912.

experiments undertaken in Madras (based on successful field results in the Basel Mission workshops and Bengal) were not really satisfactory. It was found that though the rate of weaving could be more than doubled by the use of the fly-shuttle, yet at the same time the threads of the warp were broken so frequently that the final result did not show an advantage sufficient to induce the average native weaver to take to the fly-shuttle loom. It therefore became evident to Chatterton that if the fly-shuttle loom was to come into extensive use, it was necessary to materially improve the warps; a great deal of attention was since paid both in respect to sizing and to the mechanical arrangement of the threads.[40]

Initial failures only strengthened Chatterton's resolve to pursue his experiments more vigorously. Collecting more information from other parts of the country was one part of his programme; more importantly he tried to analyse why looms which had succeeded in one place were not effective in Madras. He was convinced that weaving could be best carried on in a damp climate, and that it was climate which had had a considerable influence over the success met by the fly-shuttle loom within different parts of India—'there is no question whatever that the finest and best work has always been the product of damp districts'.[41]

While accepting that government assistance would hardly be necessary where financial prospects were good, he pointed out that in the Madras Presidency there were few people who knew anything at all of weaving

[40] Letter from Chatterton to the Secretary to the Commissioner of Revenue Settlement and Director of the Dept. of Land Records and Agriculture, dated 19 September 1905; Revenue G.O. no. 1088, 6 November 1905.

[41] Ibid.

and fewer still who understood the problems of the handweaver. Therefore, to make capital flow easily into the handweaving industry it was essential to demonstrate on a fairly large scale that the work could be carried on in a profitable manner.

At the outset the main difficulty to be overcome is the organization of a handweaving factory and the training of a sufficiently large number of hand weavers, so that they may fully avail themselves of the possibilities of the new handloom. All this work requires considerable initial outlay and as there is no possibility of making a corner in handweaving which might induce capitalists to invest considerable sums of money on the chance of ultimately getting a big return on their investments, it is not likely to be forthcoming and hence the necessity of government intervention and assistance.[42]

At first, the manufacture of Madras handkerchiefs was taken up, and though at the beginning it was not much of a success, gradual improvements were effected. Experiments with Madras kerchiefs and subsequently with other class of indigenous goods such as saris and dhotis yielded results that left no doubt that it was practicable to turn out a much large percentage of cloth on a fly-shuttle loom, that a cloth of even better texture could be produced, and that if the sizing processes could be improved there seemed to be some hope of the fly-shuttle loom coming into general use throughout the country. According to Chatterton, want of success was partly due to trying to do too many things at one time but mainly to the difficulty of getting good weavers to work regularly in the weaving shed.[43]

[42] Ibid.

[43] Chatterton, *Industrial Evolution in India*, p. 225.

In 1905, Chatterton made a tour through Bombay, the United Provinces, and Bengal. Passing orders on his report, the Madras government expressed their willingness to establish a handloom weaving factory for experimental work either in Salem or Madurai. For a variety of reasons, the former town was selected and in February 1906, the looms and apparatus situated in the School of Arts were transferred to Salem and a new start was made. In Chatterton's words, the Salem Weaving Factory was an experiment to ascertain whether it was possible to improve the conditions of handweavers in southern India:

1. By substituting for the country handloom an improved handloom which would enable the weaver to produce a greater length of cloth in a given time without in any way sacrificing the essential characteristics of the country handwoven goods;
2. By introducing the factory system among weavers so that they might work under the management of men with commercial and manufacturing experience and so that capital and organization might be introduced into the industry; and
3. By introducing, if possible, improved preparatory processes to diminish the cost of the preliminary warping and sizing.[44]

Chatterton was convinced that the amelioration of the condition of the handweavers in India depended upon the introduction of the factory system and the organization of the labour available in a more efficient manner.

In India industries are not dying because they have become so complicated that the old methods of training men to direct them

[44] Ibid., p. 226.

> have become inadequate; on the contrary they are gradually being extinguished because the methods of working continue in their primordial simplicity, and no attempt whatever has been made to take advantage of modern developments.[45]

For a number of reasons, it was difficult to get a sufficient number of capable handweavers to keep the handloom factory going. Few of the weavers were free agents. Most of them were in the hands of the cloth merchants who viewed the factory with suspicion and directed their influence against it. By sheer persistence, however, improvements were effected with the financial results each year showing considerable progress. The most useful work done at the factory was in connection with the first of the problems which Chatterton set out to solve, namely experimenting with the fly-shuttle loom. The type of loom ultimately adopted at the Salem factory was the old English fly-shuttle loom modified in the direction of simplicity so as to make it suitable for the manufacture of indigenous cloths. Numerous other types of improved looms were kept under observation and trial and, in 1908, a weaving competition was arranged at Madras with the object of procuring definite data regarding the merits of various types of loom, which then were offered to the Indian weaver. The result of the competition was to confirm the conclusions of the Salem factory—the looms which did the best all-round work were those manufactured at Madras on the lines of the old English handloom.

Efforts were made to spread the use of the fly-shuttle loom; the Salem Weaving Factory did arouse considerable interest and was the direct cause of numerous small private factories being started. A census of fly-shuttle looms in ordinary use taken in 1911 revealed the existence

[45] Ibid., p. 210.

in the eighty-nine towns and villages visited of not less than 6,528 looms with fly-shuttle sleys. Practically all these villages were in the coastal districts north of Madras and it was estimated that in these districts roughly 40 per cent of the weavers had adopted the new method of plying the shuttle.[46]

As in the case of the other industries, the Salem Weaving Factory also came under criticism by the European mercantile community. But Chatterton defended the weaving factory as one meant to experiment with various forms of handlooms on the market and as a possible way of getting handloom weavers to work under factory conditions. 'If the hand weaving industry is to be materially improved, a great deal has to be done not merely in connection with the technical details of the weaving processes, but also in connection with the training and education of the weaver himself.'[47] The commercial viability of the factory was demonstrated through the range of cloths produced and the increasing sale receipts. But this fact proved the factory's undoing. The Chamber of Commerce protested, Lord Morley's ultimatum followed shortly, and the factory was closed in September 1910.[48]

Notwithstanding the Secretary of State's drastic action, what stands out are the perceptive observations made by Chatterton about the weavers and the conditions of their work and living.

[46] See (a) Letter from Chatterton to the Secretary to Government. Revenue Department 18 January 1912, in Educational G.O. no. 406, 11 May 1912; (b) Notes connected with Educational G.O. no. 406, 11 May 1912.

[47] Chatterton, *Industrial Evolution in India*, p. 226.

[48] 'Memorandum on the Department of Industries in the Madras Presidency', Appendix J, p. 112

It must be admitted that the prospect of effecting any great change is not a very hopeful one and I think we must look to the operation of indirect measures, such as the spread of education and to the pressure of general economic forces rather than to direct attempts to effect any great change in these matters.[49]

Emphasizing the necessity of organization in the handloom weaving industry, Chatterton stated:

Everything seems to point to the fact that for any permanent amelioration in the condition of the weaver the first step is to get him out of the hands of the sowcar (moneylender) and provide him with an agency for marketing his goods on fair commercial terms. In the case of the export trade this has been done, but the difficulties in connection with the domestic trade seem to be almost insuperable.[50]

Should the Government Continue to Intervene? Differential Approaches

In 1908, the government considered that the time had come when the best method of developing the useful work commenced by the Director of Industrial and Technical Inquiries should be further considered. It was pointed out, that capital was not lacking but there was an almost complete absence of men, qualified technically and commercially, to handle manufacturing enterprises. The larger industries were almost entirely managed by Europeans and the capital invested in them was mostly

[49] Letter from Chatterton to the Secretary to Government, Revenue Department, dated 18 January 1912; Educational G.O. no. 406, 11 May 1912.

[50] Ibid.

in the same hands. The manufacturing instincts were weak and underdeveloped, and there was a vast field for government intervention in the way of pioneering work. In order to discuss in what directions the industrial development of the Presidency could be further assisted and promoted by experiments made by the department, the government held a conference at Ootacamund in September 1908 to which the representatives of the leading industrial interests of the Presidency were invited.[51]

Representatives of the private sector were more keen in confining government participation to the provision of technical education. A majority of the European community condemned the local students as being ashamed of using their hands and keeping government hours; others were more circumspect and felt that the existing condition was mostly due to the fault of the educational methods, and to a great extent due to the lack of a suitable example on the part of the Europeans.[52] It was also felt that no useful purpose would be served by a series of haphazard experiments in any particular industry or by indiscriminate suggestions as to the betterment of any industry that one happened to be personally interested in. What was required, it was pointed out, was a radical improvement in all the industries and manufactures, and this could only be brought about by a systematic plan or campaign which would take the education to the villages themselves and which would be founded strictly on the survey of

[51] See (a) Revenue G.O. no. 1421 dated 20 May 1908; (b) *The Industrial Conference Paper*, Madras: Superintendent, Government Press, 1908.

[52] See the extract of a letter from H.P. Gibbs, Chief Electrical Engineer with the Mysore Government, reproduced in *The Industrial Conference Papers*, p. 68.

existing industries contemplated by the government.[53] The difference in approach to the whole question of the industrial development of the province by the European mercantile community on the one hand, the Indian educated classes on the other, and the officials (mostly European) of the provincial government in between makes interesting reading.

A.J. Yorke, speaking on behalf of the Chamber of Commerce, expressed the feeling that the limits within which the government could promote industry in the province were not wide, unless it was by adopting far-reaching steps such as the introduction of a protective tariff which, however, was beyond the scope of the provincial government to levy. The Chamber believed that industrial business could best be managed by businessmen and was therefore of the opinion that any general policy of government experiments in connection with established industries was to be deprecated. As regards the promotion of new industries, the Chamber did not wish to advocate the government embarking on a manufacturing scale with public funds where commercial men feared to venture their own money and suggested that the Director of Technical Enquiries should devote his attention chiefly to industries where there were grounds for future success, namely, 'cottage industries'. As far as employing Indians was concerned, the Chamber vehemently asserted that in industry there was no racial question, but added that, up to a point the Indian was excellent, cheap, and reliable employee but beyond that he failed to come up to modem industrial requirements. 'The Chamber is not prepared to dogmatize as to the

[53] Letter from the Chief Engineer, South Indian Railway, Trichinopoly to the Agent, South Indian Railway; reproduced in *The Industrial Conference Papers*, p. 76.

causes of that failure or as to the educational or other remedies possible for it but the personal experience of several of its members in connection with many factories throughout India leaves no practical room for doubt of the fact mentioned.'[54]

Diwan Bahadur Rajaratnam Mudaliar, echoing largely the feelings of the Indian community in his note, submitted that the most effective means of carrying out the objects of the government in regard to the promotion of (a) industrial development and (b) technical education, was to establish a thoroughly equipped institute of technology for conducting researches and experiments on the most approved methods in certain specified branches of industry, in which, in the opinion of government and its advisers, improvements were possible and could be carried out with advantage. The fact that private enterprise had done very little towards industrial development during the past thirty years, according to Mudaliar, seemed a sufficient answer to the argument that the government ought not to intervene in the development of industries. He was also convinced that a reasonable amount of protective tariff was essential to give a fair start to some of the industries which otherwise could not be revived. Such protective duties formed part and parcel of the industrial policies of every major industrialized country.[55]

The educational system was sharply criticized both by Europeans and Indians. It must be recorded here that

[54] Note from A.J. Yorke, Chairman, Madras Chamber of Commerce, dated 4 July 1908 in *The Industrial Conference Papers*, pp. 83–5.

[55] Note on 'Industrial Development and Technical Education' by Diwan Bahadur P. Rajaratnam Mudaliar, dated 24 July 1908, in *The Industrial Conference Papers*, pp. 86–93. Chatterton, *Industrial Evolution in India*, p. 359

right through the literature on education in colonial India there runs the recurrent theme of the 'natives being indolent by nature and disinclined to physical exertion'. Chatterton himself believed that Indian engineers did not possess 'in any very large measure the grit and common sense which mark the engineer'.[56] This is a difficult subject to evaluate but, as Crane points out, this official viewpoint dampened official zeal for the extension of technical or industrial training. Further, this cliche operated to bias English entrepreneurs against risking the employment of Indians (with technical training) with the often-reported result that English foremen and technicians were imported to fill the slots in industry which required trained personnel.[57]

Imperial Interests vs Provincial Government Industries

What emerges from the above account is the near unanimity among most of the officials in the provincial government as regards the express need for state assistance in fostering indigenous industries and in helping in the encouragement/development of new industries. Every little success achieved by the government strengthened this belief and led them to seek the sanction of the GOI not only to make the provincial department of industries permanent but also to extend the scope of its functioning. In their dealings with the

[56] Chatterton, *Industrial Evolution in India*, p. 359.

[57] For an account of the development of technical education in India before World War I see Robert I. Crane, 'Technical Education and Economic Development in India before World War I', in *Education and Economic Development*, ed. C.A. Andeson, and M.J. Bowman, Chicago: Aldine, 1965, pp. 167–201.

European mercantile community and, more so, during the deliberations of the conference, the officials of the provincial government did not hesitate to point out the contradictory postures adopted by the former and in the process exposed the European mercantile community's 'selfish exploitation of the country'.[58] Deprecating the attitude of the Chamber of Commerce, Madras, towards government involvement in the chrome tanning industry, Chatterton stated vehemently:

> It seems to me obvious that from the strong opposition offered by the Chamber of Commerce and from the European mercantile community to the policy of Government assisting in the development of new industries they fear that the fostering of indigenous industries will place Madras in the same position as Bombay and that the Indians will gradually acquire a commanding position in the mercantile and manufacturing industries of the Presidency. This, I submit, is eminently desirable.... It seems to me impossible that the present state of things should be allowed to continue indefinitely. In the past the European mercantile community have displayed no great amount of energy and ability in building up the industries of the Presidency and there is less hope in the future that they will be able to achieve a better result.... only a few years ago the Chamber of Commerce advocated a *laissez-faire* policy. Now that it has been demonstrated that something can be done and that some practical results have been achieved, they say we are going too far and all that is necessary is to establish technical institutions for the training of workers for non-existent industries.[59]

[58] See Notes to Revenue G.O. no. 641, 8 March 1909, especially the observations made by A.G. Cardew and G. Stokes, senior officials in the provincial government.

[59] Demi-official from Chatterton to A.G. Cardew, Secretary to Government, Revenue Department 6 October 1908, Notes to Revenue G.O. no. 641, 8 March 1909.

The other officials in the government agreed with Chatterton's contention that the opposition of the European merchants of Madras to any attempt by the government to assist the industrial development of southern India was due to their not wishing to see the country developed for fear it should injure their export trade of raw material. While they felt that this was a natural attitude of businessmen, the government on its part could not 'hold back from its duty of trying to lead the people on to industrial development which is the only hope in the future'.[60] It needs to be recorded here that the provincial government saw its policy of intervention as one necessitated by the need to promote and establish private enterprise on a firm footing in the Presidency underlying the motive that 'the well-being of India will promote the well-being of England'.[61] This was made very clear to the mercantile community at the conference by Chatterton:

> Manufacturing enterprise in the Madras Presidency is at the present time very weak and I am not prepared to assent to the proposition put forward that government has no right to start a factory in India to demonstrate the advantages of improved methods of working in any particular industry. If they can be introduced in any other way I would gladly adopt that procedure but as a last resort I think it will be in the best interest of the country at large that government should be at liberty to demonstrate those advantages in a practical way *provided always it is willing to retire from business as soon as that object has been accomplished.*[62] (emphasis added)

[60] See observations of A.G. Cardew and G. Stokes in Notes to Revenue G.O. no. 641, 8 March 1909.

[61] D.G. Bearce, *British Attitudes Towards India, 1784–1858*, Oxford: Oxford University Press, 1961, p. 224.

[62] Note dated 12 September 1908 by Chatterton, *Industrial Conference Papers*, p. 191.

Passing orders on the resolutions passed at the Industrial Conference held at Ootacamund in September 1908, the Governor-in-Council recognized as a general principle that the exploitation of industries should be regarded not as a normal but as an exceptional function of government, and on the general question of the limitations that should be set to the functions of the state in attempting to promote industrial development, the Governor-in-Council had no hesitation in accepting the conclusions arrived at by the conference. With the restrictions which the conference had laid down, the government was convinced that the private enterprise had nothing to fear while it could have much to gain from the association of the State in the work of promoting the industrial development of the country.[63]

The government accordingly approved of the recommendation of the conference that there should be a special department under a special officer to deal with industrial questions. This officer was to be entrusted also with the control of industrial instruction, that is, instruction in the performance of definite operations not necessarily involving the teaching of general principles but only of their application. The government however considered that technical education should continue to be under the direction of the Director of Public Instruction. The officer at the head of the new department would be styled the Director of Industries. He would correspond directly with government in the Revenue Department but not through the Board of Revenue.[64]

[63] Revenue G.O. no. 2894, 17 October 1908—Passing orders on the Resolutions of the Industrial Conference held at Ootacamund in September 1908.

[64] Ibid.

In 1909, the Madras government addressed the GOI, emphasizing the need for placing the appointment of the Director of Industrial and Technical Inquiries on a permanent basis and constituting a definite department of industries. In addition to formulating the principles on which the Department of Industries should function, the conference submitted a comprehensive series of resolutions specifying in detail various directions/areas in which industrial development should be fostered in future.[65]

The Finance Department of the GOI, in its despatch to the Secretary of State recommending the proposals of the Madras government, stated:

> We concur with the local government in their view that the valuable results which Mr. Chatterton has so far achieved justify the hope that the constitution, under his direction, of a permanent department having for its principal objects the fostering of industrial development within the limits laid down by the Conference, and the control of industrial instruction as defined by them, will prove highly beneficial.[66]

On the question of the principle which was involved in the separation of the Department of Industry and industrial instruction from that of technical education, the Finance Department despatch was of the opinion that it was not necessary to insist that the development of industrial and technical education should proceed upon

[65] Letter from L.M. Wynch, Acting Secretary to the Government of Madras, Revenue Department to the Secretary to the Government of India, Home Department (Education) dated 3 March 1909, no. 4294–A/08-1; Revenue G.O. no. 3446, 27 October 1910.

[66] Despatch from the Government of India, Finance Department, to His Majesty's Secretary of State for India, dated 28 October 1909, Simla, no. 253; Revenue G.O. no. 3446, 27 October 1910.

exactly similar lines in different provinces. 'Since such a development was still in its infancy, it would be wiser to permit a certain latitude in the methods of dealing with the problems presented to enable a system to evolve over a period of time best suited to the conditions that had to be provided for.'[67]

In his despatch dated 29 July 1910, the Secretary of State, Lord Morley, took exception to the policy of creating new industries by state intervention and declared that the funds required for the extension of industrial and technical education ought not to be diverted to state-managed commercial enterprise.

> I have examined the account which the Madras Government have given of the attempts to create new industries in the province. The results represent considerable labour and ingenuity, but they are not of a character to remove my doubts as to the utility of state effort in this direction, unless it is strictly limited to industrial instruction and avoids the semblance of a commercial venture. The policy which I am prepared to sanction is that state funds may be expended upon familiarising the people with such improvements in the methods of production as modern science and the practice of European countries can suggest, further than this the state should not go and it must be left to private enterprise to demonstrate that these improvements can be adopted with commercial advantage. I accept the view of the Madras Government that a special officer is required to supervise and extend industrial education in the Presidency, and I agree to Mr. Chatterton being so employed; but am not prepared to sanction a separate Department of Industries with a separate Director.[68]

[67] Ibid.

[68] Despatch from His Majesty's Secretary of State for India to the Governor General of India-in-Council, dated India Office, London, 29 July 1910; Revenue G.O. no. 3446, 27 October 1910.

Accordingly, an order was issued stating that the Department of Industries would cease to exist with effect from 1 January 1911.

Lord Morley's orders prohibiting the employment of state funds in the pioneering of industries gave rise to a very widespread feeling of disappointment among many sections of people in the Presidency. Evidence of such feeling could be gleaned from repeated articles that appeared in the Indian press. At the Sixth Indian Industrial Conference which was held at Allahabad in December 1911, a resolution was passed expressing the deep regrets of the delegates there assembled, who came from all parts of India, at the action of the Secretary of State in directing the abolition of the Department of Industries, Madras and protesting against the prohibition of state pioneering of new industries. Further, at a meeting of the Legislative Council, which was held in Madras on 22 February 1911, a resolution was moved by a non-official member, T.V. Seshagiri Aiyar, representing the University of Madras, to the effect that the council request the Secretary of State to reconsider his decision regarding the establishment of the Department of Industries in the Madras Presidency and to sanction the proposals of the Ootacamund Conference of 1908. The speakers on this resolution, who were all non-official members of the council, urged that instruction in industrial schools was insufficient and needed to be supplemented by practical teaching in workshops where the application of the new processes could be demonstrated. They pointed out that in a place such as Madras, where industrial enterprise was backward and private workshops almost non-existent, it was desirable that the government be permitted to conduct such experiments as may be necessary to decide whether any new industrial processes could be profitably introduced.

The resolution was carried by 211 votes against 3, the official members of the council abstaining from voting. At the close of the debate, the Governor undertook to invite the Secretary of State to reconsider his decision on the subject.[69] From the discussion on this resolution and from the practically unanimous Indian vote in favour of it, it could be discerned how strongly Indian non-official opinion was in favour of the policy of state intervention to pioneer and promote industrial development.

The Governor-in-Council had no doubt that this resolution represented the feeling of a vast majority of the educated classes of southern India and he felt that the wishes of this community on so important a matter deserved the sympathetic consideration of the Secretary of State. He was convinced that there was considerable force in the argument that the difference in conditions of India and those of Europe had to be taken note of; that, in a place like south India where industrial progress had hardly commenced, it was difficult without state aid to bridge the gulf which existed between mere scholastic instruction and the practical application of industrial teaching unless factories under state management were established.[70]

While Lord Morley in his despatch had stated that his objections did not extend to the establishment of a bureau of industrial information or to the dissemination from such a centre of intelligence and advice regarding industries, it was pointed out that such a bureau could not be properly

[69] In a letter addressed to the Secretary to the Government of India, Department of Education, dated 8 May 1911. Ootacamund, A.G. Cardew, Secretary to the Government of Madras, Revenue Department gave details of the forms of protest that followed following Morley's despatch of 29th July 1910; Revenue G.O. no. 3851, 30 December 1912.

[70] Ibid.

conducted by an officer of the educational department. The functions of such a bureau, not being of an educational character, the subordination of the officer-in-charge of that bureau to the Director of Public Instruction was found in practice to be inconvenient and unnecessary. Consequently, the Governor-in-Council strongly urged that the creation of a separate department (to be styled the Department of Industries, or given any other name which was thought convenient) should be sanctioned.[71]

The Finance Department of the GOI, in their despatch to the Secretary of State, endorsed very strongly the arguments adduced by the Madras government and urged His Lordship to modify his decision on the lines indicated by the Madras government.[72]

Lord Crewe (Lord Morley's successor), however, in his despatch, reaffirmed his predecessor's decision against the extension of the activities of the Department of Industries to trading on commercial lines. He, however, had no objection to the creation of a separate department of industries provided that its functions were confined within the limits specified by him.[73] Accordingly, the Department of Industries finally came into existence on 21 March 1914. The functions of the director were defined thus:

(i) to collect information as to existing industries, their needs and the possibility of improving them or of introducing new industries;

[71] Ibid.

[72] Despatch from the Government of India. Finance Department, to His Majesty's Secretary of State for India, dated Simla, 21 September 1911. Revenue G.O. no. 3851, 30 December 1912.

[73] Despatch from His Majesty's Secretary of State for India to the Governor-General of India, dated India Office, London, 15 March 1912; Revenue G.O. no. 3851, 30 December 1912.

(ii) to carry out and direct experiments connected with local enquiries;
(iii) to keep in touch with local manufacturers, to bring the results of his experiments to their notice, and to obtain their cooperation in the conduct of experiments on a commercial scale;
(iv) to supervise the training of students; and
(v) to advise governments with regard to technical matters involving legislation.[74]

That the Secretary of State for India took strong exception to a resolution passed in the Provincial Legislative Council asking for reconsideration of his earlier decision to abolish the Department of Industries can be seen from the following order subsequently passed to all provincial governments.

> His Excellency in Council is doubtless aware that official members of the Imperial Legislative Council are not entitled to vote in favour of any measure which is at variance with the declared policy of the Secretary of State, with whom it is incumbent upon the Government of India to preserve solidarity. It is no less incumbent on a provincial government in the conduct of the business in its Legislative Council to avoid disclosing a difference of opinion in an administrative matter between the Imperial and Provincial Governments and doing anything to foster an impression that there may be opposition between the constitutional responsibilities of those governments when no such opposition either does or can exist. There is for India but one system of administration and one alone and it is only by bearing steadily in mind this fundamental principle that the solidarity of the administration can be kept unimpaired.[75]

[74] 'Memorandum on the Department of Industries', Appendix J.

[75] Letter from H. Wheeler, Secretary to the Government of India, Home Department (Public) to the Secretary to the Government of Madras—Legislative Department G.O. no.156, 2 October 1913 (confidential).

A confidential note[76] addressed to Austen Chamberlain, Secretary of State for India in 1915, outlined the urgent need for a considered central policy in the case of the manufacturing industries. It stressed the point that the people of the country had recognized their inability to carry out their programme without the help and guidance of the government, and had confined themselves for the most part to pressing their demands for assistance from the state and for a policy of tariff discrimination against foreign imports. Public sentiment had, again and again, expressed itself in the form of resolutions and questions in the Imperial and Provincial Councils, of resolutions in the Indian National Congress, and at public meetings and articles in the press. This movement, which had acquired considerable political significance in India, had generally followed two particular lines of expression. In the first place, there was the constant assertion that the British government had with malicious intent, or, if not, with malice, by their attitude of indifference allowed indigenous industries to be overwhelmed by foreign, and especially by British, competition. The second charge was that the British system of education had confined the energies of educated young people to literary pursuits and the learned professions and had created among them a demand for employment limited to government service, the law, and medicine. These contentions emphasized one aspect of the need for an industrial policy which would enable technical education in India to produce

[76] This note signed by Hardinge of Penhurst, Beauchamp Duff, Saiyid Ali Imam, W.H. Clark, W.S. Meyer, C.H.A. Hill and C. Sankaran Nair was addressed to Austen Chamberlain, Secretary of State for India—no. 51 of 1915, Government of India, Department of Commerce and Industry, dated 26 November 1915; Educational G.O. no. 46, 12 January 1916 (confidential).

its best results and which would lighten the pressure on purely literary courses and reduce the excessive demand for employment in those services and callings to which these courses led.

Lord Crewe's despatch of 1912, while it had somewhat relieved the disabilities imposed by Lord Morley, still left the GOI in a considerable degree of doubt as to the precise lengths to which they were justified in going when dealing with proposals for demonstration plants, financial assistance, and other forms of direct aid to industries.

In a resolution dated 19 May 1916,[77] the GOI made explicit its decision to take up for examination the question of the expansion and development of Indian manufactures and industries in a more comprehensive manner than had hitherto been attempted.

Thus, the rumblings generated by Lord Morley's 1910 despatch did not die a natural death. On the contrary, it had a significant impact in forcing the GOI to constitute the Indian Industrial Commission in 1916. Incidentally, Chatterton, who was then Director of Industries and Commerce in Mysore, was made a member of the commission.

[77] Educational G.O. no. 622, 5 June 1916.

CHAPTER 2

State Competition with Private Enterprise

The Case of Manufacture in Jails in the Madras Presidency

An aspect of state intervention that aroused considerable opposition among the commercial community, both in the Madras Presidency and elsewhere, was related to the question of starting and expansion of industries in jails with the help of prison labour. The issue was seen as competition of the State with private enterprise, and, with the introduction of power machinery in some jails, the cry was raised that the 'state was no longer competing with private enterprise with convict labour but with means of production which greatly enhance the output of the jails'.[1]

*Previously published as 'Prison as Factory', Studies in History and in MIDS Working Paper no. 100, 1991.

[1] See, for example, the letter from the Chairman, Chamber of Commerce, Madras, to the Secretary to the Government of India, Finance and Commerce Department, dated 20 April 1910, Judicial, Government Order (G.O.) no. 1097, 21 July 1910.

The whole issue of labour in jails has followed a long and torturous course beginning with the question of the aim of the administration in the selection of jail employment.[2] The Committee of 1836–8 (with whose appointment can be traced the history of prison reform in India) favoured increased rigour in the treatment of prisoners. It rejected all such reforming influence as moral and religious teaching, education and/or any system of rewards for good conduct and advocated the building of central prisons where the convicts might be engaged not in manufactures, which it condemned on somewhat theoretical and unsound grounds, but 'in some dull, monotonous, wearisome and uninteresting tasks in which there shall be wanting even the enjoyment of knowing that a quicker release can be got by working the harder for a time'.[3] Ever since, there had been an ongoing debate on what principles ought to govern the selection of prison labour, how 'hard' prison labour ought to be, what really constituted 'hard' labour—a term used in the Indian Penal Code and to which an offender sentenced to rigorous imprisonment was liable to.

One view held that inasmuch as the prisoner was an offender against the state, the state was justified (especially since the latter had to defray the cost of the prisoner's support) in extracting the maximum profit from the labour of the prisoner regardless of considerations such as the effect of such treatment on the person of the prisoner. Over time it was realized that such a policy, apart from being short-sighted, sacrificed any prospect of

[2] Chapter II and IX of the *Report of the Indian Jails Committee*, vol. I, New Delhi: Government of India, 1919–20, provide a good summary of the whole issue of jail employment.

[3] Ibid., p. 30.

reforming the prisoner and of turning him into a useful member of society.

The acceptance of the principle that the main object of labour to be provided in prison should be to effect the reformation of the prisoner brought forth questions such as the kind of labour to be provided, the differentiation that needs to be made between prisoners not only because of differences in their skill level but also due to the differing prison sentences being served. While it was agreed that short-term prisoners could be put into such forms of labour as did not require long training, it was really in the case of those prisoners whose sentences were for longer terms that the object of both the reformation of the prisoner and economy in the running of jails could be pursued.

Differences persisted over the question of the most beneficial form of labour as far as the prisoners were concerned. Some authorities, relying on the fact that 'over 72 per cent of the population are engaged in agriculture and that 57 per cent of male convicts admitted to jails are returned as agriculturists insist that agriculture should be the staple jail industry'.[4] This suggestion was, however, abandoned as being impracticable and the GOI in its resolutions laid down that the principal mode of employment for long-term prisoners had to be intramural.[5]

This chapter traces the controversy that arose in the Madras Presidency between the English mercantile community and the state government over the issue of

[4] Ibid., p. 119.

[5] Government of India, Home Department Resolution no.10-605-18, dated 7 May 1886—Judicial G.O. no. 1493, 7 June 1886; Government of India, Home Department, Letter no. 145–55, dated 29 April 1912—Judicial G.O. no. 981, 19 July 1912.

manufacturing in jails which the mercantile community dubbed as State competition with private enterprise.

We begin with a documentation of the principles and policies enunciated by the GOI periodically modified to take into account,

i. Governmental requirements in terms of making the jail pay for its own upkeep;
ii. Prisoners' requirements in terms of making them work not only for their own maintenance but also in the process equipping them with some industrial skill in the hope that this would help them in life after prison;
iii. The need to keep interference with private enterprise to the minimum.

Our next section deals with the functioning of jails in the Madras Presidency; the specific policies enunciated based on the GOI's guidelines, the committees set up in the State to deal with this matter, the periodic reviews undertaken not only to streamline the functioning of the jails in the Presidency but also to expand the manufacturing activities given the provincial government's commitment to foster and strengthen jail industries.

In the third section we enter into the controversy proper between the government and the mercantile community over the whole question of 'undue' interference by the State with private enterprises. The details surrounding the controversy document:

a. The utter insensitivity of the commercial community (and therefore their selfishness) to the whole question of reformation of the prisoner as revealed in their insistence on the point that 'jail labour ought to be before all things *penal*'[6] (emphasis added);

b. The differing perception of the mercantile community and government officials (both British) over the question of the role of the State, and the admissibility of the latter's intervention in areas that the English commercial community asserted belonged to the domain of the private sector.

The controversy spanned a period of almost four-and-a-half to five decades. We begin our discussion with the Resolution of the GOI on the issue in 1886 and end with the beginning of the Second World War, by which time the intensity of the controversy had petered out. The period coincides with the rise of the Indian national movement which made it imperative for the colonial government, especially after the First World War, to make some concessions to the demands for economic development, particularly industrial development. This larger question of the slow, albeit late, development of industries under Indian entrepreneurship challenging British hegemony of the industrial field is outside the scope of this chapter. But what is of immediate relevance to our concern here is that a substantial part of the rancour of the mercantile community against State promotion/initiation of industries in general[7] and in jails in particular arose from the fact that it took away from

[6] Letter from the Chairman, Chamber of Commerce, Madras, to the Secretary to the Government of India, Finance and Commerce Department, dated 20 April 1910—Judicial G.O. no. 1097, 21 July 1910.

[7] See in this context the author's paper on 'State Intervention in Industrialisation: A Case Study of the Madras Presidency' (mimeo, 1990).

British business interests their monopoly of government contracts. It needs to be mentioned here that private enterprise represented by the mercantile community did not deem it to be its responsibility to invest in order to expand domestic demand nor would it allow active State intervention in the development of industries. It is in this context of a 'neither you nor me' attitude of the mercantile community that this chapter is anchored.

Industrially Skilling Long-term Prisoners

The question of jail industries and the various issues that arose in connection with it, among which the use of power machinery was one, were discussed by the GOI between the years 1882 and 1886 and the principles then adopted were embodied in a Resolution issued in May 1886.[8] The principles laid down to regulate the policy of the government in the matter of the industrial employment of prisoners were the following:

1. Extramural labour cannot be the principal mode of employment of long-term prisoners, who must therefore be employed intramurally.
2. In central jails there must be well-regulated forms of industrial employment on a large scale.
3. Jail industries must not compete injuriously with private capitalists in the neighbourhood.
4. Jails must not be converted into steam factories. The use of steam machinery is not prohibited, but all extensions of substantial magnitude must be submitted to the Government of India for sanction.
5. Jail industries must be adapted as far as possible to the requirements of the public consuming departments and

[8] Judicial G.O. no. 1643, 21 October 1882; Judicial G.O. no. 1493, 7 June 1886.

these departments must be compelled to take articles of jail manufacture as long as they can be supplied of the same quality and at the same price as in the open market.
6. The price of jail made articles must follow as closely as possible the existing market rates for similar products made by private industry.
7. Multifarious employments must be avoided.
8. The penal element must be fully maintained.[9]

About 20 years later in 1906, the GOI felt that the time was ripe for a reconsideration of the general position and for a full enquiry into the manner in which jail industries were being carried on.[10] With regard to some of the principles enumerated above, the GOI did not feel the need to re-open the discussion. Starting with the assumption that 'there must be in the central jails intramural industrial employments on a large scale', the GOI laid down that these were to be adapted as far as possible to meet the requirements of the public consuming departments. However, the GOI realized that acceptance of the principle that jails could legitimately supply the consuming departments of the government meant that competition to some extent with private enterprise became unavoidable. 'If the jails did not manufacture articles required for the consuming departments these would be manufactured by private enterprise. To this extent the jail industries compete with private enterprise, and in the opinion of the Government of India, *do so legitimately*'[11] (emphasis added).

[9] Judicial G.O. no. 1493, 7 June 1886.

[10] Letter from the Secretary to the Government of India, Home Department (Jails) to the Chief Secretary to the Government of Madras, dated 10 August 1906—Judicial G.O. no.1814, October 1907.

[11] Ibid.

While it was realized and laid down that 'jail industries must not compete *injuriously* with private capitalists', the issue of when competition became *injurious* was never really satisfactorily settled. Certain norms were no doubt laid down by the GOI which acted as guidelines, the interpretation and operationalization of which brought forth the differing perceptions of the jail authorities and the business community and consequently the generation of much heat over the whole issue of state competition with private enterprise through manufactures in jails. Among the safeguards laid down it was emphasized that the consuming departments of government were to take articles of jail manufacture as long as they could be supplied of the same quality and at the same price as in the open market. It was recognized that there would not be a total ban on the sale to the public of any article which was being manufactured in the jails; the question that then arose was how jails were to dispose of their surplus stocks and/or limit their outturn so as not to exceed the requirements of public departments.[12]

The kind of restrictions contemplated by the GOI in such cases amounted to making it clear that 'jails do not exist for the purpose of making a profit and that, ...a profitable return from industrial employment ought not to be made the test of prison efficiency'.[13] Furthermore the advertising of jail-made wares and the maintenance of catalogues or price lists were prohibited, surplus stocks were not to be sold directly to the public but to wholesale dealers with public tenders being called for; depots for the sale of jail manufactures were to be prohibited. As regards the use of steam machinery, the government felt

[12] Ibid.

[13] Ibid.

that a jail was not to purposely handicap itself by the use of obsolete or inferior machinery. The caveat specified in proposals to install machinery for the first time in any jail was that the objects of the installation and the possibility of its interfering with private enterprise were to be thoroughly examined and if the proposal stood, the sanction of the GOI was to be obtained. 'One important aspect of this question, however, is the necessity for preserving the penal element in jail industries, and no doubt this necessity will always be borne in mind', opined the government.[14]

Among the other bodies that went into the question of prison labour and manufactures were the Indian Industrial Commission (IIC) in its Report in 1916–18 and the Indian Jails Committee (IJC) in its Report in 1919–20.[15] The latter was specially invited to deal with the remarks of the IIC on the subject of jail manufactures, their competition with the products of free labour and the use of power-driven machinery in Indian jails. The IIC did not profess to offer final conclusions on these matters but recommended that the subject be considered by experts. It, however, did make certain suggestions. After admitting that jail industries were justifiable in order to recover as far as possible the cost of the upkeep of the jails, to keep the prisoners employed, and to teach a trade that will be useful to the prisoners after their release, the report of the IIC went on to lay down that only manual labour was to be allowed to be used in jails and that the extensive

[14] Ibid.

[15] *Report of the Indian Industrial Commission*, New Delhi: Agricole Publishing Academy, 1916–18; (reprinted 1980), especially Chapter XV; *Report of the Indian Jails Committee*, vol. 1.

use of machinery was undesirable. The ambivalent and operationally contradictory nature of the suggestions made by the IIC can be discerned from its statement, that, while jails could supply the needs of government departments to a much greater extent than at present, it condemned the use of efficient and up-to-date means of manufacture without which this result could not be achieved; at the same time the IIC also condemned the manual industries which existed in jails as likely to compete with free cottage industries.

The IJC went extensively into the whole question. Most of the recommendations of this committee found favour with the local governments, based on whose replies the GOI enumerated the following principles:

a. that the main object of prison labour should be the reformation of the criminals;
b. that non-productive labour should be avoided;
c. that short-term prisoners must necessarily be employed mainly on unskilled labour;
d. that the principal mode of employment for long term prisoners should be intramural;
e. that greater benefit to the prisoner is conferred by giving him the best available instruction in up-to-date methods of labour and so fitting him for free living under modern conditions;
f. that attention should be concentrated in each jail in one or two main industries;
g. that jail industries should be adapted to meet the needs of the consuming departments of Government.[16]

[16] Letter from Dy. Secretary to Government of India to the Chief Secretary to the Government of Madras, dated 19 December 1922, Law (General), G.O. no. 217, 22 January 1923.

On the important question of the utilization of power-driven machinery in jails, the IJC stated emphatically that

> as the reformation of the prisoner is the chief object to be kept in view, and as familiarity with power driven machinery is instructive and mind awakening, the provision of such machinery subserves the true functions of jail administration; while at the same time it increases production and tends to give increased relief to the tax payer. It is therefore from all these points of view justifiable, but it should be employed in well-established and organised industries and care should be taken to avoid any interference with nascent or unorganised industrial enterprises. Subject to this safeguard, we recommend that the restriction on the development of jail manufactures by power driven machinery should be withdrawn, that consuming departments of the state should be directed to obtain their requirements from the jails and that it should be the recognized duty of the jail department to develop their industries so as to meet these requirements... In making these recommendations we are not blind to the fact that increased production in jails will imply increased competition with free enterprise and that such competition affects particular interests, especially those of the shareholders in industrial ventures, more than it does the great mass of the community... that when all is done that can be done, prison labour remains inefficient as compared with free labour, and that the total number of prisoners available for manufactures spread over all the Provinces of India, is not sufficient to have any appreciable effect on the great mass of industrial employment in the country.[17]

The GOI invited the attention of the local governments to the above recommendations of the IJC since it involved a departure from the policy of the government as laid down in 1886 and in 1906, and, since it was also at variance

[17] *Report of the Indian Jails Committee*, vol. 1, pp. 125–6.

with the recommendations contained in the report of the IIC. The replies received denoted concurrence with the views expressed by the IJC. Consequently, the Governor General in Council decided

> with the approval of the Secretary of State for India to cancel the orders on the subject contained in the Home Department Resolution no.10-605-18, dated the 7th May 1886, and in the Home Department letter no.145-154 dated 29th April 1912, as he considers that the existing restrictions on the use of power driven machinery should be relaxed and that it may be employed in well-established industries, care being taken to avoid interference with nascent or unorganised industrial enterprises though he is disposed to think that the apprehension of the possible competition of jails with established industries is more imaginary than real.[18]

Madras Presidency Jails: Nature of Activities

It would be pertinent at this stage to get an idea of the functioning of the jails in this Presidency in terms of the kind of industries permitted and those actually carried on in the different jails, as well as the departments to which the articles made in these jails were supplied—in short, the principles that governed and the practice that obtained as far as manufacturing activities in jails were concerned. We start with the first exhaustive review that was done by the provincial government in 1907, covering the whole question of jail industries and the various issues that arose in connection with it, including the use of power machinery.[19]

[18] Resolution dated 19 December 1922, Home Department, Government of India—Law (General) G.O. no. 217, 22 January 1923.

[19] Letter from Acting Secretary, Government of Madras, (Judicial Department) to the Secretary to the Government of India, dated 25 October 1907—Judicial G.O. no. 1815, 25 October 1907.

The provincial government accepted and functioned on the principle that jails must have industries and also that prison labour was best employed in meeting the requirements of the large consuming departments of government. Further, the government also frankly affirmed that government contracts should go to jails as soon as it had been satisfactorily proved that jails were capable of undertaking the work. In the Madras Presidency, manufacturing operations were chiefly carried on in eight central jails and four district jails. Table 2.1 gives an idea of the articles manufactured in these different jails and supplied to government departments. The chief industries concentrated in the different jails were:[20]

- Cotton weaving: Coimbatore, Trichinopoly and Cuddalore
- Tent-making: Coimbatore
- Pile carpet weaving and leather work: Vellore
- Woollen cumblies and blankets: Trichinopoly, Bellary and Rajahmundry
- Jute fibre and gunny *pattah* making: Vizagapatnam
- Coir fibre industry: Cannanore
- Carpentry: Cannanore and Madras Penitentiary
- Printing: Madras Penitentiary
- Iron and aluminium work: Salem
- Cotton tape and thread: Palamcottah

The only jail in the Presidency in which articles were made for private sale to any appreciable extent was the central jail at Coimbatore, where machinery obtained from England had been installed and the work carried on with steam power. The only two central jails in the Presidency in which steam machinery had been installed

[20] Law (General) Letter no. 504, 3 June 1921.

Table 2.1: *Statement Showing the Articles Manufactured in Madras Jails and Supplied to Government Departments*

1. *Military Department*
   - Corah matting
   - Tents
   - Tape
   - Rope
   - Coir
   - Dhurries
   - Money Bags
2. *Public Works Department*
   - Sail cloth
   - Bamboo chicks
   - Cloth
   - Belts
   - Ropes
   - Coir
   - Furniture
   - Bricks and tiles
   - Corah matting
3. *Stationery Department*
   - Aloe and coir ropes and mate
   - Boots
   - Tape tags
   - Gingelly oil
   - Sealing wax
   - Wax cloth
   - Ink boxes
   - Cumblies
   - Jute ropes
   - Tape
   - Twisted thread
4. *Police Department*
   - Cumblies
   - Ropes
   - Tent carpets
   - Drills
5. *Medical Department*
   - Gingelly oil
   - Sheets
   - Towels
   - Cloth
   - Quilts
   - Palliases
   - Corah mats
   - Tape
   - Carpets
   - Coir mats
   - Furniture
   - Binding work
   - Bandage cloth
   - Belts
6. *Registration Department*
   - Furniture
   - Belts
   - Record planks
   - Binding work
7. *Forest Department*
   - Cumblies
   - Tents
   - Belts
8. *Judicial Department*
   - Belts
   - Dufter cloth
   - Sheets
   - Towels
   - Cloth
   - N.S. cloth
   - Furniture
   - Binding work
9. *Revenue Department*
   - Duster cloth
   - Binding work
   - N.S. cloth
   - Belts
   - Rattan baskets
   - Furniture

10. *Treasury Officers*	12. *Agricultural Department*
Money bags	Check dusters
N.S. cloth	13. *Educational Department*
Binding work	Binding work
Canvas tape bags	14. *Miscellaneous Departments*
11. *Salt Department*	Printing
Tents	Book binding
Yellow cloth	Tailoring
Belt	Laundry work

Sources: Home (Judicial) G.O. no. 1775, 6 August 1919.

were the penitentiary for printing and the central jail at Coimbatore for weaving. The penitentiary press worked solely for the government. Initially, the power looms in the Coimbatore jail were worked by a treadmill, and a small engine was used to provide steam for and work a sizing machine. The material turned out on these looms was confined to 'drill' for the police department and for many years the outturn was supplemented by hand-woven cloth from other jails. The cloth was of inferior quality which brought forth constant complaints. About the year 1896, the treadmill broke down; by this time the looms, which had been in use for twenty years, were also found to be in bad shape. New looms were obtained and put under steam power. The work turned out was so satisfactory that not only all the cloth for the police, but the supply of other public consuming departments were also given over to this jail.[21]

Having admitted that jails could legitimately supply the consuming departments of the government, the question that then had to be considered was how such contracts could be entered into. In the Madras Presidency over the years, the civil departments that dealt with the

[21] Judicial G.O. no. 1815, 25 October 1907.

jails practically discontinued calling for tenders and year after year obtained their requirements from the jails at rates that had gradually become more or less permanent, or rather the rate was rarely changed unless there was a change of sample. In the case of military contracts, however, the jails were made to compete with private firms, and unless the jail tender happened to be the lowest the contract was placed elsewhere.[22] The Acting Inspector General of Prisons, E.H. Gadsden, was firmly of the view that, since it had been recognized that jails must have industries and since prison labour was best employed in meeting the requirements of the large consuming departments of government, 'the Government of India should not hesitate to affirm frankly that government contracts *shall* go to jails as soon as it has been satisfactorily proved that the jails are capable of undertaking the work. The objections to this procedure will occur in whatever form the jails take up the contracts'[23] (emphasis in original).

The Madras government fully concurred with the GOI and endeavoured to give full effect to the orders relating to the provision in central jails of well-regulated modes of industrial employment on a large scale, the necessity for avoiding multifarious employments, and for standardizing jail industries as far as possible. The provincial governments were asked to give their comments on the various proposals put forth by the IJC in its report in 1919–20. The Madras government in its reply endorsed the main principles put forth by the IJC that were to govern prison manufactures, namely (a) that

[22] See letter from Acting Inspector-General of Prisons to the Chief Secretary to Government, Madras, dated 23 September 1906—Judicial G.O. no. 1814, 25 October 1907.

[23] Ibid.

the reform of the prisoner was the essential feature of prison management; (b) jails were to concentrate on one or two large industries and avoid multifarious activities; (c) industries were to be so selected that they could employ prisoners profitably and teach them a trade to follow after release.[24]

The Madras government also agreed with the IJC's observation that jails were to employ modern power-driven machines and up-to-date tools and methods of production wherever large-scale production of standardized articles were required for consuming departments of government. In this context, it categorically asserted that the use of power-driven machinery in the jails of the Presidency had not been injurious to private enterprise as the output had been limited and largely consumed by government departments.[25]

Another committee that also examined the various aspects of manufacturing in jails was the Madras Retrenchment Committee in 1921. The latter then made suggestions with a view to make jails more efficient and self-supporting. Among their recommendations were the following:

i. That up-to-date machinery should be installed wherever necessary and adequate provision made, where local conditions were suitable, for the introduction of such preliminary processes as spinning, the capital required for such expansion being found by loans; and that the inspector General of Prisons should have an expert to assist

[24] Letter from Inspector-General of Prisons, to the Secretary to Government, Home (Judicial) Department, dated 2 March 1921—Law (General), Letter no. 504, 3 June 1921.

[25] Ibid.

him in supervising the jail industries and advise him on questions connected with them;

ii. That the system now adopted for the purchase of raw materials should be examined with a view to decide whether the establishment of an agency for purchase would be more economical and efficient;

iii. That in order to secure a steady market for the products of jail labour it should be made obligatory on all consuming departments of government to purchase articles of jail manufacture subject to safeguards to quality and price; and

iv. That the system of accounts maintained should be recast the possibility of introducing a commercial system of accounts being kept in view.[26]

The Madras government considered that these proposals should be subjected to a careful examination by a committee which should work out, in consultation with the expert technical officers of the government, detailed schemes for improving the efficiency of the industries in jails and also advise on the other questions raised. Accordingly, a committee was constituted in 1924.[27] The members of the committee visited most of the jails and discussed the improvements needed in particular industries with technical expert officers; their detailed recommendations were accompanied in every case by careful estimates of the expenditure involved. To sum up, their recommendations included:

(a) The installation of a power cotton spinning plant at Coimbatore, a wool spinning plant at Bellary on

[26] See Order no. 2157, in Law (General) G.O. no. 2157, dated 4 July 1925.

[27] Law (General) G.O. no. 1934, dated 30 June 1924.

an experimental scale at first, while at Salem they contemplated some simple machinery actuated by manpower in connection with the steel and aluminium manufactures, some comparatively inexpensive boot making plant, and at Cannanore they recommended the organization of coir yarn and mat industries with improved plant and under skilled supervision. They also recommended a thorough overhaul and reorganization of the more widespread carpentry industry;

(b) They advised that the services of the technical officers of the Department of Industries should be made available to the jail department in preference to the suggestion that the department should have an expert adviser;

(c) They were against the introduction of commercial accounts though they considered that large-scale industries involving the use of power should have an adequate costing system suited to the industry. They strongly recommended that the purchase of such jail articles as could be made economically and efficiently should be made obligatory on departments of government subject to certain safeguards detailed by them.[28]

The Madras government accepted almost all the recommendations of the committee after very few modifications.

In 1932, in the Madras government a review of the question whether government policy regarding jail manufacture needed revision was again undertaken. The overwhelming opinion was that the observations and

[28] Law (General) G.O. no. 2157, dated 4 July 1925.

recommendations of the Jail Industries Committee of 1924 were still valid. 'It will be observed', the government spokesperson stated:

> that it is only *after* a careful examination of the recommendations of the various committees, the jail industries have been organised in the Presidency. Even now according to the recommendations of the Jail Industries Committee only such of the articles as can be made economically and efficiently are now required to be purchased compulsorily by the departments of Government[29] (emphasis added).

Brushing aside suggestions to effect a change in policy, the government submitted that

> the installation of power driven machinery and the employment of trained instructors in the several jails have placed these concerns more or less on a permanent basis. They have cost the government enormously and any direction to recede from the steps already taken regarding these industries will result in serious loss to government. The jails department have, on the advice of committees, undertaken only such manufactures as can be advantageously carried out by the department. In the circumstances stated above there does not seem to be any real necessity for a change in the policy of government adopted in the matter of jail industries. Jails cannot obviously compete successfully with private enterprise but is endeavouring to meet the reasonable requirements of the consuming departments of government in respect of their orders. At the same time the Inspector General of Prisons should see that the jail industries are run on sound and efficient lines so that the consuming departments may not have any cause for complaint in regard to the quality of the articles supplied to them.[30]

[29] Law (General) G.O. no. 732, dated 24 February 1932.
[30] Ibid.

Opposition to State-sponsored Manufacturing in Jails

Manufacturing in jails under the aegis of the State had its critics who kept up a constant correspondence with the provincial and central governments, condemning state-sponsored manufacturing in general and the introduction of steam machinery in particular as being unfair and detrimental to private enterprise. The Coimbatore central jail, where weaving and making of cotton goods was carried out on a fairly large scale, became the prime target of attack from the Chambers of Commerce in general and M/s Binny and Co. in particular. In the beginning, for almost twenty years, that is, up to 1905, Binny and Co. addressed their complaints directly to the GOI, requesting the latter to bring pressure on the provincial government to close down and/or at least minimize manufacturing activities in jails. It was only in 1905 that the government, in one of its replies to Binny and Co. (through the Madras government), informed the company that 'in future any representations which they wish to make must be submitted through the Government of Madras'.[31] The arguments and counter-arguments in the case and the unresolvable nature of the debate, inadvertently, also reveal the differing perceptions of the mercantile community and the officials in the provincial government over the role of the State.

Mention has already been made of the installation of new machinery and expansion of weaving facilities in the Coimbatore jail towards the closing years of the

[31] Letter from Under Secretary, Government of India, to the Chief Secretary, Government of Madras dated 6 June 1905—Judicial G.O. no. 1080–1, dated 8 July 1905.

nineteenth century. Complaining against this, Binny and Co. quoted an extract from the proceedings of the GOI, Home Department resolution of 1886 to show how the action of the jail authorities was a direct violation of the expressed views of the Governor-General in Council.

> With regard to intramural employments the Governor-General in Council admits that, in Provinces having a completely organised system of Central Jails, there must be in such jails well regulated industrial employments on a large scale; but His Excellency in Council considers that Jails should not be converted into steam factories. The use of steam machinery in jails will not, however in future be absolutely prohibited, although care should be taken that limits are set to its employment in individual cases, where it is found to be incompatible with the penal character of convict labour, or where there is strong reason to believe that it enables the jails to compete injuriously with private capitalists in the neighbourhood. If any jail industry is proved seriously to injure any local trade, it should be discontinued in favour of some other kind of employment.[32]

The use of power looms in the Coimbatore jail, therefore, according to Binny and Co., enabled the jail to compete injuriously with private capitalists in the neighbourhood and was, hence, a direct discouragement to the development of private enterprise.

Cardew, Inspector General of Prisons, in his letter to the Chief Secretary to the Madras government, stated that the new machines installed in the Coimbatore jail were to replace the twenty-five-year-old machinery of the jail: 'renewals are obviously essential and such renewals

[32] See letter from Binny and Co. to the Chief Secretary, Government of Madras, dated 6 December 1898—Judicial G.O. no. 1342, dated 22 August 1899.

are evidently authorised by the para of the Home Department Resolution quoted in M/s Binny and Co.'s letter'.[33] Cardew also pointed out that the GOI had laid stress on the importance of developing jail manufactures particularly with a view to supplying the requirements of government departments.

But until the Government of India's views on the subject of manufactures undergo a change, it is impossible to allow jail manufactures to retrogress and if retrogression is to be avoided, machinery must from time to time be renewed and replaced with renewed and more efficient types. The action taken at the Coimbatore central jail has not gone beyond this and is not reasonably open to the random remarks contained in M/s Binny and Co's communication.[34]

The GOI, in its orders on the above complaint, agreed with the Madras government that M/s Binny and Co.'s petition disclosed no reasonable ground of complaint. The GOI's letter stressed the fact that while paragraph 6 of the Home Department Resolution of 1886 dealt with the general question of supplies to the public and forbade jail manufactures being carried on in such a manner as to compete injuriously with private enterprise in the same neighbourhood, paragraph 7 requested local governments and administrators to adopt their intramural industries to the needs of the public consuming departments. These departments were required to take articles of jail manufacture in preference to any other, provided such articles were supplied by the jails of the same quality and at the same price as could be obtained in the open

[33] Letter from Inspector-General of Prisons dated 3 January 1899 to the Chief Secretary, Madras—Judicial G.O. no. 187, dated 1 February 1899.

[34] Ibid.

market. Hence, the GOI letter emphasized that the 'general orders in paragraph 6 of the Resolution of May 1886 are subject to the regulations regarding supplies to public departments prescribed in paragraph 7'.[35]

In 1900, Binny and Co. forwarded, as an illustration of the extent of jail competition with private enterprise in the Madras Presidency, an extract from the *Madras Mail* containing an advertisement of the Vellore Central Jail offering to supply a number of miscellaneous articles to the public.[36] The Inspector General of Prisons tried to justify multifarious activities in the Vellore jail on the ground that it was not possible to utilize all available labour supply on the one principal industry which, in the Vellore Central Jail was tent-making. Consequently certain minor industries that offered facilities for providing prisoners with a ready means of obtaining an honest livelihood on release from jail were chosen.[37] However, orders were issued to the Vellore Central Jail to reduce the multifarious industries carried on there. This jail was also asked to desist from advertising in the local papers articles of jail manufacture.[38]

In 1905, Binny and Co. again addressed a memorandum to the Department of Industries and Commerce entitled 'Jail vs Cotton Mills' in which they lamented: 'We have at various times during the last twenty years addressed the Local Government on the subject of jail competition

[35] Letter from Inspector General of Prisons to the Chief Secretary to Government, Madras, dated 21 April 1900—Judicial G.O. no. 187, dated 1 February 1899.

[36] Ibid.

[37] Letter from Inspector General of Prisons to the Chief Secretary to Government, Madras, dated 21 April 1900—Judicial G.O. no. 757, dated 30 May 1900.

[38] Orders of the Government, Judicial G.O. no. 757, dated 30 May 1900.

with private enterprise but without satisfactory results either in the decrease of such competition or of any hope that the competition would cease at some future time.'[39] Their principal target was the cotton mill at the central jail at Coimbatore, which had added considerably to its capacity and had taken over not only the supply of drills to the Police and Madras Army Clothing departments but also material to the Supply and Transport departments. Besides, the jail had extended its efforts to cover Burmah also, the latter being supplied with sheets made at the Coimbatore jail.

Binny and Co. accordingly requested the GOI to ensure that:

(a) sale in the open market of cloths manufactured in jails was prohibited when such goods competed with existing private manufactures;
(b) an enquiry was made by government before ordering power machinery to supply cloth to government departments to ascertain whether private enterprise had expended capital in importing special machinery to meet particular government requirements;
(c) the use of power machinery by jails was limited;
(d) private manufactures were given a fair and equal chance of competing with jails for government contracts and that when the tenders of jails were found unsatisfactory, the latter was not given a special favoured chance of reconsidering their tendered rates.[40]

---

[39] Letter from Binny and Co., to the Department of Industry & Commerce, Government of India dated 13 February 1905—Judicial G.O. no. 460, dated 23 March 1905.

[40] Judicial G.O. no. 831, dated 20 May 1905; Judicial G.O. no. 1080–1, dated 8 July 1905.

The Inspector General of Prisons, Madras, and the Chief Secretary, Madras government, in their reply to the GOI, differed fundamentally from the views expressed by Binny and Co. and refused to accede to the latter's demand. Commenting seriatim on the points raised by Binny and Co., their contention was that:

(a) Requesting the Government of India to prohibit the sale in the open market of cloths manufactured in jails when such goods competed with existing private manufactures was tantamount to asking that all weaving in jails be discontinued inasmuch as all cloth, even that used for convict clothing, could be obtained in the open market and, therefore, if made in the jails must in a sense compete with private enterprise. While it was laid down that the intramural industries of the jails should be adapted as much as possible to the requirements of the public consuming departments, it was pointed out that it was not possible always for a jail to obtain contracts from public departments that would exactly keep all the looms occupied throughout the year. When government orders were not sufficient, certain articles were manufactured for private sale. In the Coimbatore jail the articles thus manufactured were only such as had been made on handlooms for the past thirty or forty years. Better machinery had merely enabled the jail to improve on these materials;
(b) Expecting the government to make an 'enquiry' as to whether private enterprise had expended capital on importing special machinery to meet particular government requirements was considered unreasonable by the provincial

government authorities. The latter referred the company to the Government of India order of 1900 in which it was explained that the intention of the order was to enable the government 'to avail itself of labour, for the maintenance of which it has to pay, in producing articles it has to purchase'. It was also considered important that the government was not to be solely dependent on private enterprise for its public wants especially when it had an institution to meet these wants;

(c) The introduction of power machinery had become necessary to meet the essential condition under which the public consuming departments were required to take articles of jail manufacture in preference to other, namely, that such articles as were supplied by the jails were of the same quality as could be obtained in the open market;

(d) As regards the request that private manufactures be given a fair and equal chance of competing with jails for government contracts, it was pointed out that Binny and Co. had misapprehended the conditions of the 'favoured chance' referred to. The correct procedure that government departments were required to adopt was that before calling for tenders in the open market, the prevailing prices of such articles as the jails could supply was to be ascertained (by private local enquiries) and the probable requirements with samples (if necessary) communicated to the Inspector General of Prisons with a view to it being considered whether the jails could undertake the supplies at those rates and according to the samples specified. It was only after the jails had declared their inability to do so that tenders were

> to be called for in the open market in which the jails were refrained from competing.[41]

In 1910, Binny and Co. tried to pressurize provincial governments through the Chambers of Commerce in India. In a letter addressed to the Chamber of Commerce, Madras,[42] detailing what it termed 'serious injury' being done to the private woollen mills of India, particularly the Bangalore Woollen, Cotton and Silk Mills, by the Bhagalpur Jail and to the Buckingham and Carnatic Mills by the Coimbatore Jail, Binny and Co. urged the Chamber of Commerce in India to unite in pressing on the GOI and, if necessary, on the Secretary of State for India, the acceptance of the principle laid down by the Sydney Congress and Chambers of Commerce that 'in no case should power machinery be employed in jails for the production of articles of trade'.[43]

Binny and Co. began their tirade against the provincial government by stating that the 'competition with private enterprise is then by Government machinery and not

[41] Ibid.

[42] Letter from Binny and Co. (Ltd) Madras to the Chairman, Chamber of Commerce, Madras, dated 7 March 1910—Judicial G.O. no. 1097, 21 July 1910.

[43] The resolution on jail manufactures as finally adopted by the Sydney Congress is worth reproducing.

'Whereas private enterprise has the right to be protected against the competition of articles of trade manufactured by convict labour at an artificially lowered cost of production; and whereas there are indications of a tendency in certain parts of the Empire to develop the commercial element of jail labour to the injury of private manufactures, this congress approves the principle that the products of jail labour should be used in Government services only but in no case should power machinery be employed in jails for the production of articles of trade.'

See Appendix A to letter from Binny and Co., Madras to the Chamber of Commerce, Madras dated 7 March 1910.

merely by Government's criminals'.[44] The various issues raised by Binny and Co. were as follows:[45]

a. Government seems never to have understood that if a Government department takes the finished products of a jail, it does not supply the raw material... The Bhagalpur jail buys its wool in the open market in competition with the private manufactures; correspondents of ours gravely complain of the impossibility of purchasing wool in the districts in which the jail is operating of the high prices paid and of the consequent demoralization for a considerable time of the market. In any manufacturing industry the price paid for the raw material is plainly of as much importance as the sales value of the finished goods and the actin of a government department which affects the one is as prejudicial as if it affected the other.
b. The Coimbatore jail not only makes no secret of its desire to sell to the public, but pushes the business by commercial method... The jail some time ago installed expensive check looms, government departments do not use checks, and there could be no clearer proof of a deliberate intention to cater for the public market than the purchase of special looms to manufacture such cloths. We have brought this fact to the notice of government without the slightest effect.
c. The effect of the jail action has been that the woollen machinery at Bangalore is now only fully employed in exceptional years. In years of moderate demand much of it is stopped. During the last six months of 1909, only half the machinery of the mill was at work. The Army clothing contracts alone would have materially altered this condition of things.
d. The Government of India requires 'extensions of magnitude' in jail machinery to be submitted to it for sanction. Both Bhagalpur and Coimbatore appear to have made such

[44] Ibid.

[45] What follows has been taken from Binny's letter to the Chamber of Commerce, ibid.

extensions but there does not seem to have been any such sanction obtained.

e. ...We do most strongly object to a system which permits the money of the state to be continually expended in larger means of competition with the private manufacturer. Unless checked, this expenditure will go on and will become more and more a serious economic factor. The example of Bengal and Madras has already led the Punjab to contemplate steam machinery in the jails of the Province, and we may look for the same action in other parts of India. There is no security that such new jail factories will be limited to the industries already undertaken and once established they will grow by the natural process of 'replacements'.
f. India is, we believe, the only country in the world which employs steam machinery in jails, or which justifies such employment for the supply of government requirements. A government controlled by public opinion would scarcely use such a pretext, and the fate of a British Ministry which turned on such grounds Parkhurst into a cotton mill or Dartmoor into a woollen factory would be sudden and memorable.
g. Treated as a commercial undertaking the jail results are contemptible, whilst the system is a failure both as regards penal discipline and the reform of the criminal.

The Chamber of Commerce, Madras, forwarded the letter containing the above allegations to the GOI (through the Madras government) and strongly urged the government on the necessity of imposing severe limitations on the employment of power machinery in jails until such time as its use could be altogether suppressed. 'There is a tendency to lay too much stress on the commercial aspect of convict labour, in forgetfulness of the principle that jail labour ought to be before all things penal', the Chamber added.[46]

[46] Letter from the Chairman, Chamber of Commerce, Madras, to the Chief Secretary to Government, 20 April 1910—Judicial G.O. no. 1097, 21 July 1910.

The response from various official quarters to the above offensive launched by Binny and Co. through the Chamber of Commerce was equally scathing.

(a) The emphasis on the retention of the penal element in prison labour came in for a lot of flak, particularly from officials directly involved with jail administration.

Gadsden, Acting Inspector General of Prisons, remarked:

> ...the commercial community in general appears to hold the opinion that, as soon as an individual is placed in jail, his labour should be lost to the country and he is no longer entitled to earn his living. There is a large prison population for which some suitable labour must be found, and I consider that the ordinary tax payer may reasonably expect that the prison population should be to some extent self-supporting, and this cannot be done without some interference with private enterprise... A well organised industry where tasks can be carefully watched and exacted is perhaps the best method of maintaining the penal element, for though the work in such an industry would not be considered laborious especially where machinery is employed, it necessitates the constant attention of the prisoner throughout the working hours and also possesses an educational element which has not, I venture to say received the attention it deserves.[47]

Col. Macnamara, Inspector-General of Prisons, Madras, in a memorandum wrote:

> Such interest as the commercial interest takes in the subject is of a personal, if not of a more or less selfish character, and they are, to all interests and purposes neither actuated

[47] Letter from E.H. Gadsden, Acting Inspector General of Prison, to the Chief Secretary to Government, dated 23 September 1906—Judicial G.O. no. 1814, 25 October 1907.

by a desire to benefit humanity at large, nor to take into consideration how matters stand from the point of view of criminal administration or reform... They never think of how prisoners are to be employed if all the fields they wish to reserve to themselves, were closed against jail goods; they never think of how the general tax-payer may be affected so long as grist can be brought to their own mills, and most important of all, they never consider the question of the reform of the criminal, which is one, if not the principal point that should dominate the whole controversy. We must therefore choose between industry and interference on the one hand, and idleness and non-interference on the other. The former means the reform of the prisoner and putting him in the way of earning his living, to the benefit of the public at large, while the latter means making him a worse member of society than when he entered the jail, and increased cost to the state, for the advantage of a few.[48]

The IJC categorically put down in its report that the main object of prison labour was reformation of the prisoner. Consequently all forms of labour that were purposeless and sterile were to be eschewed.[49]

(b) Some of the accusations levelled by Binny and Co. were not just debatable but factually incorrect.

Binny and Co. had charged the Coimbatore jail with installing expensive check looms when no government department used such cloth. Gadsden exposed the falsity of this argument by pointing out, first, that there was one department of government which did use check cloth,

[48] Memorandum on Prison Labour and Disposal of Jail Made Goods written by Lt. Col. R.J. Macnamara, Inspector-General of Prisons—Judicial G.O. no. 1061, 3 August 1908. Also reproduced in the *Report of the Indian Jails Committee*, vol. 2, Minutes of Evidence, pp. 425–34.

[49] *Report of the Indian Jails Committee*, vol. 1, p. 118.

namely the Ordnance Department. For several years the Coimbatore jail had been given the contract for check dusters for this department for which the four check looms had been obtained. Further, it was emphasized, that the outturn of miscellaneous cloth obtained from the looms during the time they were not employed on work for government departments was so trifling that it could not be regarded as injuriously affecting Binny and Co. or any other private firm.[50] As regards Binny and Co.'s accusation that 'extensions of magnitude' had been made in jail industrial machinery without government sanction, Gadsden was furious that 'a firm of Messrs. Binny and Co.'s standing should make statements without verifying the facts. Additions (to the Coimbatore Jail) were made from time to time but in every case with the sanction of Government'.[51]

Another statement made by Binny and Co., the veracity of which was contested by the IJC, was that India was the only country in the world that employed steam machinery in jails or that justified such employment for the use of government requirements. The committee, in its Report, pointed out that both in the UK and the USA, power-driven machinery of the most up-to-date character were freely employed in prisons, often realizing large profits and that, therefore, these jails had gone beyond and ahead of what had been done in India.[52]

Another accusation levelled, the content of which was discounted by Gadsden in the case of the Madras Presidency, was that, jail manufacturing activities had led

[50] Letter from Gadsden, Superintendent, Central Jail Coimbatore to the Inspector General of Prisons, dated 6 May 1910–Judicial G.O. no. 1097, 21 July 1910.

[51] Ibid.

[52] Report of the *Indian Jails Committee*, vol. 1, p. 125.

to increase in raw material prices as well as a shortage. Gadsden countered this by pointing out that, on the contrary, in taking up large government contracts, the government had benefited another company, namely, the Coimbatore Spinning and Weaving Mills, who had no looms but confined their operations to spinning. The jail obtained nearly all its yarn from this local mill and had a monthly account with the mill averaging nearly Rs.8,000–10,000, benefiting therefore a private firm to a very considerable extent without causing any inconvenience or loss to anyone in the purchase of raw material.[53]

(c) On the question of the use of power-driven machinery in jails and the consequent alleged competition of the State with private enterprise, the IJC addressed all the local governments, asking them to invite the special attention of the several Chambers of Commerce to the inquiry so that the latter might have a full opportunity of laying their views before the committee. Each and every one of the Chambers of Commerce throughout the country who sent in their replies to the IJC were categorical that power-driven machinery ought not to be introduced in jails as it would lead to increased production which in its train would bring competition with industrial concerns for disposal of the extra production.[54] Further, most of them also stressed the fact that since attendance upon power-driven machines did not involve arduous and toilsome work nor required such close attention as hand labour, 'houses of correction

[53] Letter from Gadsden to the Chief Secretary to Government, dated 23 September 1906—Judicial G.O. no. 1814, 25 October 1907; Letter from Gadsden to the Inspector-General of Prisons, dated 6 May 1910–Judicial G.O. no. 1097, 21 July 1910.

[54] *Report of the Indian Jails Committee*, vol. 1, Appendix V: Correspondence with Chambers of Commerce, pp. 415–23.

should not introduce devices which would tend to minimize the rigours of labour'.[55]

However, only one Chamber of Commerce in India, namely, the Indian Merchants' Chamber and Bureau, Bombay, thought it necessary to depute a representative to appear before the IJC. The evidence given by this person, as the IJC put it, 'speaks for itself'. He admitted that the competition of the existing power-driven cotton and jute factories in jails were so trifling as to be negligible, but nevertheless adhered to the objection to steam-driven machinery 'on principle'. When asked whether the handlooms in jail would not compete with the handloom weavers outside, he could not deny that such competition would arise and would be infinitely more harmful to the handloom weaver than the existing power-driven machinery was to the great organized industries. Finally, when invited to make constructive suggestions as to the proper employment of jail labour, all that he could suggest was stone-breaking, road-making, or agriculture, the last two of them essentially extramural forms of labour and thus impossible of adoption for the general body of prisoners.[56]

The IJC recognized that the task of finding employment for prisoners must be so conducted as to do the least possible injury to weak and unorganized traders and nascent industries. The IJC's conclusion was that the least injury to private enterprise would be caused by directing jail labour into those channels in which large organized and powerful industries were already in existence, for instance, the great jute and cotton industries. Justifying this suggestion, they pointed out that in the Presidency

[55] Ibid., especially letter from the Manager, Central India Spinning, Weaving and Manufacturing Company Ltd., Nagpur to the Under Secretary to the Chief Commissioner, Central Provinces, Nagpur, dated 10 February 1920, p. 417.

[56] *Report of the Indian Jails Committee*, vol. 1, pp. 124–5.

Jail of Calcutta there existed a power-driven factory for the manufacture of jute goods with 50 looms. The data then available to the IJC showed that in 1916–17 there were in India no less than 74 jute mills with 39,697 looms and 824,315 spindles. 'No one would, we think, be likely to affirm that the 50 looms in the Calcutta Presidency Jail or even ten times that number, could have any serious effect on the great, highly-developed and enormously prosperous jute industry of India.'[57] Similarly, in the Coimbatore jail, which had a power-driven factory for the manufacture of cotton cloth, the number of looms in the factory was 110, while the numbers of looms employed in the 236 cotton mills of India in 1916–17 was 102,781 with 6,253,610 spindles. In such a situation, the IJC concluded, the effect of jail competition must always be infinitesimally small.[58]

(d) A lot of dust was raised by private capitalists to argue that 'If the Government of India would have the accounts of these manufacturing concerns [in jails] subjected to a proper commercial audit, we are convinced that there would very soon be an end of steam machinery in jails.'[59]

The Jail Industries Committee set up by the Madras government went into the question of the system of accounts maintained by the jails in the Presidency and came to the conclusion that they were not in favour of introducing a commercial system of accounts in jails. Their contention was that the object of introducing commercial accounts into a government concern was presumably to provide data for ascertaining whether a given manufacture was being conducted at a profit or not.

[57] Ibid., p. 124.

[58] Ibid.

[59] Letter from Binny & Co. to the Chairman, Chamber of Commerce, Madras, dated 7 March 1910—Judicial G.O. no. 1097, dated 21 July 1910.

While in free industrial enterprises labour contributed a very large proportion of the manufacturing cost in jails, on the other hand, the labourer had to be fed whether he was producing or not.[60]

It comes to this, that a jail is not a commercial proposition and cannot be regarded or treated as one. Government wish to be satisfied that there is no avoidable waste in the maintenance of jails which are in effect a disagreeable necessity in all civilized communities, and that such industries as are possible are efficiently organized. The convicts must be employed on remunerative work if possible; if not, they cannot be turned away and set free. All that seems to us to be required is a costing system for jail manufacturing to ensure that a jail does not go on making articles for sale at a cost exceeding the price that can be recovered. That price is determined by the price that similar articles fetch in the open market.[61]

'Misplaced Opposition': A Defiant Provincial Government

Concerted efforts at pressurizing the government to revise its policy and lay down that 'the state shall not in any way compete with private enterprise' were repeatedly made by the private capitalists. But the provincial governments in general and the Madras government in particular held firmly to the view that manufacturing in jails would stay. The government did not consider jail industries catering to government departments (which had previously been supplied by the private sector) as being in any way 'injurious' to private enterprise; on the contrary, they felt that the suggestion by the Associated Chambers

[60] Recommendations of the Jail Industries Committee—Law (General) G.O. no. 2157, 4 July 1925.

[61] Ibid.

of Commerce—that prisoners should be employed in cottage industries[62]—was injurious to the interests of the badly organized artisan class.

On the whole, jail administrators were required to operationalize a difficult combination of objectives, namely choosing industries in such a way that both reformation and remunerative labour went hand in hand with ensuring that jails were run efficiently without loss to the government. Under the circumstances, the jails were keen on extending and improving their operations through the appointment of qualified and trained instructors, including a technical adviser for raising the standard of business efficiency of jail officers, improving jail industries, disposing of jail products, and procuring raw materials. In fact, the authorities were even keen on introducing an 'earning scheme' for prisoners—a small remuneration for work turned out in excess of the prescribed task already in force.[63]

The Sixth All-India Conference of Inspectors-General of Prisons even passed the following resolution.

> In view of the necessity of providing good forms of industry for our jail prisoners and also of reducing the cost to the tax payer of the up-keep of jails, it is essential that goods markets should be provided for jail industries, and the members of the Conference see no objection to the sale of Jail-made products to the outside public as well as to government and semi-government departments.[64]

[62] Letter from the Associated Chambers of Commerce to the Government of India—Law (General) G.O. no. 693, dated 22 February 1932.

[63] Letter from the Inspector-General of Prisons, to the Secretary Government of Madras, Home Department—Home Department G.O. no. 588, dated 11 February 1942.

[64] Ibid.

A sharper and clear divergence of views between the government and private enterprise could not be asked for regarding what constituted the legitimate sphere of state activity. The controversy over the alleged competition of jail manufactures with private enterprise (even when demonstrated through figures that the convict population engaged in manufactures was limited and incapable of expansion or contraction at the will of the employer to suit the exigencies of the market) starkly exposed the fact that the private manufacturers were not content with the lion's share of the market but needed to have a monopoly.

Equally, the determination and grit of the jail administrators of the Presidency showed in their resolve to pursue with manufacturing in jails. In the replies addressed to the Chamber of Commerce, their arguments centered mainly around the need, not only 'to keep the prisoners employed and try to effect some reform of character but also to diminish the expenditure of the department'.[65] Consequently, the Inspector-General of Prisons, in his reply to the Secretary to the Madras Government, categorically stated: 'I submit that no sort of assurance need be given to the Chamber of Commerce in regard to the further development or retrogression of jail industries. If I may be permitted, I would like, in conclusion to suggest that the outlook of the deputation is wanting in feeling and entirely lacking in public spirit.'[66]

[65] See letter dated 7 September 1932 from the Inspector-General of Prisons to the Secretary to the Government of Madras—Law (General) G.O. no. 3827, 21 October 1932.

[66] Ibid.

PART II

Post-Independence Attempts at Industrialization

Some Illustrations

CHAPTER 3

The (Un)Making of a (Non)Competitive Economy

The accent of the recent developments in the industrial policy of the country, particularly the 'opening up' of the domestic industrial sector to global competition, has been in the government's own words, to 'build on the gains already made, correct the distortions or weaknesses that may have crept in, maintain a sustained growth in productivity and gainful employment and attain international competitiveness'.[1]

The obvious evidence of poor performance of the economy coupled with the pervasive phenomenon of rent seeking (corruption in common parlance) is largely responsible for the antipathy that has developed towards state intervention, culminating in the announcement of the new policy statement. The latter privileges the market as the prime mover of development. Viewed differently, the increasing attempt of the 'liberalization' measures is to insulate the functioning of the industrial sector from

* Previously published in *Productivity*, vol. 34, no. 3, October–December 1993.

[1] 'Text of Industrial Policy Statement', *Economic Times*, 25 July 1991.

political pressures on the assumption that, in the absence of intervention, the market itself will ensure economically correct decisions and that such decisions are sufficient for successful stabilization and adjustment.

The argument this chapter hopes to develop is that, restoring dynamism and imparting competitiveness to the economy is a two-pronged affair (necessitating organizational changes at both the firm and economy levels), which needs to be pursued simultaneously and in which process the role of the State and firm is central. While there is need to differentiate between the success (failure) of firms and the success (failure) of nation-states, the character of the state-capital linkage in any economy (that is the phenomenon of 'embededness' characterizing the economy) is a crucial determinant of economic performance.[2]

State's Role in Technical Development

The imperativeness of State intervention in economic development, particularly industrial development, has formed the theme of much development literature. All third-world States have attempted to accelerate economic development through growth strategies, which however, exhibit substantial variation in content, form, degree of commitment—across countries, instruments of implementation and over time. In the context of late industrializers, the analyses offered by Gerschenkron[3] and Hirschman[4] are still very pertinent and help to refocus

---

[2] Mark Granovetter, 'Economic Action and Social Structure: The Problem of Embeddedness', *American Journal of Sociology*, vol. 91, no. 3, November 1985.

[3] Alexander Gerschenkron, *Economic Backwardness in Historical Perspective*, Cambridge, MA: Belknap, 1962.

[4] Albert Hirschman, *The Strategy of Economic Development*, New Haven, CT: Yale University Press, 1958.

attention on the centrality of the state despite neo-utilitarian attempts to reduce the state's role to the minimum.

Gerschenkron's main proposition is that, processes of industrialization are not amenable to implantation in backward countries. It is not just the speed of development that is problematic but the whole gamut of productive, organizational, and financial structures of industry by means of which development took place in the advanced countries in the first place. These differences in the speed and character of industrial development are, to a considerable extent, the result of application of institutional instruments for which there is little or no counterpart in countries that began their industrialization earlier. Thus, in late industrializing countries, it is not enough to simply provide a suitable environment; the state has to, in addition, organize crucial aspects of the market such as in the area of risk taking, serve as surrogate entrepreneur, etc.

Hirschman develops on the theme of 'inadequate' and 'timid' entrepreneurship characterizing the 'late late' developers of the twentieth-century third world. What is lacking in developing countries, according to Hirschman, is entrepreneurship in the sense of willingness to risk the available surplus by investing it in productive activities. If 'maximising induced decision-making' is the key, as Hirschman argues, then the State's role involves a high level of responsiveness to private capital. The state must provide disequilibrating incentives to induce private capitalists to invest and, at the same time, be ready to alleviate bottlenecks that are creating disincentives to investment. States that undertake the tasks outlined by Gerschenkron and Hirschman are called 'developmental' by Evans.[5]

[5] Peter Evans, 'The State as Problem and Solution: Predation, Embedded Autonomy, and Structural Change', in *The Politics of Economic Adjustment*, ed. Stephan Haggard and Robert R. Kaufman, New Jersey: Princeton University Press, 1992.

They (developmental states) extract surplus but they also provide collective goods. They foster long-term entrepreneurial perspectives among private elites by increasing incentives to engage in transformative investments and lowering the risks involved in such investments. They may not be immune to rent-seeking or to using some of the social surplus for the ends of incumbents and their friends rather than those of the citizenry as a whole. Yet, on balance, the consequences of their actions promote rather than impede economic adjustment and structural transformation.[6]

However, argues Evans, the potential existence of a positive State role creates no logical necessity of the potential being realized, inasmuch as, societies and economies that need 'developmental' states do not necessarily get them. The acid test for the State arises when faced with structural transformation, which in turn, renders the State either into a predatory one or a developmental one.

There is no disputing the fact that the economic success of the major East Asian Newly Industrialized Countries (NICs) was/is premised on the active involvement of the State. These States could not only foster rapid local industrialization but also obtain effective adjustment to changing international markets. The difference between India and the East Asian NICs lies precisely in the less developmental (more predatory) nature of the Indian State as against the more developmental (less predatory) nature of the East Asian NICs.

Import Substitution Policy

A substantive thrust of India's technology import policy has been the encouragement of domestic production to substitute for imports implemented through import

[6] Ibid., p. 148.

substitution industrialization. This, in turn, necessitated protection of the domestic industry under the infant-industry argument. The manner of implementation and operationalization of this strategy in India has led to two major negative results.[7] One is a non-competitive environment, and the other is the continued dependence of the economy on imports of production goods with substantial underutilization of capacity of the same at home. Given the inefficiency of final goods industries and hence their inability to compete in external markets through exports, a limit to the import capacity of production goods has appeared as a result of foreign exchange constraints. The net result has been a stagnant, inefficient, and non-integrated industrial sector.

The examination of such results needs to be done in a more rigorous manner than adopting the conventional argument of market inefficiency. One crucial thread of analysis revolves around the way in which technological change has been/was incorporated into and determined the industrial structure during the process of import substitution industrialization.

An interesting hypothesis that has been put forward with reference to South Korean industries is that the latter's superior performance can be attributed to a combination of selective infant industry protection and export activity.[8] Thus, it is argued that the protection of infant industries is most effective not as a part of an import-substitution regime but rather under an

[7] Kurt Unger, 'Industrial Structure, Technical Change and Microeconomic Behaviour in LDCs', in *Technical Change and Economic Theory*, ed. Giovanni Dosi et al., London and New York: Pinter, 1988, pp. 480–95.

[8] Martin Fransman, 'Conceptualising Technical Changes in the Third World in the 1980s: An Interpretive Survey', *The Journal of Development Studies*, vol. 21, no. 4, July 1985.

export-oriented one. Several reasons have been put forward to account for the positive effects that exports may have on total factor productivity, namely:

> The competitive pressure that compel improvement in product quality and reduction in cost; opportunities for international inter-firm learning that are opened up by exporting activities; economies of scale due to increased market size as a result of exporting possibilities and also fall in costs; overall improvement in productivity due to greater availability of foreign exchange and more productive inputs.[9]

Underlying this beneficial positive association between economic performance and exports is an implicit assumption; the attainment of a minimum threshold level of technological capability which can only be built up during a prior period of protected import substitution. The central role played by the domestic market in the growth of countries like South Korea and Japan has also been emphasized.[10]

However, in each of the above, the precise casual mechanisms need to be worked out. Moreover, while technical progress is necessary and occurs under both protected and more open regimes, the type of technical change may be different in each case, leading to differing consequences for the nature of growth of the economy. For example, it has been suggested that technical change may be more adaptive and less innovative under high protection, and more cost-reducing under the low protection of open economies. But no definite conclusions can be reached nor can any generalizations be drawn since one will

[9] Ibid., pp. 620–1.

[10] M. Nishimizu and S. Robinson, 'Trade Policies and Productivity Change in Semi-industrialized Countries', Report no. 52, Washington DC: World Bank, Development Research Department, 1983.

have to come to terms with the phenomenon of import-substituting industries of today becoming the export industries of tomorrow, in which case the connections between technical change for adaptation and subsequently for effective assimilation and innovation needs to be rigorously made. South Korea is a prime example of an economy that was/is both open and protected.[11]

It is our submission that statements of official policies need to be backed by sound empirical analyses of the phenomena being addressed, which by necessity implies an evaluation of the problems that the government thinks need rectification. This is because we believe that (if the economies of the East Asian countries present themselves as some sort of role models) governments do have the ability and the capacity to permanently alter the terms of international competition as well as irrevocably change the very structure of the market. In the Indian context, there are hardly sufficient studies of such an in-depth nature to warrant the (beneficial) impact that the government options will (automatically) follow from its statement of industrial policy, namely:

- The predictability and independence of action that this measure (namely the freedom to negotiate the terms of technology transfer with their foreign counterparts according to their own commercial judgement) is providing to Indian industry will *induce* them to develop *indigenous competence* for the *efficient absorption* of foreign technology; and
- Greater competitive pressure will (also) induce our industry to *invest much more in research and development* than they have been doing in the past.[12]

[11] Fransman, 'Conceptualising Technical Changes in the Third World in the 1980s'.

[12] 'Text of Industrial Policy Statement'. Emphasis added.

On the contrary, studies/data we have, while certainly critical of the ineffectiveness/even harmful nature of government intervention, point, at one level, to fundamental structural weaknesses afflicting the production system; at another level, they bring out starkly the inability of the political system to direct the economy towards certain well-defined economic goals.

Technical Performance of Indian Corporate Sector

In an earlier study we have examined in some detail the performance of the Indian corporate sector during the post-Independence period which we have divided into three phases, namely:

- Period of liberalization until the mid-1960s,
- Period of tight regulation since then and until the mid/late 1970s, and
- Period of gradual relaxation from then onwards with the pace of relaxation accelerating from the mid-1980s onwards.[13]

Summarizing the conclusions from the above examination, we note the following:

During the early phase of industrialization (until the mid-1960s), when business houses/subsidiaries of multinational corporations had freely availed of imports and foreign technical collaboration/investment opportunities, their performance—as documented by the

[13] Padmini Swaminathan, 'Bridging the Technology-Gap: How Farsighted and Dynamics is the Indian Corporate Sector', report prepared for the Development Research Group, Reserve Bank of India, 1993.

Monopolies and Restrictive Trade Practices Commission, and as indicated in the nature of R&D undertaken by them—did not in any way contribute to make them innovative enough to be internationally competitive and/or dispense with further collaborations for the same product.

An examination of the performance of the capital goods sector during the period of regulation, namely between 1973–4 and 1978–9, revealed two things: that the 'impressive' growth of the capital goods industry during the period under study could not have been possible in the absence of government policies; capital goods producers had acquired a substantial innovative capacity only in 'standard' modern technology while still being very weak in 'highly' modern technology despite the increasing R&D expenditures.[14]

Jacobson's[15] study of the engineering industry in the context of the new policy framework has brought out that while the liberalization measures were successful in improving access to foreign technology, this was at a price—in terms of both an inability to reap scale economies and a very poor innovate performance.

An examination of data provided by the Reserve Bank of India points to the dismal performance of the corporate sector in almost all indicators that one can associate with technological competence, namely expenditure on R&D, volume of goods exported, value of imports and expenditure related to technology imports that is, royalty, technical and consultancy fees, dividends, etc.

[14] Centre for Monitoring Indian Economy (CMIE), *Technology Issues in the Capital Goods Sector*, Bombay: United Nations Trade and Development, Bombay, 1984.

[15] Staffan Jacobson, 'Government Policy and Performance of the Indian Engineering Industry', *Research Policy*, vol. 20, 1991.

This lends itself to two broad conclusions: liberalization measures per se cannot impart that level of dynamism necessary to catapult a low-level economy, technologically speaking, into an internationally competitive one; this transformation requires, among other things, fundamental alterations in the production structure of the economy. There is a disjuncture in the authority structure of Indian society inasmuch as the State (which has brought into being and/or legitimated different forms of organizational enterprises in the economy) has not been able to get its economic programme implemented effectively through these enterprises. In other words, the role of the State, in general, and, more importantly, the need for the State to interact at a more intense level with business in particular given the domestic and global environment facing the country, are hard issues that need to be faced.

In a thought-provoking piece on the processes that lead to and/or hinder the accumulation of technological capability in developing countries, Bell and Pavitt[16] have come out with a number of observations that are directly relevant for India. In the early stages of development, according to the authors, the accumulation of technology is influenced by factor endowments and intersectoral linkages. In later stages, the level of technological knowledge itself can become a source of comparative advantage reflected in production know-how, the design of capital goods, and a capacity for reverse engineering and imitative research and development; firms play a central role in this process. The authors reject any distinction being

[16] Martin Bell and Keith Pavitt, 'Accumulating Technologies Capability in Developing Countries', *Proceedings of the World Bank Annual Conference on Development Economies*, IBRD/World Bank, 1992.

made between *innovation and diffusion* with its implicit assumption that technical change can easily and quickly be promoted through investment in new production capacity. Instead, they distinguish such capacity from the resources and institutions that make up a country's technological capabilities, emphasizing the evidence that the accumulation of technology does not necessarily follow from policies to achieve other objectives; it must become a policy objective in its own right. The authors therefore very emphatically conclude that the failure to recognize the firm as the central player in the accumulation of technology has been a major shortcoming of technology policy in most developing countries.

Role of Firms: Organizational Structure

A related phenomenon that is increasingly being addressed in the literature on the dynamics of industrial capitalism is the dependence of a nation's competitiveness upon the organizational and financial capabilities of its firms and their supporting institutions. The works of Chandler[17] and Lazonick[18] are particularly constitutive of this kind of analysis. Chandler examines the beginnings and subsequent growth of managerial capitalism in the US, Germany, and Great Britain, through an analysis of what he considers to be the basic institution, namely, the modern industrial enterprise.

[17] Alfred D. Chandler Jr., *Scale and Scope: The Dynamics of Industrial Enterprise*, Cambridge, MA: Harvard University Press, 1990.

[18] William Lazonick, 'Organizational Integration in Three Industrial Revolutions', in *Evolving Technology and Market Structure*, ed. Arnold Heerje and Mark Perlman, Ann Arbor: The University of Michigan Press, 1990.

Chandler's implicit thesis is that firms and markets evolve together to shape industrial outcomes. A perspective that relies on markets only as the lens through which to understand industrial development is likely to be seriously flawed. Rather the strategic and organizational choices made by managers—choices not necessarily dictated by markets and technologies—shape if not determine both firm level and national economic performance.[19]

Characterizing the US as the home of competitive managerial capitalism, Chandler points out that it was the modern hierarchical industrial firm that was responsible for America's growth. The firms that obtained market power rarely got it through artificial barriers or anti-competitive conduct. Neither did it come solely or even largely from the technical efforts of investors. Rather, it came from the ability to develop and commercialize new technologies through the three-pronged strategy of investing in manufacturing, distribution, and management systems and people. British economic development, in contrast, suffered during the second Industrial Revolution because British entrepreneurs frequently failed to make the essential three-pronged investment in manufacturing, marketing and distribution, and management:

The pioneers recruited smaller managerial teams, and the founders and their families continued to dominate the management of the enterprise until well after World War II to the considerable detriment of the British economy. Boards of directors were restricted to family and those with family

[19] David J. Teece, 'The Dynamics of Industrial Capitalism: Perspective on Alfred Chandler's Scale and Scope', *Journal of Economic Literature*, vol. XXXI, March 1993, p. 200.

connections or social position, with little place for senior managers.[20]

Developing further on the theme of organizational structures in the three Industrial Revolutions, Lazonick[21] argues that in the British case, top management tends to be segmented not only from shop-floor operators but also from technical specialists, who, in both the US and Japan are integrated into the managerial structure. The origins of British organizational segmentation lie in the combination of the legacy of craft control over work organization and the persistence of proprietary control of top management positions even in larger British firms. Moreover, notes Lazonick, the British practice of passing on control of the firm to family members, regardless of relevant career credentials, has stifled the growth of the firm and the development of organizational capability. The proprietary firm often adopted a non-expansionary strategy in order to avoid becoming dependent on outside creditors or shareholders, or to avoid becoming subservient to a bureaucracy of technical specialists and middle managers.

The relevance of the above discussion to India can hardly be overemphasized. In the first place, the 'success' of the new policy measures depends primarily on the initiative and performance of the private sector. However, the organizational structure and capability of the different forms of production characterizing the Indian private sector is hardly a point of debate. Rather, the policy statements overtly and covertly privilege the

[20] Chandler, *Scale and Scope*, p. 235.

[21] Lazonick, 'Organizational Integration in Three Industrial Revolutions'.

market over substantive firm-level organizational changes to achieve competitiveness, both at the national and international levels.

Proprietary capitalism characterizes much of the Indian private corporate sector; boards of directors, as in the case of Britain, are restricted to family and extended family members with little place for professionally qualified 'outside' personnel. Consequently, more often than not, the goal for family firms is not long-term growth and profit but the provision of a steady flow of cash to owners. In such a milieu, accumulating wealth rather than making financial commitments to the rebuilding of organizational capability becomes the primary objective.

The inability of the Indian State to operationalize its policies at the firm level is brought out very concretely in the studies done, for example, by the India-Japan Study Committee.[22] These studies are based on the experiences of the Japanese companies which were (as in 1985) in technology collaborative relations with their Indian counterparts. We reproduce a part of the responses received by the committee from Japanese companies (Tables 3.1 and 3.2); the latter were asked to write down their most earnest request to their Indian partners, relating particularly to aspects of technology transfer.

Thus, on pain of repetition, it needs to be underscored that 'opening up' of the economy to allow, among other things, easy importation of technology, constitutes only the beginning; ultimate success depends mainly on the accumulation of experience and know-how by improving upon imported technologies.

[22] The India-Japan Study Committee, 'Problems and Prospects of the Technology Transfer between Japanese and Indian Companies', mimeographed, Tokyo, January 1986.

Table 3.1: *Request by Japanese Companies to the Owners of their Indian Partners*

I. Technical Awareness
   1. Awareness on the importance of technologies and quality
      (Ex.)
      - 'First priority should be given to the improvement of product quality.'
      - 'Similar quality, delivery period and prices to those in Japan should be ensured.'
      - 'Rapid localization is not appropriate.'
   2. Evaluation on intangible technology
      (Ex.)
      - 'Intangible values (industrial properties such as patent right and trademark right as well as know-how) must be fully understood and appreciated.'
   3. Accumulation of expertise and technical information
      (Ex.)
      - 'Indian companies (although ambitious in their intentions) often try to enter new fields where they have no experience, in a total reliance on overseas technologies. This seems too easy.'
      - 'Their expertises are extremely insufficient. Any party involved in technical collaboration should be prepared to visit the partner with relevant technical data for necessary consultations. Success of a project would depend on such enthusiasms.'

II. Application and Improvement of Transferred Technology
      - 'It is not appropriate to rely completely on the licensor.'
      - 'It is necessary to develop international products (in terms of design, quality and prices) from a longer viewpoint. That will require constant improvement in the transferred technology. So far, there has been a repeated process that transferred technologies become obsolete in a few years and are replaced by new ones which are also transferred from abroad.'
      - 'They should make their own efforts to reduce local cost, instead of just requesting the Japanese partners to avoid cost increases.'

(Table 3.1 Continued)

(Table 3.1 Continued)

III. Management Method
   1. Prevention of job-hopping
      (Ex.)
      - 'Measures should be taken to prevent job-hopping of those engineers and workers who have acquired skills.'
   2. Development of human resources
      (Ex.)
      - 'More middle-class engineers (site leaders) nurtured'
   3. Decentralization of decision-making
      (Ex.)
      - 'Bottom-up management is also important in addition to the top-down management.'
   4. Others
      (Ex.)
      - 'Workers are poorly motivated. Necessary training should be provided to improve the situation.'
      - 'Class-consciousness should be lessened.'
      - 'Introduction of the Japanese style of management.'

Source: Problems and Prospects of Technology Transfer between Japanese and Indian Companies, Tokyo: The India-Japan Study Committee, January 1986, pp. 37–9.

Table 3.2: *Requests by Japanese Companies to the Engineers of Partner Firms*

I. Directly Related to Mastering Japanese Technologies
   1. Awareness on the need of improved technological level.
   2. Modesty in learning technologies
      (Ex.)
      - 'They tend to have too much pride, and should try to be modest in learning transferred technologies.
      - 'We want them to listen to our advice as far as Japanese technologies are concerned.'
      - 'It is not appropriate to overestimate European technologies'
   3. Undesirability of continued reliance
      (a) Self-aid efforts
         (Ex.)
         - 'They should not rely totally on the licensor.'

- 'We want them to try to solve minor problems on their own as much as possible.'

(b) Original modification and improvement not just copying
(Ex.)
- 'Efforts should be made to modify Japanese technologies so that they would best suit in India.'
- 'Originality should be developed'

4. Others
(Ex.)
- 'More study through literature is necessary in accumulating expertise'
- 'We want them to be more informed of the product concerned.'

II. Work Attitude of Engineers

1. Improved awareness on product quality
(Ex.) 'It is sometimes considering in India that 'similar' things would do. Accuracy, quality, materials etc. are not given first priority.'
2. Overcoming of sectionalism
(Ex.) 'Positive efforts are necessary to learn expertise and technologies even outside each person's field. They should not evade responsibilities nor make excuses.'
3. Practicality

(a) Practical work attitude
(Ex.)
- 'They are argumentative, causing a delay in work. They do not take initiative in various activities. These tendencies should be changed.'
- 'In India, production techniques are often made light of due to too much emphasis on book knowledge. This has resulted in inadequate product quality.'
- 'They tend to stick excessively to what is written in documents. Instead, efforts must always be made to make modifications for improvement and develop new applications.'

(b) Emphasis on site work
(Ex.)
- 'They tend to be 'desk' engineers. We want them to be practical engineers based on site experiences.'

(Table 3.2 Continued)

(Table 3.2 Continued)

- 'They should build up a habit of confirming site details by own eyes, not relying on knowledge or information provided. What is most important is 'management and work based on facts.'

4. Teaching of expertise to others
   (Ex.)
   - 'Know-how provided by the licensor should not be made personal properties.'
   - 'Provided expertise and technologies should not be in the possession of some individual but should be utilized jointly with others.'
5. More effective training and management of workers
   (Ex.) 'Operators should be trained and managed in a more effective manner.'
6. More effective preparation
   (Ex.) 'Work must proceed according to a pre-determined schedule.'

Source: Problem and Prospects of the Technology Transfer between Japanese and Indian Companies, The India-Japan Study Committee, January 1986, pp. 39–41.

Conclusion

We began with the argument that the making of a competitive economy requires the simultaneous interaction of state and capital. More specifically, only a more developmental (and less predatory) State will have the transformative capacity to command, monitor, and get the private sector to perform. Organizational changes within the private sector are essential for firms to respond to, assimilate, and improve upon externally acquired technologies on a continuous basis. A developmental State can facilitate this process in a number of ways, the more obvious ones being through the financing of R&D, the explicit pursuit of relevant postgraduate education (and subsequent work experience), etc. The important thing to realize, however, is that, mere government-funded R&D and postgraduate education, without matching technological capabilities and learning experience in firms, is doomed to failure. The policy of setting up government-funded R&D particularly is based on the fallacious assumption that the technology which emerges from R&D laboratories is easily transmissible and applicable.

We concur with Evans[23] in stressing the need to focus more on State capacity as an important factor in policy choice and outcomes. Seen in this light, Evans argues that the State's ability to perform administrative and other functions must be treated as a scarce good. He separates India and Brazil from the East Asian developmental states to illustrate the point that the states in East Asia not only had higher levels of capacity but greater selectivity in the tasks they undertook. The developmental states focused on industrial transformation and their strategies of promoting industry were designed to conserve administrative resources. As things stand, even if the Indian State were to accept today a more limited repertoire, we are not sure whether its existing capabilities can deliver the goods. Hence, even with greater selectivity, strengthening the capacity of the State is imperative for sustained structural adjustment. To conclude with Evans: 'Pretending otherwise would be as dangerous as from the utopianism. Transforming the state from problem to solution must be central item on any realistic third world policy agenda.'[24]

[23] Evans, 'The State as Problem and Solution'.

[24] Ibid., p. 181.

CHAPTER 4

Liberalization, Market Concentration, and Prospects for Growth

A Study of the TVS Group of Companies

The objective of the government in the 1980s was to reinforce the operation of the market mechanism in the hope this would rejuvenate the economy. A number of liberalization measures were adopted on the assumption that self-regulating markets could be relied upon to restore the Indian economy to a healthy international status.

Much has been made of the deleterious effect of the absence of foreign competition and the indiscriminate and indefinite nature of the protection granted to Indian industry. That a high order of protection (from both domestic and foreign competition) offered to industry had the effect of raising costs across the industrial sector is almost treated as an axiom. In what manner liberalization policies in general and of technology import in particular would raise the technological

* Previously published in Economic and Political Weekly, May 1988 and as MIDS Working Paper no. 59, 1985.

dynamism of the economy or accelerate the growth rate in productivity and output of Indian industry is yet to be documented though past decades of industrial growth do certainly provide a clue.

Taking the business group of T.V. Sundaram Iyengar and Sons Ltd. (TVS) we hope to establish that:

(a) Access to foreign technology for most of the manufacturing units in the group at the inception of production itself enabled the group to dominate the market for automotive ancillaries and components.
(b) Vertical integration in the production of automotive components over the years helped to perpetuate this dominance.
(c) Liberalization policies of the government facilitated automatic growth in capacity and enabled the group companies to seek 're-endorsement of enhanced capacities', thus expanding their hold over the market.
(d) Liberal approvals granted by the government for renewal of foreign technical/financial collaboration and equity participation not only led to continued payments in terms of royalty, technical know-how fees, etc., but have also thwarted any attempt at establishing domestic R&D in a big way considering the resources at the disposal of the group as a whole, their vast experience in the automotive ancillary and component field, and their long association with leading foreign manufactures in the automotive industry.
(e) With a strong domestic base to absorb, assimilate, and adapt technology, while liberalization of technology *per se* seemingly appeared to usher in

a competitive climate, its long-term implications for the domestic industrial structure in particular and of the economy in general turned out to be far worse.

Organizational Set-up of the TVS Group[1]

T.V. Sundaram Iyengar and Sons Ltd. is the parent company of the TVS group. It was incorporated as a private limited company in 1929. The shares of T.V. Sundaram Iyengar and Sons Ltd. are held by four families represented by the four sons of T.V. Sundaram Iyengar. Even though the company document filed with the Registrar of Companies classifies the holding of shares among three components—namely, bodies corporate, directors, and their relatives—and other top fifty shareholders, a study of each of the component reveals that the bodies corporate are nothing but small private limited companies promoted by one or other of the four families with shares held by the family members themselves. The four families between them hold cent per cent of the shares.

Up to 1973, only male lineal descendants (meaning male descendants in the male line only) could hold shares and be members of the company. After 1973, the word 'male' was deleted and the clause read as 'only lineal descendants of T.V. Sundaram Iyengar shall be members'. In 1979 this clause was also deleted the reason being 'so as to remove the restriction and conform to the requirements of a public company'.

[1] A study covering the organizational structure of the TVS group was undertaken by the author. See for details, Padmini Swaminathan, 'Business Houses in South India: A Case Study of the Structure and Functioning of the TVS Group', Working Paper no. 59, Madras: Madras Institute of Development Studies, 1985.

A special resolution (no. 3) passed on 27 October 1979 contained clauses (to be included as new provisions in the articles of association of the company, namely, T.V. Sundaram Iyengar and Sons Ltd.) defining a 'family' and laying down conditions under which decisions could be undertaken in a board meeting. According to this resolution, the 'family' strictly comprises the four sons of T.V. Sundaram Iyengar, their spouses, lineal descendants, and the spouses of such descendants. However, we also refer to the 'TVS extended family' in our study to make allowance for other members and close relatives not covered by the 'family' definition. Thus, for example, the daughters of T.V. Sundaram Iyengar and their spouses and children have been included by us in the 'TVS extended family' definition.

T.V. Sundaram Iyengar and Sons Ltd., the parent company, has two divisions, namely Sundaram Motors and Madras Auto Service, as well as four subsidiaries, namely Southern Roadways Ltd., Sundaram Industries Ltd., Sundaram Fasteners' Ltd., and Sundaram Textiles Ltd. Almost all the other companies in the group, specifically the existing public limited companies, have been promoted by the parent company.

We have undertaken a study of the share ownership pattern of the TVS group of companies which for convenience of analysis have been classified as follows:

(a) Eighteen public limited companies registered under the MRTP Act, 1969, as interconnected undertakings;
(b) Two public limited companies not registered under the MRTP Act, 1969;
(c) Over forty private limited companies.

There is considerable investment by TVS companies in their own group companies, especially in the case of the public limited companies. Apart from such intercorporate investment, there are holdings by 'family' members, 'extended family' members, foreign collaborators, etc. For the eighteen public limited companies, Table 4.1 gives details of the share holding pattern under the following heads, namely, holdings by,

1. TVS group companies
2. TVS 'family'
3. TVS 'extended family'
4. foreign collaborators
5. financial institutions
6. 'others'

While categories (1) to (5) are fairly clear, a few observations about the 'others' holding shares need to be recorded.

(i) In the first place it needs to be clarified that 'others' includes *corporate bodies* (other than those belonging to the TVS group) and individuals not included under the category of 'TVS family' or 'TVS extended family' but not necessarily unrelated.
(ii) In quite a few companies the same members (both corporate bodies and individuals) figure under the 'others' category (as evidenced from their names and addresses).
(iii) If the 'extended family' concept is extended further, then quite a few of the individuals included under the 'others' category are related in one way or the other to one or the other of the TVS extended family members.
(iv) Quite a few of the 'others' are employees of the TVS group of companies.

Table 4.1: Share Holding under Different Heads in TVS Public Limited Companies (Per Cent)

	T V Sundaram Iyengar and Sons Limited	*Sundaram Industries*	*Southern Roadways*	*Sundaram Fasteners*	*India Motor Parts and Accessories*	*Sundaram Textiles*	*Sundaram Finance*	*Wheels India*	*Lucas -TVS*
Percentage shares held by									
1. TVS group of companies		56.67	54.98	99.36	42.93	70.00		44.02	34.00
2. TVS 'family'	100.00	43.33	34.49	-	17.65	1.65	13.96	-	-
3. TVS 'extended family'	-	-	0.65	-	1.65	-	10.34	0.21	-
4. Foreign collaborators	-	-	-	-	-	-	-	35.91	51.00
5. Financial institutions	-	-	-	-	-	-	8.22	6.62	15.00
6. Others	-	-	9.88	0.64	37.77	28.35	67.48	13.24	-
Total	100.00	100.00	100.00	100.00	100.00	100.00	100.00	100.00	100.00
Total for TVS group of companies and 'family'	100.00	100.00	89.47	99.36	60.58	71.65	13.96	44.02	34.00
Total for (TVS group companies + family + extended family)	100.00	100.00	90.12	99.36	62.23	71.65	24.30	44.23	34.00

	Lucas Electrical Tractor Service	*Lucas Indian Service Ltd*	*Sundaram Clayton*	*Brakes India*	*Axles India*	*Sundaram Abex*	*Srichakra Tyres*	*TVS Sewing Needles*	*Sundarams Ltd*
Percentage shares held by									
1. TVS group of companies	100.00	100.00	51.04	51.00	33.00	29.88	30.00	43.25	-
2. TVS 'family'	-	-	-	-	-	0.09	-	-	70.54
3. TVS 'extended family'	-	-	-	-	-	-	-	-	8.52
4. Foreign collaborators	-	-	48.96	49.00	33.00	30.00	-	33.22	-
5. Financial institutions	-	-	-	-	-	1.09	-	23.43	-
6. Others	-	-	-	-	34.00	38.94	-	0.10	20.94
Total	100.00	100.00	100.00	100.00	*	100.00	**	100.00	100.00
Total for TVS group of companies and 'family'	100.00	100.00	51.04	51.00	-	29.97	-	43.25	70.54
Total for (TVS group companies + family + extended family)	100.00	100.00	51.04	51.00	-	29.97	-	43.25	79.06

Notes: *The details of the share holding pattern of *Axles India* have been taken from the prospectus issued by the company. Details are not yet available for public inspection.

** In the case of Srichakra Tyres the following are the details given in the *Stock Exchange Official Directory*, Bombay.

(i) 30 per cent shares reserved for TVS group of companies; (ii) 10 per cent reserved for promoters; (iii) 4.2 per cent reserved for employees; and (iv) 55.8 per cent offered to the public for subscription. Details for public inspection not available at the Registrar of Companies Office, Madras.

Source: Padmini Swaminathan, 'Business Houses in South India: A Case Study of the Structure and Functioning of the TVS Group', *Working Paper no. 59*, Madras: Madras Institute of Development Studies, September 1985.

What emerges from an analysis of the share ownership pattern of the eighteen public limited companies is the following:

(i) The shares of the parent company, namely T.V. Sundaram Iyengar and Sons Ltd., are held by the families of the four sons of T.V. Sundaram Iyengar.
(ii) T.V. Sundaram Iyengar and Sons Ltd., holds slightly over 50 per cent of the shares in each of its subsidiaries while a substantial part of the rest is held by the direct lineal descendants of T.V. Sundaram Iyengar, comprising the 'TVS family'.
(iii) T.V. Sundaram Iyengar and Sons Ltd. along with two of its subsidiaries, namely Sundaram Industries Ltd., and Southern Roadways Ltd., holds considerable proportion of the share capital of the rest of the group companies, exceptions being Sundaram Ltd. and Sundaram Finance Ltd.
(iv) There is considerable foreign equity participation by foreign collaborators in seven of the eighteen companies. In each case, the percentage of equity shares held by the foreign collaborators is 30 per cent and above with a majority holding of 51 per cent in Lucas-TVS Ltd.
(v) Apart from its holdings in the parent company, the shareholding by 'TVS family' is significantly evident in five of the eighteen companies and by the 'extended family' in two of the eighteen companies; more importantly, whatever has been disbursed to the ubiquitous 'public' (i.e. 'others') also reveals a pattern, inasmuch as the same 'public' figures in quite a few companies.
(vi) Intercorporate investment in the sense of TVS companies investing in companies other than

> their own group companies is rare and nominal. Further, the holding by financial institutions is also comparatively nominal and confined to five of the eighteen companies.

Thus, with the exception of Sundaram Finance Ltd. and Lucas-TVS Ltd. (where the majority is held by the foreign collaborators), in almost all other cases the holdings by TVS group companies and TVS family is considerable, making the business group as a whole a closely held unit.

An analysis of the composition of the board of directors of the TVS group companies reveals explicitly a case where if a family holds a majority of the shares in a company, it would be relatively difficult for non-family executives to participate in strategic control if family members seek to monopolize top executive positions for themselves. Further, while 'technical direction and co-ordination of the process of production' may seem to enhance the power of the bureaucratic hierarchy in charge of operational administration, it is important to note that a gulf exists between those executives who do participate in the exercise of strategic control and those who are merely concerned with day-to-day control over detailed operations of the enterprise.

Mention has already been made of a special resolution (no. 3) passed on 27 October 1979 which contained clauses to be included as new provisions in the articles of association of the parent company, namely, T.V. Sundaram Iyengar and Sons Ltd. Apart from defining a 'family', the resolution also laid down the conditions under which decisions should be undertaken in a board meeting. At the outset it should be recorded that in the parent company all the twelve directors belong to the TVS family with three directors from each of the four families.

Each of the said four families shall be entitled to have an equal number of directors at any time on the board including the person appointed by the concerned said family as nominated director, so long as the aggregate holding of the equity shares in the company by the concerned said family is not less than 10 (ten) per cent of the subscribed equity capital of the company for the time being.

Notwithstanding anything contained in these presents the board shall not enter into or amend any formation agreement or collaboration agreement with any company or individuals, whether Indian or foreign, unless the same is approved by a resolution at a meeting where at least one director representing each of the said four families is present and it has the unanimous consent of all the members of the board present and eligible to vote.

Any transfer of shares held by this company in any other company by way of sale, gift or pledge shall be only approved by a resolution of the board of the company passed at a meeting in which at least one director representing each of the four said families is present and it has the unanimous consent of all the members of the board present and eligible to vote. In the event any sale of such shares, the first option for purchase shall be given to the said four families in equal proportion and the said four families shall exercise the option within 30 days from the date of such offer.

According to the Companies Act 1956, 1/3 (one-third) of the total number of directors can be non-rotational directors. The present articles of the company provide that only the managing director shall be a non-rotational director. If the proposal for amendment set forth is approved there can be 4 non-rotational directors and each family can appoint one nominated director who will not be liable for retirement by rotation.

The present directors of the company are from the four families who hold the entire share capital of the company.

The fact that T.V. Sundaram Iyengar and Sons Ltd. has been the promoter of almost all the companies of the

TVS group and that T.V. Sundaram Iyengar and Sons Ltd. and its subsidiaries hold considerable proportion of the equity shares in most of the other companies of the group has already been mentioned by us. This, coupled with the contents of the above special resolution, clearly indicates where the decision-making power of the group lies. Further, in almost all the other companies of the group, the top executive positions of the board of directors are monopolized by the family members of the TVS group.

Business Carried on by the TVS Group of Companies

The business of the group as a whole can be studied under three broad heads:

a. Dealership/distributorship for automobile spare parts, accessories, and components. Of the twenty public limited companies, three are engaged in the above business.
b. Manufacture of automotive accessories/ components, etc., makes thirteen public limited companies engaged in the manufacture of various automotive products, components and accessories.
c. 'Miscellaneous' industrial category covered by the remaining four TVS public limited companies.

Data on share in production and capacity provided in Tables 4.2 and 4.3 give some idea of the predominant position occupied by the TVS group in important automotive accessories. Not only is the TVS group a 'larger house', but from the business carried on by the group it is clear that the group as a whole is very 'integrated' as far as the automotive industry is concerned. In the production of most of the important automobile

Table 4.2: Share of TVS Companies in All India Production (Percentage)

Products	*1978*	*1979*	*1980*	*1980–1*	*1981–2*	*1982–3*	*1983–4*	*1984–5*	*1985–6*
1. Brake assembly	60.58	60.38	63.89			71.77	59.51	58.88	
2. Air brakes	73.91	87.04	68.75						
3. Starter motors				85.45	73.75		80.21	81.69	65.60
4.Generators				81.31	73.46		77.86	80.90	71.79
5. Voltage regulators				83.70	80.85		69.66	89.72	59.00
6. Distributors				100.00	100.00		100.00	100.00	100.00
7. Headlamps				30.83	40.32		42.90	21.90	13.42
8. Electric horns				17.82	23.17		86.73	64.52	55.31
9. Flasher units				53.44	54.66		62.61	71.68	55.78
10. Wheels				67.94	86.62	82.68	79.39	84.79	81.31
11. Mopeds				4.58	15.06	24.5	23.01	26.10	29.50
12. Motorcycles								5.46	19.32
13. Ignition coils				100.00	100.00		100.00	100.00	100.00

Sources: (1) *Automotive Industry of India: Facts and Figures, 1980 and 1986*, Bombay: Automotive Component Manufacturers Association of India, 1986.
(2) Balance Sheets of the various TVS companies.

Table 4.3: Share in Licensed Capacity
(Percentage of All India Capacity)*

Products	*Percentage Share in Licensed Capacity*
1. Motorcycles	12.66
2. Mopeds	13.54
3. Starter motors	40.19
4. Generators/alternators	34.47
5. Voltage regulators	54.71
6. Distributors	100.00
7. Ignition coils	100.00
8. Wheels	57.29
9. Air brake assembly	74.84
10. Brake assembly	54.34
11. Brake linings	16.34
12. Head lights	27.95
13. Electric horns	16.77
14. Wiper motors	32.74
15. Tyres	3.21
16. Rear axle shaft/assembly	4.76

Note: *Total licensed capacity is of the units in production
Source: Automotive Industry of India, Facts and Figures, 1986, Bombay: Automotive Component Manufacturers Association of India, Bombay, 1986.

accessories, the group holds a semi-monopoly. Apart from manufacturing a wide range of components and accessories, the group has also established a well-knit and a far-reaching network of dealership, distributorship, and agency in the automobile industry. Sixteen out of the twenty public limited companies studied by us are in the automotive field. From the dates of incorporation of the various companies, it will be clear, that, over the years the permission to expand and/or set up new units in related fields has helped to provide a definite and permanent basis for such a vertical link.

For a number of companies, a part of the market for the components manufactured is provided by other companies in the group. For most of the companies in the group, T.V. Sundaram Iyengar and Sons Ltd. functions as the main distributor. The prospectus issued by Srichakra Tyres is representative of the group's mode of functioning.

> Of the plant and machinery required for the project, three items will be leased from Sundaram Industries Limited. The company will be appointing main distributors. T.V. Sundaram Iyengar and Sons Limited (including its divisions Sundaram Motors and Madras Auto Service) with a well-knit dealership network has an established name and reputation for supplying only quality automobile products.
>
> The company has already received enquiries from leading two-wheeler manufacturers—Sundaram Clayton Limited, Madras, manufacturers of TVS-50. The latter have, in principle, agreed to buy 75,000 numbers of moped tyres and tubes per annum.

The government's liberalization policies—specifically delicensing of industries, re-endorsement of capacities on the basis of fuller utilization of plant and machinery, automatic growth of capacity and broad-banding of licences, immensely helped the group not only to expand vertically but also diversify.

Back in 1971, a member of the MRTPC commenting on the capital structure of the TVS companies remarked:

> Most of the manufacturing activity of the group companies has been undertaken on the basis of foreign collaborations and

the collaborations have usually been on generous terms. The equity participation of the foreign companies has been quite substantial—majority participation in the case of Lucas-TVS and 45 to 50 per cent in the case of others and the whole of the remaining equity is held by group companies all of which are family concerns. A (further) result of the capital structure that most TVS companies have been having combined with a high degree of profitability due to their semi-monopoly position, has been that the accumulation of capital by the group has been rapid. Prudent and careful husbanding of resources has of course played an important role in this achievement. The group companies have kept the dividends at a reasonable level, using the undistributed profits for building up reserves which have been used either for further expansion of the same company or for developing new concerns under the auspices of the group. But from the point of view of counteracting monopoly and economic power it has to be pointed out that all this ultimately is a method of enriching the shareholders in this case one family and its foreign partners at the expense of the consumers of the product and the community at large.[2]

Technological Dependence of the TVS Group

Practically all manufacturing activity of the TVS group right from inception is covered by foreign collaboration agreements (both financial and technical). The collaborations have usually been on generous terms, for long durations, and very often have been renewed. Subsequent expansion of the group companies as also the incorporation of new companies have been on the

[2] *Reports of the MRTP Commission and Orders Thereupon of the Central Government under Sections 21, 22 and 23 of the MRTP Act, 1969*, vol. IV, New Delhi: Department of Company Affairs, Ministry of Law, Justice and Company Affairs, Government of India, Section 22, pp. 579–80.

basis of foreign collaboration. A few of them are worth looking at.

(1) Wheels India: This company was promoted by T.V. Sundaram Iyengar and Sons Limited and Dunlop Rubber Company Limited for the manufacture of automobile wheels and rims. Wheels India was registered in June 1960. The company entered into a technical aid agreement with Dunlop, UK, in June 1960 *for a period of twenty years for the manufacture of wheels*. The collaboration continued beyond twenty years and the company continues to pay royalties (emphasis ours).

(2) Sundaram Clayton: The company was jointly promoted by TVS and Clayton Dewandre Holdings Limited, UK. Sundaram Clayton was incorporated under the Companies Act in May 1962. Practically every item of the company, except mopeds, is produced with foreign collaboration. Each new product is also covered by new licence and technical assistance agreements. In each case the company agreed to pay a lumpsum fee plus a royalty of 5 per cent of the net ex-factory price of all the items sold in India and 6 per cent on their sales outside India for a period of five years.

In the case of mopeds, Sundaram Clayton was allowed to manufacture mopeds even though the item was not included in the list of industries open to large houses and foreign majority companies. While the government wanted to stipulate a 60 per cent export obligation for a period of five years extendable by another five years, the company offered to export 40 per cent of its production from the third year onward to the fifteenth year.

The statement in the 23rd Annual Report of the company (1985) is revealing and speaks for itself:

> The company from the third year of its production of mopeds is under an obligation to export. The company has not exported any moped. The company has applied to the government for a waiver of this obligation and is hopeful of getting a favourable response. Therefore, no provision has been made for liability, if any, arising out of non-performance of the above export obligation.

The 24th Annual Report of the company (1986) offered this as an explanation for the moped division not doing too well. 'In the context of factors such as *non-availability of a foreign collaborator of repute*, severe competition, etc, the future of the moped division is being considered' (emphasis ours).

(3) Sundaram Abex was incorporated as a public limited company in September 1974. The company was set up in collaboration with M/s Abex Corporation of USA who was participating to the extent of 30 per cent in the equity capital of the company. The Abex Corporation agreed, among other things, to assist the company to establish its own R&D facilities. The collaboration agreement provided for a royalty payment of 5 per cent on the net sales of the company for a maximum period of nine years within the period of the agreement 'which shall be 10 years from the date of signing of the agreement'. As of 1988, when this chapter was originally published, the R&D facility had not been established.

(4) Brakes India, which was incorporated in 1962, is another company where the collaboration

agreement has exceeded twenty years. Interestingly, the manner in which Brakes India intended to cope with the Japanese entry into the Indian automobile market was through the contracts already established by Lucas Girling UK (the foreign collaborators of Brakes India) with various Japanese brake manufacturers (*vide* Annual Report 1984–5).

(5) Ind-Suzuki (now TVS-Suzuki Limited) was incorporated in July 1982 in collaboration with Suzuki Motor Company Limited, Japan and was allowed a ten-year agreement with royalty at 3 per cent of the ex-factory value of production plus lumpsum fee of US dollar 1 million.

What does all this add up to? At the outset it should be recorded that the TVS group has a high reputation for producing high quality products and, from all accounts, this reputation is well deserved. At the same time, it cannot be ignored that the R&D effort of the group has not been consistently good. The balance sheets of only four of the TVS group companies record some kind of expenditure on R&D. By the group's own admission,[3] the kind of R&D undertaken in these concerns is 'absorptive' and 'developmental' (as opposed to 'creative') in the sense of the adaptation of foreign technology to suit domestic requirements. While it cannot be stated categorically that imports of technology have completely replaced domestic R&D, it needs to be brought out that all R&D activity of the TVS group is within the parameters specified by the foreign collaborators.

In this connection it would be worthwhile to examine the role of the foreign collaborator to understand why the

[3] Oral evidence collected. Names withheld.

R&D activity of the TVS group cannot but be confined to very limited spheres of activity. We begin with the details presented by the MRTPC enquiry in the Lucas-TVS (LTVS) case.[4]

One of the expectations with which LTVS was granted an industrial licence, favouring it over other applicants, and was also permitted favourable terms of foreign collaboration, was that at an appropriate stage the industrial unit would be developed as the basis for exports. When the representatives of the foreign collaborator were asked at the public hearing about why much progress has not been achieved in respect of developing exports, their answer was that the focus of attention throughout the period had been on import substitution rather than on export development. They further explained that many developing countries were setting up plants for the production of such items; exports to them were therefore going to be difficult. They were asked whether it was not possible to think of certain items or components which required proportionately more labour, especially skilled labour, which was available at much cheaper rates in India than in the richer countries of the West. Their answer was two-fold. First, the technology that they had developed was essentially a labour-saving and capital-intensive technology and therefore could not make much use of the cheaper skilled labour available in India for this purpose. Their own R&D had mainly focused on labour-saving technologies and not on capital-saving ones. By and large, albeit with

[4] India, Government of, Department of Company Affairs, Ministry of Law, Justice and Company Affairs, *Reports of the MRTP Commission and Orders Thereupon of the Central Government under Sections 21, 22 and 23 of the MRTP Act, 1969*, vol. II, Section 21, pp. 24–8.

some adaptations, the same technologies were in use in the unit in India. One could not therefore say there could be much saving in cost by producing these items in India. On the other hand, given the small quantum of production and the higher costs of materials, the costs of production in India were significantly higher. But they indicated that they had come to appreciate this aspect and had undertaken an examination of what items could be economically produced in India for supplying the market in the West.

The technical aid and royalty agreement with Joseph Lucas (Industries) Ltd., UK expired on 1 October 1972. The company had applied for renewal of the agreement for a further period of five years. The government agreed to the renewal on the terms and conditions stated below:

a. Royalty at 3 per cent subject to Indian taxes would be payable to the foreign collaborator on exports only.
b. No royalty would be paid to the collaborators on internal sales.
c. No further extension of the collaboration would be agreed to under any circumstances.
d. The Indian company would be free to sub-licence the technical know-how/product design/engineering design under the agreement to another Indian company should it become necessary. The terms of such sub-licensing would, however, be as mutually agreed to by all the parties concerned including the foreign collaborators and shall be subject to the approval of government.
e. Exports would be permitted to all countries except where the foreign collaborators had existing arrangements for manufacture of the articles.

LTVS and the collaborators, of course, did not agree to the new conditions laid down by the government. The collaborators proposed that regarding the products covered by the original licence which were introduced late in the ten-year period, they should continue to get royalty at the original prescribed rate for a period of ten years from the time the design was introduced, and further that royalty should be paid on new designs introduced after 1972 at the rate of 2 per cent for internal sales and 3 per cent on exports. The period for such payments, however, may be confined to seven years instead of ten. It was further suggested that an annual technical fee at 1 per cent on factory cost of any designs introduced in India under both the original and renewed licence agreements should be paid and that this should continue for a period of seven years at the end of which the position might be reviewed.

LTVS supported this proposal in the following words:

> This company needs to keep abreast of the requirements of the Indian automobile industry and to export directly its own goods which makes it essential that it keep its designs and production technique up-to date. Whilst we are doing design and development work of our own in Madras, we nevertheless feel that it is essential to the continued satisfactory progress of the company that it has full access to the extensive engineering research and development programmes carried out by our collaborators—it should be noted that their published accounts showed an expenditure running at a rate of (£ 12 ½ million) per annum. It is also considered that in the light of our experience over the last ten years it will be necessary from time to time to call in specialised assistance from our collaborators—particularly when new processes are involved. Our collaborators have also undertaken extensive training of employees of the company at their expense and we wish to continue to enjoy this benefit. Our collaborators, therefore, consider that

an annual technical fee to pay for their support would be appropriate—the fee would go towards paying for the day-to-day expense of supporting the company with a continual supply of technical information and also make a contribution to the group's expenditure on R&D—the benefits of which are freely made available to the company.

The exposition given by the representatives of the foreign collaborator and the submission made by the company clearly indicate the limitations of the R&D efforts undertaken by the company. There was, in the first place, little effort at developing a production process adapted to Indian conditions.

Further, the collaborating company did not see much prospect for developing production of electrical accessory items in India specifically for export purposes—to which their Indian counterparts agreed. When such an elaborate arrangement for foreign collaboration was allowed to continue, it is not difficult to understand why it was less worthwhile to develop indigenous R&D.

While in its terms and conditions the government had indicated that no further extension of the collaboration would be agreed to under any circumstances, it not only subsequently waived this condition, but also granted further approvals for updating technology and for manufacturing new products.[5]

A know-how contract[6] entered into in 1982 between Turbo Energy Pvt. Ltd. (TEL) (a TVS company not registered under the MRTP Act, 1969) and Aktiengesellschaft Kuhnle, Kopp and Kausch, West Germany (KKK), to manufacture turbochargers (contract products) brings to light other restrictions that nullify,

[5] *Vide* Annual Reports 79, 80, 86.

[6] A certified copy of the contract was obtained by the author from the Registrar of Companies, Tamil Nadu.

among other things, any attempt at independent R&D, given the operation of such agreements. We reproduce below some of the clauses of the agreement.

a. TEL has the right to have the contract products manufactured completely, or in part, by another manufacturer in India pre-condition being, that the manufacturer concerned can manufacture to the quality required and KKK is kept informed. TEL can, in this respect, grant a sub-licence. However, *in all other respects it is not allowed to grant a sub-licence* (emphasis ours).
b. All information received by TEL within the scope of this agreement is kept a secret by TEL, and TEL equally binds those companies to whom it sub-licenses the manufacture of the product.
c. After the expiry of the contract, the documentation, supplied by KKK will remain the property of TEL. TEL has the right to manufacture the contract products in India and to sell them in all other countries throughout the world, without restrictions. The obligation mentioned in (b) above *will apply up to the end of the third year after the contract has expired* (emphasis ours).
d. On the expiry of this contract, TEL shall have the right to license third parties for the manufacture of contract products in India.
e. For a period of three years commencing from the expiry of this contract, TEL shall not be entitled to license third parties for the manufacture of contract products outside India.
f. For a period of three years commencing from the expiry of this contract, TEL shall only be entitled to sell spare parts for turbochargers which were supplied by TEL.

Since the contract explicitly forbade diffusion of know-how, any attempt by the government to establish competition in the industry could not but lead to 'repetitive imports.' Again, explicitly started in the contract was the fact that any patentable development that took place during the period the agreement was in force had to be available to either party free of charge. The question that arises is, what would TEL stand to gain by investing resources in R&D in developing, if possible, patentable products while the contract was in force?

Those companies of the TVS group involved in some amount of R&D admitted that the adaptation of technology in which they were concentrating, was primarily in the direction of substituting locally made materials, spares, and components for imported varieties. For this they were also going to upgrade, in a big way, technological developments in the ancillary industry. For example, the 3rd Annual Report of Ind-Suzuki, 1984–5, stated:

> [Your] company has recognized the importance of ancillary development and has evolved schemes to promote and support the production of ancillaries with technological assistance to meet the stringent quality requirements. *The company also proposes to embark upon accelerated indigenization of certain critical components to reduce* dependence on imports, seeking wherever necessary, appropriate foreign collaborations (emphasis ours).

The companies also admitted that they needed their collaborators' permission to sell the know-how to others, and that they could not export their products to places/countries where the collaborators were already active and/or did not approve. In the process of adaptation to suit local conditions, the basic design of the product was kept intact; however, prior approval was needed so that change did not in any way reduce reliability.

What comes out from the TVS experience in manufacturing is the following:

a. In the first place it needs to be recorded that the TVS group successfully managed to build the capital structure of their group in a manner that kept out or kept to the absolute minimum equity participation by public financial institutions with its attendant requirement of convertibility clause and/or nominee directorship. At the same time, substantial equity participation by foreign companies coupled with the group's concentration in the automotive ancillary and component sector, enabled the group to maintain its monopolistic lead in this sector.

b. Collaboration with leading world manufacturers of automotive components, continuous renewal of collaboration agreements, further foreign collaboration approvals for every new product introduced, was the manner in which the TVS group organized its production.
c. The group's R&D activities were oriented more towards material substitution and some adaptation in manufacturing process to suit local conditions.
d. There was no economic compulsion on the group to direct its research activities to innovation. The government's policy allowing for liberal collaboration agreement removed 'the need factor' with the result that the group as a whole followed a strategy of rapid diversification under foreign licensing for every product addition to maximize the short-run profits.

The TVS study confirmed what macro studies on technology[7] pointed out—that the import of technology

[7] To name a few: K.K. Subramanian, 'Collaboration Agreements and Their Impact on Assimilation and Diffusion of know-How and Outgo of Resources', in *Science and Technology Policy in the 1980s and Beyond*, ed. M. Gibbons, P. Gummett and P. Udgonkar, UK: Longman, 1984, pp. 246–69. Mohanan P. Pillai, 'Technology Transfer, Adaptation and Assimilation', *Economic and Political Weekly*, vol. XIV, no. 47, 24 November 1979, pp. 121–6.

in India was a substitute rather than an input to Indian R&D, and the failure to adapt, innovate, and diffuse already imported technology resulted in high cost of production and drain of resources; further, assimilation was of a pseudo character and as a result technological dependence was very real.

That liberalization of technology import per se cannot by itself raise the technological level of a country unless complemented by a certain level of domestic R&D is also by now understood (whatever may be the hue and cry in certain quarters about the restrictive policy towards import of technology being the chief cause for the outmoded technology in the Indian manufacturing sector).

The question that we would like to raise in this chapter is: how can this 'certain level of domestic R&D' be achieved, and what industrial structure will make domestic R&D not merely 'absorptive' but also 'creative' in the sense of directing R&D to more original innovations? No doubt, several factors are relevant here, among them the role played by the government in supporting high-risk projects, the relative expenditure on basic as opposed to applied research, the degree of risk aversion of private firms, and the institutional framework for the adaptation of suitable foreign technology.[8]

In the context of the study of the growth and functioning of the TVS group we would like to submit the following. Given the reality of industrial activity in this country being dominated and directed by business groups/houses, and given the fact that resources, talent, and personnel at the disposal of the government are limited, industrial policy, specifically those relating to encouraging domestic R&D could be framed taking the *business house/group as a unit*.

[8] T. Blumenthal, 'A Note on Relationship between Domestic R&D Imports of Technology', *Economic Development and Cultural Change*, vol. 27, no. 2, January 1979, pp. 303–6.

Hitherto policies formulated to regulate the flow of foreign technology and to promote self-reliance, have come into conflict with the objectives of import-substitution and export promotion. The net result has been increasing imports of technology. Yet, apart from certain fiscal incentives to those firms undertaking some limited R&D, there has been no real effort at seriously pursuing 'creative' R&D in the country. While the entire blame cannot be laid at the doorstep of the government, the manner in which industrial growth in this country has been conceived (misconceived?) and pursued has led industrialists to seek maximum profits in the shortest possible time. The easiest manner of achieving this has been to tie-up with foreign manufacturers which help the domestic firm to dominate the market for the product concerned in a situation of low-volume demand.

The TVS group is illustrative of this phenomenon where a group dominating the automotive component field in the country for over two decades found it extremely lucrative to operate in a situation of continued technological dependence with absolutely no compulsion to invest in any kind of 'creative' R&D.

It would not be out of place to mention here in passing David C. Mowery's work[9] explaining the low level and inefficient organization of British industrial research (as compared to the US and West Germany). Mowery attributes the economic decline of Britain to its poor innovative record and assigns three factors as explanation:

(i) The structure of the British manufacturing firm which did not allow for a more effective exploitation

[9] David C. Mowery, 'Industrial Research, 1900–1950', in *The Decline of the British Economy*, B. Elbaum and W. Lazonick, Oxford: Clarendron Press, 1986, pp. 189–222.

of the complementarities between research activity and production activity;

(ii) The system of technical and managerial education at the secondary and university levels. The informal linkages between higher and technical education and industry, which proved to be of great importance in the industrial research system within the US and Germany, failed to develop within Britain;

(iii) Government economic policy undercut the incentive for the pursuit of competitive advantage through innovative activity.

Mowery concludes that a different set of government policies towards industrial structure and education could have substantially enhanced the level and effectiveness of British industrial research.

A study of the development of industrial research over time in India within an institutional framework is long overdue. It is sufficient to conclude this chapter by stating that regulation of foreign technology may, at best, give the country a better deal in terms of the manner and quantum of payments going out of the country. It cannot, however, tackle, first, the reality and enormity of the problem of technological dependence of the country and, second and more important, the question of the institutional changes that need to be made/introduced so that domestic R&D of a 'creative' type is more vigorously pursued.

CHAPTER 5

The Knitwear Cluster in Tiruppur

An Indian Industrial District in the Making?

Padmini Swaminathan with J. Jeyaranjan

Knitwear Exports and Tiruppur

Knitwear has come to occupy a place of pride in India's burgeoning apparel exports, particularly since the last decade. In this overall gamut, the small town of Tiruppur in Tamil Nadu has played a stellar role.

* This study is part of a larger project on 'Business Organizations in India' commissioned jointly by the Centre for Studies in Social Sciences, Calcutta, and the UNDP. An earlier version of this study was presented at a preliminary workshop held at Mysore on 26–7 August 1994. We are grateful to the participants at this workshop whose queries and comments helped in its subsequent revision. A field-based study of this nature is not possible without the active participation of a number of personnel both on and off the field. We would like to thank in particular the following: C.E. Karunakaran who was a source of help throughout; S. Neelakantan with whom we had extensive discussions on the socio-economic characteristics of the region; V. Veeraraghavan, Advocate, Tiruppur; R.M. Subramanian, Secretary, Tiruppur Exporters' Association; S.R. Sridhar of Brinda Fabrics who not only put us in touch with others in the field but also patiently

Accounting for 14 per cent of knitwear exports, Tiruppur ranks in this respect only after Delhi and Bombay. Moreover, a major chunk of exports from Tiruppur is indirect, and routed through trading agents in Bombay, Delhi, and Chennai. According to the report of the Apparel Export Promotion Council of India (AEPC), the share of knitted garments to total garment exports increased from 41 per cent in 1994 to 45 per cent (total number of pieces) in 1996. During the first quarter of the calendar year 1997, the share of knitted garments rose further to 48 per cent. The report further attributes the increase in the share of knitted garments to the steep increase in exports from Tiruppur:

> During the first quarter of 1997, exports from Tiruppur stood at 1079 lakh pieces against 2574 lakh pieces exported during the full year 1996. In terms of percentage, the share of exports from Tiruppur to the total stood at 28.97 per cent in the first quarter of 1997, against 21.73 per cent in 1996 and 18.35 per cent in 1994.[1]

The growth of Indian apparel exports in recent years is largely due to the growing demand for both cotton-based garments and knit garments in the advanced capitalist

clarified all our doubts; R. Nagarajan, Dy. Director, Apparel Export Promotion Council, Tiruppur; R. Ramamurthy, Officer-in-charge, AEPC, SITRA Knitwear and Service, Tiruppur; T.S. Sankaralingam, General Manager, Salora International Ltd, Tiruppur; M.M. Sampat Kumar of Yuvaraj International, Tiruppur; M/s Centwin, M/s Poppy's, M/s Bison, Tiruppur; C.T. Kurien, S. Neelakantan and M.S.S. Pandian for their comments on an earlier version of this paper; T. Maheswari for her assistance in bringing out this paper.

This was previously published in a book edited by A.K. Bagchi, ed., Economy and Origanization: Indian Institutions under the Neo-Liberal regime, New Delhi: Sage, 1999, pp. 94–121 and MIDS Working Paper no. 126, 1994.

[1] *The Economic Times,* 29 May 1997, Chennai.

economies. Two factors have contributed to the growth of knitwear. First, it is easier and quicker to produce fabric by knitting than by weaving and, second, knitted fabrics provide easier manoeuvrability in production with regard to design. Demand for cotton-based garments was revived when the oil shock of the 1970s curbed the production of synthetic fibres. This is especially true of cotton knitwear.[2] The 'success' of Tiruppur is thus an outcome of changes in the consumption pattern in the advanced capitalist economies and the geographical division of labour in the world garment industry.

The present study is an attempt to problematize the varied experiences and phases of Tiruppur's transition from an 'obscure hamlet' into India's premier cotton knitting and manufacturing centre. Tiruppur's phenomenal growth has been achieved through a dense and complex network linking together its '2,500 knitting and manufacturing units, 600 processing units, 300 printing units and 100 embroidery units'[3] into an industrial district. Though developed conceptually in the more developed countries to take advantage of the characteristics and functioning pertaining to particular areas, we find nevertheless that there are clearly principles of organization characterizing such an industrial district model which could very usefully be applied in other contexts and countries. Tiruppur is one such context, which in our view is amenable for analysis using this framework.[4]

[2] S. Chatterjee and R. Mohan, 'India's Garment Exports', *Economic and Political Weekly* (Review of Industry and Management), vol. 28, no. 35, 1993.

[3] Tiruppur Exporters Association, 1994, oral communication.

[4] At the end of our very first visit to Tiruppur, we concluded that Tiruppur did not fit the usual development paradigms. Though not touched upon in this paper, we realize that an important dimension that needs to be examined is why traditional economic analysis,

The Growth and Consolidation of the Knitwear Industry in Tiruppur

The town of Tiruppur, with an area of 43.52 sq. km., is situated in the dry hinterland of Tamil Nadu. With a population of 2.35 lakh according to the 1991 Census, and a decadal population growth rate of 41.55 per cent between 1981 and 1991, Tiruppur has undergone a tremendous 'boom'.[5]

While this study does not historically trace the development of the garment industry at Tiruppur, yet, an evaluation of the present 'success' of Tiruppur needs

and official policies which often take scales of operation as the major point of reference (simultaneously marginalizing the fact that multiple modes of industrialization coexist with different points of reference) are not really useful in understanding Tiruppur. In a study reviewing industrial clusters in LDCs, Nadvi and Schmitz have this to say about Tiruppur: 'Among the categories of case studies represented (in the table) the Sinos Valley shoe cluster, the Ludhiana experience and the Indian cotton knitwear industry of Tiruppur are leading examples of regional industrial successes in LDCs which conform closely with important elements of the industrial district story'.

See K. Nadvi and H. Schmitz, 'Industrial Clusters in Less Developed Countries: Review of Experiences and Research Agenda', Discussion Paper no. 399, Sussex: IDS, January 1993.

[5] Tiruppur's economic performance, outstanding by Indian standards has kindled quite a few research studies, the most notable of those we have come across being that of Pamela Cawthorne. Cawthorne did her fieldwork at Tiruppur in 1986 when Tiruppur had just begun its entry into the export market. In a later piece she attempts to fit her 1986 findings into the 'industrial district' framework. See Pamela Cawthorne, 'Amoebic Capitalism as a Form of Accumulation: ·The Case of the Cotton Knitwear Industry in a South Indian Town', PhD dissertation, Milton Keynes: The Open University, UK, 1990; Pamela Cawthorne, 'Of Networks and Markets: The Rise and Rise of a South Indian Town: The Example of Tiruppur's Cotton Knitwear Industry', *World Development*, vol. 23, no. 1, January 1995, pp. 43–56.

an examination that dynamically situates and captures the remarkable changes that have taken place in the town in all spheres. In this context, we find Brusco's[6] analysis of small firm development in Italy very useful for conceptualizing the changes that have taken place in Tiruppur over time. In an overview, tracing the genesis of the concept of industrial district, Brusco developed four models to capture the essence of the debate on small firm development that took place in Italy over forty years.[7]

The first model, that of *traditional artisan*, covers the period of the 1950s and the early 1960s, when the south of Italy was underdeveloped with a number of small artisan firms producing for the local market. The producers still employed methods of production characterized by low levels of productivity and the use of labour-intensive techniques. Skills were acquired mainly through apprenticeship and practice. The discussion that

[6] S. Brusco, 'The Idea of the Industrial District: Its Genesis', in *Industrial Districts and Inter-Firm Cooperation in Italy*, ed. F. Pyke, G. Becattini and W. Sengenberger, Geneva: International Institute for Labour Studies, 1990, pp. 10–19.

[7] Our reading of the experiences of similar industrial clusters in other countries, particularly Bangladesh (Yung Whee Rhee, 'The Catalyst Model of Development: Lessons from Bangladesh's Success with Garment Exports', *World Development*, vol. 18, no. 2, 1990) and South Korea (Myung-Rae Cho, 'Weaving Flexibility: Large-small Firm Relations, Flexibility, and Regional Clusters in South Korea,' in *Flexible Specialisation: The Dynamics of Small-scale Industries in the South*, ed. Poul Paderson et al., London: Intermediate Technology Publications, 1994), leads us to agree with the following concluding remarks made by Cho: '... there is no single pathway to a flexible specialization industrialisation paradigm. In particular, the 'new orthodoxy' based on Piore and Sabel's paradigmatic theorisation of flexibility drawing upon a single type of small-scale firm relations leaves many important questions unasked and unanswered.' See Cho, 'Weaving Flexibility', p. 127.

took place during this period pitted the large firms of the north against the small firms of the south; the fact that the small firms were inefficient and were unable to pay high wages was also stressed.

The second model, Brusco calls the *dependent subcontractor model.* Following a wave of decentralization that took place in Italy at the end of the 1960s, whole departments of production in large plants were closed down, and the activities previously undertaken in-house were handed over to small firms often situated in the vicinity. Two strong views prevailed during this period; one accepted the theory that, as the wages were low, efficiency would also be low. That is to say, the level of efficiency was inferred from the level of wages instead of looking at wages and efficiency separately. The other view, while conceding that small firms used low technology, and paid low wages, nevertheless stressed that there were some small firms that had a level of technology and an efficiency that was comparable to that found in large firms. Thus, two crucial points, stressed by the second group, and relevant for our discussion of Tiruppur, were:

1. The efficiency of a small firm could be as great as that of a large one provided the same technology was used;
2. Wages were no longer linked to productivity so that high efficiency and low wages could coexist.

The third model developed was the *industrial district-Mark I* model. This was differentiated from the fourth model, namely the *industrial district-Mark II* model, by the considerable government and non-government intervention that the latter had. The *Mark I model* grew in the mid-1970s, when a number of industries and towns became economically successful. G. Becattini applied the Marshallian concept of 'industrial district' to these territorially defined productive systems.[8] Subsequent analysts of this phenomenon contended that the unit of analysis should be no longer a single firm, but a cluster of interconnected firms located in a small area. Schematizing the products of firms and the production processes in an industrial district, three categories could be distinguished. First, there were the firms which produced a final product, with direct access to the final market, national and/or international. At the next level were the *stage firms* which were involved in one stage of production. The stage firms were not necessarily engaged in less skilled, less capital-intensive, lower technology activities, but might be engaged in any activity from the dirtiest, to the most specialized using the highest technology. The third group of firms might not produce the final product that defined the industry, or its direct inputs, but provided the services, such as transport to it. Thus, the district comprised a cluster of firms, producing basically similar products, even though they could position themselves differently on the market. Such firms cooperated as well as competed among themselves. Other factors highlighted included the role of the cultural context within which the district flourished.

The fourth model, the *industrial district-Mark II*, stressed the need for intervention. The contention was that new markets and new technologies had developed since the beginning of the 1980s, posing a problem for

[8] S. Brusco, S. 'Small Firms and the Provision of Real Services', in *Industrial Districts and Local Economic Regeneration*, ed. F. Pyke and W. Sengenberger, Geneva: International Institute for Labour Studies, 1992, pp. 177–96.

both large and small firms, but more so in the case of the latter. Production in an industrial district was carried on as a social process, by virtue of a social structure that encouraged interaction amongst thousands of people. Access to specialized services was made much more difficult by the very fact that the district has neither a head, nor a hierarchical structure. Hence, the need for intervention by the government. Some local governments in Italy coped with this problem by giving the firms 'real services'[9] rather than financial help. The problem engaging many in Italy was whether these local policy measures could be used elsewhere to transform clusters of firms into industrial districts. Could a centre for real services be used to this end, or could such a centre even induce the growth of firms where none existed?

The experience of Tiruppur can be better understood if we have the above discussion in mind. Since the 1960s, Tiruppur has undergone tremendous organizational changes in terms of: (a) the entrepreneurial caste dominating the scene; (b) the size of the units comprising the production structure; (c) the phenomenon of networking among firms across the industry; and (d) the manner in which capital-negotiated labour assumes greater control over the labour process.[10]

In the early 1960s, the caste group dominating the manufacturing scene in Tiruppur was the Chettiar caste;

[9] Ibid.

[10] Details of the early history of Tiruppur can be read from the following: S. Shanmugam, 'A Plan for Tiruppur Hosiery Town', PhD thesis, School of Architecture, Anna University, Chennai, 1988; B. Mandakini, 'History of Hosiery Industry in Tiruppur', MPhil thesis, Department of History, Bharathiar University, Coimbatore, 1984; C. Vijayakumar, 'A Study of Hosiery Entrepreneurs at Tiruppur, Tamil Nadu', PhD thesis, Kerala University, Kerala, 1986.

production then was organized in what was known as 'composite units', there being hardly any subcontracting system of production. During this period, according to Krishnaswami,[11] all the knitting units employed more than twenty workers and were registered under the Factories Act. Workers were employed on a permanent basis and paid on a time-rate system with statutory benefits. From 1962, quite a few factory-level strikes of varying intensities and a prolonged industrywide strike finally led to several permanent closures, and resulted in the decline of the composite unit form of production.

The period also witnessed the entrepreneurial rise of the Gounder caste in Tiruppur. Gounders are basically a peasant caste. The rapid depletion of groundwater around Tiruppur, and the ever-growing investments involved in the deepening of wells and the attendant uncertainties rendered agriculture less profitable than before. Gounders then started investing in the small-scale knitwear units of Tiruppur. Quite a few of them had also been employed previously as workers; this experience enabled them to quickly double up as workers in their factories in the event of labour shortage either due to strikes, absenteeism, or other factors.

The more interesting aspect of the organizational change during this period, and one which helps us understand Tiruppur's then (and still current) organizational mode of production is the manner in which the (Gounder) entrepreneur-employers encouraged their loyal workers to start subcontracting units. This encouragement was backed up, very often, with capital and the placing of orders. The ensuing change in the character of production

[11] C. Krishnaswami, 'Dynamics of Capitalist Labour Process: Knitting Industry in Tamil Nadu', *Economic and Political Weekly*, 17 June 1989, pp. 1359–69.

organization had an immediate negative impact on the labour front: workers were no longer guaranteed time-rate wages with statutory benefits; the dominant mode of payment became piece-rate, with hardly any benefits.

These organizational changes notwithstanding, almost up to 1980, the knitwear industry in Tiruppur was characterized by low levels of production catering largely to the local market. The little that was exported were indirect exports of innerwear to countries like Afghanistan as well as some African and East European countries. The industry was managed largely by family members with the help of a few workers. It produced only innerwear—vests, briefs, etc. While this seems to fit Brusco's traditional artisan model, it differs from the Italian experience in an important way—the wage levels at Tiruppur, even during this phase, were on par with that prevailing in the industrial town of Coimbatore.

Tiruppur started catering to the export market from 1980 onwards, and the industry began to grow. However, much of the exports during the 1980s were indirect, in the sense that Tiruppur firms were selling their goods to the international markets through selling agents/export houses situated outside Tiruppur, namely Bombay and Delhi (the dependent subcontractor model). Until 1985, the export growth was slow but steady, and confined to t-shirts. From the late 1980s, however, the industry diversified very quickly, and took up manufacturing as well as *direct* exports of outer garments (besides t-shirts), namely cardigans, jerseys, pullovers, ladies' blouses, dresses and skirts, trousers, nightwear, sportswear, and industrial wear.

During the boom which began in the mid-1980s, and peaked in 1993–4, profit margins were high—around 30 to 40 per cent—and led to a huge inflow of both capital and labour into Tiruppur. The mad rush almost doubled the number of units during a short time span. Many new entrants assumed the high margins to be eternal. Unproductive investments in huge buildings (both for housing and factories) locked up their existing capital and blocked future flows. Such investments sent land prices soaring. Along with this, the rental charges galloped. Conspicuous consumption found its expression in investments in cars, jewellery, etc.

Simultaneously, the mushrooming of small units resulted in the undercutting of prices and the squeezing of profit margins. The phenomenal increase in yarn prices compounded the problem. The escalation due to higher input prices, the increase in the working capital requirements due to increased rent, the crash in the output prices, all these pushed the system to an 'adjustment phase' in the beginning of the 1990s. Many new entrants, who had worked out their economic and business logic based on a 30 to 40 per cent margin, were squeezed out of business. Since their capital as well as future earnings were locked up in unproductive investments, they had little elbow room to wriggle out of the squeeze. Further influx of capital into Tiruppur slowed down as the boom abated.

Many view 1994–5 as a watershed for the Tiruppur knitwear industry when exports began to even out after a decade-long growth. As one commentator put it:

> The year brought home truths to many in the industry. The scores of new entrants in the export business who pitched their tents in boom time could no longer pursue their business in the same uneven scales of economy. . . In the aftermath of the phenomenal input cost escalation, cut-throat competition and price war in exports, manufacturers also received complaints and suffered due to defaults in payments. The great shake-out

that followed in the Tiruppur knitwear industry is history now, and to some extent an inevitable antidote that has come about as a technical correction required by the industry. . . . The post-1995 knitwear sector has thus seen the accelerated pace of modernisation taking place within Tiruppur knitwear industry.[12]

The well-established old hands, and the cautious new entrants had not locked up their surplus earned during the boom in unproductive investments. Hence, they were under no compulsion to continue to produce even under unprofitable conditions. These units used this 'adjustment phase' to consolidate their position in the international market. By then they realized the need for superior technology so as to address the higher value markets. The surplus generated during the boom period was available, and their direct exposure to the world market provided them with the know-how of the latest in technology, machinery, design, etc. Spheres of the production processes—which were hitherto dominated by local machines—were focused upon, like knitting and processing.

According to Mr A. Sakthivel, President, Tiruppur Exporters' Association, between 1995 and 1997, 1,000 sophisticated knitting machines and oyer 300 compacting machines had been installed. In addition, substantial volumes of new-generation dyeing and printing machines had also been imported by the processing industry, which enabled the dyeing units to gain high-volume continuous bleaching and printing capability. An estimated Rs.800 crore was reported to have been invested in imported machinery during 1995–7.

The question that remains unresolved, however (in the absence of disaggregated product-cum-value data),

[12] *The Business Line*, Chennai, 29 May 1997.

is to what extent did value-added manufacture help the exporters realize higher export earnings, in terms of per unit value? If one goes by the data provided by the AEPC on the exports from the region, there does not seem to be much visible value appreciation in dollar terms. For example, the overall exports in 1996 (for the eleven-month period ending November) showed a rise of about 28 per cent in both value and volume terms over the 1995 levels. But the per unit value realization in dollar terms hovered at around US $2.21 for the year, almost the same as, or slightly lower, than the previous levels. However, Mr Sakthivel maintained that the market share of high-value garment exports from Tiruppur had gone up substantially, though this may not have been reflected in the average piece-rate unit. This is, because, according to him, out of the total volume, high-value garments constituted 60 per cent and were exported to the quota countries. They carried a higher price tag than non-quota exports. This may not, therefore, have been actually reflected in the per piece-rate value analysis. And, as a result, therefore, according to Sakthivel, there had been a value-wise growth of 38 per cent for knitwear in 1995 and 1996.[13]

Locating Tiruppur in the Global Economic Framework

The emphasis laid on 'cultivating industrial districts' through national industrial development policies, assumes that these centres of local/regional growth have the potential to shape and determine their future. However, local allegiance, cooperation, trust relations, and social and institutional solidarity leading to the emergence of

[13] Ibid., 2 January 1997.

a cluster in no way guarantee its self-sustaining growth. As Amin and Robins very rightly point out:

> . . . they (these local production complexes) are still tightly locked into a wider international division of labour and a set of hierarchical relationships over which they have limited control. These new production spaces . . . are not the masters of their own destiny. . . [The] map is one of places with different roles in the international division of labour, different states of economic well-being, and different degrees of local productive synergy.[14]

The question of the sustainability of the Tiruppur industry in its present organizational form is importantly linked to the location of Tiruppur in the international clothing market, particularly the question of what scope, if at all, this location provides Tiruppur, to manoeuvre price, design, scale of order, etc.

Gereffi's[15] concept of a 'commodity chain' offers an important analytical framework for understanding both productive and spatial interdependencies at a global level. In the global manufacturing system of today, production of a single good commonly spans several countries, with each nation performing tasks in which it has a cost advantage. This is true for traditional manufacturers, such as footwear and garments, as well as for modern products, like automobiles and computers. In analysing the implications of this global division of labour, Gereffi stresses the need to

[14] A. Amin and K. Robins. 'These are Not Marshallian Times', in *Innovation Networks: Spatial Perspectives*, ed. Roberto Camagni, London: Belhaven, 1991, p. 114.

[15] G. Gereffi, 'New Realities of Industrial Development in East Asia and Latin America: Global, Regional and National Trends', in *States and Development in the Asian Pacific Rim*, ed. Richard Appelbaum and Jeffrey Henderson, Newbury, Park, CA: Sage, 1992, pp. 85–112.

include forward as well as backward linkages. He argues, moreover, that the extension of commodity chains beyond production to include the flow of products to the final consumer market has important implications for where economic surplus is concentrated in a global industry. In the case of knitwear, the comparative advantage of Tiruppur lies primarily in knitwear *production* because of the relatively low labour costs. A corollary of this fact is that the main source of economic surplus within the garment commodity chain generally is not at the production stage, but at the last stage in the chain, where service activities predominate (i.e. the marketing and retailing of garments). Product differentiation by means of heavily advertised brand names and the use of diverse retail outlets allow core-country firms, rather than those in the periphery and semi-periphery, to corner the lion's share of economic rents in this industry.

At this juncture, we need to introduce an important caveat. So far, our reasoning has followed the argument put forward by the New International Division of Labour (NIDL) school.[16] The apparel industry has often been characterized as an example of the NIDL. According to this argument, advances in transportation and communication technologies allow multinational corporations to move manufacturing facilities to whichever part of the world that can provide the most profitable combination of capital and labour. Labour-intensive activities are thus decoupled from capital-intensive activities, and dispersed to low-wage areas around the globe, while capital-intensive activities remain in industrialized nations.

[16] For details of the argument of the NIDL school and that of the 'transaction-cost and embeddedness' schools, see B. Christerson and Richard P. Appelbaum, 'Global and Local Subcontracting: Space, Ethnicity and the Organization of Apparel Production', *World Development*, vol. 23, no. 8, 1995, pp. 1363–74.

According to this argument, since apparel production is highly labour-intensive, production shifts to developing nations to take advantage of cheap labour.

In spite of this tendency however, over 60 per cent of clothing produced, say, for the US market is still produced in the US, while high-wage European nations such as Italy, France, and Germany are still among the top exporters of apparel in the world. Thus, the industry cannot be characterized *exclusively* according to the NIDL argument.

The market niche within which a firm is producing often determines where that product will be produced. Fashion trends in industrialized countries in the last few decades have moved from an emphasis on practicality, simplicity, and standardization to individuality, freedom of expression, and a breakdown of clear conventional standards of dress. Fashion-oriented apparel production tends to be more labour-intensive, which makes offshore sourcing to low-wage areas more attractive. For products that tend to be highly standardized, and which change little in style over time, production can be automated. It is sometimes cheaper to make jeans and t-shirts in the US using automated production than to produce them in low-wage areas. With styles that continually change, however, work becomes more labour-intensive, and volumes, smaller. This makes cheap labour more important.

One of the key organizational mechanisms by which production is dispersed to new low-wage locations in the apparel industry, is known as 'triangle manufacturing.'[17] Under this arrangement, US and European firms place

[17] G. Gereffi, 'The Organisation of Buyer-Driven Global Commodity Chains: How U.S. Retailers Shape Overseas Production Networks', in *Commodity Chains and Global Capitalism*, ed. G. Gereffi and M. Korzeniewicz, Westport: Praeger, 1994, pp. 95–122.

orders with agents or factories in established locations, such as Hong Kong, Taiwan, or South Korea. These firms then subcontract the work to factories in lower-wage locations in order to reduce production costs This arrangement has transformed the role of apparel firms in these higher-wage, established locations, from contractors and manufacturers to traders, which link US and Europe-based firms with low-wage factories all over the world.

Even within the Third World, Gereffi[18] stresses the need to differentiate the role played by each country in the world economy. Focusing on export production, he outlines five basic types of international economic roles into which (Third World) countries can be characterized: (a) the commodity export role; (b) the commercial subcontracting role; (c) the export platform role; (d) the component supplier role; and (e) the independent exporter role.

The *commercial-subcontracting role*, to which we believe Tiruppur belongs, refers to the production of finished consumer goods by locally owned firms, where the output is distributed and marketed by large chain retailers and their agents. The salience of the above discussion for our purpose lies in the arguments outlined below.

First, Tiruppur's role in the world clothing industry can be identified as one of *commercial subcontractor*. However, within this delineation, the market niche to which Tiruppur caters is the low-volume, narrow, fashion-oriented garments which are prone to volatile changes in style and design. This particular market does not easily lend itself to automation.

Second, the 'triangle' manufacturing phenomenon correctly identifies and locates the (international) market

[18] Gereffi, 'New Realities of Industrial Development in East Asia and Latin America', p. 106.

addressed by Tiruppur as evident from our field data discussed a little later.

Third, seen from an international perspective, Tiruppur does fit the NIDL argument which emphasizes the decoupling of labour-intensive activities from capital-intensive ones, and the dispersal of labour-intensive activities to low wage areas of the globe. However, the organization of production *within* Tiruppur follows very closely the characterization of the transaction-cost and 'social embeddedness' schools of economic organization. Our discussion of the organization of production in Tiruppur will (concretely) explicate this in detail.

The Organization of the Production Process in Tiruppur

The knitwear industry is classified under the Small Scale Industrial (SSI) category, and hence subject to the rules and regulations of the SSI sector. Designation of this sector as SSI, however, masks the common ownership of otherwise spatially separate units of production. This common ownership includes the phenomenon of both horizontal expansion and vertical integration. The relaxation of rules since 1991 relating to investment levels, employment, scrapping of excise duty, etc., has not drastically altered the character of the cluster, in that it has not led to the setting up of large units and/or vertical integration. On the contrary, we find in Tiruppur the continued dominance of small units of production with inter-unit transactional relationship increasing rather than becoming *rigidly hierarchical*. Between the two poles of market and hierarchy, one finds a whole range of arrangements—putting out, subcontracting, franchising, joint ventures, etc.—giving rise to varied interactions. In a dynamic context, this *process of organizing* itself gets continuously transformed. Pre-existing social ties have facilitated the emergence of networks (hierarchical but not necessarily ruinous) which in turn have enabled firms to overcome legal restrictions and minimized risk of opportunism as regards quality, delivery schedules, etc.

Analytically, the entrepreneurs in Tiruppur can be divided into three categories: (a) direct exporters; (b) subcontractors and job workers to direct exporters; and (c) ancillary product producers. These three groups of entrepreneurs can be perceived as constituting a pyramid. The subcontractors are in the middle sandwiched between the direct exporters at the top and the ancillary product producers at the bottom. This pyramidical structure is defined by access to the market. While the direct exporters are the nodal points of interaction with the market, the rest are to work in tandem with them. Importantly, this pyramidical structure is not rigid. The subcontractors and the ancillary producers cater to any number of direct exporters and hence the dependency on any single exporter is minimized. At another level, exporters own many ancillary units which cater to other subcontractors and exporters as well. An understanding of the complexity and flexibility of this network indicates the danger inherent in perceiving clusters as mere spatial phenomena under which units are specialized in the manufacture of a particular product and assembled together in one location without any interconnections between them. The much publicized advantage of clusters enjoying the economies of scale is possible *only* with networking.

Our discussions with entrepreneurs revealed near unanimity among all categories of entrepreneurs about the quantum jump over time in initial capital required (despite the phenomenon of networking among units), if the unit aspires to procure export orders. The fast-changing nature of international orders, coupled with intense rivalry at both the international and domestic levels to procure orders, has now required even beginners to contemplate investing in better and more sophisticated machines—a situation quite in contrast to the pre-1985 days. An important caveat needs to be entered here. The quantum of investment requirements today also needs to include a component for land/lease of building, the prices of which have appreciated tremendously since the export boom.

The need to stick to delivery schedules and maintain internationally acceptable standards in quality, finish, etc., has had its own impact on production organization. It has not led to all operations being brought under one roof. On the contrary, particularly the large exporter-manufacturers and merchant-exporters have teamed up with several enterprises covering different segments of the production process. The mutual exchange of information and assistance provided (if necessary) between the members of the network (in technology and market on the one hand, and expertise relating to the different processes on the other) has enabled each of the segments to run in tandem.

Even those large enterprises which have all operations under their control, through the numerous units that they instituted under the SSI sector, have to rely on outside facilities to fulfil their orders on time. Hence, the vertical integration of different processes by large entrepreneurs does not obviate the need to network with others.

Reflections on Technology and Labour at Tiruppur

Technological Change at Tiruppur

Much has been written about the technological backwardness of the industry at Tiruppur. Seen statically and in isolation, this would appear to be a major drawback. However, perceived over a longer period, it would highlight both the strengths and weaknesses of the functioning of the system in Tiruppur.

By international standards, the old Ludhiana-made circular knitting machines—used extensively in Tiruppur until the late 1970s and early 1980s—are outdated, with relatively low productivity levels, as compared to imported ones. But it is important to note that exports of garments worth the name began only after the middle of the 1980s.

As exports grew, technology upgradation also took place as the following indicate:

1. Imported stitching machines, apart from chain lock (Singer) machines, replaced the indigenous machinery.
2. Imported fabrication machines were increasingly being used, as they processed five to six times the quantity, and were of better quality. Yarn wastage was minimal in the case of imported machines. Moreover, in recent years, machines for different kinds of fabric were also installed.
3. Computer-aided designing was tried out in some of the big export firms.
4. Jet dyeing and soft floor dyeing units were set up by a few firms. These technologies imparted a degree of evenness in dyeing.
5. Rotary printing is now more frequently used.
6. Embroidery has been almost completely computerized. Intricate designs can be quickly embroidered.
7. Compacting, unheard of in Tiruppur till 1990, can be done now in a number of units. This is to prevent fabric shrinkage.
8. Raising, mercerizing, yarn dyeing, fabric roll checking and tumble drying are some of the other

new process innovations that were gradually introduced in response to market demand.

To us, the more important aspects relating to the issue of technology (considering the knitwear cluster as a whole), would appear to be the following:

- The latest machinery in almost all the processes of production were available at Tiruppur itself, complete with spare parts and components;
- The level of awareness of the existence and availability of such machines was also high among almost all sections of the entrepreneurs coupled with the ability to decide what combination of the machines would enable them to stay competitive in the international market;
- Those interviewed were unanimous in their faith in the ability of their own workers in repairing and maintaining the machines, both domestic and imported; and
- Individual exporters (particularly the large entrepreneurs) benefited considerably from technology upgradation. But the sharp polarization that one would have expected between those going in for new imported machines, and those still working with domestic machines did not lead to large-scale closure of units on this score. This has a lot to do with the networking aspect unique to Tiruppur, since the facilities (even if not owned) were available to all irrespective of scale of operation.

Innovation, in the strict sense of the advent of new machines *from* Tiruppur, did not take place, but the incremental innovation needed to adapt, assimilate, and diffuse technology continued successfully in Tiruppur. The development of technology in this field, however, was directly related to the state of knowledge in the country on micro-electronics. The use of CAD systems greatly increased the productivity of individual designs, particularly in the developed countries.[19] It also enormously simplified the entire time-consuming and skill-intensive range of activities in the assembly process, namely, pattern-making, grading, nesting, marking, and cutting. At another level, a CAD system interfaced with a modern telecommunications network made it possible to separate skill-intensive activities from the locations where the purely labour-intensive activities were taking place, without sacrificing necessary information linkages. In the application of micro-electronics-aided applied technology in designing processes and in telecommunications, both Tiruppur and the country have a long way to go.

Two aspects related to technology that have been noted at the global level, were found to be corroborated at the micro level in Tiruppur:

1. Notwithstanding the fact that units in Tiruppur had to artificially peg their operations at a particular scale to beat the legal system, it has been established that increasing the scale of operations in individual plants did not generally seem to be an efficient way of raising current levels of productivity. Besides, given the highly fashion-oriented nature of the business, short production runs were more effective in promoting

[19] Dean Spinanger, 'The Impact on Employment and Income of Structural and Technological Changes in the Clothing Industry', in *Industry on the Move*, ed. Gijsbert Van Liemt, Geneva: International Labour Office, 1992, p. 96.

flexibility than the use of cost-reducing specialized production equipment. Moreover, imported technology is costly. Therefore, while many individual entrepreneurs at Tiruppur may have gone in for specialized machinery, the industry as a whole could not upgrade its technology on a large scale. But through networking, such technological services were made available to all.

2. The introduction of newer and better technology into Tiruppur did not lead to labour displacement; on the contrary, there was a steady intake of labour at various levels, particularly since the export boom.

At a crude level, we found any number of signboards hung outside unit gates advertising vacancies for specific jobs. The CITU trade union office-bearers categorically told us that labour displacement on account of modernization was not an issue in Tiruppur.

Labour in Tiruppur

The discussion on labour in Tiruppur is charged with very strong emotions depending on how and who approaches the question, and from what angle, ideology, etc.

According to Krishnaswami,[20] the organizational changes that accompanied the change in ownership from Chettiar to Gounder[21] were motivated solely by the desire 'to attain control over the labour process and to maximize the surplus value extraction'.

[20] Krishnaswami, 'Dynamics of Capitalist Labour Process', p. 1359.

[21] There is need to explore this phenomenon of change in the caste composition of the entrepreneurial group in Tiruppur as recorded by Krishnaswami here. We heard a different version which stressed only a relative decline of the *Chettiars* and the rise of the *Gounders* to a dominant position in the industry.

Similar sentiments were expressed in a *Business India* report on Tiruppur: 'In the industry's eagerness to hold down costs, scant respect has been shown to labour laws or even to elementary human concerns like health.'[22] The report also castigated the low wages paid to women and children as compared to males, based on the classic argument that men attend to *skilled* jobs and women to the *unskilled* ones.

In Cawthorne's[23] opinion, the process of expansion at Tiruppur can 'also be seen as a generalized process of skill acquisition. Workers have tended to acquire a range of different skills in different workshops . . .' Further, because of the concentration of units in a cluster 'an island of labour shortage (amidst labour surplus) is created'. This coupled with the fact that 'knowledge and information (as well as the work itself) are easily acquired in an area where nearly everyone is working in similar kinds of jobs—is in part responsible for the very large number of small one-man firms that get set up by workers who have become highly skilled in the course of working in a number of different jobs.'

However, she also notes the segmentation of the work and rates of wages by gender and age. All categories of workers across gender and age, frequently worked twelve hours a day, six days a week, and often even longer when a particular order had to be completed. Therefore, pitching her argument on the relative 'cheapness' of labour for employers, and, comparing the level of wages to that of the regulated mill sector, Cawthorne[24] concludes thus:

> . . . the situation in Tiruppur is about the classic sweating of labour—long working hours, the intensification of work through

[22] *Business Line*, Chennai, 29 August 1984, p. 82.
[23] Cawthorne, 'Amoebic Capitalism as a form of Accumulation'.
[24] Ibid.

the use of piece-rate payments and the use of children who are paid a (relative) pittance (although one owner mentioned a kind of productivity trade-off in employing children). Both long working hours and the work practices which allow the intensification of the amount of work performed in a given time, means that the labour force is compensating in labour time for the need to improve productivity—the only other route to which is higher productivity machines.[25]

It is undeniable that the wage-rates (even if better in Tiruppur than in other informal sector clusters) were exploitative, the hours and the intensity of work were inhuman, child labour was pervasive, and that all parties concerned got away with abysmal working conditions largely because of a collective (non-written) decision to render infructuous or non-operable existing labour legislation.

There are, however, other interesting aspects relating to labour in Tiruppur that need to be problematized apart from the issue of conditions of employment. These include:

1. The enormous amount and range of skill and experience that the cluster, as a whole, encompassed as compared with other clusters;
2. The kind of autonomy that labour (particularly among the more skilled and experienced) came to acquire, which in turn allowed them to negotiate terms and conditions of employment;
3. The hope and scope that the industry provided workers, which enabled the latter to become entrepreneurs. This fact, to some extent, also conditioned the manner in which labour conducted itself, in that, while being militant, labour did not resort to any form of destructive militancy which would undermine the industry.

[25] Ibid.

We had earlier alluded to the incremental innovations that continually took place in Tiruppur which facilitated adaptation, assimilation, and diffusion of imported technology. We were given to understand that the use of existing machinery to produce nearly the quality obtainable from the latest imported machinery was pervasive. Hence the quality of labour obviated to a large extent the need to continually import expensive machinery and also lent a competitive edge.

A concrete manner in which particular segments of labour did exercise some degree of autonomy was brought home to us in the discussion on how to cost a particular piece of garment. The more experienced among the workers also took part in the deliberations on how an order was to be executed, how complicated designs were to be operationalized, etc. In the process leading up to the final figure to be quoted to the buyer, the workers could also decide whether they would be better off being piece-rated or time-rated.

There was frequent switching between time and piece-rate modes of payment at Tiruppur with considerable participation by labour in this decision. And therefore one could not simply deploy the stereotyped notion that workers on piece-rated wages were always worse off than those on time-rated wages, and also that 'informal' labour always was in a hopeless situation with no space to negotiate a better deal.

There are several related issues which make it difficult to subscribe to stereotyped visions of conflicts of labour versus capital.

In the first place, kinship and caste play an important role, particularly in the appointment to posts such as foreman. In the course of time, when the owner decided to expand his operations, very often, the unit entered into a contract with the foreman; the latter was provided with machinery and fabric and was given a small commission for the job executed. Quite a few job workers came up in this manner. Krishnaswami, however, views this as a mechanism to subordinate labour.

> The most loyal workers are rewarded in the form of fringe benefits. The highest form of reward can be helping the worker to set up a subcontract unit. The most common reward is to provide a loan to a worker when he is undergoing a real financial crisis. Giving enough freedom inside the factory, providing a subcontract within the factory, arranging a loan to set up a factory, employing the workers' relatives in the factory, providing work even during the slack period, etc., are the other major rewards given to loyal workers.[26]

Viewing the relationship solely as one of patronage, as Krishnaswami does, masks the enormous economic mileage that accrues to the owner as well as to the industry as a whole given the pervasiveness of the phenomenon. But from the workers' point of view, this relationship together with the institution of *kashtakkoottu*, seems to be almost the only way in which they could aspire to branch out independently.

The institution of *kashtakkoottu* is unique to Tiruppur and the surrounding region. *Kashtakkoottu* is an arrangement whereby a skilled labourer is taken as a partner in a joint venture; the other partners are not skilled, but pool their financial resources for a specific business venture. The skilled partner is entitled to a share in the profit that ranges from 10 to 25 per cent.

[26] Krishnaswami, 'Dynamics of Capitalist Labour Process', p. 1359.

This profit-sharing arrangement enables accumulation. Further, the market for second-hand machines that obtains in Tiruppur provides the scope for skilled workers to become entrepreneurs in their own right. The (inherently) dynamic institution of *kashtakkoottu* has over a period of time, enabled the simultaneous growth in entrepreneurship and in the mobility of labour, precisely because this arrangement enabled the coming together of persons with skill (but insufficient, or no financial resources) and those with financial resources (but little or no skill). Hence, neither the lack of skill, nor inadequate resources constrained industrial investment in the region.

Almost all the big names among the exporters today in Tiruppur are those who have come up from the ranks. Besides that, there is a constant attempt by workers to join the ranks of entrepreneurs; among entrepreneurs, the struggle continues to move up from local production to subcontractors to the position of direct exporters. Of course, there is also a large number of failures among entrepreneurs. But given the social milieu which privileges the capability, honesty, and integrity of an entrepreneur, a 'failure' can start all over again.

This brings us to another important issue, namely, the premium that *industrial experience* commands over *educational qualification.* By and large, wages are linked to years of experience in the industry, and not to educational qualifications. Hence those who come into the industry after completing school find themselves being paid less than those with no formal education, but with considerable experience in the industry. This privileging of work experience over education also provides them (employers, parents and unions) the justification for the employment of children.

We would argue that the state should ban child labour in any form, and not just in X or Y industry. The industry on its part also needs to actively participate in vocational training institutes so that a semblance of relevance is imparted to the current educational system.

Hardly 10 per cent of the workers are unionized in Tiruppur. However, it is widely acknowledged that the influence of the unions, particularly the CITU, which has the largest membership, goes far beyond that measured by the number of enrolled members. But union activity has been effective only in the area of wages; workers have been able to achieve wage revisions every three years. Neither labour legislation nor trade union militancy has been able to address the issues of intensity of work, hours of work, benefits, and allowances other than wages, occupational health issues, and/or the issue of the employment of children.

What Makes Tiruppur a Potential Industrial District?

What we have covered so far is largely the analytical dimension of *external* economies, particularly the phenomenon of networking among Tiruppur's innumerable production units right across the industry. In this section, we intend to discuss the second of the analytical dimensions of the Marshallian 'industrial district', namely, the aspect of *agglomeration* economies to explain the emergence and growth of Tiruppur. This has more to do with the socio-cultural practices underlying the production networks, apart from holding Tiruppur together. In the process, we hope to move beyond the tautological circle according to which 'industrial districts are successful economies and they are successful because they are industrial districts'.[27]

Networking: A Necessity and a Way of Life of the Local Community

While the need for networking can be explained to some extent by economic necessity, this by itself is not a sufficient condition, since networking does not automatically emerge wherever it is needed. In Tiruppur, what facilitates production networks is the structure of the overall network of relations that characterize its local community. As of now, the industry is dominated by two major communities—the Kudiyanava Gounders and the Senguntha Mudaliars—who have come into the industry through entirely different routes. One particular sect of the Mudaliars (the ones in Tiruppur) has traditionally been craftsmen specializing in weaving, whereas the Gounders have moved over from agriculture. But the two share common traits and values, namely an extraordinary capacity for work under inhospitable conditions, and a strong work ethic that is shared by all members of the family. There are underlying tensions between the two communities, however, particularly in the matter of control of formal institutions, in the approach to be adopted towards political parties/leaders in representing local grievances, and so on. But, so far, this antagonism has not been carried over into the work atmosphere.

Another interesting aspect about Tiruppur is the manner in which quite a few non-local entrepreneurs, particularly north Indians, have not only settled down,

[27] G. Grabher, 'The Weakness of Strong Ties: The 'Lock-in' of Regional Development in the Ruhr Area', in *The Embedded Firm: On the Socio-Economics of Industrial Networks*, ed. G. Grabher, London: Routledge, 1993, p. 256.

but have got absorbed into the Tiruppur ethos. The Tiruppur community, in this sense, is not a 'closed one'; on the contrary, there is a continuous in-migration of population into the district. This does bring about its own problems of social integration which are, as Becattini[28] points out, *ceteris panbus*, 'an increasing function of the cultural distance between the alien and the native, and of the power of assimilation of the district'.

Competition and Cooperation

There is considerable horizontal competition, in the sense that enterprises in the same process of production compete intensely for orders. The large entrepreneurs particularly are constantly on the move, exploring markets, establishing contacts, setting up units outside Tiruppur and even abroad in a bid to beat the quota restrictions, etc. These entrepreneurs admit to sharing some information but not all; for example, the installation of a new machine or an improved version of an existing one is generally thrown open for visits to other entrepreneurs, but adaptations made, extra attachments acquired, and designs developed are not disclosed. Thus the willingness to share information has subtle elements of competition built into it.

Cooperation in Tiruppur works at various levels. While there is intense rivalry to bag orders, the successful completion of an order requires the services of even those who have not got any of their own: this in turn means that failure to get orders does not automatically lead to the closure of units.

[28] G. Becattini, 'The Marshallian Industrial District as a Socio-Economic Notion', in *Industrial Districts and Inter-Firm Cooperation in Italy*, ed. F. Pyke, G. Becattini and W. Sengenberger, Geneva: International Institute for Labour Studies, 1990, p. 40.

Real Services

Over the years, and particularly from the time direct exports from Tiruppur began expanding substantially, the need for common action on a wide variety of fronts has brought into existence new institutions or, activated existing institutions, particularly industrial associations in Tiruppur. The most important and aggressive among these happens to be the Tiruppur Exporters' Association (TEA) set up in 1990. The kind of activities undertaken by TEA, coupled with the approach it has adopted, indicates the commitment of its members to sustain the industry, improve the *collective* efficiency[29] of the district, and carry forward the district as a whole. In 1996–7, TEA had 285 regular members and 149 associate members. Within a span of six TEA years, was been able to plan and execute the following:[30]

1. An exclusive export knitwear industrial complex at Mudalipalayam, 9 km from Tiruppur, at a cost of Rs 14 crore (Rs.140 million). Built in a record time of ten months, the complex houses 157 units each with 4,000 sq. ft. space. The complex was self-financed by the exporters;
2. A modern processing complex in Sirukkinar village, near Dharapuram, about 35 km. from Tiruppur, was planned, for which 450 acres of land were acquired. Out of this, the association

[29] We have borrowed this term from Schmitz who introduces it to denote and capture the gains from a particular form of industrial organization, one in which small firms cluster around a set of related activities. For details, see H. Schmitz, 'Small Firms and Flexible Specialization in Developing Countries', *Labour and Society*, vol. 15, no. 3, 1990.

[30] Information provided by the Tiruppur Exporters Association (TEA) from a report produced by them in 1994.

expected to develop 150 acres of land into a model agricultural farm using treated effluent water. At the time when this chapter was written the project was awaiting clearance from the various departments of the Tamil Nadu government but has failed to see the light of day;

3. A project by way of backward integration was the proposed mini-spinning mills, each having 300 spindles for captive consumption of the knitwear exporters;
4. TEA was actively lobbying, with the central government, to help it set up a Fashion Institute at Tiruppur. Besides, TEA also started conducting annual trade fairs, which, among other things, brought buyers from all over the world to Tiruppur; and TEA proposed setting up its own facilities, including an inland container terminal, a sewage plant, and a 400-line private telephone exchange, but these being in the realm of the central government, no permission was given for private investment in such facilities.

Another important institutional development in Tiruppur was the collaboration between the Apparel Export Promotion Council (AEPC) and the South India Textile Research Association (SITRA) for establishing a R&D-cum-Testing Laboratory and a training institute. The testing services were particularly useful for the small unit owners who (on their own) could neither set up the facility, nor employ the technicians needed to do the job.

At one level, the activities of TEA and of AEPC-SITRA could be characterized as 'real services' benefiting the district as a whole; it is difficult, however, to gauge which particular group of entrepreneurs benefited, and to what extent, from the different services, and/or establish any causal connection between the provision of these services and the 'success' of Tiruppur.

The emergence of the cluster was spontaneous; institutional interventions in the form of TEA, SITRA, etc., came later and their roles became more intense and diverse once exports really took off. Hence, it becomes problematic to suggest (as a policy measure) the adoption of similar policies elsewhere in other clusters. The activities of TEA and SITRA really enhanced the capability of an existing cluster to perform better, and to respond to new challenges. A loosely coupled, but linked, production network was already in place in Tiruppur which enabled institutions to build on existing linkages. In other words, TEA, AEPC- SITRA, were the products of a dynamic Tiruppur; they did not create Tiruppur.

By Way of Conclusion

From very humble beginnings, Tiruppur now has a visible presence on the international knitwear market. It is essentially a buyer-driven cluster. Its main strength, in our opinion, lies in its internal structure that enables it to convert external challenges into opportunities, despite poor infrastructure and very low levels of support from public authorities. Whether or not Tiruppur will sustain in the long run depends to a large extent, on the quality, nature of operations, and coverage of the *real services* that are being set up by public and private authorities.

The sensitivity of the various agencies to the complex problems of the industry is evident from the measures initiated by them. However, we ought to highlight the crucial lacunae in the manner in which policies were conceived and implemented in Tiruppur. We have dwelt at length on the centrality of networking (among the different categories of entrepreneurs), as constituting the fundamental principle of business organization in Tiruppur. This implies that Tiruppur is not a mere cluster of units with spatial proximity. It is not so much the size and number of units that is important, as the network relation between firms within the pyramidical hierarchy. Hence, it is important to conceive and implement real services that would cater to the entire network, rather than operate in a manner that encompasses only one link in the chain. To take the concrete case of financing of the units, our field survey confirmed the conventional approach of the financial institutions (including those specifically meant for small-scale units) in targeting individual units fulfilling the usual norms of lending. Given this approach, the coverage has been confined to direct exporters and some subcontractors, but has excluded numerous ancillary producers.

A really innovative policy would be one that would include (in its scheme of finance) the entire range of subcontractors and ancillary producers needed to execute a particular order. Such a format of targeting a group of units across the hierarchy of production, rather than single units, would, in our opinion, not only strengthen existing networking, but also quicken the development of an entrepreneurial base. In the continuing phase of burgeoning exports, and capital deepening of the processes of production in Tiruppur, there is every danger of polarization, because of existing unequal access to finance for different groups of entrepreneurs. This could, in turn, result in the break-up of networks, thereby destroying the collective efficiency of the cluster. The recognition of clustering as a form of organization has not resulted in any change in the methodology of identifying and financing the beneficiaries.

Similarly, in order to improve conditions of employment and eliminate child labour, institutions need to make it mandatory that in the execution of an order (which involves several different categories of entrepreneurs), all participating units will adhere to critical minimum norms of employment.

The generalization of this approach has significant implications for the state's small-industry policy as well, since clusters, or a region of clusters, should be targets of policy-making rather than individual units within a cluster.

Small-industry promotional agencies need to map out for the country *regions* that contain different clusters. At the first stage, an attempt must be to locate a spectrum of clusters, ranging from the most dynamic to the stagnant ones. This will also reveal (at a superficial level), whether dynamic clusters are themselves clustered within a particular region and vice versa. Once a region is taken up for study, clusters making up the region will need to be identified. At the regional level, one will need to explore what accounts for the dynamism or characteristics common to the region as a whole. Each cluster thereafter will need to be studied as an entity by itself. This identification of the logic of functioning of a cluster is essential for policy formulation precisely because it would help in unravelling factors that 'foster either an erosion or a lock-in of networks'.[31]

[31] Grabher, 'The Weakness of Strong Ties', p. 26.

CHAPTER 6

Regulating Industrialization through Public Action and Legal Intervention

Interpreting an Experiment in Tamil Nadu

The Context

In a collaborative study of the Tiruppur knitwear cluster published during the latter half of the 1990s,[1] we attempted a contextualization of the varied experiences and phases of Tiruppur's transition from

* Previously published in K. Das, ed., *Globalization and Standards*, India Studies in Business and Economics, New Delhi: Springer, 2014. I am extremely grateful to members of the Noyyal Committee for use of the data from submissions made to the high court of Madras. However, I alone am responsible for interpretations of the data.

[1] The Report of the Study on the Knitwear Cluster of Tiruppur, sponsored by the Small Industries Development Bank of India, Bombay, was submitted in September 1996. Subsequently, a paper based on this Report was published as P. Swaminathan and J. Jeyaranjan, 'The Knitwear Cluster in Tiruppur: An Indian Industrial District in the Making', in *Economy and Organization: Indian Institutions under the Neoliberal Regime*, ed. A.K. Bagchi, New Delhi: Sage, 1999.

an 'obscure hamlet' into India's premier cotton knitting manufacturing centre in terms of the principles of organization characterizing the 'industrial cluster' model. In the process, we found that:

1) The economic vitality of the industry in Tiruppur did not rest solely or even largely on the technical superiority of the individual strategies of firms within the market place. Rather, the evidence seemed to indicate that the dynamism of the industry at Tiruppur and the particular growth path and pattern of growth that Tiruppur has followed, depended to a large extent on a specific social and economic order.
2) The spatial and sectorally specialized clustering of firms in Tiruppur allowed the firms to enjoy economies of scale at the level of 'one or a few machines not just whole factories'. Efficiency in production was achieved by rapid responses to market needs based on a flexible organizational structure and substantial subcontracting to other small firms to allow specialization and maximum use of existing plants and equipment. These strategies increased rather than decreased interfirm dependency.

While the above-mentioned study concentrated mainly in capturing the dynamics of production organization within Tiruppur, there was no engagement whatsoever with 'environmental' issues that had begun to surface consequent to indiscriminate emphasis on increasing output and foreign exchange earnings through exports. Among the several 'environmental issues' that have become increasingly visible, this chapter is concerned with:

- Understanding the nature of damage that the growing industry has caused to the Noyyal River flowing through the town
- Mapping the consequences of river water pollution to agriculture and livelihood of farmers in the area
- Documenting the steps being taken to address pollution consequent to intervention by the judiciary in the matter
- Attempting an interpretation of the steps being taken in the name of environmental protection and sustainable development.

Clusters of small firms specializing in various stages of production for an industry are seen as possible engines of industrial growth in low-income economies. This is in contrast to earlier perceptions of small firms operating in the informal sector as vestiges of a backward production structure. This change in perception is largely a result of the success of such small firm clusters in the advanced capitalist economies. These firms in the latter countries could not only successfully compete in the international market when the bigger firms were going through a crisis but also offered decent work conditions for labour. More importantly, it was realized that workers in such clusters were found equipped with multiple skills that enabled them to work 'efficiently' in flexible product markets that required production structures to switch and cater to different product markets. In the course of time, stringent implementation of environmental laws, growing concern for the health of workers in developed economies and long-term interest of these countries in conserving their resources led to, both, relocation of the more polluting parts of these industries from developed to developing countries, and to sourcing of products based on non-renewable raw materials from developing economies; for the latter countries, while this relocation and sourcing signified growth in terms of income and employment, the concomitant conditions of work that obtained in developed countries did not apply.

In the specific case of the garment industry of Tiruppur under study, dyeing and bleaching are important components. However, these components, apart from being both chemical and water intensive, are also extremely polluting. In Tiruppur, with growth in export orders, the demand for the output of the dyeing and bleaching industry has also increased, which in turn has accelerated the quantum of discharge of effluents from these industries; this discharge has accumulated in the Noyyal River. Further, and over time, the discharge into the river was allowed to accumulate into a dam built on the river—the Orathupalayam dam. This dam, which was completed in 1992, was able to service the agricultural sector through irrigation for an extremely short period of time, namely, *only* through the years 1992–3 to 1995–6. Thereafter, the polluted water accumulating in the dam became a source of land degradation, yield reduction, and ground-water contamination, which in turn adversely impacted the health of villagers, cattle, and livelihood of the area and of households in general.

Struggles by Farmers' Associations and Court Intervention

Aggrieved by the total failure of the State as well as the Pollution Control Board (PCB) to check pollution, farmers' associations began approaching the courts to direct the PCB to take action against the polluting dyeing and bleaching units. In response to a writ petition, an interim order was passed on 6 March 1997, by which the court ordered the PCB, among other things, to close 114 units (enumerated in the PCB's detailed report filed before the court) and to ensure that the said units did not operate till they had installed the devices to prevent pollution and obtained the consent of the PCB. The order also required that Common Effluent Treatment Plants (CETPs) should be constructed before 10 June 1997. The affected parties filed a joint memo on 11 February 1998 containing an agreement arrived at among the parties which specifically provided in Clause 5 that:

> the bleaching and dyeing units agreed to contribute such amount as may be decided by the Court as and when this Court decides the liability of all the polluting units in the upstream of Bhavani River, for the purpose of undoing the damage caused by pollution and especially with regard to the cleaning up of Orathapalayam dam.

After recording the agreement as per the joint memo, the court passed its final orders on 26 February 1998: '. . . The PCB will be at liberty to open the units covered by the memo for three months . . . If they fail to obtain consent within three months, the PCB is directed to implement the Pollution Control and Environmental Laws forthwith. No further extension will be granted in any eventuality.'

In spite of the final order passed on the joint memo filed by the parties, no steps were taken to implement the said order and no efforts were made to get the units to install the necessary equipment and machineries to clean the polluted river water stored at Orathapalayam dam. Neither did the association of the dyeing and bleaching units (to whom the PCB had issued a letter dated 14 August 2003, estimating cleaning operations of the Orathapalayam dam to be of the order of Rs.12.50 crores) comply with the PCB's letter of 14 August 2003.

The Farmers' Association approached the Court again (vide Writ Petitions nos. 29791 and 39368 of 2003) seeking enforcement of the Joint Memo dated 11.02.1998. By Order dated 5.5.2005, the Court appointed an Expert Committee which was directed '*to go into all the terms of reference... and then make an interim report by giving the ways and means to clean the stored water and release the treated water in the river, and for removing the sludge that has formed in the dam area, without delay, and also to suggest an immediate action plan for remediation of the Noyyal river and for preventing the discharge of polluted trade effluents into the Noyyal river*'. (emphasis mine)

Apart from describing the work of the committee and the attempts still in progress to address and bring together different stakeholders to arrive at a workable solution, this chapter attempts to reflect on sets of questions raised by the whole exercise undertaken by the committee, of which the author is a member. An important set of questions has to do with interpreting the act of the court in constituting this committee with a set of Terms of Reference (ToR). These include, for example: does the constitution of the committee and the nature of the exercise undertaken by the committee to operationalize its ToRs constitute 'environmental management' (EM) that may ameliorate the more visible environmental consequences of industrial production but may not necessarily lead to environmental sustainability? If so, are present attempts to address environmental issues by the Indian State and its provincial governments through their ministries of environment, PCBs, and such other institutions more about political sustainability rather than about addressing fundamental environment problems?

Salient Features of the Committee's Work, Its Findings and of Submissions Made Before the Committee

It would be pertinent to begin by recording here the methodology that the committee adopted throughout to arrive at its recommendations that were then forwarded to the high court from time to time for appropriate directions. Given the nature and complexity of the problem involving a range of stakeholders affected, but also interested in arriving at a reasonable and workable solution, the committee adopted a democratic process right from the beginning that strove to bring all parties to the discussion table. Before almost every visit by the committee to the Noyyal Basin, the agenda prepared by the committee was made known in advance to different stakeholders; time was set aside to meet all parties together or in groups. Besides, the committee was open to meet (either at Chennai where members were based or on the field) whosoever either had a specific grievance to share, or a suggestion towards a possible solution to one or several of the components of the 'pollution problem'. The committee also received several written depositions from across a range of people. Further, in the quest for appropriate technology to achieve zero liquid discharge (ZLD), which would go a long way to save the D&B industry from folding up, the committee undertook to visit (not just in Tiruppur and surrounding areas) plants/units in other areas to assess the suitability of the technology for the specific nature of processes required by the garment industry in Tiruppur.

In sum, while particular stakeholders or even interested members of the public may have stayed away from getting in touch with the committee, the committee itself has not consciously denied access to anyone wanting to depose before the committee. To some extent, every interim report filed before the high court by the committee contains details of the particular process adopted by it for the nature of deliberations that eventually led to the recommendations contained in that specific interim report.

Between May 2005 and October 2011, the committee filed nineteen reports before the high court of Madras, one after every visit to the affected areas. What follows is an account of the process/methodology adopted by the committee to operationalize specific tasks that were required to be undertaken against each of the ToRs and the 'progress' of work till 2011.

The very first meeting of the committee consisted in studying in detail the ToR, the operationalization of which made it clear that the committee would have to: (a) collect a range of data from several departments of the government, (b) generate data wherever necessary by initiating certain processes and plans of action so that data became available within a reasonable time period, (c) undertake field visits periodically and at various levels so that all stakeholders were covered, and (d) devise systems to monitor and report on the progress made towards the ultimate objective of the committee's constitution, namely, 'arrive at a plan for remediation of the Noyyal river'. We begin with a factual account of the committee's efforts to piece together a coherent picture of the dimensions of the problem, and the steps that it took to address the problem on the ground, based on its assessment of the problem.

An important department of the state government directly mandated to deal with issues of environment in general and pollution in particular is the Tamil Nadu Pollution Control Board (TNPCB). It is significant that, very early on, the committee realized that the TNPCB was part of the problem given its inability even to answer the basic question of what role it had played in addressing the problem of pollution of the river, how it perceived the problem, and what information it had, if any, regarding the bleaching/dying industry, level of pollution, and the environment in general. At the committee's insistence, the board collected and furnished the following information (in May 2005) on the dyeing and bleaching units in Tiruppur and Coimbatore areas:

Table 6.1: *Dyeing and Bleaching Units in Tiruppur, 2005*

Area	*Coimbatore*	*Tiruppur*	*Total*
Total units	87	737	824
Units with common effluent treatment plants	47	281	328
Units with individual effluent treatment plants	10	420	430
Units that do not treat effluents	30	36	66
Quantity let into Noyyal in KLD	6520	87,800	94,320

Source: Government of Tamil Nadu, Pollution Control Board, Chennai, 2005.

According to the TNPCB, of the 824 units, 650 units were discharging their effluent into the Noyyal River, 155 units were discharging their effluent onto the land, and 19 units were recycling their effluent. Some of the units were using the treated effluent for casuarina plantations within the factory premises.

The TNPCB also stated that the *permitted quantity of effluents* of the 737 dyeing and bleaching units of Tiruppur was 87.80 Mega Litres per Day (MLD). However, neither the TNPCB nor the units concerned had any measuring devices to record the flow at the outlets. Moreover, the TNPCB was/is not able to explain how '*permitted quantity*' was arrived at initially and for how long and in what circumstances did it continue to hold.

In its very first (interim) report to the high court, the committee made it clear that in its opinion, the role of the TNPCB left much to be desired; at the least, the committee hoped that the TNPCB would be made to undertake measurement of effluents from individual outlets by suitable measuring devices to arrive at the exact quantum of effluents. Further, the committee also realized that there were no devices by which one could arrive at the quantum of inflows into the reservoir. Since the reservoir came under the jurisdiction of the Public Works Department (PWD), the latter had to be directed to install suitable measuring devices. Till date, the issues of line department coordination as well as of generation of data relating to quantum of effluent discharge remain unresolved.

The committee inspected the Orathupalayam dam in May 2005 and several times thereafter. In May 2005, the committee checked the quality of water stored in the dam. The water was dark in colour, indicating the presence of residual dyes and suspended solids. By using a portable instrument, the Total Dissolved Solids (TDS) values were checked and found to be as high as 5350 mg/l. The committee then undertook the exercise of estimating the quantity of water stored in the dam. The level of the dam on the date of inspection was 11.68 m (Full Reservoir level is 12.00 m). From the capacity table of the Orathupalayam reservoir, the storage corresponding to this level was 16.23 m^3 (573.325 mft^3) whereas the Full Reservoir capacity was 17.44 mm^3 (616 mft^3).

The committee then inspected the dam and its components. Leakages were observed in the spillway gate. The Executive Engineer in charge of the dam informed the committee that due to accumulation of chemically laden water in the reservoir for over nine years, regular maintenance of the dam and its components could not be undertaken. The river sluice shutter was completely corroded and damaged and could not be operated. The sluice shutter would have to be broken if water was to be let out through the river sluice. The engineers were aware that the spillway gates, sluice shutters, and steel ropes were due for replacement; however, the exercise of repairing the spillway shutters and river sluice could be taken up only after depleting the water from the reservoir. The fact that the authorities concerned allowed accumulation of polluted water to collect in the dam also, inadvertently, disabled regular maintenance work of the dam.

The committee had to grapple with the implications of emptying an entire reservoir of water containing 580.235 mcft. of water. During floods, and if the water quality is normal, this amount of water could be emptied within two days. However, the committee was aware that discharge of such large quantities of highly polluted water would create pollution problems downstream in the Noyyal River and even in the Cauvery River, which catered to the drinking water needs of many municipalities and the corporation of Tiruchirappalli. A less-hazardous method would be to discharge quantities with such high TDS when the flow in the Cauvery just above the Noyyal confluence was large enough to dilute the polluted water of the Noyyal. Considering all factors, the committee decided that water from the Orathupalayam dam could be released during the monsoon season, preferably in August or September 2005.

Another major issue was finding a place to dump the sludge removed from the reservoir basin. While participating in the discussions relating to the nature of action to be taken with regard to the sludge in the reservoir basin, the TNPCB forcefully opined that, since the sludge and solid waste were 'hazardous', their disposal called for the following precautions, namely that:

1. After identifying a place for dumping of the sludge, an Environmental Impact Assessment (EIA) has to be carried out.
2. The waste should not be so dumped that, during rains or due to other causes, the sludge found its way and spread into nearby areas. Some structural measures like sealing the sides and bottom of the dumping yard had to be taken to prevent the entry of hazardous material through seepage. Otherwise, this would pollute the ground water all around the area.
3. The people living nearby had to be convinced that the dumping would not affect their area. For this purpose, a 'Public Hearing' had to be carried out.

What astonished the committee was that, even while the PCB made the above deposition before the committee, the latter observed that huge quantities of the same solid waste had accumulated and was kept in bags in the compounds of all the dyeing units visited by the committee; equally huge amounts of the waste were also dumped along the river banks and along the sides of the roads. This, the committee discovered, had been going on for more than ten years. When confronted with these visible signs of 'hazardous' waste, the TNPCB officers simply admitted that for want of a dumping place, the waste had been allowed to accumulate. The committee took strong exception to the callous attitude of the TNPCB and recorded that action should have been initiated by the TNPCB on this issue much earlier.

The committee took into consideration the request made by several farmers' representatives that the stored water in the dam be emptied without delay. The farmers on both sides of the river bank stated that the impounded polluted water in the Orathupalayam reservoir had led to deterioration of the ground water. It was brought to the committee's notice that the river course was caused by incises and that the bottom was a rocky bed. Hence, while flowing water would quickly drain without seeping into the ground, stagnant water would find entry into the ground through the sides of the banks and affect the ground water. This was observed in the tests undertaken during field inspection by the committee. The committee also realized that damage to ground water would spread further the longer the polluted water was stored in the dam. The livelihood of farmers depended upon wells for irrigation, and, with polluted water seeping into their wells, they had lost their only source of livelihood, namely agriculture. Further, drinking water scarcity was acute in the villages around the dam, both in the case of human beings and for livestock.

After discussing the pros and cons of releasing water and de-silting the dam, the committee took the view that that the dam could be emptied during the period when the water could be sufficiently diluted by the flow of the Cauvery River. Immediately thereafter, a baby channel could be excavated in the dam along the old river course to lead the flows from both runoff water and effluent water to the river sluice. More important, the committee felt that the river sluice should be kept open until permanent remedial measures were in place to address the problem of effluent discharge.

The committee organized several meetings with representatives of different stakeholders at various sites. The first such meeting, held at the Collector's Office at Erode in May 2005, brought together a large number of farmers, office bearers of farmer associations, representatives from panchayats, members of the Legislative Assembly from Karur constituency, officers from the PWD, TNPCD, Revenue Department, Agriculture Department, and Tamil Nadu Water Supply and Drainage (TWAD) Board. Between May 2005 and October 2011, the committee met representatives of the different stakeholders and officials of the Tamil Nadu government, either jointly or individually. The following provides a summary of the views expressed by the different representatives.

Opinions of Farmers and Spokespersons of Farmers' Associations

- When the dam was built in 1992, it was hoped that it would irrigate and provide water to the surrounding areas. However, because of pollution, 20,500 acres of land were degraded and people of almost twenty villages had been affected. Availability of drinking water was a major problem in all these villages; people were forced to fetch water from far-off villages. The people were aware that polluted water flowing in the river may not affect the ground water due to incisions and the rocky bed, *but stagnant water in the dam* had adversely affected ground water and the wells. When earlier, the farms yielded paddy, sugarcane, banana and turmeric, there was very little of cultivation activity now. The question that keeps recurring was: when new technologies and equipments had been introduced by the dyeing industries, why could these industries not introduce new and cleaner production processes? (President of a Farmers' Association).

- Monitoring of industries had not been undertaken by the authorities. As they (the industries) earned foreign exchange, the stakes were high and the industrialists tend to ignore norms; they also did not operate the treatment plants at night. Who was to monitor this? The New Tirupur Scheme should not receive water if they (the industries) did not adopt reverse osmosis (RO) process and attained zero discharge. The TNPCB had failed in its duty of preventing setting up of new industries within 5 km. from the river. (President of a second Farmers' Association)
- Members of several other farmers' associations elaborated on the impact of ground water pollution in the vicinity of the dam on agriculture and livestock. Coconut trees had started withering. While theoretically, drinking water for humans could be arranged from elsewhere, cattle tended to drink the polluted water, which, according to the farmers, had resulted in infertility and reduced fertility capacity among cattle. The specific kinds of health problems identified among humans included hair loss, cancer, and joint pain. Another visible indicator of the growing health problems because of water and environmental pollution was the phenomenal increase in the number of doctors, clinics and growth of speciality hospitals in Erode district.

- The farmers' compared the operation of the industrial units in Tiruppur with the adage: 'Buying a picture by selling one's eyes'. According to them, the long staple cotton from Egypt was sent to Tiruppur for dyeing and bleaching to protect the Nile River from pollution. European countries had all the technical knowhow but did not undertake dyeing and processing in their own land; these processes were done in other developing countries so that their countries could be saved from pollution. According to many farmers, treatment of effluents had gone beyond the realm of the remedial and the only solution would be to close the dyeing units and stop export of garments.
- Most farmers were critical of the TNPCB and asserted that the continuing problem was not for want of powers to the TNPCB but because of the inability of the latter to function in an effective manner.

Perceptions of Industry Representatives

- The President of the Dyers' Association of Tiruppur made a plea for government subsidy of 50 per cent (25 per cent each by the provincial and central governments) towards installing effluent treatment plants to achieve zero discharge norms. The emphasis of his presentation was on making the committee recognize the importance of dyeing and bleaching to the hosiery industry of Tiruppur, the importance of Tiruppur in the global export garment market, and the need for government to step in so that competition from countries, such as China, could be met. He therefore not only wanted the government to assume half the financial burden for installation of treatment plants but also provide the industry with a breathing room of ten months to install a zero-discharge system.

- A former Member of the Legislative Assembly (MLA) and a representative of the Centre of Indian Trade Union (CITU) deposed before the committee stated that the livelihoods of almost 6 lakh workers were directly dependent on the textile industries of Tiruppur while another 1.5 lakh people depended on it indirectly. Hence, according to him, the government should build the treatment plants and recover the cost from the industry. The former MLA also stressed the point that the government was itself a party to the pollution of Noyyal: why had the government permitted industries in the prohibited area of 1 km. from the river? He wanted the committee to provide a solution that would save the employees and industries of Tiruppur.
- The industry representatives were able to provide concrete evidence of the improvement in technology that enabled them to, for example, drastically reduce the quantum of water used for dyeing and bleaching; however, except for a handful of large units, most units could not provide similar evidence of the innovations made for treating polluted water before the latter was discharged into the river or land as the case may be.

Observations from Discussions and Interactions with Government Officials

It became clear to the committee that the complete lack of coordination between the line departments of the government contributed in no small measure to the problem of continuing pollution in Noyyal.

The government had no database and no clue to what kind of database needed to be created for monitoring and assessing the pollution created by the textile industry in general and the dyeing and bleaching industry in particular. The problem was further compounded by the fact that, in addition to industrial pollution, the Noyyal and its tributaries were also the recipients of raw, untreated sewage waste and water.

The committee put in place the following: one, a basic framework and a time-bound agenda for collection of data at various levels and by different agencies; two, the committee initiated and/or encouraged experiments with new technology to ascertain the degree to which these technologies contributed to making processes of production cleaner and/or the degree to which they allowed water to be reused for industrial purposes; three, the committee sought data on the status of drinking water supply in the areas stated to be affected by the dam, as also a report on the health condition of Noyyal riverside villages; four, the committee desired that the ground water, especially with reference to the TDS, should be collected by the Agriculture Department from the records of various departments and collated for the period before and after the commissioning of the Orathupalayam dam to develop a justifiable basis for attributing deterioration in agriculture consequent to water pollution in the dam.

Nature of 'Action' Taken

The Orathupalayam dam was depleted of its polluted water in August 2005, the release having been undertaken in a phased manner.

However, the committee, during their visits from 2006 through 2011, found that untreated water continued to flow in the river. Their inspection also revealed that most industries were not treating the effluents but discharging them directly into the river. Test results of effluents indicated that the effluent water entering the Noyyal River was not meeting standards set by the government and therefore the interests of communities in and around the Noyyal and those dependent on the river continue to be harmed. Clearly, the monitoring mechanism of the TNPCB could not cope with the situation.[2] In this connection, it needs to be pointed out that despite compensation having been awarded by the Loss of Ecology Authority to affected farmers, the same could not be implemented fully for the following reason: the Loss of Ecology Authority, Chennai, had passed an order that a sum of Rs.24.79 crores had to be collected from 793 industries and disbursed to 28,944 affected landowners. The industries had been directed to remit their dues in bimonthly instalments from 1 April 2005. Sixteen industries in Erode had remitted their first instalment, totalling Rs.4,20,736. The Collector, Erode, informed the committee that the industries were not forthcoming in remitting the subsequent instalment amounts in spite of his best efforts. The Collector had initiated action to recover the amount under the provisions of the Revenue Recovery (RR)

[2] The committee did not receive specific directions from the High Court of Madras subsequent to the note that it presented to the court in 2009. However, on 28 January 2011, the High Court of Madras acting on a contempt of court petition, ordered the closure of all dyeing and bleaching units on the banks of the Noyyal River. As per newspaper reports, the court also directed action against the TNPCB officials who had failed to comply with the court directions to prevent the pollution of the river. See *Times of India*, Chennai edition, 29 January 2011.

Act. Three industries had filed writ petitions in the high court against the use of RR Act for recovering the dues from them for the above purpose. As there were legal impediments in collecting the second and subsequent instalments, the compensation amount could not be collected and disbursed to the affected land owners. The affected land owners, on their part, continue to represent their case to the district administration for expeditious settlement of the compensation amount due to them.

At present, there are two categories of dyeing and bleaching industries operating in Tiruppur. The first are those who have complied with the directions of the court and installed RO plants to ensure zero discharge; the second, those who have not. Hence, the problem of untreated effluent being discharged into the river continues. A Monitoring Committee of the high court, consisting of lawyers, in their report dated 5 August 2006, had recommended a system of imposing fines on free riders. The quantum of 'fine/penalty' suggested was related to the savings made by the CETPs and/their member units who had not implemented the zero-discharge concept but had gained commercial advantage of lesser production costs when compared to those units who had faithfully implemented the court order and incurring additional costs in reaching zero discharge. So as to neutralize the commercial advantage gained by the defaulters over compliant units, until they (the defaulters) completed the installation and effect zero discharge, the Monitoring Committee recommended the following: all non-complying CETPs were to be subjected to an ascending fine from 6 paise a litre beginning 1 August 2006, increasing month after month to 10 paise a litre till December 2006. Thereafter, if a CETP was not in a position to operate the RO plan, the CETP and its member units would be shut down till such an achievement was possible.

The Monitoring Committee also recommended that these monies, along with the fines already levied by the court on individual units and CETPs, be segregated and used for remediation of the Noyyal River and other water bodies such as the Sarkar Periyapalayam Eri, which had been the recipients of polluted water, after the Orathupalayam Dam was cleared of accumulated sediment. The money was also to be used as a reserve for compensating downstream farmers for continuing damages suffered after the period for which compensation was ordered by the Loss of Ecology Authority.

The high-court-appointed committee endorsed the recommendations of the Monitoring Committee in its submission to the court. In addition, the committee had repeatedly asked the court to direct the TNPCB to spell out its institutional mandate. The committee also noted that municipal waste continued to be dumped into the river. It was distressing for the committee to seek court direction to get a wing of the government to stop the practice of emptying waste into the river and to get it to install sewage treatment plants.

In its visit undertaken in July 2007, the committee inspected, among other things, the RO plants still under erection by the industry. For the first time, the industry admitted that, forced to contend with the pollution that its activities were generating, it had to source appropriate technology that not just treated effluents but *ensured zero discharge*. Further, locating such technology was one part of the problem; the industry had no clue to the level and intensity of civil works required to install the technology and had, in fact, underestimated the time required to install the RO plants. Hence, for the industry, as the deadline extended the penalties also mounted.

During the committee's visit to the dam area subsequent to the depletion of dam water, the representative of a farmers' association informed the committee that he could observe and feel the improvement in quality of water in the wells after the dam has been emptied. However, farmers were apprehensive that any decision to impound polluted water in the Orathupalayam dam in future would reverse the achievement and cause deterioration in quality of their wells; farmers therefore wanted the existing arrangement of keeping the shutters of the dam open till the dyeing industries ensured zero discharge.

While the TNPCB clearly failed on all fronts, its environment cell division at Coimbatore was active in finding ways to reclaim land affected by polluted water. The cell experimented with various kinds of vegetation on soil degraded by polluted water. The committee inspected various kinds of trees planted on the banks of the Noyyal River. Some species of tree plants with high rate of transpiration had been planted as an experimental measure in these areas by the Environmental Cell Division and the Social Forestry Department. The committee observed lush green growth of the plantations on the banks of the Noyyal. The partly treated effluents were used to irrigate the plants on alternate days. The polluted water was absorbed by the trees and evaporated. This serves two purposes: one, the development of green cover and, second, removal of polluted water from the ground. The committee requested the Environmental Cell Division to monitor the soil ingredients and the ground water quality in the locality periodically along with the quality of water used for irrigation.

Issues at Stake: Interpreting the Constitution of the Committee and its Work

How Does One Understand/Interpret the Work of the Committee?

At the outset, it needs to be recorded that the authorities (in this case, the TNPCB, the sole authority to issue pollution clearance certificates mandating that production units meet certain 'standards' howsoever questionable these may be) had precipitated a situation by their inaction, forcing farmers to petition the court; the latter were initially granted a stay that allowed impounding of the polluted water that the authorities had allowed to accumulate in the dam. Subsequently, since the impounded water posed a grave threat to ground water, the court constituted a committee to suggest to them a remedial course of action.

In the author's opinion, the constitution of a department like the TNPCB, and directing it to 'regulate' the environment through a 'command and control' policy that involves setting air and water quality standards, emission, and discharge limits, etc., is, at one level, an acknowledgement that an 'environment' problem exists, that the present system is not sustainable, and that change is needed. Nevertheless, this rhetoric does not translate into action that is commensurate with the nature and scale of the problem, which in the present case would amount to questioning the basis on which the dyeing and bleaching industry is allowed to grow in the name of earning foreign exchange for the country and because of the scale of employment that the garment industry as a whole generates. As Handmer and Dovers[3] point

[3] J.W. Handmer and R.S. Dovers, 'A Typology of Resilience: Rethinking Institutions for Sustainable Development', *Organ Environ*, vol. 9, no. 4, 1996, p. 501.

out, 'Many responses to environmental change, and much else besides, are shaped by what is perceived to be politically and economically palatable in the near term rather than by the nature and scale of the threat itself.' In fact, 'From the perspective of global survival, the thrust of these changes—as distinct from the rhetoric—may be further entrenching unsustainable practice. Yet the minor adjustments and policy statements may give the appearance that the problem is being addressed properly'.[4]

At another level, the state's actions in constituting an Expert Committee and authorizing the latter to seek directions towards redressal of the problem directly from the court, could be explained by what Davidson and Frickel[5] describe as 'efforts of state actors to maintain legitimacy among a given set of civil society actors'. However, and as our description of the committee's work reveals, the preoccupation by nation-states to respond only to concerns of legitimacy has resulted in a situation where:

> nation-state environmental activity will continue to be characterized by incremental, incoherent, and at times directly conflicting political actions that are more often designed to appease political interest groups rather than address environmental degradation and have the potential to become dominated by corporate interests based on this group's ability to co-opt environmental discourse to its own advantage.[6]

The fact that the nature of ToRs given to the committee and the latter's suggestions to address the ToRs were not commensurate with the problem on hand

[4] Ibid., p. 504.

[5] D.J. Davidson and S. Frickel, 'Understanding Environmental Governance: A Critical Review', *Organ Environ*, vol. 17, no. 4, 2004, p. 487.

[6] Ibid.

is illustrated below with three of the several ToRs dealt with by the committee:

Box 6.1

ToR (1) To explore and suggest ways and means to clean the stored water and then release the treated water in the river, by adopting any technical industrial process, its estimated cost and the likely time that the process might take, and its feasibility.

Committee's Suggestions to Address ToR (1) Above

Based on discussions with the farming community and their associations, various Knitwear Associations and their representatives, field visits undertaken by the Committee to the various types of polluting industries and observations of damage that it has done to the Noyyal river basin and Orathupalayam reservoir water and dam in particular, the following suggestions with respect to ToR (1) were made:

- Dilution of the polluted water in Orathupalayam dam.
- Once the dam is empty, arrangements have to be made to safely conduct the incoming raw effluent after treatment. The transport can be effected either through a pipe line or through a lined baby channel constructed within the reservoir bed to lead the water safely to the river sluices.
- At the inlet to the river course, it is suggested that Ozonised Activated Centrifugal Aeration Treatment process (OACT) be adopted as a pilot measure.
- After depleting the dam, if the sludge is found hazardous, proper precaution to be taken to dispose of the sludge in a safe dumping place, identified and cleared by the TNPCB.
- River sluices will be kept open till the polluted water entering gets considerably reduced by effective zero discharge or other remedial measures.
- After successful depletion of Orathupalayam dam, the river shutters will be closed and opened alternatively (on and off) to flush the groundwater aquifer located below the Oruthupalayam Dam.

Many of the above suggestions, the committee felt, could be implemented in the near term except the last two, which were of a longer duration and needed to be properly monitored in order to reclaim the degraded land and prevent further deterioration of ground water.

Box 6.2

ToR (2) To suggest an immediate action plan for remediation of the Noyyal River and in particular the Orathupalayam Dam and the canals.

With respect to ToR (2), the Committee suggested the following remediation measures for immediate implementation in the short term followed by measures to be taken in the medium- and long-term:

Immediate measures:

- Repair to river sluice gate
- Repair to surplus spillway gate
- Repair to canal sluice gate
- Dam to be inspected on its upstream side after reservoir depletion, identify the affected areas and take remedial measures.

Catchment and Command Area Treatment to be implemented in the Medium- and Long-term

- Construction of check dam and percolation ponds for rainwater harvesting
- Rehabilitation of tanks and ponds including de-silting of the tanks to reclaim the ground water.
- Treatment to the command area through land reclamation, crop diversification, and water management.
- Rejuvenation of Noyyal River through improved maintenance and management of river course.
- Strict adherence to zero discharge and maintenance, monitoring and management.

Box 6.3

ToR (3) To suggest ways and means for preventing the discharge of polluted trade effluents either directly or indirectly into the Noyyal River by the cluster of industrial units in and around Tiruppur during the process of cleaning of the dam area and later. With regard to ToR (3), the committee sought the direction of the court for speedy implementation of the following:

- The committee stressed the point that ensuring zero discharge into the river by the polluters is the only solution.
- Based on the information furnished and through discussions, the committee felt that the time required to arrive at zero

discharge would be 12 months. However, to arrive at a reasonable and realistic estimate of time, a detailed study would need to be carried out.

- The industries should be directed to commence installation of treatment plants towards zero discharge level and complete it on a war footing.
- Sewage disposal, as well as municipal waste, is being dumped into the river. The TWAD Board and the local bodies concerned have to be directed that this practice be stopped forthwith. Particularly the TWAD Board should be directed to install sewage treatment plants within 9 months and treated effluent should be recycled.
- The PCB and other concerned government departments may be directed to play a proactive facilitator role to implement the zero discharge facilities by the industries.
- The industrial units may be directed to produce concrete evidence on their part of having commenced installation of facilities for zero discharge within a period of 3 months.
- An independent monitoring unit appointed by the court to review and report the progress of assigned works by the Industries, TWAD Board, TNPCB and PWD once in 3 months to the Court and based on the progress, advice the stakeholders accordingly.
- The TNPCB was directed to adopt uniform standards for either ordering closure or revoking of the Industrial units.

Author's Interpretation of the Committee's Role

- Broadly, the committee's attempt to rid the Noyyal River of its pollutants as well as the committee's suggestions to rejuvenate the river can be read as creating a context and an environment that makes capitalism and development sustainable rather than developing sustainability in the ecological sense. The emphasis on clean and cost-effective technology centre stages the concept of 'efficient' production—so crucial to mainstream economics.

- The committee, to borrow a phrase from Castro,[7] 'tends to be technologically optimistic'. Thus, the emphasis on RO plants and the attainment of zero discharge become virtuous ends in themselves. Seen from another perspective, the fact that industry has already invested substantially in fixed capital makes change a costly proposition and politically unpalatable. Hence, 'intense phases of bureaucratic activity in the face of pressure on environmental issues (committees, inquiries, commissioning reports, etc.) ...is unlikely to advocate substantial change or to question the overall direction of society'.[8]
- The preoccupation with technology to achieve 'environmental sustainability through efficiency' has completely blanked out discussions on fundamental issues such as the scale of resource exploitation, the length of such exploitation, etc., since market-led growth places the onus of deciding what constitutes sustainability on buyers and sellers being satisfied with their transactions, even if the latter leads to extensive resource exploitation. The government, clueless at best on how to account for environment, and/or seeing itself as facilitator of market-led efficient growth at worst, is comfortable with interpreting sustainable development as capitalist development.
- It needs to be recorded, however, that unlike the State, the courts[9] have a far more holistic understanding

[7] C.J. Castro, 'Sustainable Development: Mainstream and Critical Perspectives', *Organ Environ*, vol. 17, no. 2, 2004, pp. 195–225.

[8] Handmer and Dovers, 'A Typology of Resilience', p. 505.

[9] The cases cited in the text are all contained in a comprehensive Court Order dated 22 December 2006 of the Madras High Court in connection with the Writ Petition [no. 29791 of 2003] filed by the Noyyal River Ayacutdars Protection Association.

of 'environment' and 'sustainable development' as discernible from the following observations in various judgments relating to cases of industrial pollution and damage to forests:

1. '(Therefore) there is a Constitutional imperative on the state authorities and bodies like the PCB not only to ensure and safeguard proper environment, but also an imperative duty to take adequate measures to promote, protect and improve the environment, man-made and natural' [Order dated 22.12.2006 on WP nos. 29791 and 39368 of 2003].
2. In Indian Council for Enviro-Legal Action etc. Vs. Union of India, Justice Jeevan Reddy observed: 'Sections 3 and 5 of the Environment [Protection] Act 1986, apart from other provisions of Water and Air Acts, empower the government to make all such directions and take all such measures as are necessary or expedient for protecting and promoting the "environment"...This power includes the power to prohibit an activity, close an industry, direct and/or carry out remedial measures, and wherever necessary, impose the cost of remedial measures upon the offending industry' (J. T. 1996 (2) S. C. 1996).
3. In Vellore Citizens Welfare Forum versus Union of India the court rejected the argument that leather industry in India is a leading exporter and a major foreign exchange earner and that any adverse order would affect the flow of foreign exchange in the country. The court observed as follows: 'It is no doubt correct that the leather industry in India has become a major foreign exchange earner and at present, Tamil Nadu is the leading exporter of

finished leather accounting for approximately 80% of the country's export. Though the leather industry is of vital importance to the country as it generates foreign exchange and provides employment avenues, it has no right to destroy the ecology, degrade the environment and pose as a health hazard. It cannot be permitted to expand or even to continue with the present production unless it tackles by itself the problem of pollution created by the said industry' (J. T. 1996 (7) S. C. 375). The court discussed the 'polluter pays principle' as well as the 'precautionary principle' and the concept of sustainable development and held, in the light of the constitutional and statutory provisions we have, that they are part of the environmental law of the country.

4. The 'Precautionary Principle' means: (i) Environment measures must anticipate, prevent and attack the causes of environmental degradation; (ii) Where there are threats of serious and irreversible damage, lack of scientific certainty should not be used as a reason for postponing measures to prevent environmental degradation; (iii) The 'Onus of proof' is on the actor or the developer/industrialist to show that his action is environmentally benign.
5. The Polluter Pays Principle means: 'Once the activity carried on is hazardous or dangerous, the person carrying on such activity is liable to make good the loss caused to any other person by his activity irrespective of the fact whether he took reasonable care while carrying on his activity. The rule is premised upon the very nature of the activity carried on. Consequently, the polluting industries are absolutely liable to compensate for the harm caused by them to villagers in the affected area, to

the soil and to the underground water and hence, they are bound to take all necessary measures to remove sludge and other pollutants lying in the affected areas. The Polluter Pays principle as interpreted by this court means that the absolute liability for harm to the environment extends not only to compensate the victims of pollution, but also the cost of restoring the environmental degradation. Remediation of the damaged environment is part of the process of 'Sustained Development' and as such, polluter is liable to pay the cost to the individual sufferers as well as the cost of reversing the damaged ecology' (Order dated 22.12.2006 on WP nos. 29791 and 39368 of 2003).

Nevertheless, however radical the observations of the courts may have been, hardly any of this radicalism was translated into operational details, so necessary for transformations on the ground. At the end of the day, the courts' directives have to be operationalized, if at all, by the same structures and bodies, that failed to act and deliver in the first place.

- Seen from another angle, the committee's work can be characterized as EM, which seeks to find a harmony between economic and environmental interests even while furthering private corporate interests.[10] Levy explicates the ideological character of the four central assumptions of EM, namely: that the environment can and should be managed, that corporate managers should be doing the management, that EM is a win–win opportunity, and that traditional management functions and concepts are appropriate tools.[11] The

[10] D.L. Levy, 'Environmental Management as Political Sustainability', *Organ Environ*, vol. 10, no. 2, 1997, pp. 126–47.

[11] Ibid., p. 127.

underlying principle informing the constitution of the Committee by the Court centrally endorses Levy's point, namely, that the environment can be managed.

- Further, the committee in turn worked towards mitigating adverse environmental effects of growth without questioning the goal of increased production and consumption. The set of measures put in place by the committee were aimed largely to deflect attention away from demands for more radical changes that would seriously challenge capitalism's hegemony. In this sense, what the committee's work ensured was political rather than environmental sustainability. Forced to grapple with the Habermasian 'crises of legitimacy' situation, because of growing public protest over land and water degradation, consequent loss of livelihoods, scarcity of drinking water, etc., the state/court had to step in to forestall the crises from not only challenging existing hegemonic positions but from leading thereon to major social transformations.
- In sum, therefore, the committee's EM process ensured accommodation and compromise but had no scope for 'a broader debate over economic goals, organizational governance mechanisms and alternative approaches to addressing environmental problems'.[12]

By Way of Conclusion

What the Above Case Holds for Our Understanding of Industrialization and Its Interface with Environmental Issues

As already mentioned above, the circumstances leading to the constitution of the committee and the ToRs given to it

[12] Ibid., p. 142.

did not provide an occasion for the committee to question the broader and more serious questions of continued increase in production and consumption to satisfy global and local demands. This constraint need not, however, inform academic interpretation and/or engagement with the adverse environmental fallouts of industrialization. It would be pertinent to locate the contents of the above case within the framework of the Treadmill of Production Model developed by Schnaiberg.[13]

When Schnaiberg first developed the theory of the Treadmill of Production in 1976, this was an exercise in empirical deduction. As a social scientist with a technical/scientific background, Schnaiberg tried to understand why US environmental conditions had declined so precipitously since the Second World War. No matter where he turned or what he read, the dominant narrative always seemed to start with changes in economic production as the major determinant of the trajectory of ecosystem impacts. From a logical perspective, it was production changes that, according to him, caused environmental disruption.

The primary reason that Schnaiberg's Treadmill of Production Model of socio-environmental dynamics emphasizes production rather than consumption is that:

> production is prior to consumption . . . Consumers may opt not to consume specific produced items. But they are not empowered by market processes to determine how such items will and will not be produced. In this sense, they are not seriously empowered to alter the ecological impacts of production decisions . . . Consumers can choose Pepsi

[13] And as explicated in K.A. Gould et al., 'Interrogating the Treadmill of Production: Everything You Wanted to Know about the Treadmill, but were Afraid to Ask', paper prepared for the symposium on Environment and the Treadmill of Production, University of Wisconsin, Madison, 31 October–1 November 2003.

or Coke or some low-calorie, green alternative soft drink. Yet this is largely irrelevant if the ownership and control over all these products is in the hands of producers who are simultaneously displacing workers, taxing the state's resources, and placing great burdens on the ecosystem. Clothing is another 'consumption' example. *Unless consumers in the North produce their own clothes, they leave producers the appealing option of producing virtually all clothing in sweatshops that exploit labourers, and typically produce various ecological disruptions (in both agriculture and transportation). So long as owners are free to invest in low-wage countries (or engage low-wage immigrants in industrial countries), consumers exercise little control over these production processes* (emphasis added).[14]

The question of how much we are consuming (that is, growth), is rarely challenged, the focus is on only changing what we are consuming. This is perhaps not surprising, as consumerist approaches are fundamentally about protecting the right to consume as much as they are about corporate and social responsibility. A policy focus on consumption is almost always the easy path: it generally absolves industry and the state of responsibility for a host of problems:

- It leaves production largely undisturbed.
- It fails to challenge the fundamental structure of the industry in question.
- It often blames poor populations for not engaging in 'enlightened', 'responsible', and, 'conscious' consumer practices.[15]

Transnationalization of the economy and deepening global inequality makes the possibility of avoiding distributional

[14] Ibid., pp. 5–9.
[15] Ibid., pp. 9–12.

politics in pursuit of green objectives decreasingly plausible. Inequality provides the basis for environmental injustices, insatiable material aspirations, anti-ecological survival strategies, and treadmill support even in the face of ever-diminishing social returns. Our case study above amply demonstrates the practically nil manoeuvering capacity of the Indian government, *either* to withdraw from the global market (and risk loss of earnings as well as employment) *or* enforce a pattern of consumption compatible with sustainable environment standards.

Coming to the theme of sustainability, we find Handmer and Dovers'[16] approach in terms of systems and responses to change (what they term as resilience) very useful and relevant to our case. They suggest the following three-way classification of resilience, defined in terms of the response to threats of disturbance:

Type 1: Resistance and Maintenance
Type 2: Change at the Margins
Type 3: Openness and Adaptability

Type 1 resilience, according to them, is characterized by resistance to change, where the system or individual in authority does its utmost to avoid change and typically denies that a problem exists, where enormous resources could be expended in maintaining the status quo.

Type 2 resilience is characterized by acknowledgement of the problem, discussion of the implications, and promulgation of reforms that do not challenge the basis of societies but that may lead to changes in the emphasis at the margins. Here, there could be clear acknowledgement that the present system is not sustainable and that change

[16] Handmer and Dovers, 'A Typology of Resilience', 1996.

is needed. The rhetoric will be there, but only minor changes occur, largely directed at alleviating symptoms.

In Type 3 resilience, the underlying structural causes of the problems are identified, the options explored, and changes put in place. This seems straightforward, Handmer and Dovers opine, but also ask why it has not happened: 'One powerful constraint is vested interests, in that major change is likely to alter the power structure substantially'.[17]

On the whole, Handmer and Dovers conclude that:

> the whole ethos of public management is to limit the debates to type 1 and 2 (denial and management of symptoms) and to avoid even discussing type 3 (tackling the underlying causes) . . . the precautionary principle is currently a key policy response to the sustainability challenge. It is an official recognition of pervasive uncertainty, and a statement that awaiting positive proof that an activity is harmful may no longer be tenable. Nevertheless, in implementation, the principle seems unlikely to take us beyond type 2 responses—although a complete reversal in the burden of proof should move action strongly toward type 3.[18]

Without labouring the point further, any discerning reader of our case study will immediately realize that the nature of intervention in Tiruppur belongs to the Type 2 classification, where, as already underlined, the action was nowhere commensurate with the rhetoric, namely, that of cleaning the Noyyal River and ridding it of all pollutants, now and forever.

[17] Ibid., p. 502.
[18] Ibid., pp. 504–6.

PART III

Industrial Growth, Employment and Education

The Missing Link

CHAPTER 7

Technical Education and Industrial Development in the Madras Presidency

Illusions of a Policy in the Making

It is said that we ought to secure the cooperation of the native public, and that we can do this only by teaching Sanskrit and Arabic. I can by no means admit, that, when a nation of high intellectual attainments undertakes to superintend the education of a nation comparatively ignorant, the learners are absolutely to prescribe the course which is to be taken by the teachers.[1]

* Previously published in *Economic and Political Weekly*, July 1992 and MIDS Working Paper no. 106, 1992. This paper is part of an ICSSR-sponsored study on the growth of the corporate sector in the Madras Presidency. I am extremely grateful to the commissioner and staff of the Tamil Nadu Archives from where substantive part of the material for the paper has been drawn; the staff at the National Archives of India, Delhi; my colleagues C.T. Kurien, S. Neelakantan, M.S.S. Pandian and Nasir Tyabji for their comments and suggestions on an earlier draft of this paper; T. Maheswari for painstakingly word processing several drafts of the paper; needless to add, I alone bear responsibility for the views expressed in the paper.

[1] T.B. Macaulay's Minute, dated 2 February 1835, reproduced in H. Sharp, ed., *Selections from Educational Records*, part I: 1781–1839, Calcutta, Superintendent Government Printing, India, 1920, p. 112.

The Natives must either be kept down by a sense of our power, or they must willingly submit from a conviction that we are more wise, more just, more humane and more anxious to improve their condition than any other rulers they could possibly have.[2]

An official documentation of the need to provide technical education to the people of India can be traced to the Educational Despatch of 1854:

Our attention should now be directed to a consideration, if possible, still more important, and one which has been hitherto, we are bound to admit, too much neglected, namely, how useful and practical knowledge, suited to every station in life, may be best conveyed to the great mass of the people, who are utterly incapable of obtaining any education worthy of the name by their own unaided efforts, and we desire to see the measures of Government more especially directed for the future, to this object, for the attainment of which we are ready to sanction a considerable increase of expenditure.[3]

Following the despatch came the *Report of the Education Commission* in 1883. Unfortunately, technical instruction was one of the few matters connected with education on which the commission was not required to report.[4] But they could not ignore the question altogether and among other things observed that:

It has been felt in all provinces, and urged by many witnesses that the attention of students is too exclusively directed to University

[2] Minute by J. Farish, dated 28 August 1838, Quoted in the Gauri Viswanathan, 'Introduction' *Masks of Conquest: Literary Study and British Rule in India*, London: Faber and Faber, 1990.

[3] J.A. Richery, ed., *Selections from Educational Records*, part II: 1840–1859, Calcutta: Superintendent Government Printing, India, 1922, p. 376.

[4] We have not been successful so far in locating material explaining why 'technical education' did not come under the scope of enquiry of this Education Commission.

studies, and that no opportunity is offered for the development of what corresponds to the 'modern side' of schools in Europe. It is believed that there is a real need in India for some corresponding course which shall fit boys for industrial or commercial pursuits, at the age when they commonly matriculate, more directly than is effected by the present system.[5]

The commission recommended a bifurcation of studies into two divisions in the upper classes of high schools—one leading to the entrance examination of the universities and the other, of a more practical character, intended to fit youths for commercial or non-literary pursuits. The GOI, in its review of the commission's Report, gave the recommendation the fullest significance by passing the following Resolution in 1884: 'The bifurcation of studies suggested by the Committee is of special importance at the present time. Every variety of study should be encouraged which may serve to direct the attention of native youth to industrial and commercial pursuits.'[6]

In July 1886, Macdonnell, the Home Secretary drew a note examining the condition of technical education in the various provinces and the steps taken by each local government to give effect to the 1884 orders of the GOI enforcing the necessity of improvements in the matter of practical and industrial training. Macdonnell noted that nowhere, except in Madras, had any practical steps been actually taken in giving effect to the orders in question.[7]

[5] K.D. Bhargava, ed., *Selections from Educational Records of the Government of India*, vol. IV, Technical Education in India, 1886–1907, National Archives of India, Delhi, 1968, p. 13.

[6] Ibid., p. 15.

[7] Macdonnell's Note on *Technical Education in India* reproduced in Bhargava, *Selections from Educational Records of the Government of India*, pp. 9–84.

The attempt in this chapter is to bring out the educational manifestations of colonialism through a study of the development of technical education in the Madras Presidency. The model, method, curriculum/content, and the organization for developing a system of technical education that was initiated in the Madras Presidency around 1885 was largely based on the experience of England. Simultaneously, efforts were underway in the Madras Presidency to stimulate some form of industrial activity in the state—largely through the pioneering efforts of Alfred Chatterton who took over as Superintendent of the School of Arts in Madras in 1897.[8]

The closing decades of the nineteenth century and the first decade of the twentieth century saw intense activity in the Madras Presidency in the form of debates, discussions, memoranda, conferences, and resolutions covering the following issues:

(a) The need to bring the scheme of technical education into relation with the industrial needs and conditions of the country;[9]

[8] See 'Memorandum on the Department of Industries in the Madras Presidency' in Home (Education), G.O. no. 141, Mis, 7 February 1917 (all Government Orders [G.O.] refer to those issue by the Madras government and maintained at the Tamil Nadu Archives, unless otherwise specified).

[9] Given the circumstances of the period, at one level it was futile to talk of relating technical education to the industrial needs and conditions of the country. And yet, in the Madras Presidency, to some extent, the Department of Industries under Chatterton tried to push through a scheme which:

(a) Recognized and stressed the need to study those artisan-based industries that could be made commercially viable by improvements and,

(b) Looked to the state to launch new ventures in order to ameliorate the deteriorating conditions of the vast majority of

(b) The insulation of the artisan classes from any form of formal instruction in schools that could be classified as industrial or technical schools and therefore the inability of the system to tackle 'the real problem of industrial education';
(c) The extreme illiteracy of the vast majority of the population which meant that fundamental or necessarily preliminary instruction had to be imparted before going on to specialized technical instructions;
(d) The need for government intervention in fostering industrial development and embarking on a series of industrial experiments worked out on a comparatively large and commercial scale to make industrial and technical education really take off.

For convenience of analysis the paper is divided into three sections. Section I gives a brief outline of the chronological developments in policy aimed at fostering technical education from an all-India perspective. Section II forms the nub of our analysis. Here we document the evolution of the policy relating to technical education in the Madras Presidency, which, while trying to function within the framework of the imperial dictat, attempted to evolve a model of its own in the light of what it perceived as being suited to the conditions obtaining in the province. The early phase of enthusiasm (beginning with the closing decades of the nineteenth century and the opening decade of the twentieth century) ended in a near disaster with the imperial government ordering the closure of the Industries Department of the Presidency.

---

the poor. In this limited sense there could be said to be some awareness of the need to impart those skills that would help the artisan to hold his own.

Thereafter, even the customary service to the magnitude of the problem became few and far between until almost the eve of Independence when the Scientific and Technical Man-Power Committee was set up at the all-India level. Whatever else this body may not have done, it certainly brought out the depressing scenario as far as the country's technical and scientific manpower was concerned, the Madras Presidency included.[10] In Section III we conclude with certain observations borne out of our study of the whole issue.

Technical Education Policy in India: Chronological Developments

The *Report of the Education Commission of 1883* had recommended the introduction of secondary school courses preparing boys for industrial or commercial careers. Upon this subject, the GOI in 1886 circulated a memorandum to all local governments in which the position of industrial schools then existing was set forth and it was shown that hitherto little progress of a substantial character had been made in promoting technical education.[11] Since then the subject had received much attention both from the public and the various local governments. One consideration which had forced the question into prominence had to do with the need of industrial occupation for a population rapidly outgrowing the means of support supplied by a too-conservative system of agriculture.

[10] 'Technical Education: Scientific Manpower Committee' in Education G.O. no. 633, dated 23 March 1948.

[11] 'Resolution on Industrial Education and Industrial Survey of India' in Home Education B. Proceedings, January 1891, nos. 14–15, National Archives of India, also reproduced in Bhargava, *Selections from Educational Records of the Government of India*, pp. 85–8.

It was realized that, in India, the application of capital to industry had not then developed to the extent which in European countries had rendered the establishment of technical schools on a large scale an essential requisite of success. But the extension of railways, the introduction of mills and factories, the exploration of mineral and other products, and the expansion of external trade was expected to create a demand for skilled labour and for educated foremen, supervisors and managers. The conspicuous insignificance of what had been attempted in India, then, by way of promotion of technical education, prompted the Governor-General in Council to suggest that local governments were to take action in two ways: (1) collect information on the extent, character, and circumstances of important local industries in every province of India; and (2) each government was to form a committee of educational experts and professional men who would make suggestions from time to time for the supply of appropriate means of technical education, and at the opportune time establish a technological Institute for the enlargement of the provincial Schools of Art and Design and for the larger cooperation of the university in the promotion of the object in view.[12]

In 1901, the government of India requested E. Buck to enquire into and submit a report on the position and progress of practical education in each province.[13] The conclusion that Buck drew from his examination of the position throughout India was that the general intention of all the educational departments was in accordance with the principles of the Imperial Resolutions but

[12] Ibid.

[13] E. Buck, *Report on Practical and Technical Education*, Home Education A Proceedings, December 1901, no. 20, National Archives of India, reproduced in Bhargava, *Selections from Educational Records of the Government of India*, pp. 116–95.

that the measures taken were not always clearly defined and were in some provinces insufficient. In some of the provinces no definite scheme had yet been drawn up on the basis of the resolutions of 1895 and 1897, no final considerations had been given to these resolutions, no modifications made in the curricula. Progress effected in the teaching of teachers was slow while some of the school books even went against leading principles enunciated.[14]

Buck noted that the Educational Despatch of 1854, on which the educational scheme of the country was founded, had divided the classes for whom a different kind of instruction was needed under three heads—high, middle, and low. This division, according to Buck, though sufficient half a century ago for the purposes of initial organization, was not adequate but needed further differentiation and a determination of the line which was to separate the functions of the educational staff from those of the administration of industrial and technical schemes.[15]

Buck provided a chart of the different types of primary and technical schools that he came across in the various provinces (reproduced in Table 7.1). He found that the schools of type VI were the favourite type of industrial schools in India where a good deal of literary education was given at the same time that minor trades, of which the most prominent were carpentry and smithy work, were taught. This type, originally founded by missionaries, had been more or less copied in most of the industrial schools established by official authorities. The sale of the articles made in the school provided for the maintenance of the school. The method of instruction in these schools, according to Buck, was faulty, the boys

[14] Ibid., p. 134.

[15] Ibid, p. 148.

Table 7.1: Types of Primary and Technical Schools in Various Provinces

	Class of School		*Provinces in which found*
Primary			
I	In which no teaching is given by practical methods, i.e. kindergarten, object lessons, illustrations, etc.	I	North-Western Provinces
II	In which object lessons and elementary science are optional subjects.	II	Madras
III	In which practical methods are employed.	III	More or less in every province. More perhaps in Bombay and the Central Provinces than elsewhere.
IV	In which hand and eye and manual training are added to III.	IV	Central Provinces town school; North-Western Provinces English Schools; Bengal vernacular schools.
Technical			
V	Manual work schools on the 'disciplinary' system which prepare boys by manual exercises for manual occupations.	V	All industrial schools in Bombay.
VI	Schools which give literary instruction combined with teaching a trade under school officials.	VI	Aided Schools, chiefly missionaries in Bombay, Madras, North-Western Provinces and Central Provinces.
VII	Special trade schools not giving literary instruction for teaching improvements in an industry or for teaching a new industry under school officials.	VII	Sericulture school in Bengal; aluminium school in Madras; art schools in Bengal, Madras, Bombay and Punjab; Rurki College Industrial class.
VIII	Special schools, for training artisans in foundries, workshops etc.	VIII	Lahore

(Table 7.1 Continued)

(Table 7.1 Continued)

	Class of School		*Provinces in which found*
IX	Special Schools for higher class employees	IX	Victoria Jubilee Institute, Bombay
X	Special trade schools for teaching industries under native artisan teachers on the Naples system.	X	To be introduced at Lucknow: recommended for all towns.

Source: E. Buck, *Report on Practical and Technical Education*, Home Education: A Proceedings, December 1901, no. 20, National Archives of India, Reproduced in Bhargava, *Selections from Educational Records of the Government of India*, p. 151.

being taught by a salaried artisan who had no personal interest in the success of the work turned out while the literary education was too advanced for those who were meant to follow a manual occupation. Buck found that the largest number of such schools existed in the Madras Presidency, where the number of missionaries were more than in any other province. Chatterton, in a note, condemned the type as having a double object in view and failing in both.[16]

[16] Chatterton wrote in his note: 'Schools under Class VI have a double object in view, and as a rule they fail to achieve success in either branch of the work. *I therefore think that the establishment of such schools should not be encouraged.* This, I think, also is the opinion of the European managers of many of the Mission Schools, though some advocate, for their own requirements, the establishment of schools of the type described in class V, in which the boys get a preliminary knowledge of handicraft, and then when they have attained a certain degree of manual skill and completed their course of general education, they are drafted into a special trade school (class VII). This, I think, has been the idea from the very outset and schools of class VI have arisen through the inability on the part of the managers to clearly recognise the necessity for keeping schools of class V and class VII perfectly distinct' (emphasis as in original). Ibid., p. 153.

The compulsions of the government apart, the arguments put forward by Buck highlight various aspects of the complexities of the situation. At one level, to derive maximum benefit from the instruction imparted in industrial schools, the government felt that instruction was to be differentiated for different classes. At another level, caste domination of particular trades made it difficult for those outside the castes to learn a trade. It was here that the missionaries played a significant role by providing an avenue to the native Christian community to learn trades which otherwise would have been out of bounds to them. On principle, the government expressed its abhorrence over entering into commercial transactions (which would have been the only way to make a dent in occupations dominated by caste) and wanted the trades selected in industrial schools to be capable of improvement by expert instruction or the introduction of scientific methods.

Summing up the main defects of the then industrial schools, Buck enumerated the following: that general and technical education were combined, that instruction was not differentiated for different classes, that disproportionate attention was given to carpentry and smithy work, that aims and objects were not defined, or, if they were, not kept in view, that if a trade was taught it was not followed, that attempts at working for a market lead to embarrassment, and that the leading defect of all was that no clear principles were laid down.[17]

An important observation made by Buck relevant from the Indian point of view (considering that England's experience formed the model for the setting up of technical schools in India) was that England could no longer claim the monopoly she once possessed of modern

[17] Ibid, p. 160.

manufactures. Austria and Germany had embarked on a serious training programme of their subjects in scientific, technical, and artistic training.

> In England people are still content to repeat that trades cannot be taught in a school. The Austrians and Germans have discovered that trades cannot be efficiently taught *without* a school. In many towns employers are required to send their apprentices to a technical school for a certain number of days a week, and a breach of the law is followed by fine or imprisonment. Nor are the schools confined to a few large towns. In Austria, in particular, a great point is made of carrying technical training to the small towns and even to the villages.[18] (emphasis in original)

A Conference on Technical Education was held at Simla in 1901. Before going into the resolutions passed at the conference, a point to be noted that is the conference proceedings were kept secret, and, more important, no Indian was invited to it, even though, as Aparna Basu has pointed out, representatives of the Indian educated class had been found competent to advise the government on the framing of the educational policy in 1882.[19]

The conference recommended the institution of a number of State Technical Scholarships for the encouragement of the further studies of Indian students in the higher branches of technical education. The proposal was accepted by the GOI who were prepared to institute ten scholarships a year, two each to the presidencies of Bombay, Bengal, and Madras and the remaining four

[18] Ibid., pp. 194–5.

[19] Aparna Basu, *The Growth of Education and Political Development in India, 1898–1920*, New Delhi: Oxford University Press, 1974, pp. 19–20.

to be distributed among other local governments and administrations in whose territories technical instruction had not advanced sufficiently.[20]

The Simla Conference had come down heavily on the lack of organization and the want of purpose of the then existing industrial schools in the country.[21] The GOI therefore decided in 1901 to appoint a committee to visit the different provinces in connection with the institution of industrial schools to examine what had already been done and with what measure of success, and to confer with local educational officers and others as to the best means of establishing such schools.[22]

The GOI wanted the local governments to examine the lines on which a practical beginning could be made.[23]

Despite the 'torrents of words',[24] both the government of India and the local governments were in a maze as to

[20] Letter from J.P. Hewett, Secretary to the Government of India, to Local Governments Regarding Encouragement of Technical Education, dated 20 November 1901, Home Education: A Proceedings, November 1901, no. 57, National Archives of India, reproduced in Bhargava, *Selections from Educational Records of the Government of India*, pp. 196–202.

[21] 'Resolution of the Simla Conference (1901) on Technical Education', reproduced in *Papers Relating to Technical Education in India, 1886–1904*, Calcutta: Superintendent Government Printing, 1906, pp. 251–3.

[22] 'Resolution of the Government of India on Report of the Committee on Industrial Schools in India', in ibid., pp. 257–61.

[23] Letter from H.H. Risley, Officiating Secretary to the Government of India, Home Department (Education) to the Secretary to the Government of Madras (Educational Department), 30 September 1903, Educational G.O, no. 313, Press, 12 May 1905.

[24] G.S. Forbes, an official in the service of the Madras Government, was quite critical of the statement made at the Ootacamund

the course to be followed. Their exasperation was all the more acute given the realization that ordinary education, which formed the preliminary to technical instruction, was so little advanced among the population at large and especially among the classes and castes who were likely to adopt an industrial life. The cause for the slow progress was blamed on the character of the people themselves.

> They do not trust one another and they are unable to adopt cooperative methods. Of all those who have received in the high schools and the university a scientific training upon which they would readily found a technical education, the numbers who have so applied that training during the last quarter of a century would be counted upon the fingers of one's hand.[25]

The increasing realization of the importance of technical education led in some quarters to the demand for the creation of a separate department, despite the fact that the creation of a Department of Technical

---

Conference of 1908 to the effect that technical education was a matter of interest to a very large section of the public in the Presidency and that there was a 'popular demand' for the same. He noted: 'Out of 40 million of population there are not 300 who care a brass farthing one way or the other. We have had torrents of words, but almost entirely from those classes of the people, who will do nothing themselves in the direction suggested but *talk* and whose sons with an education which would fit them to take up scientific or technical instruction steadily decline to embark on scientific or industrial enterprises. Most of those I refer to are actuated largely by political motives: if they really cared as much as they profess for industrial reform they would do something themselves instead of urging the government to act for them.' See Notes to Revenue G.O. no. 2894, Press, dated 17 October 1908.

[25] Ibid.

Education separate from the Educational Department had failed so conspicuously in England.[26] Some of those who advocated such a separation were led to this view by the consideration of the inability of the education departments, as then organized, to add to their burdens by undertaking the supervision of a new branch of work.

In September 1912, the GOI felt that the time had come to endeavour to connect educational institutions more closely with business firms, railways, and other employers of labour, to enquire how the former could better meet the requirements of the latter and to pinpoint the way to further the employment of Indians in them. Colonel Atkinson and Dawson were selected to conduct the enquiry in the leading industrial centres of India. The GOI was keen on eliciting the opinions

[26] The administration of technical education in England was controlled for many years by the Science and Art Department, which was in the first instance an offshoot of the Board of Trade. It was then an independent department by itself and was afterwards a department nominally united with the education department by virtue of a common minister but really almost separate and independent. After forty-six years of independent functioning in England, the Education Department and the Science and Art Department were brought together in 1899 and were fused into one department under a single permanent secretary. 'So great were the evils of the separation of administration of technical education from that of general education, and so signal has been the success of uniting them, that there is not a single person in England having any acquaintance with the subject who would propose to revert to the *status quo ante* 1899 or who would not concur as to the advantages gained by the measure of consolidation then carried through.' See Letter from H.W. Orange, Director-General of Education in India to the Secretary to the Government of India, Home Department, Simla, dated 21 October 1908. Educational G.O. no. 572, Press (Confidential), 22 October 1909.

of the local governments on recommendations made in the report.[27]

Tressler, Superintendent of Industrial Education in the Madras Presidency, in his note on the report, pointed out that the investigations made by Atkinson and Dawson had transformed into an enquiry about the nature of the combination needed to produce the class of workers required in modern industry.[28]

Tressler felt that under existing conditions it was only in the matter of school training that the Educational Department could influence industrial education. Such training, however excellent it might be intrinsically, could not be expected by itself to lead to a complete solution of the problem under consideration. School training could teach a pupil the principles of his trade but the real solution to the problem, according to Tressler, lay with the employer of labour over whom the government had no control.[29]

In 1915, a confidential note submitted to the Secretary of State drew attention to the growing discontent among the population, which followed two particular lines of expression.[30] In the first place, there was the constant asseveration that the British government had with malice intent or, if not with malice, by their attitude of indifference, allowed indigenous industries

[27] Letter from H. Sharp, Joint Secretary to the Government of India, Department of Education, to the Secretary to the Government of Madras, Educational Department, Simla, dated 27 September 1912, Educational G.O. no. 798, Press, 26 August 1913.

[28] A general note by K.T.B. Tressler, Superintendent of Industrial Education, in Educational G.O. no. 798, Press, 26 August 1913.

[29] Ibid.

[30] Note addressed to Austen Chamberlain, Secretary of State for India, Delhi, dated 26 November 1915, in Educational G.O. no, 46, Miscellaneous (Confidential), 12 January 1916.

to be overwhelmed by foreign and especially by British competition. The second charge was that the British system of education had confined the energies of the educated young men to literary pursuits and the learned professions, and had created among them a demand for employment limited to government service, the law, and medicine. These contentions emphasized one aspect of the need for an industrial policy which would enable technical education in India to produce its best results, lighten the pressure on purely literary courses, and reduce the excessive demand for employment in the services and callings to which the courses led up.

In a resolution dated 19 May 1916,[31] the government made explicit its decision to take up for examination the question of the expansion and development of Indian manufactures and industries in a more comprehensive manner than had hitherto been attempted. In discussing the functions of the provincial departments of industries, the commission proposed that the control of technical and industrial education should be vested in the Department of Industries, with the government reserving the right of deciding whether particular schools should be controlled by the educational or industries department, such as, the reformatory schools and the schools of art. Another proposal of the commission was the constitution of an imperial department of industries. Among the latter's function was included the need to advise local governments regarding the conduct of industrial and technical education and this advice was to be tendered through the medium of 'thoroughly qualified visiting experts', the implication being that these 'itinerant experts' would replace the provincial inspector of

[31] Educational G.O. no. 622, 5 June 1916.

industrial schools. This move was opposed by the Director of Industries, Madras, among others.[32]

Around this time the Montagu-Chelmsford Reports on Constitutional Reforms was also published. Both the reports emphasized the need for rapid industrialization of the economy with active state participation. However, while the Indian Industrial Commission's (IIC) Report emphasized the need to centre direction in the government of India, the Reforms Committee emphasized the need to minimize central supervision and direction of provincial activities.

A reading of the administration reports of the Department of Industries brings out clearly the limited impact that the department had on the industrialization of the province, despite organizational changes keeping with the recommendations of the above bodies.

Provincial autonomy was accompanied by financial stringency leading to retrenchment, which was accentuated further in the depression and post-depression years. This slowed down industrial development and technological progress. Nothing significant by way of educational policy/resolutions was announced in the 1930s and 1940s though the establishment of stray institutions here and there did take place.[33]

The magnitude of the task facing the country on the eve of Independence in terms of the paucity of scientific

[32] See letter from C.A. Innes, Director of Industries, Madras to the Secretary to Government, Revenue (Special) Department, dated 20 January 1919, in Revenue (Special) G.O. no. 791, Press, 28 April 1919.

[33] For details see, for example, Saugata Mukherji, 'Some Aspects of the Policy on Technical and Industrial Education in India under Colonial Rule from Late Nineteenth Century to Independence', Occasional Paper no. 123, Centre for Studies in Social Sciences, Calcutta, June 1990.

and technical personnel and the extremely poor base from which post-Independence India had to build, can be gauged from the following statistics provided by the Scientific and Technical Man-Power Committee set up by the GOI in April 1947.[34] The committee could not obtain up-to-date statistics concerning the annual output of scientific and technical personnel from institutions and had to make do with figures concerning the whole of British India for the year 1940:

Students passing the various examinations:	
Matriculation or its equivalent	92,555
Intermediate arts	19,000
Intermediate science	5,453
BSc (pass)	2,499
BSc (Honours school)	359
MSc	428
Medical degree	875
Agricultural degree	293
Engineering (civil, mechanical & electrical, mining and metallurgy) degrees	638
Doctorate (arts, science, medicine) degrees	38

The committee expressed the opinion that they had no reason to suppose that conditions in 1947 were remarkably different from that obtaining in 1940. Uncertainty as to the extent of development of Indian industries in subsequent years and the inadequacy of information available to them, made it difficult for the committee to assess with reasonable exactitude the

[34] What follows, including the statistical details have been summarized from the Committee's Report, Educational G.O. no. 633, 23 March 1948.

requirements for technical personnel for the following five years. The committee therefore made an approximate assessment by analyzing the new capital flotation allowed by the government and from this tried to infer India's requirement for technicians. We reproduce a table given by the committee that showed the position of new capital issues for some of the industries in January 1946 together with a column showing the number of additional technical personnel that would be required for the successful running of these industries (Table 7.2). The technical personnel were divided into three categories:

'A' – Experts
'B' – Technicians with superior qualifications
'C' – Lower grade technicians including mechanics

From a comparative study of the figures of the estimated output with those giving the immediate requirements of industry alone, leaving aside the requirement of governments for their contemplated large-scale public works, the committee found that they had to plan for at least a four-fold increase in the output of all categories of personnel, if the needs of the next four or five years had to be met. In this context, a note was prepared for the committee giving a statement of the facilities available in various Indian universities, and the urgent measures which should be given effect to, in order to increase the outturn of research workers as well as the probable numbers of additional men each university would be in a position to admit in the immediate future. From such data it was found that only the Universities of Calcutta, Bombay, Andhra, Benaras, Lucknow, Allahabad, Aligarh, Dacca and Punjab had fairly well-equipped postgraduate research departments while the Universities of *Madras*,

Table 7.2: Additional Technical Personnel Required in Selected Industries

	Industries	*New Capital Issues Allowed in 1946 (Rs. in lakhs)* 'A'	*Estimated requirements (Number in Grades)* 'B'	'C'	
1.	Glass and Ceramics	213	10	30	200
2.	Chemicals and Drugs	570	20	100	250
3.	Soap and Oil (excluding edible oils and vanaspati)	110	8	10	100
4.	Rayon and Art Silk	402	6	30	200
5.	Paper, Board, etc.	281	10	50	150
6.	Plastics	50	10	40	200
7.	Leather	85	5	13	35
8.	Cement	463	10	20	80
9.	Woollen	137	10	36	100
10.	Rubber	117	70	94	188
11.	Engineering	1242	25	150	1000
12.	Electrical	910	25	150	300
13.	Non-Ferrous Metals	98	6	45	250
14.	Machine Tools	122	100	400	1000

Note: The output of graduates in engineering and technology in 1946 was estimated as follows:

1.	Aeronautical Engineering	15
2.	Architecture and Building Construction	20
3.	Civil and Municipal Engineering	467
4.	Chemical Engineering and Chemical Technology	244
5.	Electrical Engineering	285
6.	Mechanical Engineering	258
7.	Metallurgy	27
8.	Mining	27
	Total	1,343

Nagpur, Delhi, Patna, *Annamalai* and Agra *were not so in this respect* (emphasis added).[35]

An observation made by the committee (relevant in the Indian context even today) was that a good proportion of the available scientific manpower in the country had not been made use of in a fruitful way inasmuch as owing to the then existing conditions of recruitment to services and other factors many qualified men had not suitable opportunities of contributing all they could in the sphere of scientific and industrial activity.

Technical Education Policy Initiatives in the Madras Presidency

A systematic attempt to develop technical education in Madras owed its origin to Sir Mountstuart Grant Duff who was Governor of the Presidency from 1881 to 1886.[36] Despite the fact that in Madras the College of Engineering, the Agricultural College and the School of Arts were already in existence, no attempt had been made to develop technical education systematically.

[35] Ibid (note prepared by S.S. Bhatnagar and appended to the Main Report).

[36] For details of the scheme aimed at introducing a system of technical and industrial training in the Presidency, see (a) H.B. Grigg, *Scheme for the Development of Scientific and Technical Education in Madras*, Madras: Department of Home Affairs, 1891; (b) *Papers Relating to Technical Education in India*, pp. 103–16; (c) Macdonnell's note on Technical Education in India, Home Education A Proceedings, July 1886, no. 27, National Archives of India, reproduced in Bhargava, *Selections from Educational Records of the Government of India*, pp. 57–67; (d) 'Note on Technical Education in Madras' in *Papers Relating to the Industrial Conference held at Ootacamund in September 1905*, Madras: Superintendent, Government Press, 1908, pp. 7–20.

In September 1884, Grigg, then Director of Public Instruction, was asked to submit proposals for the encouragement of scientific and technical education in the Presidency. Grigg's proposals were based on the experience of his 'predecessors of a similar path at home (England) and abroad' and the package contained a scheme of examinations, supplemented by a system of liberal grants-in-aid, making at the same time provision for a supply of well-instructed and professionally trained teachers; in addition, steps were to be taken to develop the scientific and art institutions then existing in the Presidency so that they could provide courses in all or most of the sciences and arts of which need was then felt, but also that both supply science and art teachers and the models for private effort.

Grigg's scheme of development was divided into three main sections. The first place was given to the establishment of a system of higher examinations in technical subjects. The second part of his scheme included the provision of grants-in-aid to institutions providing facilities for industrial and technical education and the grant of scholarships to pupils undergoing such instruction, besides grants for machinery, plants, apparatus, and chemicals. Third, Grigg proposed the development of the College of Engineering, the School of Arts, and the Agricultural College into institutes dealing with the several connected branches of technical works. The College of Engineering was to teach the various branches of engineering with subsidiary subjects, machine construction and the like. The School of Arts was to add to its curriculum decorative metalwork, wood carving, cabinet making, furniture and architectural wood-work, pottery, glass manufacture, and carpet-weaving. The Agricultural College was to teach, besides agriculture, agricultural chemistry, geology, physiography, forestry and surveying, plan drawing, and veterinary surgery and medicine. Improved provision for instruction in biology and chemistry was to be made in the chief first-grade colleges while practical training in industries was to be provided in the workshops of the Madras Municipality and Madras Railway.

Grigg's proposal was favourably received by government and high appreciation was expressed for the care with which the scheme had been drawn up.[37] The government gave the first place to examinations and prompt action to start these tests was taken. The committee appointed to fix the character of the syllabus and the details of the examination submitted its report in November 1885 recommending examination in sixty-three subjects (revised to include ninety-three subjects in 1892). In December 1891 the name of the examination was changed to the 'Government Technical Examinations' and their objective was declared to be 'the encouragement of scientific and technical instruction with special reference to manufactures and industries and generally to the necessities of the practical side of life'.[38] However, the extension of the scope of work undertaken at the College of Engineering was negatived and no notice was taken of the suggested use of railway and municipal workshops for practical training.[39]

[37] Resolution of the Government of Madras, no. 377 (Educational), order dated 3 June 1885, in *Papers Relating to Technical Education in India*, pp. 116–17.

[38] 'Note on Technical Education in Madras'.

[39] It is pertinent in this context, to recall Krishna Kumar's observations on examination culture, wherein, whatever could not be examined within the norms of the examination system was kept out of the curriculum, howsoever useful, relevant, and interesting it

Though some progress had been registered in technical education since Duff first drew attention to the subject in 1884, the Director of Public Instruction's Report for 1906–7 remarked that the general result was far from satisfactory. 'Out of the large population of this Presidency', he wrote,

> less than three thousand children were receiving technical instruction in the various handicrafts and of these less than nine hundred were non-brahmin Hindus, the class of the community to which the bulk of hereditary workers in wood and metal and textile fabrics belong. There is as yet little demand for technical education, and the little advance that has been made has practically left unaffected the great mass of the industrial population.[40]

Among the causes attributed to the failure of Grigg's scheme of 1884–5 was the fact that only part of the scheme was carried out, while some of the most valuable suggestions contained in it had been passed by. The attempt, moreover, it was pointed out, to create examinations without first providing qualified teachers and adequately equipped training institutions reversed the true order of progress. Most important, it was mentioned,

---

might be: 'This is how theoretical, especially literary study acquired a dominant place in Indian schools and colleges. Literary study fitted nicely within the frame of textbook culture and written examination. Practical or vocational skills and subjects dependent on practical skills such as all the science subjects, were a misfit in the frame'.

See Krishna Kumar, 'Origins of India's Textbook Culture', vol. 47 of Occasional Papers on History and Society, New Delhi: Nehru Memorial Museum and Library, 1987, p. 17.

[40] 'Note on Technical Education in Madras', in *Papers Relating to the Industrial Conference held at Ootacamund in September 1905*, Madras: Superintendent, Government Press, 1908, p. 14.

was the neglect to bring the scheme of technical education into relation with the industrial needs and conditions of the country. Even in providing scholarships for the encouragement of handicrafts, sufficient care was not taken to see that they were reserved for members of the artisan classes—the scholarships too often fell to youths who had not the least intention of following the industry as a livelihood and who merely drew the scholarship while it lasted and then betook themselves to the role of clerk, peon, policemen or whatever the customary occupations of their class might be.[41]

Remarking on the general character of the industrial schools in the Presidency, the Acting-Director of Public Instruction noted that the industrial schools in the Presidency were more in the nature of charity schools designed to feed, house, and clothe a certain number of poor children than schools where young people were taught scientific principles of the theory and practice of industrial arts. Further, their influence in improving the industries of the Presidency were practically nil; few managers of such schools ever placed such an aim before them.[42]

Among the steps that had been taken for the encouragement of technical education in the Presidency, the establishment of the Victoria Technical Institute (VTI), which was expected to take an important part in fostering technical education in the Presidency, may be mentioned. In his memorandum recommending the setting up of the VTI, John Adam, member of the sub-committee on technical education, emphasized that

[41] Ibid., p. 15.

[42] 'Note by the Director of Public Instruction on Technical Education in Madras', in *Papers Relating to Technical Education in India*, p. 87.

'humbler but very useful work must be performed before high class technical instruction can be appreciated by any but a small minority'.[43] While Adam strongly underlined the fact that it was not the task of the institute to impart general instructions, however, in the absence of pupils so instructed, it was essential that the institute encouraged and assisted in the spread of general technical instruction before going on to more specialized instruction.

On the question of artisan education, Adam pointed out that every effort to impart technical instruction to such children had failed because they were totally devoid of general education and because their parents were unwilling to lose the value of their labour during the time spent in acquiring what appeared to be useless knowledge.[44] Apart from want of money, want of teachers, want of teachable material (which acted as obstacles to immediate or extensive action in directing the institute towards special technical education), Adam stressed another obstacle, namely want of knowledge (as to the extent and condition of various industries, how these could be improved by the application of scientific principles and methods, and what sort and amount of instruction was best calculated to lead to much improvement).[45]

In a despatch in November 1893, the Secretary of State questioned whether the Schools of Art in India served any useful purpose, and suggested that they might be converted into elementary technical schools and

[43] John Adams, 'Memorandum on the Proposed Victoria Technical Institute', in *Papers Relating to Technical Education in India 1886–1904*, Calcutta: Office of the Superintendent of Government Printing, India, 1906, pp. 91–100.

[44] Ibid., p. 94.

[45] Ibid., p. 98.

transferred to the control of municipalities or of private bodies. On receipt of this despatch, the GOI convened an art conference at Lahore and, later, invited the opinions of the local governments on the resolutions of that conference. Duncan, Director of Public Instruction, Madras, in his reply to the government, contended that the institution was the only one of its kind fitted to supply schools with art teachers and of industries capable of ornamental treatment; that it had helped to train the young of the artisan and working classes to earn a better livelihood than they could otherwise have earned. He simply insisted on the retention of the school as a government institution.[46] In a subsequent ruling the government also laid down that the School of Arts would continue to devote itself to what could be called artistic industries and would not be developed, or rather transmuted, into an institute for teaching the application of science to mechanical manufacturing processes.[47]

In 1897, Chatterton took over as Superintendent of the School of Arts in Madras. Initially at his own expense, and later with the help of a small grant from the provincial government, Chatterton began experiments in the manufacture of aluminium vessels which subsequently became an integral part of the work of the School of Arts. Coppersmiths and bell-metal founders were employed; indigenous ways of working were initially adopted with changes being introduced very slowly and at convenient opportunities. From the outset there was a good demand from the military authorities and from Europeans for aluminium vessels, and by, establishing agents and subsidiary

[46] For a detailed summary see note by H. Tremenheere in Notes Connected with Educational G.O. no. 500, Press, 11 October 1900.

[47] Ibid.

workshops at various places the Indian demand was also stimulated.[48] By 1899 so much progress had been made that the government applied to the Secretary of State for permission to employ Chatterton for a term of three years in furthering the progress of technical and industrial education in the Presidency.

In a letter to the local governments, generally endorsing the conclusions of the Simla Conference on the subject of the Schools of Art, J.P. Hewett, Secretary to the GOI, Home Department made a specific reference to the 'successful establishment and extension of the aluminium industry in Madras' by Chatterton.[49] Hewett acknowledged that, but for the development of the aluminium industry, the articles formally produced by the workmen might have been supplanted in the Indian market by articles manufactured in other countries. But Hewett was quick to add that the government considered work of that nature to be outside the scope of the Education Department: 'If any local government feels that special efforts are required to organise or to help any particular industry from the mercantile point of view, they should either invoke the assistance of private enterprise or should arrange for its development by means of special officers not connected with the Education Department.'[50]

[48] For details on the aluminium industry, see Padmini Swaminathan, 'State Intervention in Industrialization: A Case Study of the Madras Presidency', Working Paper no. 99, Madras Institute of Development Studies, Madras, January 1991.

[49] Letter nos. 501–8, 20 November 1901, from J.P. Hewett, Secretary to the Government of India, Home Department to Local Governments, in *Papers Relating to Technical Education in India, 1886–1904*, Calcutta: Office of the Superintendent of Government printing, India, 1906, p. 249.

[50] Ibid., p. 250.

Chatterton, in his comments on Hewett's letter, pointed out that the industrial condition of the Madras Presidency was such that little good could be done in technical or industrial schools unless there were industries in the Presidency which would give employment to those who had passed through these institutions. The mercantile community of the Presidency were merely middlemen and it was not likely that they would risk capital to build up a manufacturing community, which, if successfully established, would be largely at the expense of the foreign trade of the country. Under the circumstances it was only to the government that labour could turn for help, and the government could render them effective assistance only by becoming pioneers in new lines of business.[51]

While industrial education of some kind or the other was given in a large number of schools in the Presidency, the majority of them offered only very elementary instruction and were of no industrial importance. In a very rudimentary state there were several industries practised in various parts of the Presidency which could be investigated and possibly developed.[52] From his experience in the aluminium industry, Chatterton opined that there was need to set up industrial schools with a view to producing goods to compete with imports all over India since demand from a single Presidency was in many cases insufficient to build up a business. Industrial schools, therefore, were not to be regarded as purely provincial institutions; it was to be brought to

[51] Note by Chatterton on Letter no. 501 by J.P. Hewett, 20 November 1901, from the Home Department of the Government of India, Educational G.O. no. 114, Miscellaneous (Confidential), 4 March 1902.

[52] Ibid.

the notice of the Committee of Exports that where new industrial developments were to be attempted through the agency of schools under a technological department, the work throughout India was to be coordinated and organized so that no institution trespassed on the field taken up by another.[53]

An examination of the facts concerning the chief local industries in each district, the list of schools which could be classified as industrial or technical schools, the subjects taught in these schools, and the numbers of the different classes of the community attending them, revealed that the total number from the community classed under 'non-brahmin caste Hindus' (whose hereditary occupation was an industry) reported to be studying in industrial and/or technical schools was 983. If from this number was taken away those studying commercial subjects like telegraphy, music, and drawing, those in carpentry classes in schools (which were manual occupation classes), and also those in the reformatory school, an analysis of the remainder made it quite clear that there were not even a hundred pupils in the whole Presidency who were then receiving instruction in the methods and processes of their hereditary caste occupations or in the principles underlying the same.

So that I think we may say that the existing schools while doing useful work in other ways, for instance, teaching Native Christians and others a trade and affording instruction to all classes of the community in certain technical subjects are doing nothing towards what I call the real problem of industrial education. I am not condemning the existing schools, they

[53] Letter from A.G. Bourne, Director of Public Instruction, Madras, to the Secretary to Government, Educational Department, 26 June 1904.

fulfil to a greater or less extent a useful purpose. The particular field which the Government of India have in view is however at present almost a blank' (emphasis added). Bourne, who made the above observations, was also skeptical about teaching principles of industrial processes to children when the industries themselves were on their last legs, and there was no sign of capital forthcoming to put into practice the new processes that the children may have learnt. Instruction, under such circumstances would be tantamount to 'offering them a stone when they ask for bread'.[54]

While Chatterton fully acknowledged the objection to any scheme aimed at exploiting Indian industries with government funds and under government control, yet, he felt that, because in the south of India industrial enterprise was almost non-existent, it was therefore useless to provide for technical and industrial education, unless at the same time efforts were made in some way or the other to improve the status of existing industries and provide for the introduction of new ones. Whilst, therefore, he considered that it would be necessary in the immediate future for the government to undertake the working of industrial experiments on a commercial scale, he emphasized that that was to be regarded as exceptional. He was strongly of the opinion that the College of Engineering in Madras was to be developed and made the centre of all educational effort in the Presidency which did not come under the term 'general education'. Private enterprise in the Presidency being very weak, it was Chatterton's suggestion that for the successful introduction of new industries or important improvements in existing industries, it would be

[54] Letter from A. Chatterton to the Director of Public Instruction, Madras, 13 November 1903, Educational G.O. nos. 313–14, Press, 12 May 1905.

necessary for the government to set up temporary special industrial schools analogous to the erstwhile Aluminium Department of the School of Arts. He was also critical of the College of Agriculture and lamented that the latter had not materially influenced agriculture in the Presidency.[55]

In order to promote industrial development in the Presidency it was proposed in 1905 to sever technical education completely from general education, to create a separate department to deal practically with the promotion of industries by experiment and advice as well as with the imparting of theoretical instruction in technical schools and colleges, and to place the department under an officer styled the Director of Industrial and Technical Inquiries.

In passing orders on these proposals, the Secretary of State stated in his despatch in August 1906, that he was unable to anticipate with much confidence the attainment of satisfactory results from the direction of state effort towards the creation of industries but he was, however, willing that the experiment should be tried in view of the special circumstances of the Presidency and of the talents and enthusiasm which rendered Chatterton well fitted for the proposed appointment. He sanctioned the appointment provisionally in the first instance for a period of five years.[56]

On receipt of the Secretary of State's sanction, Chatterton was appointed Director of Industrial and

[55] For a brief outline of the history of the appointment of a Director of Industrial and Technical Inquiries and the need for a definite Department of Industries, see letter from L.M. Wynch, Acting Secretary to the Government of Madras (Revenue Department) to the Secretary to the Government of India, Home Department (Education), 3 March 1909, Revenue G.O. no. 3446, Press, 27 October 1910.

[56] Ibid.

Technical Inquiries. He was directed to follow the lines on which he had been working since being placed on special duty in 1900 for the purpose of subjecting to a detailed examination each of the more important industries of the Presidency in turn and indicating the lines on which improvement might best be effected, devoting special attention to the chrome leather industry, the improvement of the handloom industry and the development of irrigation by pumps driven by oil-engines. Chatterton was, in addition to his other functions, entrusted, subject to the control of the Director of Public Instruction, with the inspection of eighteen technical schools, in which instruction was given in engineering subjects, in wood and metal work, and in the preparation of textile fabrics.

The satisfactory results achieved by Chatterton in these directions convinced the Governor-in-Council in Madras of the desirability of enlarging the scope of his work. In order to determine the lines on which action could be taken, a conference of persons either concerned or interested in the conduct of the chief industries of the Presidency was summoned and met in September 1908. The deliberations of the conference took shape in the form of sixty-eight resolutions.[57] On the general and cardinal question whether State intervention was desirable or necessary in fostering industrial development in a country in which private industrial effort had hitherto been either spasmodic or practically non-existent, the opinion of thirty-five out of the thirty-eight gentlemen who composed the conference laid down that, subject to the restrictions therein specified, the government could

[57] For details covering the papers printed for the use of the members of the conference, the proceedings of the conference, and the resolutions passed, see *Papers Relating to the Industrial Conference held at Ootacamund in September 1908*.

undertake as a pioneer the introduction of new industries or industrial processes for the purpose of training students or apprentices, or for demonstrating that such industries could be commercially viable/successful.

Lord Morley, the Secretary of State, however, thought otherwise and vetoed the Madras government's move to establish a separate department of industries with Chatterton as director. The policy which Lord Morley was prepared to sanction was one where State funds could be expended upon familiarizing the people with such improvements in the methods of production as modern science and the practice of European countries could suggest; further than this, it was to be left to the private enterprise to demonstrate that these improvements could be adopted with commercial advantage.[58]

On the abolition of the Department of Industries by the Secretary of State in October 1910, Chatterton was appointed to the newly created post of Superintendent of Industrial Education in the Educational Department. This appointment he held until late 1911, when it was found impracticable to carry on pumping and boring operations under the arrangement in force and Chatterton was accordingly placed on special duty in the Revenue Department in charge of these operations, his place as Superintendent of Industrial Education being taken by Tressler.[59]

[58] Despatch from the Secretary of State for India to the Governor-General of India in Council, dated 29 July 1910, Revenue G.O. no. 3446, Press, 27 October 1910.

[59] Details contained in the letter from K.T.B. Tressler, Acting Superintendent of Industrial Education to the Director of Public Instruction, 29 May 1912, submitting the report on the progress of industrial education in the Madras presidency for 1911–12, in Educational G.O. no. 765, Press, 22 August 1912.

In a note submitted to the Revenue Secretary to the Government, Chatterton came down heavily on the proposal to divide the work carried on by the Department of Industries between two officers, one under Education and the other under Revenue, which according to Chatterton would seriously curtail the amount of useful work done by either officer. While the Secretary of State had sanctioned the appointment of experts in tanning, weaving, and dyeing, these men had to work in the Education Department, thereby dissociating them to a large extent from the work going on in the country. But the practical action that Chatterton wanted the government to adopt contained within it the seeds for perpetuating and accentuating the class-cum-caste-wise division of the population. Chatterton wanted industrial education to be provided at two levels: (i) operatives or their allies who would be mainly drawn from the existing artisan classes; and (ii) masters and foremen who would control industrial undertaking and who would probably be mainly drawn from the upper ranks of the educated Indian population.

> For the indigenous industries [therefore] it seems inevitable that we must have recourse to industrial schools, but I would suggest that instruction in each industry should be confined to the sons and relatives of those actually engaged in the industry at the present time: that is to say, we should carry on the industrial schools on a caste basis. The indigenous industries have suffered very severely from foreign competition and it will not help the people still dependent on these industries for a livelihood to have added to their difficulties the competition of locally trained people belonging to the non-artisan castes.[60]

[60] See enclosure (ii) entitled 'Industrial Education' by Chatterton, 8 March 1911, in Educational G.O. no. 274, Press, 12 May 1911.

The Madras government had accepted the principle that industries had to exist for any useful results to accrue from provision for technical education in such industries. This meant that the pioneering of industries had to precede technical education but the orders of the Secretary of State precluded the government from taking up such work. Chatterton strongly urged the government to approach the Secretary of State for a reconsideration of the latter's orders prohibiting governments from carrying commercial work in pioneering new industries.

While Chatterton was emphatic that the local government had to pioneer and demonstrate the commercial viability of industries, either existing or new, in order to make technical education really meaningful, his successor, Tressler, was more concerned in getting the government to spell out its objectives clearly as far as industrial education was concerned.[61] According to Tressler, the most characteristic feature of the educational methods then followed in industrial schools was their absolute lack of common or definite objective. Each school was a law unto itself, each school imparted instruction over an entirely arbitrary range of subjects in a different manner with a different object in view. Further, the system according to which the extent and nature of State aid to be given to industrial schools was determined, was equally vague. Apart from minor considerations the main condition for recognition was that the teaching staff had to possess certain prescribed qualifications. If this condition was fulfilled a school

[61] Letter from A.G. Bourne, Director of Public Instruction, Madras, submitting 'Notes on Industrial Schools' by Tressler, to the Secretary to Government, Educational Department, to the Secretary to Government, Educational Department, 26 March 1912, in Educational G.O. no. 833, Press, 16 July 1914.

could receive financial assistance to the extent of half the net cost of maintenance. The nature of teaching then provided in industrial schools, however, made it clear that the qualifications then called for, excellent though they were from an academic point of view, constituted no test of a teacher's practical acquaintance with industrial requirements and was therefore in most cases valueless as a criterion of his ability to teach an industrial subject.

What the system therefore represented was manual training, and hence Tressler felt that if the object was merely to multiply the number of workmen irrespective of quality, the then existing system was satisfactory enough though it had to be clearly recognized that it did not represent industrial education. On the other hand, any objective of making education truly industrial had to be done only by workshop training conducted under conditions of efficient manufacture. 'If we accept the first alternative then manufacture does not come within our sphere at all, and should be entirely ignored. Most of the industrial schools provide a very fair course of manual training which, however, they almost inevitably associate with manufacture of a more or less inefficient character.'[62]

Given the politics of the time, the government was not interested in a consistent and coordinated programme of development involving intense regulation of the economic life of the country, including the activities of the private sector. Being forced by circumstances to act, their method of approach was to select piecemeal certain lines of development and to concentrate on them individually without considering the economy as a whole. This attitude towards economic development and this method of approach failed to achieve any substantial

[62] Ibid.

improvement with large sections of the population not being touched at all.

Prior to 1926, the policy of the local government in regard to industrial development included the starting of pioneer factories with a view to ascertaining the commercial possibilities of manufacturing articles not produced in the Presidency. In view of the so-called facilities afforded by the State Aid to Industries Act when it became law in 1923, the policy of government in regard to the pioneering of industries underwent some modification in 1926, and it was laid down that the experimental work of the Department of Industries should not ordinarily proceed beyond the stage of laboratory tests, and that pioneer manufacture on a commercial scale should be left mainly, if not entirely, to private enterprise. It was also considered advisable to concentrate the attention of the department on the organization and development of small industries preferably on cooperative lines, particular stress being laid on the importance of village or rural industries with special reference to their suitability as subsidiary occupations during the slack season for the agriculturists. The policy was followed in subsequent years with little or no change.[63]

More Doubts than Clarifications: Unresolved Conceptual and Practical Issues

To a large extent the question of inadequacy, inefficiency, and vagueness that characterized the whole course of technical education in the province, as well as the recurring and inconclusive debates that went on from time to time

[63] For details see 'Review of State Action in Respect of Industries', memorandum submitted to the Government of India Development Department, G.O. nos. 360–1, Miscellaneous, 3 March 1935.

around the theme of how to make technical education 'more practical' and/or how much of 'practical education' was to be introduced into 'technical' instruction, had to do at one level with the larger and more fundamental question of how deep and how far the State was to involve itself in such questions. At another level the colonial impact has been deep and structural, revealing itself in many ways: in the manner in which long years of foreign rule has shaken the confidence of the people in the viability of their own culture and institutions; in the continuing impact of colonialism wherein the essential structure of the educational system, inherited from colonial days, has been retained intact along with curricular orientation, the language of instruction and of intellectual discourse, and books and journals.

The indecisiveness that marked the whole approach to the problem of technical education can be gathered from the periodic doubts that were raised as to what constituted technical education—an issue that was never really satisfactorily dealt with at any level.

The most scathing comments, attacking the lack of conceptual clarification on the subject of technical education, came from John Wallace, the editor of the *Indian Textile Journal*, whose piece is worth quoting at some length:[64]

> One of the rarest things in India is to hear a definition of technical work. It is generally assumed to consist of a mixture in no fixed proportion of science and art; the science being mathematical, mechanical and chemical, and the technique—the art of some kind of work in wood and metals. . . .

[64] John Wallace, 'Technical Education for the Workman', *Indian Textile Journal*, reproduced in *Papers Relating to the Industrial Conference held at Ootacamund in September 1908*, pp. 136–41.

The confusion of the terms technical and scientific are exemplified in two institutions in the Bombay Presidency. In the College of Science, Poona, various physical sciences are taught, and illustrated by means of work in wood and metals for the training of engineers or roads, bridges and canals. In the Victoria Jubilee Technical Institute, Bombay, various physical sciences are taught, and illustrated by means of work in wood and metals for the training of students in mechanical or electrical engineering and textile work. It is not easy to guess on what basis the titles of the two institutions were chosen, but they illustrate the popular acceptation of the terms science and technique.

The cause of the present state of technical education in India is traceable to the constitution of the Educational Department which is controlled by University men, whose ideas of education are so built upon reading and writing as a foundation that they have overlooked the true relation of technique to science in a country whose industrial training is still in a very backward condition. In every other country, which has reached any industrial eminence, the knowledge of handicraft preceded by many generations, that of reading and writing.

India has yet to recover from an educational impulse in the wrong direction. Reading and writing, which have been of incalculable value of certain classes, are not of use at all, and they become positively pernicious when they entice young men away from a sure living by handicraft to the overcrowded ranks of clerical labour.

For a full assessment of the colonial legacy even at the provincial level, it would be essential among others, to examine critically and in depth the components that made up what passed for technical and industrial education.[65]

[65] In the Madras presidency these comprised the following:

'I. (a) Technical Scholarships Abroad: Number of scholarships tenable at a time—four (b) Government Institutions: consisting of The Government School of Technology, The Government Industrial and Trades School, Aided Industrial Schools, The Government Leather Trades Institute.

The scope of our study has not been expanded to include an examination of this component. However, a paper tracing the development of the Engineering College at Madras has made some important observations, relevant to the argument in this chapter.[66] It is pointed out that only in 1911 was the need for an institution capable of generating knowledge for local requirements expressed and plans made to convert the Madras Engineering College 'into a high-class technological institute capable of dealing not only with the immediate but also the prospective needs of the Presidency'. In 1922 again came the recommendation that 'the College of Engineering at Guindy should be expanded in due course and developed into a technological institute'. Despite all these exhortations, the paper points out, the college failed to become an advanced centre of research until after India achieved its independence.[67]

Again, the comparison between the Madras Engineering College and the Engineering College established at Tokyo, Japan is revealing.

The establishment of this college [Tokyo Engineering Colleges] has been claimed as an important milestone in Japanese

---

(c) Scholarships to students tenable at: (i) The Indian Institute of Science, Bangalore; (ii) The Victoria Jubilee Technical Institute, Bombay; (iii) Benaras Hindu University; (iv) The Indian School of Mines, Dhanbad; (v) Jamshedpur Technical Institute; (vi) Scholarships for sugar manufacturing technology; and (vii) Aided industrial schools.

(d) Institutes (cottage industries): comprising (i) The Government Textile Institute; (ii) The School of Arts and Crafts.

II. The Engineering College, Madras.'

See 'Review of State Action in Respect of Industries', memorandum submitted to the Government of India, Development Department, G.O. no. 360–1, Miscellaneous, 7 March 1935.

[66] S. Ambirajan, 'The Content of Science and Technology Education in South India During the Colonial Period', mimeo, Madras, undated.

[67] Ibid.

development because it was this college that acted as a catalytic agent for the emergence of Japanese technical eminence in the future. Within 30 years of the establishment of this College, nine other major technical institutions teaching civil engineering, ship building, electrical engineering, mining and metallurgy, and with a total strength of 1,200 students, were brought into existence. By 1903—thirty years after its establishment—the Tokyo Engineering College had a staff strength of 24 professors, 24 assistant professors and 22 lecturers. By contrast, in 1909—50 years after the Madras Engineering College was established—it had no more than four professors and 12 instructors.[68]

While there never was any sustained/single-minded expansion of technical education in India, even the feeble efforts at spreading the same could not have had any positive effect in broadening the base of 'steam intellect'[69] given that official policy at the same time was overtly and covertly antagonistic to any large-scale industrialization taking place in India. When exceptional individuals like Chatterton tried to create a demand for technical education by involving the State in entrepreneurial activity, a lot of hairsplitting took place over whether that was the right method of instruction and over where State promotion ended and commercial interest took over. Chatterton's efforts were frowned upon by the higher authorities. J.P. Hewett, Secretary to the GOI, made it clear in no uncertain terms that

> the success achieved by Mr Chatterton has been due to his peculiar qualifications for the work which he has undertaken.

[68] Ibid.

[69] S. Ambirajan, 'Steam Intellect and the Raj: Technical Education in South India in the Nineteenth Century', in *The Steam Intellect Societies—Essays on Culture, Education and Industry Circa 1820-1914*, ed. Ian Inkster, Nottingham: Department of Adult Education, University of Nottingham, 1985.

Such qualification are not ordinarily to be expected or desired in an educational officer, and the government of India wish it to be distinctly understood that commercial enterprises, such as this must not be undertaken, as a part of the scheme of Technical Education in India.[70]

A 'carefully planned and meticulously executed policy' of defrauding and exploiting India cannot be drawn from studies with a limited scope such as ours. However, from a concatenation of events, from statements of officials who mattered, and from an examination of the legacy that has been left behind, it is possible to infer and establish with some amount of certainty the fact that in colonial education there occurred simultaneously an obliteration of the roots of the colonized and the denial of the wherewithal to change except on limited terms. Further, the tension between the upward mobility promised by modern studies and the limited opportunities open to the colonized for advancement exposed the fundamental paradox of British

[70] Letter from J.P. Hewett, Secretary to the Government of India, Addressed to the Local Governments Regarding Encouragement of Technical Education, 20 November 1901, in *Papers Relating to Technical Education in India, 1886–1904*, Calcutta: Office of the Superintendent of Government Printing, India, 1906, pp. 253–4.

It is interesting to note the different position taken by J.P. Hewett as Lieutenant Governor of the North-West Provinces and Oudh. In his inaugural address to the Industrial Conference held at Nainital in August 1907 he observed, '[But] it does seem to be an axiom that there is *a very close connection between education and the progress of industries and trade*. Undoubtedly this truth has not been sufficiently recognized in India, and to my mind its backwardness in industries and trade is largely due to the failure to recognize the importance of organizing on a proper basis its system of education' (emphasis added). Reproduced in Bhargava, *Selections from Educational Records of the Government of India*, p. 274.

imperialism: economic exploitation required the sanction of higher motives, but once colonial intervention took on a moral justification[71]—that is, the improvement of a backward people—the pressure to sustain expectations of the people and match the educational opportunities with job opportunities created new internal stresses. At the same time, official statements like Wood's Despatch clearly articulated the material interests of a capitalist society while endorsing an educational system that reproduced division of labour directly and caste structure and social inequalities indirectly.[72]

[71] For a well-documented elaboration of the colonial discourse on education (to which both English and Indian intellectuals contributed) and which implied a morally superior teacher and a society whose character was in need of reform, see Krishna Kumar: 'Colonial Citizen as an Educational Ideal', Occasional Papers on History and Society, second series, no. XIII, Nehru Memorial Museum and Library, New Delhi, November 1988.

[72] For an excellent overview of the educational manifestations of colonialism see (a) P.G. Altbach and Gail P. Kelly, eds., *Education and Colonialism*, New York: Longman Inc., 1978, specially, the Introduction; (b) Viswanathan *Masks of Conquest.*

CHAPTER 8

Making Sense of Vocational Education Policies

A Comparative Assessment

The Context

In the space of just two years the central Planning Commission of India constituted two committees to examine the 'problem' of growing incidence of unemployment and under-employment in the country.[1] Our purpose here is not to discuss the politics of why, within a space of two years, we have had two official committees set up by the same department to examine the same theme. Rather, for us the important aspect in both the reports[2] of the two committees is the very considerable

[*] Previously published in *The Indian Journal of Labour Economics*, vol. 48, no. 3, 2005.

[1] The first committee, chaired by Montek Singh Ahluwalia, submitted its report in July 2001. It went by the name of Task Force on Employment Opportunities. The second committee, chaired by S.P. Gupta, submitted its report in May 2002. This committee was called the Special Group on Targeting Ten Million Employment opportunities.

[2] GoI, *Report of Task Force on Employment Opportunities*, New Delhi: Planning Commission, Government of India, 2001; and GoI, *Special Group on Targeting Ten Million Employment*

emphasis that has been placed on the lack of interface between employment and what passes for economic development in the country. In the process, both the reports have discussed the aspect of 'quality'[3] of existing employment and of that being generated in the economy.

Both the reports[4] emphasize the fact that there has been a steady decline in the job creating capacity of the economy, which has accelerated since 1993–4. This decline needs to be noted in the context of a deceleration in population growth, a significant deceleration in labour force growth, but a significant acceleration in GDP growth between 1983–4 and 1993–4 and between 1993–4 and 1999–2000 from 5.2 per cent to 6.7 per cent per annum. The above-mentioned reports point out that the growth in GDP is accompanied by a significant decline in labour intensity in production in almost all sectors, barring a few, and also in the aggregate; the labour intensity (measured as employment elasticity to value added) declined from 0.52 to 0.16.[5] As a result of the decline in labour intensity of production, the employment growth fell to 1.07 per cent per annum

---

Opportunities Per Year, New Delhi: Planning Commission, Government of India, 2002.

[3] We are aware that the term 'quality' is highly loaded. For the purpose of our discussion, quality of employment encompasses the following: whether being employed enables the person to rise above the poverty line; the quality of employment, namely whether employment is regular, casual or temporary; does the employment impact adversely on health; what is the nature of interface between employment and education. Through a combination of quantitative and qualitative data, some of these aspects have been discussed in the paper.

[4] GoI, *Report of Task Force on Employment Opportunities*; and GoI, *Special Group on Targeting Ten Million Employment Opportunities Per Year*.

[5] GoI, *Special Group on Targeting Ten Million Employment Opportunities Per Year*, p. 24.

(between 1993–4 and 1999–2000) from 2.7 per cent per annum in the past (that is, between 1983 and 1993–4) in spite of acceleration in the growth of domestic product from 5.2 per cent (between 1983 and 1993–4) to 6.7 per cent (between 1993–4 and 1999–2000). This in turn means that the capacity of job creation per unit of output went down about three times as compared to that in the 1980s and early 1990s. The organized sector's employment-generating capacity (measured in terms of employment elasticity) came down to near zero; in the public sector, it has been negative in most cases. Thus, the major source of employment generation and for labour absorption is the unorganized sector of the economy whose employment weightage is as high as 92 per cent (of the total employed labour force).[6]

On examining all major sources of information, the above-mentioned committees found that the rate of unemployment in India had increased significantly in 1993–4 and was above 7.3 per cent in 1999–2000 as compared to 6.0 per cent in 1993–4 on Current Daily Status (CDS) basis.[7] The number of unemployed

[6] GoI, *Report of Task Force on Employment Opportunities*, p. 34; GoI, *Special Group on Targeting Ten Million Employment Opportunities Per Year*, pp. 2 and 26.

[7] The National Sample Survey Organization (NSSO) of India collects detailed information on the employment status of the population through large-scale, nation-wide sample surveys in which individuals are categorized as employed or available for work but not employed, using different criteria. Rates are calculated as percentages of the total labour force. The NSSO provides four different measures of employment and unemployment, each of which captures different facets of the employment-unemployment situation. One of these is the Current Daily Status (CDS). Based on the reported time disposition

increased from 20.13 million in 1993–4 to 26.58 million in 1999–2000. Nearly 74 per cent of the unemployed were in rural areas, while 60 per cent of the unemployed were educated (higher secondary and above).

A point that both the committees stressed is the fact that an unemployment rate of 7.3 per cent should not be read as implying that those employed have 'decent' jobs; on the contrary, the committees extensively discussed the phenomenon of the quality of existing employment and of that being generated in the economy. One dimension of this 'quality' is the level of income that the employment provides. That a large part of the employment generated in the economy provides very low levels of income is very evident from the fact that whereas unemployment even according to the most expansive measure, namely CDS measure, was only 7.3 per cent, the percentage of population in poverty was as high as 26.1 per cent. Thus, being employed did not necessarily enable an individual/household to rise above the poverty line.

An equally important issue flagged by both the reports borne out of their exercise of disaggregating unemployment data was that the rate of unemployment

---

of the person on each day of the reference week, person-days in employment (unemployment) are aggregated to generate estimates of person-days in employment/unemployment. The person-day unemployment rate is derived as the ratio of person-days in unemployment to the person-days in the labour force. This measure captures the within-week unemployment of those classified as employed on the Weekly Status. The CDS-measure of unemployment is widely agreed to be the one that most fully captures open unemployment in the country (GoI, *Report of Task Force on Employment Opportunities*, pp. 15–16).

was higher among the educated than among those with lower levels of education. Thus, recorded one of the reports,[8] measuring unemployment rates on usual principal and subsidiary status (UPSS) basis, the unemployment rates for the illiterate was as low as 0.2 per cent rising to 1.2 per cent for literates up to primary school and 3.3 per cent for middle school. For the category of 'educated labour' (that is, education level of secondary education and above), the rate was 7.1 per cent—more than three times the unemployment rate on the UPSS basis for the population as a whole.[9] The starkness of the mismatch increased when the criterion of education was combined with age. While between 1993–4 and 1999–2000, the incidence of unemployment among educated youth, both for general and technical education, declined sharply, these rates for youth were still high at 14.8 per cent of secondary education and 23.7 per cent for all types of technical education.[10] The report says thus:

> The high rate of unemployment among educated youth is in many ways the core of the problem because it creates a sense of despair across a wide section of the population including not only the educated youth but also their parents and families. It needs to be emphasised that the aspirations of this group cannot be met just by creating any employment opportunities . . . The problem of unemployment in this category can only be solved if *high quality* employment is created.[11]

[8] GoI, *Report of Task Force on Employment Opportunities.*
[9] Ibid., p. 26.
[10] Ibid., p. 28.
[11] Ibid., pp. 28–9. Emphasis added.

The GoI report[12] compared unemployment rates arrived at by the NSSO using UPSS, UPS, CWS and CDS methods.[13] According to this report, the UPSS estimates (which give the lowest unemployment rates) included large numbers of under-employed. This report therefore used the CDS measure. This report emphasized a third dimension of the problem of unemployment in the country, namely the inter-state differentials in unemployment rates. More significantly, it attempted to relate SDP and employment growth and came up with interesting results. These included the following: of the sixteen major states, there were three with very high and increasing unemployment rates. These were Kerala, Tamil Nadu, and West Bengal. Of the three, Kerala had comparatively lower growth rate of GDP but higher employment elasticity, whereas Tamil Nadu and West Bengal had high growth (above 7 per cent) but with very low employment elasticity. The report therefore recorded that, GDP growth rate *or* high labour intensity in production *exclusively* would not reduce unemployment: 'For reducing unemployment, the challenge is to combine a high growth rate with high employment elasticity (that is, labour intensity in production) by proper sectoral and technology choice.'[14] The GoI reports[15] also highlighted

[12] GoI, *Special Group on Targeting Ten Million Employment Opportunities Per Year.*

[13] UPS = Usual principal status; CWS = Current weekly status; CDS = Current daily status.

[14] Ibid., p. 31.

[15] GoI, *Report of Task Force on Employment Opportunities*; and GoI, *Special Group on Targeting Ten Million Employment Opportunities Per Year.*

the growing incidence of unemployment among the educated youth, but went beyond by disaggregating the data by state and gender.

The regional dimension on employment-unemployment and among youth is important since recent data[16] indicate an explosive growth of technical institutions in the south, particularly Tamil Nadu.

The emphasis on youth unemployment and educated youth at that, requires, in our view, an exploration of not just the interface between growth and employment generation but an intensive engagement with (i) what passes for vocational/technical education in the country to assess also the employability of our 'educated' youth; (ii) who are the actors involved in imparting this vocational/technical education to our youth; (iii) what role do employers play or do they at all have a role in this sector of education; (iv) who facilitates or should facilitate some level of coordination between employers, educators and potential workers; and (v) how do we bring about and, more importantly, maintain this coordination.

This chapter in no way pretends to answer all or even some of these questions. Rather, the burden is to briefly sketch the kind of vocational education imparted in a few developed countries to bring home the point that piece-meal attempts to tinker with our existing 'vocational' educational system, and/or exhorting our industrialists to invest more in vocationalizing higher education, without a framework in place to understand what systemic changes such vocationalization would require, cannot but be a non-starter.

[16] GoI, *Revitalizing Technical Education: Report of the Review Committee on AICTE*, New Delhi: Ministry of Human Resource Development, September 2003.

Vocational/Technical[17] Education in India

The GoI reports[18] do not deem it their responsibility to define the various terms in them, most importantly, vocational and/or technical. The significance of bringing up the question of the precise connotation of such terms lies in the manner in which countries that have vocationalized their educational systems have imparted to these terms not only specific meanings but also whole

[17] A scathing comment attacking the lack of conceptual clarity on the subject of vocational/technical education made in 1908, which we reproduce below, retains its relevance even today, for the sheer complexity of the issues involved and with which we need to contend with, if and when we seriously get down to unravelling, comprehending and concretizing our notions of higher education, vocational and technical education: 'One of the rarest things in India is to hear a definition of technical work. It is generally assumed to consist of a mixture in no fixed proportion of science and art; the science being mathematical, mechanical and chemical, and the technique – the art-of some kind of work in wood and metals . . . The cause of the present state of technical education in India is traceable to the constitution of the Educational Department that is controlled by university men, whose ideas of education are so built upon reading and writing as a foundation that they have overlooked the true relation of technique to science in a country whose industrial training is still in a very backward condition. In every other country, which has reached any industrial eminence, the knowledge of handicraft preceded by many generations, that of reading and writing... India has yet to recover from an educational impulse in the wrong direction. Reading and writing, which have been of incalculable value for certain classes, are not of use at all and they become positively pernicious when they entice young men away from a sure living by handicraft to the overcrowded ranks of clerical labour'. See J. Wallace, *Technical Education for the Workman in Madras*, Papers Relating to the Industrial Conference held at Ootacamund in September 1905, Tamil Nadu Archives, Chennai, 1908, p. 141.

[18] GoI, *Report of Task Force on Employment Opportunities*; GoI, *Revitalizing Technical Education: Report of the Review Committee on AICTE.*

operational institutions and systems. We begin with a brief summary of the development of technical education as recounted in the GoI report.[19]

The GOI, through a resolution passed on 30 November 1945, set up the All India Council for Technical Education (AICTE) to supervise all technical education above the high school stage. The Council, as constituted, consisted of representatives of the Ministries of Education, Labour, Industry, and Commerce, the Inter-University Board, the Central Advisory Board of Education, the Association of Principals of Technical Institutions, the Institution of Engineers, the Indian Legislature and the provincial governments. As constituted, the AICTE was an advisory body with no statutory powers; nevertheless, it played an important role in the development of technical education in the country.[20] *While the expansion of technical institutes in the 1950s was done with the approval of the AICTE and the Government of India, the expansion in the eighties was localized mostly in the four southern states and was primarily in the self-financing sector without the approval of the AICTE and the Government of India.*[21]

The National Policy on Education, 1986, made a specific mention of the need to vest the AICTE with statutory powers; accordingly, among other things, it laid down that: (a) The AICTE would be vested with statutory authority for planning, formulation, and maintenance of standards, accreditation, funding of priority areas, monitoring and evaluation, maintaining parity of certification and awards, and ensuring the coordinated and *integrated development of technical and*

[19] GoI, *Revitalizing Technical Education: Report of the Review Committee on AICTE.*

[20] Ibid., p. 23.

[21] Ibid., emphasis added.

management education (emphasis ours); and (b) In the interest of maintaining standards and for several other valid reasons, the commercialization of professional and technical educations would be curbed.[22]

In December 1987, the AICTE became a statutory body through an Act of Parliament. Apart from setting up the AICTE and providing it with statutory powers, the GOI also came out with Technology Policy Statements (most notably in 1958 and again in 2003) wherein it reiterated the central role of science and technology 'in raising the quality of life of the people of the country, particularly of the disadvantaged sections of society, in creating wealth for all, in making India globally competitive...'.[23] The implementation plan of these policies emphasized human resource development. Thus, for example, the Science and Technology Policy Statement of 2003 states: '. . . There is need to progressively increase the rate of generation of high quality skilled human resource at all levels . . . In order to encourage quality and productivity in science and technology, *mobility of scientists and technologists between industry, academic institutions and research laboratories will be ensured.*'[24]

Viewing the development of technical education from the demand side, the GoI[25] offered the following perspective on the changing employment scenario since the enunciation of the first of the Technology Policy Statements. It acknowledged that there had been a:

> rapid expansion of supply of technical personnel, far in excess of the absorptive capacity of the economy, leading

[22] Ibid., p. 24.
[23] Ibid., p. 34.
[24] Ibid., p. 35. Emphasis added.
[25] Ibid.

to under-employment and even unemployment of graduates and a deterioration of their real-income levels. It has also led to a degree of substitution, whereby, in many cases, degree holding engineers are taking up employment opportunities that could have gone to the diploma holders . . . Manufacturing, the traditional user of technical manpower, does not exhibit an ability to provide significantly expanded employment opportunities for technical persons. The growth of the manufacturing sector has been largely jobless, due to its low employment elasticity, almost close to zero . . . Compared to the past, employment opportunities would be more sensitive to the quality of the graduates. In an internationally competitive environment, it is the quality and not numbers that would matter. Graduates of sub-standard programmes and institutions will find it increasingly harder to get employment even if they are prepared to sacrifice on the income level. Past pattern of long-term employment in a particular enterprise or even in the same industry is beginning to break down. Ability to keep up-to-date with changing knowledge and skill requirements in the wake of frequent technological restructuring and making significant lateral shifts and across disciplines, would be crucial for remaining employed. *The implication for the technical educational system is two-fold: (a) the pedagogy should focus relatively more on the development of higher-order, generic, transferable skills and autonomous learning strategies, and (b) more opportunities for non-formal education and training, continuing education and training, and distance education, should be offered by the system.*[26]

We have dwelt at some length in reproducing the above observations from the GoI,[27] since the current ground reality in terms of, *on the one hand*, (i) the unplanned and unregulated quantum leap in technical institutions that have come up; (ii) the absolute shortage

[26] Ibid., pp. 37–8. (Emphasis added).
[27] Ibid.

of technical teachers; (iii) the low quality of teaching; and (iv) the low levels of formal coordination between educational institutes, industry, trade unions and the government (the latter through, say, the AICTE), *and on the other*, the inability of the economy to absorb the products of these institutes, makes us wonder whether there is a fundamental flaw in the way we have comprehended (or not comprehended) the two broad institutions of 'school' and 'work', with which vocational/technical institution is intimately connected and deeply embedded.

With respect to vocational/technical education, it would be useful to present some numbers to give an idea of the dimensions of the problem under consideration. At one level, we are told that the number of degree engineering colleges practically doubled in the decade 1980 to 1990, from around 158 institutions to over 337; during the next decade, 1990–2000, it increased from 337 to 776, three-quarters of which were self-financed. In early 2000, there were 1,208 engineering colleges including 986 self-financing institutions with a total intake of over 3.5 lakh students. Equally spectacular has been the growth of MCA and MBA degree institutions, which in early 2000 stood at 1,006 and 930, respectively, with an intake of over 53,000 and 64,000 students. At another level, data put out by the National Technical Manpower Information System (NTMIS) reveal that considerable numbers of engineering graduates remain unemployed even two years after completion of their graduation; the then estimates indicated that the unemployment rate of engineering degree holders could have exceeded 20 per cent.[28] The story of the growth in PG institutions in engineering is similar.

[28] Ibid., p. 47.

Several aspects of the above growth in technical institutions need to be explicated. One, data on region-wise and state-wise distribution of institutions and sanctioned intake of students reveal the highly skewed geographical distribution of institutions across the country with more than 52 per cent of the institutions located in the south and south-west, whereas the east and north account for just around 7 per cent and 10 per cent, respectively. Likewise, 43 per cent of MBA institutions and 59 per cent of MCA institutions with an intake of 35 per cent and 57 per cent of students, respectively, in the above disciplines are in the south and south-west, almost equal to the total number of MBA and MCA institutions and their sanctioned intake in the entire region of the country covering central, east, north and north-west regions.

Two, analysing the status of faculty availability to impart technical education to such levels of student intake, the GoI records that:

> as of today, going strictly according to the prescribed norms, there is shortfall of over 26,000 PhDs and 30,000 MTechs for meeting the teaching requirements in the engineering institutions alone. Even if the teacher to student ratio is relaxed to 1:20, the shortfall in PhDs and MTechs should still be over 18,000 and 20,000 MTechs. The faculty position in other disciplines such as MCA, management education, pharmacy, architecture and town planning is as bad, if not worse . . . many of the private colleges, in particular, employ fresh graduates passing out of the college with poor grades as teachers, thus totally compromising on the quality of teachers. It must be recognised that mediocrity in the teaching fraternity can only multiply mediocrity and cannot lead to the creation of excellence.[29]

[29] Ibid., p. 77.

The largest shortfall of teachers is in the southern region with Tamil Nadu alone accounting for almost 50 per cent of the shortfall.[30]

Three, a serious issue of concern recorded by the GoI[31] is that over 90 per cent of technical and engineering graduates were studying in non-accredited institutions. A compounding problem was the inability of most of these institutions to ensure even minimum quality of education.

> In Tamil Nadu where expansion has been greatest in recent years, in a recent semester examination conducted by the Anna University, no student passed in 5 colleges, 28 had less than 5 per cent passes, 78 had less than 10 per cent passes, 108 had less than 15 per cent passes and only 17 had more than 40 per cent passes, with only 8 having more than 50 per cent passes.[32]

The GoI[33] approached the theme of labour skill through a discussion of the NSSO Survey of Employment-Unemployment (1993–4), which collected information on the possession of thirty specific marketable skills by persons in the labour force.

The results of this component of the survey are summarized in Table 8.1. The skilled percentage is evidently very low; hardly 10 per cent of the male workers and 6 per cent of female workers in the rural areas possessed specific marketable skills. The urban areas returned relatively better figures but still abysmally low by any yardstick—19.6 per cent of male workers and 11 per cent for female workers.

[30] Ibid., p. 76.
[31] Ibid.
[32] Ibid., p. 174.
[33] GoI, *Report of Task Force on Employment Opportunities*.

Table 8.1: Percentage Distribution of Persons by Possession of Marketable Skill, 1993–4

	Rural		*Urban*	
Possessing	*Male*	*Female*	*Male*	*Female*
No skill	89.9	93.7	80.4	88.8
Some skill	10.1	6.3	19.6	11.2
Total	100.0	100.0	100.0	100.0
Sample Persons	(183,464)	(172,835)	(106,067)	(99,283)

Source: GoI 2001, p. 128

Table 8.2 provides a comparative picture of the percentage of youth (age group 20–4) with vocational skills across several industrial countries. Only 5 per cent of the Indian labour force in this age category has vocational skills whereas the percentage in industrial countries is much higher, varying between 60 per cent and 80 per cent. It may be argued that in developing countries like India, economically productive skills are acquired not only in formal training/education institutions but also through the family. But it also needs to be stressed that currently the traditional artisan classes are among the poorest, in economic terms, in the country. 'The developing countries listed have percentages that are significantly lower than the developed countries, but they are still much higher than India, example, Mexico at 28 per cent and Peru at 17 per cent. Differences in definitions may make comparisons somewhat unreliable but the level in India is clearly far too low'.[34]

The GoI[35] has devoted considerable space in its report to discuss the nature of vocational education and

[34] Ibid., p. 128.
[35] Ibid.

Table 8.2: Proportion of Vocationally Trained among the Youth in Labour Force: International Comparison

Country	*Age Group*	*Vocationally Trained (percentage of those in labour force)*
India	20-24	5.06
Developing countries		
Botswana	20–4	22.42
Colombia (1998)	20–9	28.06
Mauritius (1995)	20–4	16.08
Mexico (1998)	20–4	27.58
Developed countries		
Australia (1998)	20–4	64.11
Canada (1998)	20–4	78.11
France (1997)	20–4	68.57
Germany (1998)	20–4	75.53
Israel (1998)	18–4	81.23
Italy (1997)	20–4	43.88
Japan (1997)	15–4	80.39
Korea Republic (1998)	20–4	95.86
New Zealand (1997)	20–4	63.03
Russian Federation (1998)	20–4	86.89
Singapore (1998)	20–4	66.24
United Kingdom (1998)	20–4	68.46

Source: GoI 2001, p. 129.

Note: Only those who have received formal vocational training are shown as trained in this table. To the extent that training and skills in India are acquired through informal methods, including training in the family, the Indian figures are understated; estimates are based on distribution of persons by technical education in India adjusted by labour force participation rate by sex. The corresponding percentages by sex and residence are rural female 1.7, rural male 2.3, urban male 9.4 and urban female 17.0. See NSSO Report no. 409 on Results of 50th Round (1993–4), Survey on Employment and Unemployment, Table 20.

training, and the system of apprenticeship available to students in India. Its overall assessment of the situation is as follows:

> The actual number of persons expected to enter the labour force (on the 1.8 per cent labour force growth assumption) is about 12.3 million per year. Allowing for underutilization of seats in training institutions and some overlaps, the percentage of those entering the labour force with some degree of formal training is probably around 1.5 million or about 12 per cent of the gross new entrants into the labour force. While a significant number of the new entrants will be absorbed in various types of unskilled labour in agricultural and non-agricultural occupations, where skills are not needed, the level of skill endowment of new entrants to the labour force revealed by these numbers is clearly not consistent with triggering a process of rapid economic growth and high-quality employment generation. The inadequacy of training capacity in quantitative terms is not the only problem. *There are also serious problems relating to quality.*[36]

An added feature of the GoI[37] report is that it has tried to map the 'school-to-work' transition systems in several countries, and has even provided an elaborate table comparing the vocational training systems of India and the Republic of Korea.[38] Our point of departure with this report lies in the complete silence that ensues thereafter on how other countries have been able to not only operationalize their 'school-to-work' transition-enabled vocational education and apprenticeship systems but also make it as broad-based as possible to cover large numbers of their school-going population—a feature conspicuous by its absence in India.

[36] Ibid., p. 133. Emphasis added.
[37] Ibid.
[38] Ibid., p. 146.

The German System

Apprenticeship training in Germany is referred to as a dual system of vocational education.[39] Trainees receive both school education at special vocational schools and on-the-job training at firms. The law lays down both the length of training and its objectives. This applies both to in-company and school-based training. In-company training normally lasts three years. The training objectives are specified in training ordinances, which are adjusted from time to time according to social, economic, and technical changes. These ordinances are prepared by the Federal Institute for Vocational Education and developed in cooperation with employers, trade unions and the state governments under the auspices of the federal government.[40]

An important corollary is that training curricula in Germany—while they are formally signed into law by the federal government—are in fact negotiated between the employers' association and the union of the specific industry. The government acts according to what is called the 'consensus principle'. It will decree only after the 'two sides of industry'

[39] This section is a summary based on the following: W. Franz and D. Soskice, 'The German Apprenticeship System', *Discussion Paper FS/94-302*, Berlin: Wissenschaftszentrum Berlin fur Sozialforschung, 1994; D. Dettke and C. Weil, eds., *Challenges for Apprenticeship and Vocational Training in the 1990s: German and American Perspectives*, Bonn, Germany: Friedrich-Ebert-Stiftung, 1992; and K. Wagner, 'The German Apprenticeship System After Unification', *Discussion Paper FS/98-301*, Berlin: Wissenschaftszentrum Berlin fur Sozialforschung, 1998.

[40] B. Buck, 'Qualification Concepts in Vocational Training in the Federal Republic of Germany', in *Challenges for Apprenticeship and Vocational Training in the 1990s: German and American Perspectives*, ed. D. Dettke and C. Weil, Bonn, Germany: Friedrich-Ebert-Stiftung, 1992, p. 23.

have agreed. As long as there is disagreement over even a comma, the government will postpone action until both sides return with an agreement. That is important because the government thus relies on the knowledge of organised social groups and attempts to utilise the experience of the private sector rather than trying to legislate unilaterally. Firms and unions have the chance to organise themselves and to reach consensus before the government adds its comparative advantage of public accountability and legal binding.[41]

Streeck[42] emphasizes in particular the institutions and policies that sustain the German training system. His piece, outlining the lessons that one can learn from the German case, highlights the structural elements that characterize the German system. While Streeck draws out these learnings for the United States, they are nevertheless relevant for any country that is keen on addressing *simultaneously* issues of (youth) employment, education, and accumulation of skill.

According to Streek,[43] three general recommendations follow from observations of the German system: (a) *Strategic use of training*: 'The German system of training is not just reactive to the needs of firms. In fact, mechanisms in the system make firms responsible for training beyond their individually perceived needs at a given moment. An apprentice learns more than necessary for a specific job';[44] (b) *Workplace as the place*

[41] W. Streeck, 'Institutional Mechanisms and Structural Elements of Vocational Training in Germany and the United States', in *Challenges for Apprenticeship and Vocational Training in the 1990s: German and American Perspectives*, ed. D. Dettke and C. Weil, Bonn, Germany: Friedrich-Ebert-Stiftung, 1992, p. 43.

[42] Ibid.

[43] Ibid.

[44] Ibid., p. 52.

of training: 'A very important general lesson from the German system and also from the Japanese system, is to recognise the extreme importance for learning of the work process and of experiential knowledge...Where products and manufacturing processes change very fast, workers always must improvise. In improvising they have to rely on experiential skills which must be emphasised in training and can only be acquired in the workplace';[45] and (c) *Avoid a technocratic perspective on training* and emphasize the political and institution-building dimension of training systems. The first crucial aspect of the German system is that training is defined on a sectoral and/or regional or national level. To understand the German system, one must understand why it relies on collective action among firms and binds firms together in larger units. If all or most firms in a region or sector offer training according to identical standards and curricula, the incentives *not* to train declines for individual firms.

The German system also offers several lessons for trade unions. According to Streek,[46] the politics of training are both extremely complicated and important from a trade union perspective. Training programmes can enable the generation of general, transferable skills; such skills can enable workers to quit one job for another, a possibility that may not be available if their training were to give them firm-specific skills. Further, since training in Germany follows standardized, obligatory training profiles that apply to all firms' training for a particular occupation, such training generates excess skills that can serve as reserve skills for later use. Another valuable

[45] Ibid., p. 42.
[46] Ibid.

lesson from the German system is its emphasis on skill profiles—a task that is accomplished by consensus between unions and the employers' associations; the broad-based training that emanates from this, in turn, enables greater coordination and adjustment on the shop floor, thereby increasing the competitive strength of firms and of the industry in general. Equally crucial to note is that, it is the private sector, namely the firm, that is the main actor in training. The public sector facilities private action. The German system also places considerable emphasis on training of trainers and the certification of firms that take part in workplace-based training. Institutionalized accountability is built into the German system, which therefore lends it credibility. An aspect that trade unions find difficult to accept and which therefore remains a bone of contention is the special employment status of apprentices. The employer is under no obligation to continue the employment of individuals beyond their apprenticeship term. Similarly, apprenticeship wages are significantly lower than the wages of skilled workers. The apprenticeship period is an investment whose cost needs to be shared between the apprentice and the employer; hence the lower wages are considered appropriate. Further, it is also argued that, the more closely the apprenticeship wages approach those of skilled workers, the greater is the pressure to use apprentices for production work.

That apprenticeship should culminate in an examination is another point that is stressed by the German system. For each trade and region, evaluating committees participate in about 600,000 theoretical and practical examinations each year. These committees also consist of representatives of labour, management, and the vocational schools. Unions are represented with about 100,000 individuals.[47] Examinations not only provide the apprentices with a certificate but also test the employer who has trained the apprentice; apprentice failure may be a very important reason for a firm to lose its training license.

There is growing concern within Germany about the viability of its apprenticeship model. Questions regarding the relevance of the curricula for the emerging new forms of work organization, the adaptability of the system of training to new challenges such as lean production with its emphasis on continuous improvement processes, flexible machine tools, close supplier relationships and rapid innovation, etc., are increasingly being raised.[48] Other macro-level problems, such as unification and recession contribute in no small measure to strengthen these doubts. However, scholars analysing these doubts in the context of the changing global and local (within Germany) scenarios argue that the German dual system is not in crisis but that it needs to react flexibly to changing market conditions.[49] Wagner's analysis reveals several other features of the dual system, particularly from the industry side, which are worth considering given AICTE's anxiety to make Indian industry more proactive in technical/vocational education.

Wagner notes that German employers incur high gross training costs, which differ according to the size of firms, the type of apprenticeship, and the training year

[47] M. Ehrke, 'German Apprenticeship System: A Trade Union View', in *Challenges for Apprenticeship and Vocational Training in the 1990s: German and American Perspectives*, ed. D. Dettke and C. Weil, Bonn, Germany: Friedrich-Ebert-Stiftung, 1992, p. 30.

[48] Wagner, 'The German Apprenticeship System After Unification', p. 1.

[49] See ibid.

of the apprentice. However, what is not highlighted, according to Wagner,[50] is the nature of direct and indirect benefits that accrue to companies by their being part of the apprenticeship programme. One, over the years, companies have realized that:

> the risk of hiring a skilled person who does not fit the job, the team, or the company culture is much higher than hiring an apprentice who has been educated for over three years in the firm and whose personality and technical skills are well-known . . . The pressure to hire the right person, and hence the benefits from the lengthy screening period apprenticeships provide, is particularly important in Germany, given the relatively high costs and difficulties of firing employees.[51]

Two, large companies derive not only goodwill but also benefit financially from being part of the apprenticeship programme. Companies' balance sheets always include long accounts of their training activities; the performance of trainees in exams itself acts as an advertisement for the company concerned since such news is well advertised in newspapers and business magazines; many German readers associate well-trained people with high quality goods. 'The correlation between training and reputation has recently been used in press releases of the ministry and of the chambers to increase the willingness of companies to train by publicly disclosing the names of those companies that do not train'.[52] In addition, training costs are tax deductible; hence, even if variable net costs are much higher for larger companies, the after-tax cost of training apprentices is, to that extent, reduced.

[50] Ibid.

[51] Ibid., p. 8.

[52] Ibid., p. 11.

The Japanese Experience

The structural differences between Japan's economy and that of other industrial nations continue to evoke considerable interest. One important structural difference is the interaction between the markets for higher education and labour.[53] Mosk and Nataka,[54] in their study of the comparison between American and Japanese higher education, posit it, among other things, as a difference between the demand-driven nature of American higher education versus the supply-driven nature of Japanese higher education.

An important observation made by Mosk and Nataka is the paramount influence that the Japanese Ministry of Education has over national universities, 'where its budgetary authority permits it to choose which fields are staffed and which laboratories are to be equipped'.[55] While emphasizing that posing the problem as one of demand versus supply should not be read as ruling out altogether the influence of demand from the Japanese economy, Mosk and Nataka however point out that: (a) the two major business organizations

[53] Based on C. Mosk and Y-F. Nataka, 'Education and Occupation: An Enquiry into the Relationship between College Specialisation and the Labour Market in Postwar Japan', *Pacific Affairs*, vol. 65, no. 1, Spring 1992, pp. 50–67; P. Bennell and J. Segerstrom, 'Vocational Education and Training in Developing Countries: Has the World Bank Got It Right?', *International Journal of Educational Development*, vol. 18, no. 4, 1998, pp. 271–87; and K. McCormick, 'Japanese Engineers, Lifetime Employment and In-company Training: Continuity and Change in the Management of Engineering Manpower Resources', in *International Comparisons of Vocational Education and Training for Intermediate Skills*, ed. P. Ryam, London: The Falmer Press, 1991, pp. 159–182.

[54] Mosk and Nataka, 'Education and Occupation'.

[55] Ibid., p. 53.

in Japan exercise considerable influence over policies adopted by pro-business liberal political parties. The authors cite the instance of business pressure leading to an expansion in the number of engineers during the period 1959–70;[56] and (b) since government policy plays a significant role, the more powerful elements in the Japanese business community attempt to shape disciplinary composition of college graduates through a political process.[57] Analysing the supply component in some detail, the authors point out that the Ministry of Education in Japan has a strong hand in formulating curriculum guidelines to be followed by all schools, and these guidelines are stringently administered; more importantly, the curriculum compels students to work especially hard in mathematics and science. Further, the ministry's special emphasis on engineering and science has translated into one national university in each of Japan's forty-seven prefectures. While the ministry's sway over private universities is relatively weak, it does make its point by accrediting universities and by providing subsidies for departments and projects that it wishes to promote.[58]

An equally important observation recorded by Mosk and Nataka is that Japanese economy is not insulated from supply and demand coordination failures; however, 'the point is that extensive company retraining of workers is a response which Japanese companies can and do use when there is a coordination failure of supply and demand for certain specialties'.[59]

[56] Ibid., p. 53.
[57] Ibid., p. 54.
[58] Ibid., p. 63.
[59] Ibid., p. 65.

McCormick's detailed engagement with the Japanese 'lifetime employment system'[60] brings out, from the company side, the rationale for their continued commitment to the concept. In his own words: 'The main lesson to be learned from international comparison is not necessarily the need to spend more money but the need to re-think the nature and purpose of training in relation to business and employment strategies'.[61] In McCormick's view, the 'lifetime employment system' has had a significant influence on the way in which Japanese corporations develop their graduate-level engineering manpower resources. To quote him in some detail:

It [the life time employment system] has had a significant influence on the recruitment and selection policies of companies. The system encourages the concentration on entry ports to the companies immediately after graduation, a preoccupation with potential for development rather than readily applicable skills, the use of the educational system as filter to identify such potential, and attempts to develop long-run relations with universities as part of the recruitment process...It has had a significant influence on the locus, content, mode, and agencies of training and employee development. The system emphasises a preoccupation with company-specific knowledge and skills and hence a preoccupation with in-house training; it lays stress on the importance of making new recruits into

[60] According to McCormick ('Japanese Engineers, Lifetime Employment and In-company Training'), the term lifetime employment system means: (a) entry to employment directly on graduation from school or college, (b) a strong moral expectation of employment from that sole employer until retirement, (c) continual training, and (d) mandatory retirement at 60, after the increase of mandatory company retirement from 55 to 60. Lifetime employment covers about 85 per cent of the labour force of the large companies and about 30 per cent of total national labour force. See ibid., p. 161.

[61] Ibid., p. 159.

company members [and hence it lays stress on organisational skills]; it uses on-the-job training as the main mode of training; and it uses line managers as major agents in human resource management.[62]

Several other aspects highlighted by McCormick include what he refers to as the 'structural peculiarities of Japanese capitalism';[63] the ownership and financial structure of the Japanese corporation are so organized that shares tend to be held largely by other companies rather than by individuals; two, Japanese companies have a high ratio of debt, typically bank loans, to equity. The net effect of these features is that they insulate Japanese corporations from individual shareholders, thereby providing them more scope to engage in long-term goals. On the other hand, McCormick notes that, in the Japanese corporations the ties between regular employees and the corporation appear closer because of the lifetime employment system:

Three mechanisms link lifetime employment to organic growth objectives. First board members tend to come through the management ranks of the company as lifetime employees and strongly identify with the company. By organisational socialisation and current structural relations these board members are sensitive to the pressures of their middle management and regular employees. Second, under lifetime employment middle management and regular employees are keenly interested in growth in order to satisfy their aspirations for career and salary advancement within their own company. Finally, growth by acquisition is both difficult and problematic with this distinctive pattern of ownership and employment system.[64]

[62] Ibid., pp. 161–2.
[63] Ibid., p. 163.
[64] Ibid., p. 165.

The latter point needs to be noted in particular; Japan provides several examples of companies that have grown by diversification based on technology. Among others, this has important implications for the manner in which countries, companies, and labour acquire and accumulate skill over time. We will return to this point in our concluding section.

The 'Japanese employment system' has had a number of apparently beneficial effects for graduate engineers: the broad educational base has provided a strong foundation for subsequent learning: the mutual commitment of employer and employee to training has meant the development of a 'learning organisation' in which those sent on on-the-job training have an obligation to share their learning with the work group; the homogeneity of training experiences has built a company-wide technological culture which leads to closer integration between functions such as R&D and production; the system of rotation and the lack of identification with specialisms has aided the movement of engineers to ease 'bottlenecks' and the development of new activities; finally the emphasis on company identification and the spread of features of lifetime employment to blue collar workers has reduced the social distance between engineers and blue collar workers.[65]

The South Korean Experience

Among the HPAEs (or the East Asian Miracle Economies) held up by the World Bank[66] as role model for other

[65] Ibid., pp. 177–8.

[66] World Bank, *The East Asian Miracle*, New York: Oxford University Press, 1993.

developing countries is the Republic of Korea;[67] however, while the World Bank would like all to believe that it was the private sector that to a large extent satisfied the demand for higher education stimulated by the government, Bennell and Segerstrom[68] dispute this claim. In the case of Korea in particular, they point out that

> on the whole, the role of enterprises in skills training appears to have been passive and limited in terms of both quality and quantity. Most Korean enterprises relied on the government for high quality trained manpower . . . during the early stages of the industrialisation process in South Korea which were characterised by the predominance of semi-skilled workers, good quality basic education and limited on-the-job training were sufficient to meet skill requirements. Once, however, the industrialisation strategy shifted in the early 1970s to the more skill-intensive heavy industry and chemical sectors, the state had to take initiative in establishing formal training capacity in critical areas of skill formation.[69]

The South Korean experience with vocational education is being recounted here with a view to emphasize the fact that: (1) Unlike the German and/or Japanese systems that show an uncommon level of institutional organization, information, and dialogue between social partners, in the Korean case the initiative came from the central

[67] Based on W. Georg and K. Rutters, eds., *Vocational Education and Training, Employment and Labour Relations in the Republic of Korea*, Baden-Baden, Germany: Nomos Verlagsgesellschaft, 1991; Bennel and Segerstrom, Vocational Education and Training in Developing Countries; and M. Carnoy, *Higher Education in a Global Innovation Economy*, paper prepared for a seminar co-hosted by CHET and the Human Sciences Research Council, 31 July 1998.

[68] Bennell and Segerstrom, 'Vocational Education and Training in Developing Countries'.

[69] Ibid., p. 275.

government and not from industry.[70] The organization and contents of vocational training in Korea are marked by the dominance of State regulation and planning; (2) A second 'congenital defect', according to Georg,[71] of the Korean system lies in the strict isolation of the new training system from the general education system, which manifests itself not only in the political responsibility divided between the Ministry of Education on the one hand and the Ministry of Labour on the other, but also in the mutual exclusiveness of the certificates, in the way that the transition between the systems is blocked, and in the discrimination over the status of the students who qualify;[72] (3) The loss of attractiveness of vocational training institute-trained personnel is aggravated by the fact that the qualifications it offers are scarcely recognized in employers' recruitment and staffing policies. As Schilling[73] notes: 'Most Korean companies consider it necessary to provide newly graduated engineers with a thorough working-in period whose length depends on the level of work and the complexity of the technologies which are to be mastered.'[74] However, Schilling also adds that companies must share the responsibility for this as long as they stick to recruitment policies in which formal educational attainment holds priority over vocationally trained personnel.[75] The companies, on their

[70] Georg and Rutters, *Vocational Education and Training, Employment and Labour Relations*.

[71] Ibid., p. 19.

[72] Ibid., pp. 19–20.

[73] E.G. Schilling, 'Occupational Aspects of Higher Education', in *Vocational Education and Training, Employment and Labour Relations in the Republic of Korea*, ed. W. Georg and K. Rutters, Baden-Baden, Germany: Nomos Verlagsgesellschaft, 1991.

[74] Ibid., p. 49.

[75] Ibid.

part, according to Schilling, have learned to live with the necessity to invest a lot in the training of fresh graduates from engineering colleges who come along with hardly any practical competencies. 'So long as occupational recruiting practice and social estimation discriminate between academic and occupational qualifications, choices of school will continue to be determined by the cost/benefit expectations of pupils and parents, whereby the benefits comprise much more than merely material advantages'.[76]

Where Do We Go from Here: Lessons Not Learnt

The levels of unemployment among the educated has led to demands to reduce the intake and/or, close down particular streams of higher education, declare certain other streams as non-utility courses, etc. At another level, the State in India, faced with the embarrassment of having to answer for large numbers of formally illiterate persons as well as for large numbers of 'out of school' children, has reacted by turning the issue into one of competing resources between higher and elementary education. The excuse of competing resources flies in the face of the fact that, in India, only 7 per cent of the population in the age group 17 to 24 attend higher educational institutions as against 92 per cent of the eligible age group population attending higher educational institutions in USA, 52 per cent in the UK, and 45 per cent in Japan.

The interface that education has with economic development in general and employment in particular, or the lack of it, has merited very little academic attention in India. The controversy around the report by Ambani and

[76] Ibid., p. 19.

Kumaramangalam[77] submitted to the Prime Minister's Council on Trade and Industry provides an illustration of the particular nature of our concern. Briefly, Ambani and Kumaramangalam argue, among other things, for an overall change in the approach to higher education, one where there is full cost recovery from students of public higher education institutions and immediate privatization of higher education except those areas of education involving 'disciplines that have no market orientation'.[78] The report has drawn flak from all over, particularly academicians. While, very rightly, these critiques[79] have condemned the report and its authors for perceiving higher education as largely a profitable industry, not a single critique that we have read so far, has taken the industrialist-authors to task for not including even a single line outlining the industry's responsibility towards the products of higher education. The state in India, for its part, is bent on downsizing higher education through starving universities of resources, freezing appointments, and encouraging commercialization.[80]

[77] M. Ambani and Birla Kumaramangalam, *A Policy Framework for Reforms in Education*, report presented to the Prime Minister's Council on Trade and Industry, New Delhi, 2000.

[78] As quoted in T. Ravi Kumar and Vijender Sharma, 'Downsizing Higher Education: An Emergent Crisis', *Economic and Political Weekly*, vol. 38, no. 7, 15–21 February 2003, p. 607.

[79] See for example, the following: K. Panikkar, 'Whither Indian Education', Inaugural Address to the National Convention Against Communalisation of Education in India, organized by SAHMAT, 4–6 August 2001, New Delhi, India; Vijender Sharma, 'WTO, GATS, and Future of Higher Education', *People's Democracy* (Weekly Organ of the Communist Party of India, Marxist), vol. 26, nos. 6–8, 10, 17 and 24 February 2002; and 'Teachers' Panel Opposes Report', *The Tribune*, Chandigarh, 2 March 2002, p. 5.

[80] Ravi Kumar and Sharma, 'Downsizing Higher Education: An Emergent Crisis'.

The GoI report[81] has devoted a whole chapter to labour force skills and training. This chapter, among other things, refers to the experiences of countries that have in place a system of labour training and vocal education and which includes the experience of the three countries (namely, Germany, Japan, and Republic of South Korea) as discussed above. However, the section entitled 'Suggested Remedial Steps', ostensibly to strengthen vocational education in India,[82] leaves a lot to be desired. It is not the disparate set of steps suggested that is the problem but the complete absence of a theme linking the different steps and actors. In short, in the absence of a clear exposition of the underlying philosophy outlining why, how, when, and with what levels of commitment these actors have to come together, it is not off the mark to state that the recommendations are a non-starter.

The GoI[83] again has detailed recommendations: for industry, for government, for the AICTE itself, etc. While none can quarrel with the spirit of each of the recommendations, the inability of this report to situate and contextualize these recommendations within an overall economic and social system is visibly glaring. For instance, McCormick[84] explicates this point very succinctly when discussing the feasibility of replicating the Japanese system in Britain:

> [Thus], even if the innovative and higher value-added strategies of Japanese companies are similar to those advocated for

[81] GoI, *Report of Task Force on Employment Opportunities*.

[82] Ibid., p. 135.

[83] GoI, *Revitalizing Technical Education: Report of the Review Committee on AICTE*.

[84] McCormick, 'Japanese Engineers, Lifetime Employment and In-company Training'.

British companies, and even if more career development policies through internal labour markets in Britain echo lifetime employment policies, the scope for implementing these business and human resource strategies will be severely restricted if they are dependent on the peculiar financial structure of Japanese companies. Similarly, the emphasis on group work cannot simply be seen as the logical outcome of an internal labour market. Behind group work lies the influence of Japanese language and culture, where the language encouraged heavy dependence on oral communication and pre-industrial work.[85]

McCormick also notes other 'peculiarities' of Japanese society that the British may not want to emulate, namely long working hours, curbs on individual liberties, company management of careers, etc.

An examination of the systems of vocational education in other countries is no doubt essential to enable us to understand to some extent the kind of institutions that have been put in place, the nature and depth of interactions among these institutions, etc., so that it becomes possible to gauge how smoothly or otherwise students are able to make the transition to work. A more significant purpose of this exercise, however, is the hope that it will initiate in India the kind of discourse that preceded these arrangements in these countries in the first place, and the changing nature of the discourse over time.

[85] Ibid., p. 178.

CHAPTER 9

Education and Skill Development in the Context of the Declining Rate of Formal Employment Generation

Issues for Discussion

The Context

In an earlier paper[1] we had traced, historically, the growing disjuncture between education and employment in India. In the process we had shown that successive governments in independent India have come nowhere close to matching the alacrity with which the colonial government in the Madras Presidency, for example, attempted to address the issue. In conclusion, we had argued thus:

Research to unravel and understand the interface between education and economic development has hardly begun

* Previously published in *The Indian Journal of Labour Economics*, vol. 51, no. 4, 2008.

[1] Padmini Swaminathan, 'The Interface between Employment and Education: The Need for a Discourse', in *Education and Social Change in South Asia*, ed. Krishna Kumar and Joachim Oesterheld, New Delhi: Orient Longman, 2007.

in India. Even so, the levels of unemployment among the educated has led to demands to reduce the intake and/or, close down particular streams of higher education, declare certain other streams as non-utility courses, etc. At another level, the state in India is faced with the embarrassment of having to answer for large numbers of formally illiterate persons as well as for large numbers of 'out of school' children, has reacted by turning the issue into one of competing resources between higher and elementary education. The excuse of competing resources flies in the face of the fact that, in India, only 7 per cent of the population in the age-group 17 to 24 attend higher educational institutions as against 92 per cent of the eligible age group population attending higher educational institutions in USA, 52 per cent in U.K. and 45 per cent in Japan (Geetha Rani, 2003) . . . It is important to point out in this context that in much of the literature covering particularly the developed as well as the East Asian (miracle) economies, the state has played an instrumental role, either through direct interventions or by facilitating the setting up of appropriate institutions... the models of state intervention in each of these countries and within each country at different points in time are extremely diverse, with equally diverse outcomes; not all of these outcomes have been equally benign for their respective population and certainly not from a gender perspective. The bottom line however, in all of this is the recognition that, howsoever difficult, states need to constantly engage with the challenge of matching education with employment and, more important, of maintaining the relevance of this match. Economies like India, faced with growing imbalance between the output of the school system and the absorptive capacity of their labour markets for such types of educated personnel, are attempting to reform the contents of education without questioning their development strategies or development goals.

In the recent past the subject of higher education in general and of the skill level of the population in particular, has received considerable official recognition. The

Reports of two Task Force Committees on Employment set up by the Central Planning Commission[2]—the Report of the Review Committee on All India Council for Technical Education (AICTE)[3] and the Report on Conditions of Work and Promotion of Livelihoods in the Unorganized Sector[4]—have, in different ways, addressed the theme of the mismatch between the products of higher education and the absorptive capacity of the economy. Similarly, a World Bank study on Skill Development including the system of Vocational Education and Training in India (January 2008) dwelt at considerable length on the nature, scope and adequacy of existing facilities for training in the public and private sector. Among the reports mentioned above, the Report of the Review Committee on AICTE, given its mandate to suggest steps to revitalize technical education in the country, has frontally addressed a major component of higher education-based skill development, namely engineering education.

The main aim of this chapter is to examine and contextualize the findings of the AICTE Review Committee Report and of positing it against those of others. This helps us to understand and compare their various approaches to the issue and the different conclusions arising from them.

[2] Planning Commission, *Report of Task Force on Employment Opportunities*, New Delhi: Planning Commission, 2001; Planning Commission, *Special Group on Targeting Ten Million Employment Opportunities per Year*, New Delhi: Planning Commission, 2002.

[3] Government of India, *Revitalizing Technical Education: Report of the Review Committee on AICTE*, New Delhi: Government of India, Ministry of Human Resource Development, 2003.

[4] NCEUS, *Report on Conditions of Work and Promotion of Livelihoods in the Unorganised Sector*, New Delhi: National Commission for Enterprises in the Unorganised Sector, 2007.

Official Speak on Higher Education and Skill Development: Salient Findings

Planning Commission Task Force Reports on Employment and Unemployment (2001, 2002)

In the space of just two years the Central Planning Commission of India constituted two committees to examine the 'problem' of growing incidences of unemployment and under-employment in the country.[5] Our purpose here is not to discuss the politics of why, within a space of two years, two official committees were set up by the same department to examine the same theme. Rather, for us the important aspect in both the Reports is the very considerable emphasis that was placed on the lack of interface between employment and education. In the process, both the Reports have expanded the definition of 'quality' of employment to include the 'skill' component of those employed and of those returned as unemployed.

Both reports emphasize the fact that there has been a steady decline in the job-creating capacity of the economy, which accelerated from 1993–4. For example, the Reports point out that the employment growth fell to 1.07 per cent per annum (between 1993–4 and 1999–2000) from 2.7 per cent per annum in the past (that is, between 1983 and 1993–4) in spite of acceleration in the growth of domestic product from 5.2 per cent (between 1983 and 1994–4) to 6.7 per cent (between 1993–4 and 1999–2000). This in turn means that the capacity of job creation per unit of output went down about three

[5] The first committee, chaired by Montek Singh Ahluwalia, submitted its Report in July 2001. It went by the name of Task Force on Employment Opportunities. The second committee, chaired by Dr S.P. Gupta, submitted its Report in May 2002. This committee was called the Special Group on Targeting 10 Million Employment Opportunities.

times compared to that in the 1980s and early 1990s. The organized sector's employment-generating capacity (measured in terms of employment elasticity) came down to near zero; in the public sector, it has been negative in most cases. Thus, the major source of employment generation and for labour absorption is the unorganized sector of the economy whose employment weightage is as high as 92 per cent (of the total employed labour force).[6]

On examining all major sources of information, the committees found that the rate of unemployment in India had increased significantly in 1993–4 and was above 7.3 per cent in 1999–2000 compared to 6.0 per cent in 1993–4 on Current Daily Status (CDS) basis.[7] The number of unemployed increased from 20.13 million in 1993–4 to 26.58 million in 1999–2000. Nearly 74 per cent of the

[6] Planning Commission, *Report of Task Force on Employment Opportunities*, p. 34 and Planning Commission, *Special Group on Targeting Ten Million Employment Opportunities per Year*, pp. 2 and 26.

[7] The National Sample Survey Organisation (NSSO) of India collects detailed information on the employment status of the population through large-scale, nation-wide sample surveys in which individuals are categorized as employed or available for work but not employed, using different criteria. Rates are calculated as percentages of the total labour force. The NSSO provides four different measures of employment and unemployment, each of which captures different facets of the employment-unemployment situation. One of these is the Current Daily Status (CDS). Based on the reported time disposition of the person on each day of the reference week, person-days in employment (unemployment) are aggregated to generate estimates of person-days in employment/ unemployment. The person-day unemployment rate is derived as the ratio of person-days in unemployment to the person-days in the labour force. This measure captures the within-week unemployment of those classified as employed on the Weekly Status. The CDS-measure of unemployment is widely agreed to be the one that most fully captures open unemployment in the country. See Planning Commission, *Report of Task Force on Employment Opportunities*, pp. 15–16.

unemployed are in rural areas, while 60 per cent of the unemployed are educated (higher secondary and above).

Another dimension of the employment-unemployment problem is the serious mismatch between the expectations of the new entrants to the labour force and the quality of employment opportunities available to them, as revealed by the very high unemployment among certain groups, especially among educated youth.

Given the high expectations of the increasingly better educated new entrants to the labour force the employment problem for this group cannot be addressed by creating more jobs of the same low quality that exist at present. What is needed is a strategy that will create more high-quality jobs that generate higher levels of income.[8]

This despite the fact that, overall, educational levels of the labour force in India are very low. About 44 per cent of all workers in 1999–2000 were illiterate and another 22.7 per cent had schooling only up to the primary level.

If we define the minimum level of education necessary to function in a modern economy as schooling up to the middle level, then only about 33.2 per cent of the labour force had schooling of that level and above. The percentage was higher at 57.4 per cent for the urban labour force, but it was correspondingly worse in rural areas, with only 25.4 per cent for the rural labour force meeting these standards.[9]

The regional disaggregation of unemployment data raises further issues of concern. The unemployment rate (on the CDS basis) was higher in high literacy states, almost 21 per cent in Kerala; next is West Bengal with 15

---

[8] Ibid., p. 41.

[9] Planning Commission, *Report of Task Force on Employment Opportunities*, p. 124.

per cent followed by Tamil Nadu at 12 per cent of their respective labour forces. Further, in each of these states, the incidence of unemployment among youths was even higher and more so for females. Among female youth in Kerala, the unemployment rate was as high as 46 per cent, in West Bengal it was 39 per cent and nearly as high in Tamil Nadu. Once again, this feature of higher incidence of unemployment among youths needs to be juxtaposed against the positive aspect of increasing levels of education discernible among the younger age groups of the population.[10]

The statistics discussed above relate to general education, which is not the same thing as possession of 'marketable skills'. At the same time, it is not easy to quantify the level of skills in the labour force since such data are not readily available. However, in 1993–4 the National Sample Survey Organisation of India (NSSO) conducted a survey where information on the possession of thirty different marketable skills by persons in the labour force was sought. The results of this component of the survey reveal that hardly 10 per cent of the male workers and 6 per cent of female workers in the rural areas possessed specific marketable skills. The urban areas returned relatively better figures but still abysmally low by any yardstick—19.6 per cent for male workers and 11 per cent for female workers.

Both the committees emphasize the painful fact that the level of vocational[11] skills in the labour force in India

[10] Both the Planning Commission Reports give a large number of tables containing state-wise data relating to the nature of employment generated, the level of unemployment disaggregated by sex, age and level of education.

[11] For a description of what constitutes formal vocational education in India, see Planning Commission, *Report of the Task Force on Employment Opportunities*, p. 129.

compares poorly with the position in other countries. Only 5 per cent of the Indian labour force in the age category 20–4 years has vocational skills whereas the percentage in industrial countries is much higher, varying between 60 and 80 per cent. It may be argued that in developing countries like India, economically productive skills are acquired not only in formal training/education institutions but also through the family. But it also needs to be stressed that currently, the traditional artisan classes are among the poorest, in economic terms, in the country. 'The developing countries... have percentages that are significantly lower than the developed countries, but they are still much higher than in India, example, Mexico at 28 per cent and Peru at 17 per cent. Differences in definitions may make comparisons somewhat unreliable but the level in India is clearly far too low'.[12]

One of the committees[13] devoted considerable space in its Report to discuss the nature of vocational education and training, and the system of apprenticeship available to students in India. Its overall assessment of the situation was as follows:

> The actual number of persons expected to enter the labour force (on the 1.8 per cent labour force growth assumption) is about 12.3 million per year. Allowing for underutilization of seats in training institutions and some overlaps, the percentage of those entering the labour force with some degree of formal training is probably around 1.5 million or about 12 per cent of the gross new entrants into the labour force. While a significant number of the new entrants will be absorbed in various types of unskilled labour in agricultural and non-agricultural occupations, where skills are not needed, the level of skill endowment of new entrants to the labour

[12] Ibid., p. 128.
[13] Ibid.

force revealed by these numbers is clearly not consistent with triggering a process of rapid economic growth and high-quality employment generation. The inadequacy of training capacity in quantitative terms is not the only problem. There are also serious problems relating to quality.[14]

An added feature of the above committee's Report was that it tried to map the 'school-to-work' transition systems in several countries, and even provided an elaborate table comparing the vocational training systems of India and the Republic of Korea.[15] Our point of departure with the committee's report lies in the complete silence that ensues thereafter on how other countries have been able to not only operationalize their 'school-to-work' transition-enabled vocational education and apprenticeship systems, but also make it as broad-based as possible to cover large numbers of their school-going population—a feature conspicuous by its absence in India. An examination of the systems of vocational education in other countries would enable an understanding of institutions that have been put in place as well as the nature and depth of interactions among them, so that it becomes possible to gauge how smoothly or otherwise students are able to make the transition to work. Much more significant, however, in our opinion, is the need to capture the kind of discourse that preceded these arrangements in these countries in the first place, and the changing nature of the discourse over time. It is our contention that a large part of the explanation for the poor record in vocational training and the almost complete lack of interface between even this miniscule vocational education and employment in

[14] Ibid., p. 133.
[15] Ibid., p. 146.

India has a lot to do with the absence of any worthwhile discourse on this subject in post-Independence India, and the consequent inability to set up appropriate institutions and systems to forge such an interface.

NCEUS Report on Conditions of Work and Promotion of Livelihoods in the Unorganized Sector (2007)

A signal service of the National Commission for Enterprises in the Unorganized Sector (NCEUS) is the collation and analysis of data to provide as comprehensive a picture as possible of the segment of the economy that employs the bulk of the country's labour force, namely the unorganized sector. According to the commission's estimate, in 2004–5, total employment (principal plus subsidiary) in the Indian economy was 458 million, of which the unorganized sector accounted for 395 million, constituting 86 per cent of total workers. The commission's estimates showed that between 1999–2000 and 2004–5, of the total incremental employment generated, only about 14 per cent was absorbed in the organized sector while 86 per cent was absorbed in the unorganized sector. Within the unorganized sector, wage workers (that is, those employed by others), constituted only 36 per cent of the workers, and the remaining 64 per cent were self-employed. Three major structural features of employment in the Indian economy highlighted by the commission are: first, that the informal sector is hugely preponderant in the Indian economy; second, that the increases in employment have been of the informal kind; and third, that within the informal sector, there is a huge preponderance of self-employed workers.

The commission analysed the educational status of various groups of workers, that is, workers in the organized and unorganized sectors, formally and informally employed workers, by social and gender status, etc. In 2004–5, the share of the population 15 years old and above who were illiterate or below primary education level comprised 47 per cent. The share was higher among women (58 per cent) and in rural areas where more than 50 per cent of the population were illiterate and below primary. While 13 per cent of the population had primary education, 16 per cent had middle school level of education. The share of educated persons, that is, those with secondary education and above was higher at 24 per cent. The share of educated persons was higher, as expected, among men and in urban areas. The commission noted that low levels of education and skills were one of the primary reasons leading to a hierarchy of work relationships, segmentation of the workforce, and vulnerability.

Using NSSO data from Round 2004–5, which collected information about the skill profile of youth (15–19 years old), the commission pointed out that only 11.5 million of those in the age group 15–29 years received or were receiving formal training while 22.3 million were being trained informally and 253.7 million received no training. Data also revealed significant differences in skill training by gender and urban/rural location; further and equally significant is the fact that only 2.1 per cent of the youth population had acquired (or was acquiring) formal skill training in rural areas, in urban areas this percentage was much higher at 7.3 per cent.

Similar to the findings of the Planning Commission Task Force Reports mentioned earlier, the NCEUS found that, across states, the pattern of skill acquisition varied quite considerably. The largest share of youth population with formal skills was in Kerala (15.5 per cent), followed by Maharashtra (8.3 per cent), Tamil Nadu (7.6 per cent), Himachal Pradesh (5.6 per cent), and Gujarat (4.7 per cent). The lowest incidence of formal training was in Bihar (0.5 per cent). Among those trained or undergoing formal training, Maharashtra accounted for 21.7 per cent share. Kerala and Tamil Nadu had more than 10 per cent share in the skilled youth population of population with formal skills. Gujarat and Andhra Pradesh too had a relatively higher share of skilled population in the 15–29 age groups. Thus, the commission noted, the southern and western states formed a continuous zone wherein the share of population with formal skills was relatively higher; together, the above six states accounted for 63 per cent of formally trained people. Primarily, these are states which either have more industries, a higher level of education, and a higher availability of training infrastructure and training capacity both in the public and private sectors.

Again, similar to the Planning Commission Task Force Reports, the commission showed how low levels of education and formal training resulted in a majority of workers being excluded from participating effectively in development processes.

The World Bank Study on Skill Development in India: The Vocational Education and Training System

The above study makes some telling comments on the state of vocational education and training in India. One, using NSSO data, it observes that:

> There is growing demand for workers with secondary education but that the same cannot be said of workers with technical/vocational education or training. Since the

early 1980s, the relative wages of workers with secondary education have been growing even as these workers have become relatively more abundant. However, the relative supply of workers with technical/vocational skills has declined throughout this period while their relative wages have also come down since the early 1990s.[16]

Two, the study finds that:

Labour market outcomes for graduates of the training system are fairly poor. Even three years after graduation, over 60 per cent of all graduates remained unemployed. Although a significant proportion of apprentices find employment, close to two-thirds are not employed in the trade for which they were trained—a third of these had been trained in obsolete trades. There appear to be three reasons for this: (a) limited growth and labour demand in the manufacturing sector; (b) mismatch between skills attained and those actually in demand, and (c) mismatch between the skills taught and the graduates' own labour market objectives.[17]

Three, the study notes that:

These poor outcomes arise owing to the public training system facing many constraints. These include the following: the management of the system is fragmented. While different authorities have clearly specified functions on paper, there is little coordination between them leading to diverse accountability. Furthermore, preoccupation with providing and financing training has resulted in government neglecting a key role—providing information about the availability and effectiveness of training programmes. Institutions do not have

[16] World Bank, *Skill Development in India: The Vocational Education and Training System*, Human Development Unit, South Asia Region, January 2008.

[17] Ibid.

incentives to improve their performance; Industry involvement in the vocational training system is nascent.[18]

Four, unlike other Reports, the World Bank study engaged to some extent with the interface of vocational education/training with employers. According to the study, skills rank below other constraints as more important than 'skills and education of available workers'. The top three constraints are 'tax rates', 'policy uncertainty' and 'access to finance'. This, according to the study, may account for manufacturing establishments in India providing less in-service formal training than the average for Europe, East Asia, and Latin America. To the study's surprise, it found that in-service training in India was also lower than other countries in the South Asia region. No more than 7 per cent of employees received training in a given year and there were also significant variations in the provision of training across states.

The fifth observation is:

> Almost no attention is paid to using financing as an innovative means to encourage either good quality public training, private training or as a way of providing incentives to enterprises to train their workers . . . The funding model used by the states is largely ineffective. Although the resources available to the states are limited, no state seems to follow a transparent funding formula in funding vocational education or training. Once an institution begins to receive funding, subsequent funds are guaranteed irrespective of the institution's performance. The same levels of finance are allocated to poorly performing institutions with high drop-out rates as to those that maintain a high quality of teaching and performance.[19]

[18] Ibid.
[19] Ibid.

The sixth point worth noting is:

there is little capacity in vocational education and even that is under-utilized. Ministry of Human Resource Development's (MHRD) original intention was to place 25 per cent of all grade 11–12 students into vocational courses by the year 2000. This has not happened. Only 6,800 schools have received grants and the total enrolment reported is only about 5 per cent at most. In fact, this figure more closely approximates the capacity of schools to offer vocational education rather than enrolments. More recent information suggests that the enrolment figure is less than 3 per cent of the students attending Grades 11–12 . . . It would also imply that less than one per cent of students who had entered Grade 1 over the last decade or so would have eventually participated in vocational education.

Seven, the study finds that:

A survey of 55 enterprises by FICCI (Federation of Indian Chambers of Commerce and Industry in late 2001 assessed the quality and relevance of vocational/technical training from an industry perspective. Close to 60 per cent of the respondents felt that institutions were not geared to meet the challenges of the global economy and over 43 per cent that academic institutions were not aligned to the needs of industry. 87 per cent felt that institutions should have greater exposure to industrial practices. They stressed the importance of a collaborative approach between academia and industry as a means of ensuring a better match between what industry wants and what the institutions produce . . . Until recently, it has been hard to detect the hand of industry in the vocational training system . . . There also seems to be a lack of employer interest in the apprenticeship system. Regulations require public and private sector employers in designated industries to engage apprentices according to set ratios of apprentices to workers for prescribed trades . . . despite the legislation, only 1,900 private establishments were registered for the Apprenticeship Scheme in 2001; compared to some 16,000 other establishments, essentially government agencies and enterprises. This lack of private sector interest compares to the 2,50,000 establishments covered by the Employee Provident Fund.

The eighth point of note is:

The quality of teachers appears to be poor. A slightly dated survey conducted of over 262 ITI teachers in 14 states showed that 61 per cent of teachers have less than 12 years of schooling, and a third had no industrial experience. Of those who had some industrial experience, a significant majority had less than two years of experience. Furthermore, two-thirds of instructors had not received any training in the past five years.

Revitalizing Technical Education: Report of the Review Committee on AICTE

The GOI, through a resolution passed on 30 November 1945, set up the AICTE to supervise all technical education above the high school stage. The council consisted of representatives of the Ministries of Education, Labour, Industry, and Commerce, the Inter-University Board, the Central Advisory Board of Education, the Association of Principals of Technical Institutions, the Institution of Engineers, the Indian Legislature and the provincial governments. As constituted, the AICTE was an advisory body with no statutory powers; nevertheless, it played an important role in the development of technical education in the country.[20] Significantly, *while the expansion of technical institutes in the fifties was done with the*

[20] *Report of the Review Committee on AICTE*, p. 23.

approval of the AICTE and the Government of India, the expansion in the 1980s was localized mostly in the four southern states and was primarily in the self-financing sector without the approval of the AICTE and the Government of India (emphasis added).[21]

The National Policy on Education, 1986, made a specific mention of the need to vest the AICTE with statutory powers; accordingly, among other things, it laid down that:

a) The AICTE will be vested with statutory authority for planning, formulation, maintenance and standards, accreditation, funding of priority areas, monitoring and evaluation, maintaining parity of certification and awards, and ensuring the coordinated and *integrated development of technical and management education* (emphasis ours); and,
b) In the interest of maintaining standards and for several other valid reasons, the commercialization of professional and technical educations will be curbed.[22]

In December 1987, the AICTE became a statutory body through an Act of Parliament. Apart from setting up the AICTE and providing it with statutory powers, the government also came out with Technology Policy Statements (most notably in 1958 and again in 2003) wherein it reiterated the central role of Science and Technology 'in raising the quality of life of the people of the country, particularly of the disadvantaged sections of society, in creating wealth for all, in making India globally competitive....'[23] The implementation plan of these policies emphasized human resource development. Thus, for example, the Science and Technology Policy

[21] Ibid.
[22] Ibid., p. 24.
[23] Ibid., p. 34.

Statement of 2003 states: '...There is need to progressively increase the rate of generation of high quality skilled human resource at all levels . . . In order to encourage quality and productivity in science and technology, *mobility of scientists and technologists between industry, academic institutions and research laboratories will be ensured*' (emphasis added).[24]

Viewing the development of technical education from the demand side, the Report[25] offers the following perspective on the changing employment scenario since the enunciation of the first of the Technology Policy Statements. In more than one place the report emphasizes the point that, there has been a:

> rapid expansion of supply of technical personnel, far in excess of the absorptive capacity of the economy, leading to under-employment and even unemployment of graduates and a deterioration of their real-income levels. It has also led to a degree of substitution, whereby, in many cases, degree holding engineers are taking up employment opportunities that could have gone to the diploma holders . . . Manufacturing, the traditional user of technical manpower, does not exhibit an ability to provide significantly expanded employment opportunities for technical persons. The growth of the manufacturing sector has been largely job-less, due to its low employment elasticity, almost close to zero . . . Compared to the past, employment opportunities would be more sensitive to the quality of the graduates.
>
> In an internationally competitive environment, it is the quality and not numbers that would matter. Graduates of sub-standard programmes and institutions will find it increasingly harder to get employment even if they are prepared to sacrifice on the income level. Past pattern of long-term employment

[24] Ibid., p. 35.
[25] Ibid.

in a particular enterprise or even in the same industry is beginning to break down. Ability to keep up-to-date with changing knowledge and skill requirements in the wake of frequent technological restructuring and making significant lateral shifts and across disciplines, would be crucial for remaining employed. *The implication for the technical educational system is two-fold:* (*a*) *the pedagogy should focus relatively more on the development of higher-order, generic, transferable skills and autonomous learning strategies, and* (*b*) *more opportunities for non-formal education and training, continuing education and training, and distance education, should be offered by the system* (emphasis added).[26]

We have dwelt at some length in reproducing the above observations from the Report for the following reasons. On the one hand we notice: (i) the unplanned and unregulated quantum leap in technical institutions that have come up; (ii) the absolute shortage of technical teachers; (iii) the low quality of teaching; (iv) the low levels of formal coordination between educational institutes, industry, trade unions and the government (the latter through, say, the AICTE). On the other, the inability of the economy to absorb the products of these institutes, makes us wonder whether there is a fundamental flaw in the way we have comprehended (or not comprehended) the two broad institutions of 'school' and 'work', with which vocational/technical institution is intimately connected and deeply embedded.

It would be useful to engage with the numbers of technical institutes and personnel provided by the AICTE Report in order to get an idea of the dimensions of the problem being considered by the Review Report. At one level, we are told that the number of degree engineering

[26] Ibid., pp. 37–8.

colleges practically doubled in the decade 1980 to 1990, from around 158 institutions to over 337; during the following decade, 1990–2000, it increased from 337 to 776, three-quarters of which were self-financed. As of 2003, there were 1,208 engineering colleges including 986 self-financing institutions with a total intake of over 3.5 lakh students. Equally spectacular was the growth of MCA and MBA degree institutions, which in 2003 stood at 1,006 and 930, respectively, with an intake of over 53,000 and 64,000 students. At another level, data put out by the National Technical Manpower Information System (NTMIS) reveal that a considerable number of engineering graduates remain unemployed even two years after completion of their graduation; the then estimates indicated that the unemployment rate of engineering degree holders could exceed 20 per cent.[27] The story of the growth in postgraduate institutions in engineering is similar.

Several aspects of the above growth in technical institutions need to be explicated. One, data on region-wise and state-wise distribution of institutions, and sanctioned intake of students reveal the highly skewed geographical distribution of institutions across the country with more than 52 per cent of the institutions being located in the south and south-west, whereas the east and north account for just around 7 per cent and 10 per cent, respectively. Likewise, 43 per cent of MBA institutions and 59 per cent of MCA institutions with an intake of 35 per cent and 57 per cent of students in the above disciplines are in the south and south-west, almost equal to the total number of MBA and MCA institutions and their sanctioned intake in central, east, north and north-west regions.

[27] Ibid., p. 47.

Two, analysing the status of faculty availability to impart technical education to such levels of student intake, the AICTE Report recorded:

> As of today, going strictly according to the prescribed norms, there is shortfall of over 26,000 PhDs and 30,000 MTechs for meeting the teaching requirements in the engineering institutions alone. Even if the teacher to student ratio is relaxed to 1:20, the shortfall in PhDs and MTechs should still be over 18,000 and 20,000. The faculty position in other disciplines such as MCA, management education, pharmacy, architecture and town planning is as bad, if not worse...many of the private colleges, in particular, employ fresh graduates passing out of the college with poor grades as teachers, thus totally compromising on the quality of teachers. It must be recognized that mediocrity in the teaching fraternity can only multiply mediocrity and cannot lead to the creation of excellence.[28]

The largest shortfall of teachers is in the southern region, with Tamil Nadu alone accounting for almost 50 per cent of the shortfall.[29]

Three, a serious issue of concern recorded by the AICTE Report was one of accreditation. The AICTE instituted an accreditation programme to ensure quality education in all technical institutes under its purview, and also established the National Board of Accreditation (NBA) as an autonomous body. Accreditation is based on an assessment of the physical infrastructure, availability of competent and qualified faculty, teaching learning process being followed, R&D work being carried out, placement of students and other aspects of relevance. Accreditation by the AICTE follows the report of the

[28] Ibid., p. 77.
[29] Ibid., p. 76.

expert committee members appointed to carry out the above task.

> As on May 2003, only 895 programmes from 202 institutions have been accredited as against a total of about 28,000 programmes in 3,589 accreditable institutions. 53 of these are Government-aided institutions (9.3 per cent) out of a total of 567 such institutions and the rest 149 are private institutions (4.9 per cent) out of a total of 3,022 . . . It is a matter of great concern to find that over 90 per cent of technical and engineering graduates are studying in non-accredited institutions.[30]

A compounding problem flagged by the Report was the inability of most of these institutions to ensure even minimum quality of education.

> In Tamil Nadu where expansion has been greatest in recent years, in a recent semester examination conducted by the Anna University, no student passed in 5 colleges, 28 had less than 5 per cent passes, 78 had less than 10 per cent passes, 108 had less than 15 per cent passes and only 17 had more than 40 per cent passes, with only 8 having more than 50 per cent passes.[31]

Observations and Recommendations of the AICTE Review Report: A Discussion

Based on its mandate of reviewing the functioning of the AICTE, and seized with the burning desire to revitalize technical education in the country, the Review Report made certain very specific observations and recommendations, that, in our opinion, could have had far reaching social and political implications if adopted.

[30] Ibid., p. 87.
[31] Ibid., p. 174.

Further, these observations and recommendations, when posited against the observations of the Reports of the Planning Commission Task Forces, NCEUS, and the World Bank, immediately bring home the diametrically opposed nature of suggestions for action offered to the government by the different Reports depending on the differing assumptions, understandings, and approaches to the theme and problem of skill development of the Indian population.

One, the AICTE Review Committee recommended:

> a much stricter control in giving further approvals to new institutions especially in the South, Southwest and Western regions, to slow down further proliferation of such institutions . . . even for a sustained economic growth rate of 8 per cent per year, the country can at best support 4–5 per cent growth in the technical personnel, as against the current 15–20 per cent annual growth in the intake of undergraduate technical students. The committee, therefore, strongly recommends that no further expansion of UG technical institutions should be allowed and approvals for new institutions should be stopped for a period of at least 5 years, in states where the intake for UG technical education exceeds the national average of about 350 per million population. As expected, it is these states which have a very severe scarcity of qualified faculty, which justifies the suggested bold step. This will not only improve the quality of existing institutions by enabling the AICTE to provide better support and prevent the social unrest that can ensue from unemployment of qualified technical personnel but also indirectly assist in promoting the establishment of quality institutions in areas/states suffering from severe scarcity of technical institutions.[32]

[32] Ibid., pp. 47–52.

Two, the committee noted:

It is increasingly clear that the organised sector in any country and particularly in India can only provide a limited number of jobs. Even the job availability in the manufacturing industries is generally smaller than the percentage of growth. The vast majority of technical graduates have to find jobs either in the service sector or preferably be trained to seek independent jobs and become entrepreneurs . . . The Committee believes that the Government must make it mandatory for all industries, including small-scale industries, to employ qualified diploma holders or engineers for all technical jobs in order to become competitive in the global market. The existing or presently employed personnel who do not have technical qualifications must be sent for training by the industries to enable them to acquire knowledge of the latest trends and practices, of quality control and production techniques.[33]

Three, the committee's solution to the growing mismatch between 'what the economy can support and what has been sanctioned by the AICTE', was to 'conduct a systematic study to determine the numbers that will be reasonable for intake into technical education'.

Four, the committee observed that:

So far, the AICTE has left the issue of quantitative expansion to market forces, and permitted unchecked growth without reference to the actual manpower requirements of the country. Taking advantage of the large demand from students, and ignoring the realities of economic conditions, many over-enthusiastic (and some unscrupulous) entrepreneurs have over-expanded technical education. Hence the AICTE should shrink excess flab in technical institutions in a relatively painless

[33] Ibid., p. 162.

manner by insisting that student admissions should be strictly to the number that can be handled by the available faculty and no more. The AICTE should even close institutions, which are not up to minimum standards.[34]

It is immediately clear from the above that the AICTE Review Committee provided important and thought-provoking details of the pattern of quantitative growth of technical education in the country, and also highlighted the nature of problems afflicting this growth in terms of: (a) the lopsided nature of geographical development of technical education institutes; (b) the severe shortage of qualified faculty: and (c) the unaccreditable nature of growth of institutes. However, as all of these compromise the quality of technical education provided, the recommendation of the Review Committee to place a moratorium on expansion of technical education institutions, among others, is unacceptable, not only because of its politically explosive overtone but also, more importantly, from the point of view of achieving socially just economic development. As the Reports of the Planning Commission Task Forces, NCEUS, and World Bank have pointed out, the percentage and levels of formally trained technical population/workforce in this country is unacceptably low, the uneven nature of growth regionally, notwithstanding. These Reports have also provided data that, in different ways, unambiguously depict how segmentation of the workforce and hierarchy of work relationships take place because of low levels of education and skills.

The problems of shortage of qualified faculty, of lopsided geographical spread of technical education institutes, poor performance of students, etc., alluded to by the AICTE Review Report are systemic in nature; each

[34] Ibid., p. 173.

of these factors, either individually or taken together, does not warrant a moratorium being placed on further expansion of technical education institutions.

However, an important problem flagged by the AICTE Review Report, largely because of which it has recommended putting on hold further expansion in technical education institutes, was the inability of the growing Indian economy to absorb those passing out of these institutions. In a different way, the AICTE Review Report echoes the point made by all other Reports, namely the gross inability of the Indian economy to generate formal employment. What is problematic about the observation made is the manner in which all of the Reports seem to take this phenomenon, namely that of the economy's inability to generate formal employment, *as given*. In fact, the AICTE Review Report goes further and laments that had the country made proper use of the data generated by the National Technical Manpower Information System (NTMIS) (despite all its limitations) 'for real decision-making', the country could have avoided investment in such large numbers of technical educational institutions, and thereby the numbers of educated unemployed could have been considerably reduced. The concern of the AICTE Review Committee begins and ends with analysing the growth and expansion of technical education institutions in the country. There is no attempt to situate this growth within the larger context of the developments in the educational sector over time (wherein, with economic development, larger numbers would be opting for higher/technical/vocational education in their quest for formal degrees to be able to access formal employment); there is also no attempt to relate this growth to the need of a growing and diversifying economy for skilled personnel. This inability of the

AICTE Review Report to contextualize its findings and observations makes it unable to expand the scope of its review to grapple with the issue of why the economy is not able to absorb even the miniscule numbers of formally trained technical personnel. In addition, Section 10(e) of the AICTE Act stipulates that it would be the duty of the AICTE to 'formulate schemes for promoting technical education for women, handicapped and weaker sections of society'. On this, the Review Committee merely noted:

> In so far as the mandate of the Council for formulating schemes for women, and physically disabled is concerned, the AICTE has not evolved any separate scheme except for providing some relaxation in age limit under the scheme of Career Award for Young Teachers and in Project and Travel Grant Schemes. In so far as schemes for promoting technical education for weaker sections of the society are concerned no specific schemes have been formulated by the Council.[35]

In its recommendations, the Review Committee was content to suggest that disaggregated data be collected by AICTE separately for male and female enrolment in various disciplines, that AICTE conduct studies to ascertain the problems faced by women, the handicapped, and the weaker sections of society regarding access to technical education and subsequent employment, and also address the problem of lack of accommodation for women students in all institutions.

Issues for Discussion

If none of the Reports deem it their responsibility or mandate to engage with and/or examine the theme of why the Indian state's paradigm of development is unable

[35] Ibid., p. 71.

to generate formal employment of the quantum and kind that will enable larger numbers of formally trained personnel to be employed, it is apparent that none of these Reports would be concerned with the quantity, quality, and skill level of the working population—particularly of the vast majority condemned to work in the unorganized sector.

Having stated the above, it is important to take note of the implications of several of the observations in the Reports discussed above.

One, the NCEUS, in its drive towards formalizing the informal/unorganized sector, not only makes a case for expanding general education given the present abysmal levels of education of the bulk of the general and working population; more significantly, the NCEUS asserts that the skills necessary for the unorganized sector should be 'formally' provided. Formal provision, according to the NCEUS, would involve the processes of accreditation, certification, and standardization. The World Bank study goes further and notes that the lack of evaluative evidence on the impact of vocational education or training makes it difficult to make informed decisions on the effectiveness of such programmes, even if these were to be 'formally' provided. Hence the need, according to the World Bank study, is 'to define transparent criteria that are easily measured but not easily manipulated'.

Two, unlike the NCEUS, the World Bank study, and to a limited extent the AICTE Review Committee, bemoans the lack of employer participation in skill development programmes. In fact, the World Bank study puts it forcefully thus: 'Critical to the success of any reform in public training system is buy-in from employers and their participation in decision-making not only at the national and state levels but also at the institutional level'. It is important to engage with the nature of industry involvement in training substantively so that issues of standard setting and overall process of certification of courses, contents, and performance evaluation of students are linked and work within a framework agreed upon by the government as facilitator and industry as the implementer.

Three, the World Bank study and the AICTE Review Report flagged the issue of poor quality of teachers and teaching in most vocational training/education institutions. A major obstacle identified is the way training institutions are governed. Most vocational training institutions are part of the government and therefore teachers and trainers are civil servants, while resources are part of the government budget. The space for innovation, experimentation, so crucial for improving performance, are practically nil in such a set-up.

Four, except the AICTE Review Report, all others Reports clearly demonstrate the miniscule scale of the institutional set-up for vocational education and training in India, and the low level of in-service training provided.

Despite the different entry points of each of the Reports, a common theme that emerges is that vocational education/training/skill development has to be addressed forthwith, howsoever intractable the problem may seem to be. What our engagement with each of these reports, individually and collectively, seems to suggest is that evolving a framework to address the theme in all its complexity seems more intractable than the problem itself. A major reason for the growing frustration on this issue could also be the assumption with which almost all the Reports begin—that is, that the ability of the economy (then, as well as well as now) to generate quality employment is limited or nil. Any attempt at resolving this issue will necessarily have to begin by examining why the Indian economy cannot be made to generate quality employment for its citizens. The reason for emphasizing the need to frontally confront this development paradigm that is not geared towards formal employment generation is also to underscore the point that merely increasing the base of formally provided vocational education/training will not by itself serve the purpose of enabling larger numbers to participate in development processes. While broad-basing vocational education/training is necessary, for the cause of social justice to be sufficiently and effectively served, the material base also needs to be expanded simultaneously.

CHAPTER 10

Patriarchy and Class

A Study of Women's Education in the Madras Presidency

Introduction

The drive for a rapid development in the education of women came largely from a perception summed up aptly in the following statement by Arthur Mayhew: 'Women's education is the condition on which ultimately the success of male education depends—the fundamental basis of any real and permanent regeneration of Indian National Life'.[1] Following G. Paradise Kelly,[2] this chapter attempts at studying women's education by 'putting women at the centre of research' in an effort to bring out the manifest presence of patriarchal attitudes in the processes by which schools, through their location,

[*] Previously published as MIDS Working Paper no. 110, 1992.

[1] Arthur Mayhew and H.R. James, *Education and Politics in India*, New Delhi: Booklovers, 1986, p. 84.

[2] G. Paradise Kelly, 'Failures of Androcentric Studies of Women's Education in the Third World', in *For Alma Mater: Theory and Practice in Feminist Scholarship*, ed. Paul A. Treichler, Urbana and Chicago: University of Illinois Press, 1985, pp. 292–306.

curriculum, and structure, produced the kinds of asymmetrical outcomes that research on women's studies have thus far documented.

Chanana has highlighted the differential spread of women's education in India particularly in the early twentieth century—both interregional and intraregional—and argues among other things that these variations are embedded in a socio-cultural milieu.[3] We take off from the overview provided by Chanana and hope to initiate an in-depth study of women's education in the Madras Presidency with particular reference to the beginnings of higher education for women. The emphasis will be on the policies formulated to further formal education for women and the debates that these policies (or the lack of them) generated in the Presidency. It is our contention that the complex issues surrounding the educational process, including women's access to education, and educational outcomes are so steeped in the gender-linked social relationships through which women are defined, that a 'cultural constraint' theory forms only part of the explanation.

Theoretical Framework: An Outline

Placing women at the centre of research on education is imperative to address fundamental questions such as why women go to school (or fail to go), how education affects institutions that women do not control and which, in most instances, oppress women. The official approach to women's education in the Third World is premised on either denial or unquestioning acceptance

[3] Karuna Chanana, 'Social Change or Social Reform: The Education of Women in Pre-Independence India' in *Socialization Education and Women: Explorations in Gender Identity*, ed. Karuna Chanana, New Delhi: Orient Longman, 1988, pp. 96–128.

of patriarchy. Instead, the problem is posed as one of 'access' to education, assuming in the process that schools are neutral institutions that make no distinction between males and females. Solutions therefore consist in advocating the setting up of more schools, more trained school teachers, 'relevant' curricula, etc., without addressing the realities of women's lives—that women's participation in activities outside the domestic sphere is profoundly affected by marriage, childbearing and childrearing, and in ways very different from men's.[4]

An approach to a study of women's education by unravelling its *patriarchal* content will, in our opinion, go a long way in explaining why expansion in schooling facilities, in curriculum (to include scientific knowledge and technical skills), and in teachers' training, cannot fully account for the persistence of inequalities in educational opportunities between men and women. The dominant approach (as far as social science methodology is concerned) stresses the significance of the changes in gender relations with the rise of capitalism. Feminist scholarship has, however, put paid to such claims by documenting the subordinate status of women in the already industrialized nations of western Europe and North America; neither are critics of the capitalist system able to explain why sexual divisions/differences in education persist in socialist systems inspite of the abolition of private ownership of the means of production. Patriarchy, thus, has to be identified as distinct from capitalism and 'sometimes antagonistic to it'[5] in order to document the process through which relations of male domination are reproduced within education.

[4] Kelly, 'Failures of Androcentric Studies of Women's Education in the Third World', p. 195.

[5] For an elaboration see Mica Nava, 'Gender and Education: A Discussion of Two Recent Books', *Feminist Review*, vol. 5, 1980, pp. 69–78.

Following Sylvia Walby, we define patriarchy as a system of social structures and practices in which men dominate, oppress, and exploit women. 'The use of the term social structure is important here, since it clearly implies rejection both of biological determinism, and, the notion that every individual man is in a dominant position and every woman in a subordinate position.'[6] An historical account of women's education in the Indian context has also to contend with the phenomenon of colonialism. Among the characteristics that Gail Kelly and Philip Altbach isolate as essential to a colonial relationship, and especially to the colonial education process (which we find relevant to our discussion), are the following:[7]

(1) The colonized group is assumed to be intellectually, morally and physically inferior;
(2) The colonial educational system is controlled by the dominant group and is detached from the culture of the colonized and colonizer as well;
(3) The history of the colonized is either denied or reinterpreted in such a fashion that colonial education constitutes a fundamental assault on the identity of the colonized group;
(4) The substance of the colonial education is different from that given to the colonizer;
(5) A plausible outcome of the colonial situation is that the colonized began to identify with their oppressor, to assume the superiority of his values

[6] Sylvia Walby, *Theorizing Patriarchy*, UK: Basil Blackwell, 1990, p. 20.

[7] Quoted in Bonnie Cook Freeman, 'Female Education in Patriarchal Power Systems', in *Education and Colonialism*, ed. Philip G. Altback and Gail P. Kelly, New York: Longman Inc., 1978, pp. 208–9.

> and knowledge, to see themselves as weak and ignorant, and finally to depend on the colonizer for a definition of the situation, 'protection', and other resources.

A gendered account of the colonial education process (which is what we have attempted in the pages that follow) demonstrates that the characteristics listed above by Kelly and Altbach did not always have the *same* impact on male and female education. Patriarchal attitudes that formed the basis for the education policy in Britain were imported into India and found expression in various official/unofficial pronouncements. More important, in the course of time, educated Indian men in their official capacity endorsed and adapted these same pronouncements while concretizing policies relating to women's education. It follows therefore, that, as in the case of capitalism, 'patriarchy has to be differentiated from colonialism and treated as a distinct analytical category'. It also follows that 'patriarchy' is not a historical constant. Changes in the manifestations of patriarchy over time can be studied through changes in the *degrees* and *forms* of patriarchy.[8] Degrees of patriarchy refers to the intensity of oppression on a specified dimension—for instance, the differential service conditions imposed on women teachers, and the size of the wage gap between men and women teachers. Forms of patriarchy refers to the overall type of patriarchy as defined by the specific relations between different patriarchal structures. For instance, *private* and *public* are two forms of patriarchy: 'They differ on a variety of levels; firstly, in terms of the relations between the structures, and, secondly, in the institutional form of

[8] We have made use of Sylvia Walby's categories for our analysis. See Walby, *Theorizing Patriarchy*, p. 174.

each structure. Further, they are differentiated by the main form of patriarchal strategy exclusionary in private patriarchy and segregationist in public patriarchy.'[9] The expansion of women's education has brought women into the public sphere but not on equal terms. They are subordinated within the public sphere through, say, the 'inferior' quality of the education imparted to them, or the emphasis on a particular kind of 'socialization'[10] message included in the courses taught to them. The increase in the number of girls attending schools led to an increase in the demand for women teachers. However, the opening up of teaching as a profession for women indicated a 'shift from an exclusionary strategy to a segregationist one since it meant a movement from attempting to exclude women from paid work to accepting their presence but confining them to jobs which were segregated from and graded lower than those of men'.[11] In summary, therefore, while access to hitherto-barred public spheres in society may appear to constitute a reduction in the *degree* of patriarchy, such access has simultaneously provoked a change in the *form* of patriarchy.

It is important to introduce a caveat at this juncture. Our chapter deals with 'education' as conceived at the

[9] Ibid., p. 178.

[10] We have used the term 'socialization' in the sense in which Mangan has used it, namely that 'socialisation may be considered to be the total process by which the culture of a community, or section of a community, is passed on from one generation and assimilated, in whole or part, by the next.' Mangan concentrated essentially on the ideologies, processes and practices of formal education that shaped and were shaped by imperial values, attitudes, and behaviour in Britain and its empire. See J.A. Mangan, ed., 'Introduction', *Benefits Bestowed? Education and British Imperialism*, Manchester and New York: Manchester University Press, 1988, pp. 1–23.

[11] Walby, *Theorizing Patriarchy*, p. 179.

official level. The debates/discussions on various aspects of education and the educational process that took place at various levels (among women's groups, members of different communities, different political parties) do not find a place in this chapter. This 'official education,' however, became, as Krishna Kumar points out:

> a programme to train a small minority of property holders in the attitudes and skills of colonial rulers. Education enabled one to place oneself above the masses, intellectually and morally, and see oneself as a legitimate candidate for a share in the colonial state's power and the privileges that went with it. None of the skills, crafts, arts and knowledge that the illiterate masses possessed could impress the educated Indian, including teachers, as being worth learning. These forms of culture became symbols of ignorance and decadence and, as such, became irrelevant to education.[12]

For convenience of analysis the rest of the chapter is divided into four sections: Section I provides some idea of the efforts made by the Madras government to give an impetus to the development of women's education. This part of our discussion is based largely on a survey that was undertaken in the Madras Presidency (on the recommendation of a Conference of the Gazetted Women Officers of the Education Department held in August 1927 on the position of women's education), the results of which were embodied in a report published in 1929.[13] This section essentially highlights the manner in which the colonial government tackled the 'accessibility' question—drawing girls from the *private* to the *public*

[12] Krishna Kumar, *Political Agenda of Education: A Study of Colonialist and Nationalist Ideas*, New Delhi: Sage, 1991, p. 15.

[13] Report on the Development of Women's Education submitted by the Director of Public Instruction, Educational G.O. no. 578, 23 March 1929.

sphere. Apart from indicating the differential accessibility levels between boys and girls, it also brings out the differential impact the government's efforts had on the various communities, with particular reference to the girls within these communities.

Section II deals with two aspects: the training of teachers and the entry of women into the educational field in an administrative capacity. The deliberations surrounding these issues bring out clearly what in feminist terminology has come to be termed as the *feminization* of the teaching profession, particularly at lower levels. More importantly, this section concretely highlights what we had outlined earlier, namely the fact that the movement from the private to the public sphere really meant a movement from an *exclusionary* to a *segregationist* strategy. While Section I points to the change in the form of patriarchy from private to public, Section II highlights the degree and therefore the intensity of patriarchy.

The debates/discussions centring around government involvement in promoting higher education for women and the issue of what should constitute the 'appropriate' content of courses for females to pursue, forms the subject matter of Section III. Here, the question is not merely one of colonialism and patriarchy but also that of *class*, with express emphasis being laid on promoting a curriculum suited to middle-class interests.

In Section IV we bring together various issues thrown up by our chapter and also outline the future course of our study on this subject.

An Overview: British India

In 1915, a memorial on the subject of the education of girls in India was presented to the Secretary of State. The memorial emphasized points which had long caused anxiety to the GOI—the insignificant number of girls under instruction, the disparity in this respect of the condition of the male and female portions of the population, and, '*the consequent danger to the social well-being of the Indian community*'[14] (emphasis added).

One cannot, however, dismiss the progress made in girls' education since 1882 (when the Indian Education Commission came out with its Report) as negligible.[15] The total number of girls at school in British India at the time of the Education Commission was 1,27,000. In 1915–16 it was 11,86,000 and in 1917–18 it was 12,64,000. In 1882 again the proportion of boys to girls under instruction was 1:20. In 1917–18 it was 1:5.3. However, turning to figures indicating girls at different grades of education it was found that more than nine-tenths of the girls under instruction were in the primary stage while something less than 2 per cent were in the secondary stage. As far as collegiate education was concerned, the number of girls studying in Arts College in 1917–18 was 914. The Calcutta University Commission in its Report[16] had declared that the intermediate classes did not properly form a part of collegiate or university education. If this proposition was accepted, then the number of girls who were doing real university work was infinitesimal. In the three colleges in Calcutta the commission found that there were only 543 students attempting such work. The GOI, however,

[14] A gist of the memorial has been reproduced in Home (Education) G.O. no. 1334, 31 October 1919 (Press).

[15] The figures on female education that follow have been taken from the *Resolution of the Government of India on Female Education*, Home (Education) G.O. no. 1334, 31 October 1919 (Press).

[16] Some views of the Commission have been reproduced in the *Resolution* cited in ibid.

were 'impressed' with the success of the two women's colleges in Madras.[17]

Madras Presidency

It must be emphasized at the outset that literacy as such among the total population of the Presidency was very poor and this was repeatedly brought to the notice of the government. But compared to other provinces in British India, the achievement of the Madras government in the field of girls' education was way ahead and was even commended in the Report of the Progress of Education in India, 1927–32.[18] Statistics relating to (a) enrolment of girls in all institutions, (b) expenditure by the government on girls' education, (c) the proportion of trained to untrained teachers, (d) the enrolment in co-educational institutions, and (e) the number of government-run institutions, point to a clear lead by Madras on all counts. However, data also reveal that, inspite of highest enrolment, the rate of retention at the primary level was very low in the Madras Presidency.[19] Further, the most prominent and disquieting feature in the development of education was the great disparity that existed between boys and girls and the rapid increase in this disparity during the quinquennium 1922–7 just before the survey[20] was undertaken. Table 10.1 gives details of this disparity.

[17] Ibid.

[18] Government of India, *Progress of Education in India*, Quinquennial Review, vols. 1–2, Delhi: Manager of Publications, 1927–32. Also quoted in Chanana, *Socialization Education and Women*, 1988.

[19] Chanana, 'Social Change or Social Reform', p. 108.

[20] Findings of the survey contained in the Report on the Development of Women's Education submitted by the Director of Public Instruction, Educational G.O. no. 578, 23 March 1929.

Table 10.1: Disparity in Education: Sex-wise

	1912	*1917*	*1922*	*1927*
Percentage of males at school	5.1	6.5	7.0	9.5
Percentage of females at school	1.0	1.5	1.8	2.5
Disparity	4.1	5.0	5.2	7.0

Source: Education, G.O. no. 578, 23 March 1929.

The percentage increase in disparity between 1912 and 1917 was 0.9, between 1917 and 1922 it was 0.2, but between 1922 and 1927 it was 1.8, practically double that of the two preceding quinquenniums. By the government's own admission, the marked increase in disparity between 1922 and 1927 was due to a special effort made during the period to accelerate the extension of elementary education among boys by opening an elementary school for boys in each schoolless centre with a population of 500 or above, with the aid of provincial subsidy. For girls, contrary to the policy in the preceding quinquennium ending 31 March 1922, no provincial subsidies were granted for opening new elementary schools. Further, by handing over control of the then existing government elementary schools for girls in 1922 to local bodies, no provincial funds were expended on developing these schools and the expansion of elementary education was thus left entirely to the initiative of local bodies and aided agencies.[21]

The disparity between the stages of development in girls and boys education in the various grades of education can be seen from Table 10.2.

[21] Ibid.

Table 10.2: Sex-wise Disparity in the Various Grades of Education

Year	*Pupils in Arts Colleges*			*Pupils in Secondary Schools*			*Pupils in Elementary Schools*		
	Men	*Women*	*Proportion of Men to Women*	*Boys*	*Girls*	*Proportion of Boys to Girls*	*Boys*	*Girls*	*Proportion of Boys to Girls*
1926–7	11,770	448	24:1	164,776	19,896	8:1	1,714,501	501,206	3:1
1921–2	7,843	384	20:1	153,466	16,471	9:1	1,199,300	347,285	3:1
1916–17	7,540	184	41:1	138,260	11,632	12:1	1,071,636	293,185	4:1
1911–12	4,893	46	106:1	101,890	8,446	12:1	829,331	199,719	4:1

Source: Education, G.O. no. 578, 23 March 1929.

Date pertaining to sex-wise distribution of population attending school in each district in the Presidency revealed that:

(i) In general, the districts which were the most advanced in boys' education were also the most advanced in girls' education, that those which were backward in one were also backward in the other, and that, on the whole, the disparity between the two types of education was greatest in the more advanced areas and less in the more backward;

(ii) That the order of advancement of the four leading districts was the same for boys and girls, but the disparity between boys and girls' education was greater in the two most advanced than in the other districts of the Presidency.[22]

Disparity in facilities provided, and therefore in access to education for the two sexes, was seen clearly in the figures provided by the government. In Madras city, for instance, where disparity in elementary education was comparatively small and girls' education was well advanced, there was one elementary school for every 139 boys of school-going age while there was only one elementary school for every 423 girls of school-going age. The authorities acknowledged that during the quinquennium ending 1921–2, attention was concentrated on the development of boys' education, which in the more advanced and receptive areas did have a positive effect on public opinion. While the need for a similar concentration on girls' education was considered necessary (but never materialized), it was also realized

[22] Ibid.

that the complete withdrawal of the government from responsibility in the matter of elementary education for girls was not desirable and that the contribution of provincial subsidies towards the provision and development of elementary schools for girls should have formed an integral part of a sound educational policy.[23]

Again, it was stressed that if progress was to be achieved in the dispersion of education, no scheme for the introduction of compulsory education into any area was to be approved unless it provided for the introduction of compulsion for boys and girls simultaneously; further, it was pointed out that while compulsion would take a longer time to be really effective in the case of girls, nevertheless, the result of omitting them altogether would mean complete cessation of development, or at least a retardation in the development of girls' education in the area into which compulsion for boys alone was introduced.

An examination of the figures showing the percentage of male and female populations under instruction in the various communities showed clearly the exceptional backwardness of Hindu girls in relation both to Hindu boys and to girls of other communities, and also the relatively satisfactory position of Muslim girls when compared to Muslim boys.[24] The percentage of the male Christian population at school was nearly double the percentage of the female Christian population at school; it was exactly double in the case of Muslims but in the case of Hindus it was four times as great (Table 10.3).

Table 10.4 illustrates the ratio of boys to girls in each grade of institution for the various communities.

[23] Ibid.

[24] What follows has been summarized from the survey report contained in Educational G.O. no. 578, 23 March 1929.

Table 10.3: Population under Instruction: Community-wise and Sex-wise

Community	*Census Figures of 1921*		*Figures for 31st March 1927 from the Quinquennial Report for 1922-27*			
	Male Population	*Female Population*	*Males at School*	*Females at School*	*% of Male Population at School*	*% of Female Population at School*
Europeans including Anglo-Indians	674,047	687,437	121,700	72443	18	10
Hindus	18,777,933	19,311,477	1,550,778	388,520	8	2
Muslims	1,404,000	1,436,488	86,727	54,781	6	4
Others	14,769	12,834	34,318	6,554	11	2
Total	20,870,749	21,448,236	1,793,523	522,298		

Source: Education, G.O. no. 578, 23 March 1929.

Table 10.4: Proportion of Scholars (Sex-wise and Community-wise) under instruction in Public Institutions in Several Grades on 31 March 1927 (Agency Schools being Omitted)

Community	*Boys*	*Girls*	*Proportion of Boys to Girls*
University			
European (including Anglo-Indians)	49	74	7:1
Indian Christian	1,150	289	4:1
Brahman	8,054	87	92:1
Non-brahmans	4,473	130	34:1
Depressed classes	45	2	22:1
Muhammadan	462	4	115:1
Others	13	2	6:1
Total	11,426	588	24:1
Secondary			
European (including Anglo-Indians)	3911	3,873	1:1
Indian Christian	15,192	7,586	2:1
Brahman	51,775	2,466	21:1
Non-brahman	81,079	5,133	16:1
Depressed classes	2,395	252	9:1
Muhammadan	9,656	335	29:1
Others	768	251	3:1
Total	164,776	19,896	8:1
Elementary			
European (including Anglo-Indian)	865	875	1:1
Indian Christian	100533	59,736	1.6:1
Brahman	80871	55,849	1.5:1
Non-brahman	1135457	286,159	4:1
Depressed classes	186629	38,244	5:1
Muhammadan	176609	54,442	5:1
Others	33537	5,901	6:1
Total	1711501	501,206	3:1

(Table 10.4 continued)

(Table 10.4 continued)

Community	*Boys*	*Girls*	*Proportion of Boys to Girls*
University + Secondary + Elementary			
European (including Anglo-Indian)	4825	4,822	5:5
Indian Christian	1021675	67,611	5:3.5
Brahman	140700	58,402	5:2
Non-brahman	1221009	291,442	5:1.2/7
Depressed Classes	189069	38,498	5:1
Muhammadans	86727	5,4781	5:2.5

Source: Education, G.O. no. 578, 23 March 1929.

In the European and Anglo-Indian community the total number of boys undergoing university education were two-thirds of the girls, but in the secondary and elementary stages the number of boy and girl pupils at schools were approximately the same.

In the Indian Christian community, the ratio of boys to girls gradually increased in the higher stages of education but showed less disparity at practically every stage than in any other section of the community.

Among brahman girls who were relatively more backward compared to brahman boys than Muslim girls were to Muslim boys, 97 per cent were to be found in elementary schools. Among non-brahman girls the proportion of boys to girls reading in secondary schools and universities was still lower, although the education of non-Brahman girls as a whole was much farther behind that of non-brahman boys than was the case between the boys and girls of any community other than the depressed classes.

The accepted policy in the Madras Presidency was the introduction of free compulsory education for all non-Muslim boys between the ages of 6 and 11, for

Muslim boys between the ages of 8 and 13, and for all girls between the ages of 5 and 10. Certain exceptions had, however, been made in practice, Muslim girls being excluded from all schemes for the introduction of compulsion. This meant that the introduction of compulsory education for girls was permissible but was not yet regarded as fundamental either by the government or by any organization responsible for the development of education in the Presidency. The Corporation of Madras and the Municipal Councils of Erode and Cochin were the only exceptions to this as they had recognized the needs of girls as far as non-Muslim pupils were concerned. But the needs of girls who came forward voluntarily were neglected even in areas where compulsion was introduced. For example, the Corporation of Madras, which had excluded Muslims from the operation of the scheme of compulsory education, failed to make proper provision for Muslim girls who came forward in such large numbers for education that it was not possible to provide for them in the then existing schools in which Urdu was the medium of instruction.[25]

The exclusion of girls from practically all schemes for the introduction of compulsory education, it was recognized, was one of the reasons for the great increase in disaparity between the development of education for boys and girls during the quinquennium 1922–7. It was also realized, the gendered perspective notwithstanding, that

> if the total exclusion of Muslim girls is continued there is no doubt that this community will fall rapidly behind all others in the matter of education for boys and girls, since it is impossible to bring *boys* of uneducated parents to the same standard of

[25] Ibid.

education as *boys* who come from homes in which the women as well as the men are educated (emphasis added).[26]

The class and gender bias of the members comprising the Conference of the Gazetted Women Officers of the Education Department is clear from the following statement recorded by them while deliberating on the findings of the survey on female education:

> Generally speaking, secondary education is intended for the wealthier classes who can afford to pay for it and a good elementary education free or at a low cost should be provided for girls who cannot afford to pay the fees of secondary schools. On the other hand, there are a considerable number of girls who would profit by secondary education but who are prevented from doing so by actual or relative poverty . . . It is *inevitable* in such cases, *even if the parents are not actually poverty-stricken* that the money available must first be spent in equipping the boys who are to be wage earners and that in many cases the girls must do without secondary education. (emphasis added)[27]

Teachers and Administrators

The subtle manner in which colonial (gendered) perspectives on education were transplanted into the colony is amply demonstrated by the argument that, keeping with the trend elsewhere in the world (meaning largely England) 'it will be necessary in the first place to replace all men teachers of the lower classes by women

[26] Ibid.

[27] The views and recommendations of the Conference of the Gazetted Women Officers of the Department have been reproduced in Educational G.O. no. 578, 23 March 1929.

and subsequently to combine these classes with similar classes in schools for girls and thus to institute mixed primary classes'.[28] Jo Anne Preston, in her article on school-teaching in nineteenth-century New England, has examined the way in which state school officials actively promoted the feminization of teaching by writing extensively about women's 'aptness' to teach because of certain 'natural' feminine qualities.[29] Similar views were echoed by the officials in Madras:

> So far in the Madras Presidency it has been customary to staff all schools for boys with men teachers from the first class upward. In all countries it has been found that women are more efficient than men as teachers of very young children and there is no doubt that this is true of Indian women also. Ideally children of both sexes should be taught together below the age of nine in schools staffed entirely by women teachers and inspected by women officers who have received special training in methods of educating young children.[30]

A different dimension was added by Mayhew to this aspect of the feminization of teaching when he argued that: 'It has been shown that the absence of women teachers for the lower classes of boys' schools increase the financial burden of mass education.'[31] This is not to deny that very genuine cultural problems existed which needed solutions of a particular kind. But the issue of patriarchy (manifested here in the feminization of the teaching profession,

[28] Ibid.

[29] Jo Anne Preston, 'Female Aspiration and Male Ideology: School-teaching in Nineteenth Century New England', in *Current Issues in Women's History*, ed. Arima Angerman, London: Routledge, 1989, pp. 171–82.

[30] Educational G.O. no. 578, 23 March 1929.

[31] Mayhew and James, *Education and Politics in India*, p. 223.

especially at the lower level) and the lack of girl's schools/ women teachers to cater to girl students belonging to particular communities need to be segregated from the analysis of gender discrimination in education.

Among men teachers, on 31 March 1927, there were approximately 13,000 of the higher elementary grade and 26,000 of the lower, that is, in the proportion of 1:2. Among women, the corresponding figures were 4,000 and 2,000, the proportion being the reverse that for men. This was considered 'satisfactory' by the authorities. The provision for training Christian women teachers was fairly adequate. In contrast, the supply of Hindu and Muslim women teachers were grossly inadequate. Hindu and Muslim women, unlike Christians, it was recorded, were accustomed to study only in local day schools; if these were not available they did not come forward for education, nor did they travel far to seek for training, and unless facilities for training existed within easy reach of their homes they did not take up teaching.[32]

The location of Mission Training Schools, as in the case of Mission Secondary Schools, usually prevented the attendance of Hindu women at them as day scholars. This phenomenon was illustrated by the number of Hindu and Christian teachers in training schools as on 31 March 1927. In Mission Training Schools, there were 860 Christian students and 17 Hindus, while in the Government Traning Schools the numbers were 407 and 457, respectively. The Muslim students, of whom there were 80, were entirely confined to government schools. Mission agencies were unable to provide for Hindu and Muslim women, and there were few, if any, non-mission aided agencies who were likely to assist in the development

[32] Educational G.O. no. 578, 23 March 1929.

of training institutions. It was clear to the authorities that if the number of trained Hindu and Muslim teachers were to be increased, the necessary training schools had to be maintained by the government.[33] While data revealed that the districts in which the public had been prepared to accept co-education were the ones which had seen the most advance in girls' education, the Conference of Women Officers, in their discussion on the possibility and desirability of developing co-education in the Madras Presidency, resolved that pupils below the age of 8 '*should* be taught together by women teachers'; as regards pupils above this age they reached the following conclusion:

> that co-education was not objected to by the backward classes or by the educationally advanced but there was a strong feeling against it in the middle classes and that, *as it was amongst this class that most rapid progress could be made at present*, co-education on any considerable scale could not be introduced effectively now (emphasis added).[34]

It was seen that the progress of elementary education for girls did not vary directly with the provision made for training women teachers. However, based on the fact that, of the ten districts in which there were no elementary training classes for girls in the local vernacular, eight were found in the thirteen most backward districts, it was clear that the progress in the provision of good supply of trained women teachers was one of the factors which controlled the development of elementary education for girls.[35]

While it was felt that good progress could be made if suitable men teachers were appointed, in general,

[33] Ibid.
[34] Ibid.
[35] Ibid.

however, it was asserted that the appointment of women teachers in a girls' school was essential if the duration of the school life of girl pupils was to be lengthened sufficiently to ensure that the pupils would be permanently literate on leaving school. The plea always given by local bodies when pressed for additional girls' schools, more teachers, or better pay for women teachers was absence of finances. But an examination of the distribution of money, however, pointed to the conclusion that, if a more systematic procedure were adopted for the provision of educational facilities for both boys and girls in the area under the control of each local board, much more adequate and equitable provision could be made for pupils of both sexes for the same amount expended. Another disability with regard to girls' elementary education was the smaller contribution made by aided agencies in the spread of education for girls.[36]

In the case of higher education, there existed a dearth of women teachers for science and medicine. Whereas there were five colleges for women in the Presidency and two in Travancore, of which three were on the west coast, the first grade colleges for women in which science courses were provided were in Madras city. 'It was generally agreed that only comparatively wealthy girls could afford to take their university courses in Madras and that the poorer students of the West Coast had no alternative but to take History, English or Philosophy since these were the only courses provided on the West Coast (emphasis added).'[37]

The Director of Public Instruction, in his letter to the Secretary to Government, Educational Department, Madras, recorded that the Inspectresses of Girls' Schools

[36] Ibid.

[37] Ibid.

had brought to his notice the demand for a larger provision of secondary education for girls in institutions under entirely unsectarian management.[38] Admirable though the mission schools were from most points of view, there seemed no room for doubt that high-caste Hindu parents hesitated to send their girls to these schools and that there was consequently need for increasing the number of government secondary schools for girls. The Director also noted the need for shifting the Presidency Training School for Mistresses from Egmore to Triplicane (the brahman-dominated residential suburb) so that there was an increase in the number of high-caste women taking up the teaching profession.

> It is an established fact (?) that we must look to the *class of widows for our chief supply of caste women teachers*, and, that, unless the supply can be steadily increased little progress can be made with the higher education of caste girls, since the only alternative, the employment of Indian Christian women is repugnant to popular feeling (emphasis added).[39]

Women in the Educational Field in an Administrative Capacity

Women's entry into the educational profession as teachers, principles, inspectresses, etc., and the service rules that governed them was/is another aspect that clearly revealed the existence of two sets of norms. On the one hand, the new social and political commitment to equality of educational opportunities to women did not by the same token lead to the questioning of old beliefs

[38] Letter from Sir Alfred Bourne, DPI Madras, to the Secretary to Government, Educational Department, dated 5 March 1913, Educational G.O. no. 586, 21 June 1913 (Press).

[39] Ibid.

asserting the rightness of inequality and the rightness of a distinction between men and women in their capacities and proper roles. The deliberations surrounding the subject of the reorganization of women's educational service illustrate, among other things, how assumptions about women's nature set up stumbling blocks for the advancement of women in the educational profession.

In 1917, when the GOI adressed local governments on the subject of the reorganization of educational service based on the recommendations of the Public Service Commission, they made it clear that the commission's recommendations for women would not be taken up along with men.[40] It was only *after* proposals in respect of men's educational service had been submitted to the Secretary of State that the GOI took up the question of the reorganization of the women's educational service for which they solicited the views of the provincial governments on various points.[41]

A loaded memorandum prepared by the Acting Director of Public Instruction, Madras, on the subject of women engaged in the educational services brings out subtly not only what Altback and Kelly refer to as 'the educational manifestations of colonialism' but also, more significantly, a gendered approach to what was otherwise supposed to further the cause of women in the educational profession.[42] The memorandum begins

[40] Home (Education) G.O. no. 950, 17 July 1918.

[41] Notes connected with Home (Education) G.O. nos. 1349–50, 1 November 1919.

[42] See P.G. Altbach and G.P. Kelly, eds., 'Introduction', *Education and Colonialism*, New York: Longman Inc, 1978, pp. 1–49; Note by R. Littlehailes, Acg DPI, on 'Women Engaged in the Educational Services under the Government of Madras', Notes connected with Education G.O. no. 504, 9 May 1916 (Mis).

with the unqualified premise that, notwithstanding the strides that had been made in the advancement of female education, yet the large majority of the people of India were opposed to female education, while an extremely small minority were in favour of advanced female education. In fact, the social customs of India obstructed any proposals for an advance in the higher branches of instruction among women, which was so essential to produce locally efficient teachers and a suitable female inspecting staff.[43]

The fact that male members in the educational profession in England were uniformly paid more than women was taken as sufficient justification for paying Indian women teachers less than their male counterparts. Giving details of wages, the acting DPI pointed out.

a) That the pay of an Inspector in Madras was Rs.500–1000 while that of an Inspectress was Rs.400–600.
b) That, in India, Madras stood first in the actual number of women engaged in inspecting work, but the city had an absolute as well as a relatively larger number of low-paid appointments (Rs.200 or less per mensem) than any other province in India.
c) Turning to salaries in secondary and training schools in India, it was observed that Madras had 32 appointments reaching to Rs.100 per month or over, Bengal 23, Bombay 22 and the other provinces and Native States even less. Madras thus appeared to be far ahead of the other parts of India in the number of higher-paid appointments in secondary and special education.

[43] Note by R. Littlehailes, Acg DPI, on 'Women Engaged in the Educational Services under the Government of Madras'.

d) A perusal of the statement showing the salaries then being paid to women teachers in elementary schools in India indicated that in Bombay the maximum pay was Rs.70, in Madras Rs.65, and in Bengal Rs.50 p.m., while the majority had pay about Rs.10 to Rs.12 per mensem.[44]

In England, the 'natural maternal' instinct argument led to the feminization of the teaching profession, which was especially marked in elementary education.[45] This in turn led to the elementary teacher being considered of a lower social status than the teacher in, say, a secondary school, and, this factor legitimized the payment of a lower salary to the elementary school teacher. But the relative disparity in pay of elementary school women teacher in England and in India was so great that the acting DPI was constrained to note that the question of the appointment of European-trained teachers to elementary schools in India was, for financial reasons, outside the range of practical politics.[46]

Even if we could persuade them to come, we should be doing our country women an injustice if we brought them out to this country on a salary less than that which would permit them to live as gentlewomen, and this country (that is, India) cannot afford Rs.350 per mensem for its elementary school teachers.[47]

The assumption and presumptions regarding Indian social customs and the modes of life among the different

[44] Ibid.

[45] Refer to Preston, 'Female Aspiration and Sale Ideology', and Alison Oram, 'Embittered, Sexless or Homosexual': Attacks on Spinster Teachers, 1918–39', in *Current Issues in Women's History*, ed. Arima Angerman, London: Routledge, 1989.

[46] Notes connected with Educational G.O. no. 504, 9 May 1916.

[47] Ibid.

communities led to definitive statements justifying payment of different salaries to women members of different communities; however, all women teachers, irrespective of the community to which they belonged, were paid less than men doing similar work.[48] The DPI observed thus:

It is desirable that no women teacher receive a salary less than Rs.12 per mensem, but so long as Indian thought continues (?) unchanged with regard to the relative positions in the social life of men and women, and, so long *as questions of economy remain of prime importance*, just so long will it be impossible to raise the minimum pay of a woman in this country above that of a man who does similar work, even though such course were considered—a doubtful assumption—desirable on a survey of the relative needs of the normal life of men and of women' (emphasis added)[49]

It was assumed that the mode of life of a Eurasian demanded a higher wage than that required by the Hindu, but it was argued that it was not possible to fix the salaries of teachers in elementary schools at a figure that would attract the Anglo-Indian: 'Such a salary would suffice for the employment of several Hindu women teachers if such were only available'.[50]

For the establishment of the Queen Mary's College the Madras government requested the GOI to sanction two Indian Educational Service lady professors.[51] Of the two ladies, the senior was to be the Principal, and the

[48] Ibid.

[49] Ibid.

[50] Ibid.

[51] Letter no. 615, Ootacamund, 27 May 1914 from the Acg Secretary to the Govt. of Madras to the Secretary to the Government of India, Dept. of Education, Education, Progs., nos. 117–27, December 1914, National Archives of India.

salaries recommended were 500-25-750 and 400-20-500, without exchange compensation allowance. The lower rate (400-20-500) was the *usual amount* paid to Indian Educational Service inspectresses.[52] The GOI in its recommendation pointed out that while the payment of nil exchange compensation allowance *was in accordance with* the government's reorganization proposal, the classification of the two recruits under the Indian Educational Service would create a piquant situation. Inclusion in the service could not be accompanied by a deprivation of a concession that was admissible to all other members of the service. To get over the problem, the course suggested by the government was to place the ladies recruited *outside the regular cadres* so as to make them inelligible for the exchange compensation allowance.[53] It was only after the college was placed on a permanent footing that the posts were included in the service. And yet, while inclusion in the service standardized women's services it did not give them equal remuneration vis-à-vis their male counterparts.

The Public Services Commission had recommended, that, as in the case of the service for men, there would be a women's educational service to comprise Class I, Class II and special appointments, and also a subordinate service. Class I was to comprise, on the *collegiate* side, principals of all arts colleges, principals of professional colleges (excepting law and medicine), professors of all first-grade arts and professional colleges, and the headmaster of the Central High School, Mercara. On the

[52] Ibid.

[53] Letter no. 416 from the Finance Dept. of the Govt. of India, addressed to the Secretary of State for India, dated 11 December 1914, Education, Progs., nos. 117–27, December 1914, National Archies of India.

administrative side, Inspectors of Schools, and the then existing appointments of Deputy Director and Personal Assistant to the Director of Public Instruction were to be included. *Class II* was to include on the *collegiate* side all lecturers, assistant professors and assistant lecturers in all arts and teachers' colleges, and on the *administrative* side, Assistant Inspectors and other officers of equivalent rank.[54] For all the posts, as far as pay was concerned, the proposals submitted by the DPI, Madras, was lower than those recommended by the GOI; in fact, the DPI felt that the GOI proposals were *more than what was necessary to secure suitable recruits in the South of India* (emphasis added).[55]

Table 10.5 gives a comparative statement of the scale of pay recommended for male members of Class I and that suggested by the government for women. Tables 10.6 and 10.7 give rates of salary for Class I and II women recruits, indicating the then existing scale of pay and those recommended by the various bodies, central and local.

The lesser scales of pay recommended for women was sought to be argued away simply by stating that 'as it is the practice everywhere to pay women with similar qualifications at lower rates than men, the Governor-General in Council accepts the (discriminatory) rates of pay as suitable'.[56] Much was made of the 'climate of the

[54] Note from the Govt. of India, Dept. of Education, dated 19 August 1919, no. 887, Home (Education) G.O. nos. 1349–50, 1 November 1919 (Press).

[55] Note by the DPI dated 8 September 1919, Home (Education) G.O. nos. 1349–50, 1 November 1919 (Press).

[56] See for example the letter (no. 1350) from the Secretary to the Government of Madras to the Secretary to the Govt. of India dated 1 November 1919, Home (Education) G.O. no. 1349–50, 1 November 1919 (Press).

Table 10.5: Recommendation of Differential Pay Scales for Men and Women Teachers

Class I		
Service for Men	*Scale Finally Recommended*	*Service for Women*
Scale recommended by the Government of Madras	By India to the Secretary of State for Men's Service	Scale suggested by the Govt of India
a) Rs.400-50-1,250 per mensem. Selection grade up to 15 per cent of the cadre Rs.1,300-50-1,600 per mensem.	Rs.550-30-1550 Selection up to 15 per cent 1,500-50-1,750.	Rs.400-25-850 per mensem
b) Special compensatory allowance of one-third of the pay of Europeans and to Indians recruited in Europe subject to a maximum of Rs.2,000 per mensem.	To be allowed to all officers with European qualifications irrespective of place of recruitment. Allowance of Rs.150 to Principals and one allowance of Rs.250 to a selected Principal	Selection grade up to 20 per cent of the cadre Rs.900-50-1,100 per mensem.

Source: Home Department (Education) G.O. no. 1349–50, 1 November 1919 (Press).

plains' being 'more trying to a woman's constitution than to a man's' and hence the Governor-General in Council recommended that women officers were to be given more generous terms as far as leave facilities were concerned.[57] Again, it was stated that since 'women inspecting officers in the Presidency are put to much inconvenience and have to incur also heavy expense when on tour for want of

[57] Ibid.

Table 10.6: Salary Scales for Class I Women Members as Recommended by Various Bodies

Rates of pay allowed to the lady members of the Indian Educational Service 1	*Rates recommended by the Public Services Commission* 2	*Rates proposed by the Government of India* 3	*Rates suggested by the Director of Public Instruction, Madras* 4	*Rates suggested by Home (Education) Madras* 5
One Principal (400-20-500-25-750) plus local allowance Rs.200	First five years-400-20-500 Thereafter 500-25-600 (no reference to the payment of any allowance to the Principal or other officer).	Ordinary grade 400-25-800 Selection grade for 20 per cent of the number of posts – 900-10-1000 (no reference to the payment of any allowance to the Principal or other officer).	400-20-500-25-750 with a duty allowance of Rs.150 for any officer who has been for five years on the maximum and an allowance to the Principal of a College and to the Senior Inspectress (amount not stated).	Same as in column (3) plus a local allowance of Rs.150 to the Principal of the College only
One Professor (400-20-500-25-750),				

(Table 10.6 continued)

(*Table 10.6 continued*)

Rates of pay allowed to the lady members of the Indian Educational Service	*Rates recommended by the Public Services Commission*	*Rates proposed by the Government of India*	*Rates suggested by the Director of Public Instruction, Madras*	*Rates suggested by Home (Education) Madras*
1	2	3	4	*5*
One Professor (400)				
One Inspector (500-20-600)				
One Inspector (450-10-500)				
One Inspector (400-10-450)				
One Superintendent, Egmore Training School (350-10-450)				

Source: Home Department (Education) G.O. no. 1349–50, 1 November 1919 (Press).

proper conveyances and properly furnished rest houses at the places they visit', they were to be compensated to some extent by the grant of a higher rate of travelling allowance than was then admissible.[58]

The discussions on the conditions for payment of pension to women was another terrain where the enmeshing of colonial and gender perspectives was clearly discernible. As early as 1908, in a letter forwarded to the GOI, the DPI, Madras, requested modification of the pension rules as applicable to Indian women.[59] The argument ran something like this:

> Under article 358(a) of the Civil Service Regulations (4th edition), an officer's services does not in the case of superior service qualify for pension till he has completed twenty years of age. *Indian women, especially in this Presidency, are, by their nature and climatic influence,* fitted to commence service qualifying for superior pension much earlier than at the age fixed in the regulations. Moreover under article 114 of the Madras Educational Rules, native women teachers become eligible to be trained for teaching work at the age of 14, so that, they are in a position to enter government service when 15 or 16 years old; *but they are unfit as a rule for efficient work after their 50th year*. In these circumstances I request you to be so good as to obtain the sanction of the Government of India to the following additions being made to article 358(a) referred to above:
>
> 'but in the case of *non-European women teachers* in Madras, service qualifying for pension on the superior scale commences after an officer has completed sixteen years of age' (emphasis added).[60]

[58] Ibid. See also the discussion among the officials on the subject recorded in Notes to Home (Education) G.O. no. 1349–50, 1 November 1919 (Press).

[59] Educational G.O. no. 723, 21 October 1908 (Press).

[60] Ibid.

In her evidence before the Public Service Commission Mrs. Drysdale, Chief Inspectress of girls' schools, echoed similar views. She stated that inspectresses should receive a pension after twenty years' service *as that was quite long enough for a woman to work in India*.[61] The GOI also proposed that women were to be permitted to retire after twenty years service on proportionate pension reckoned in the usual way subject to a maximum of Rs.4,000 but that they should not be allowed any increase beyond the maximum of Rs.5,000 then permissible after twenty-five years' service, since '*service beyond that period is not to be encouraged in the case of women*' (emphasis added).[62]

The Beginnings of Higher Education for Women: Government Initiatives

The 'desirability for a separate non-sectarian college for women'[63] formed the basis for the setting up of the first government college for women. In the deliberations surrounding this proposal we highlight the manner in which the missionaries objected to any form of government intervention in the field of education. The government, thus, had to grapple, at one level, with a dominant body with powerful backing in England; at another level, it had to adapt its policies to the dominant viewpoint among the colonized.

At the budget meetings of 1911 and 1912, Rao Bahadur T.S. Balakrishna Ayyar urged the government

[61] See note under 'Conditions of Pension', Notes to Home (Education) G.O. no. 1349–50, 1 November 1919 (Press).

[62] Ibid.

[63] Note from the DPI dated 20 November 1913, ROC no. 9323, Educational G.O. no. 125, 29 January 1914 (Press).

Table 10.7: Salary Scales for Class II Women Members as Recommended by Various Bodies

As recommended by the Public Services Commission	*The scale which the Government of India proposed to recommend*	*As recommended by the Director of Public Instruction*	*As proposed by the Department*
Rs.200-10-400	Rs.200-500 (details to be fixed by the local government)	The Director of Public instruction did not advocate the formation of a definite class II service. For the posts which could be considered as equivalent to those which India contemplated placing in class II, he proposed rates of salary varying from Rs.125 to Rs.250 exclusive of allowance to heads of secondary and training schools.	Scale suggested by Government of India together with a selection grade for 20 perc ent of the officers with an ultimate maximum of Rs.750. Further details were to be worked out.

Source: Home Department (Education) G.O. no. 1349–50, 1 November 1919 (Press).

to consider the desirability of establishing a college solely intended for women in the Presidency.[64] The then existing institutions for collegiate instruction of non-European women were the Sarah Tucker College, Palamcottah, and the United Free Church Mission College, Royapuram, both of which were of the second grade, the latter being unaffiliated to the university. As on 31 March 1912, the former institution had eight pupils on its rolls and the latter seven. With the exception of only one, all the students belonged to the Indian Christian community. Besides, there were thirty women students reading in the arts colleges for men. Nineteen of them were in the institutions in Madras, the rest in the mufassal colleges. It was not known from what communities these students were drawn. But according to the DPI, not many would have been drawn from the Hindu community.[65]

The intention of the government to open a separate college for women brought forth protests from the Missionary Educational Council of South India whose spokesperson, Sir Andrew Fraser, Chairman of the Interdenominational Committee on Education in the Mission Field, in his letter to Lord Pentland, Governor of Madras, made it clear that, 'It is better to have the arrangements for women's colleges made by private agency.'[66] He apprised the Governor about the decision arrived at during the World Missionary Conference

[64] See Notes connected with Educational G.O. no. 125, 29 January 1914 (Press).

[65] Details taken from Public Instruction Report for 1911–12, vols. I–II, also quoted in Educational G.O. no. 125, 29 January 1914 (Press).

[66] Demi-official from Sir Andrew Fraser to Lord Pentland, Governor of Madras, dated 5 March 1914, See notes connected with Educational G.O. nos. 614–15, 27 May 1914 (Press).

to establish a Christian Arts College at Madras with a special training department. Fraser also hinted that Miss McDougall, a recognized and trained teacher from London, would be its first Principal.[67]

Miss McDougall and Miss E. Roberts (another trained teacher from London) had travelled in India in the winter of 1912–13 and recorded their impressions of the work that was being done for the education of women and girls in India.[68] In the context of the Madras government's proposal to start a college, and Fraser's letter indicating the Christian Mission's plan of starting a college with McDougall as Principal, the conclusions that McDougall and Roberts had been 'inevitably led' by their acquaintance with Indian university women, are worth quoting:[69]

> The college, i.e., a college for women, should be on a distinctly and avowedly Christian basis. There are many reasons for this, but two in especial seem to me very cogent in India.
>
> In the first place, parents of all creeds will more willingly entrust their daughters to Christian care than to any other. Some anxiety is felt about possible change in religion, but these are outweighed by the confidence that the girl will be in good moral atmosphere, that her health will be carefully guarded that she will be treated with sympathetic kindness and above all that she will be protected from moral danger. In the second place work in secular education will never attract to

[67] Ibid.

[68] The general impression of Misses M.E. Roberts and E.M. McDougall contained in their letter to Sir Harcourt Bulter, Education, Progs., no. 5, January 1914 (Deposit), National Archives of India.

[69] Ibid. See also demi-official from Lord Pentland, Governor of Madras to Sir Andrew Fraser, dated 9 May 1914, notes connected with Educational G.O. nos. 614–15, 27 May 1914.

Indian women of the type most needed for the new college. A university women bred at one of the English residential colleges has a number of interesting and lucrative careers open to her at home in comparison with which India with its trying climate, its distance from home, its scanty pay and limited possibilities of advance offers no attraction. Of course there are exceptions but in our experience of Indian schools and colleges, it is only a sense of vocation that brings out from England, women of the best type, intellectual, moral and social to take up the very trying work of a teacher in India.

Lord Pentland, in his reply to Fraser, was highly critical of the stand taken by the Missionary Council and particularly of McDougall's observations. While acknowledging that the Madras Presidency owed perhaps more to Chrisitan effort in education than any other part of India, he nevertheless, pointed out that there was in south India, a strong orthodox caste Hindu opinion, which, according to Lord Pentland, 'growingly sensitive of the influence of christianity in public education, is peculiarly distrustful of its influence upon Hindu women and girls'.[70] This was seen as a real obstacle to the progress of education among Indian women.

At one level the provision of college education by the government (ostensibly on secular lines) was expected to lead to a progressive increase in the number of Hindu women students. At another level, the government explicitly realized that college education would provide 'the opportunities desired by the increasing number of *higher caste* and *wealthy Indian young women* who under no necessity or desire to seek University distinciton but wishing to continue their education for its own sake

[70] Notes connected with Educational G.O. nos. 614–15, 27 May 1914.

are not willing or not allowed to do so under definitely Christian influence'.[71]

Missionary protest to any proposal from the government to set up educational institutions was not new, specially to the Madras government.[72] When in the year 1910, the government of Madras, in pursuance of the GOI policy to establish government high schools in each district, proposed to convert ten board and five private high schools in certain districts into government model schools, the Missionary Council on aided education in Madras approached the government and protested that the scheme as likely to hamper the progress of aided education in that Presidency. The local government thereupon gave up the original idea.[73]

Again, a similar protest was made in 1913, this time in respect of the wording of clause (iii) of paragraph 11 of the Resolution of February 1913, which laid down that the 'expansion (of primary education) should be secured by means of board schools except where this

[71] Ibid.

[72] See in this connection the following G.O.s (All from the National Archives of India):

(a) Education A, October 1906, no. 31
(b) Education A, June 1910, nos. 43–4
(c) Education A, March 1911, nos. 195–9
(d) Education A, April 1911, nos. 91–111
(e) Education A, November 1911, no. 64
(f) Education A, August 1912, nos. 8–21
(g) Education A, October 1912, nos. 17–22
(h) Education A, March 1913, nos. 103–8
(i) Education A, July 1913, no. 42
(j) Education, September 1913, no. 19

[73] Letter from the Government of Madras no. 998, Educational, 22 August 1914, Educational, Progs., nos. 15–16, October 1914, National Archives of India.

is financially impossible when aided schools under recognized management should be encouraged'.[74] The missionaries immediately feared that the opening of board schools would be harmful to the progress of aided education and prayed that in the contemplated expansion of primary education the work of aided bodies would be fully recognized and suggested certain safeguards to this end.[75] The Madras government's reaction to this memorial was quite scathing as revealed in the notings of various officials some of which are worth reproducing:[76]

a) The memorial is one of series of documents. The missionaries of South India seem to have a sort of political organization (with agents at home) whose object is to push the case of missionary schools. They are not bound by educational principles and would, for example, rather have the country overrun with inefficient missionary schools than with good government schools.
b) Their (missionary) attitude is to the effect that they have vested rights in Indian education. They talk of the 'rights of aided education.' They also assume that the Government of India is forever bound by somewhat unsound statements of their predecessors (example, the 1882 Report).
c) They are now attempting to get a definite declaration of policy that will tie the hands of Government and what they propose is practically that their societies shall have the monopoly of extension—they should extend where they please, while Government should not make any extension without consulting them.

[74] Ibid.

[75] Memorial dated 20 March 1914 addressed to the Government of India by the Missionary Educational Council of South India, Education., Progs, nos. 15–16, October 1914, National Archives of India.

[76] Letter from the Government of Madras no. 998, Educational, dated 22 August 1914, Education, Progs., nos. 15–16, October 1914, National Archives of India.

d) The argument that missionaries have fostered education for many years has no weight. It is not quite correct: they have and do only use 'education' as a means to their own end, which, however worthy it may seem, is not the end desired by the people of India.[77]

Despite the protest, the government of Madras decided to go ahead with its plans to open a college for women on the following lines, namely:

(i) That the Presidency Training School for Mistresses, Madras, would be developed into an institution providing for collegiate instruction for girls;
(ii) That arrangements would be made for opening therein a junior intermediate class first and a senior intermediate class the following year;
(iii) That two women teachers with first class qualifications, recruited in England would be provided for the purpose.[78]

With reference to the above decision of the government, the office of the DPI came up with the following proposals:[79]

a) The Director suggested the opening of a women's college for one year on a temporary basis with a view to avoid the delay which would be

[77] Ibid.

[78] See in this context letters from: (a) J.H. Stone, Acg DPI, Madras, to the Secretary to Government Educational Dept., dated 3 April 1914; and (b) W. Francis, Acg. Secretary to the Government of Madras, Educational Dept. to the Secretary to the Govt of India, Dept. of Education, dated 27 May 1914. Both (a) and (b) contained in Educational G.O. no. 614, 27 May 1914 (Press).

[79] For details see Notes connected with Educational G.O. no. 614–15, 27 May 1914 (Press).

occasioned by recruitment of lady professors in England and also with a view to test the extent of the demand that existed for a purely secular college for women.

b) As regards subjects for instruction, the Director suggested that only group III of the intermediate course would be taught initially. Under University Regulation 179, students for the intermediate examination had to undergo the following courses of study:
   I. English language and literature
   II. Composition in one of the vernaculars, or translation into English from one of the classical and foreign languages named in Regulation 176.
   III. One of the following optional subjects:
      i. Mathematics, Physics and Chemistry
      ii. Natural Science, Physics and Chemistry
      iii. Any three of the following subjects:
         a. Ancient History
         b. Modern History
         c. Logic
         d. A classical language
         e. A second classical language, i.e. one of the foreign or Indian vernacular languages mentioned in Regulation 176.

The DPI's suggestion that students of the women's college would take up group (iii) of item III (in addition, of course, to the compulsory items I and II) was approved. Any attempt to take science subjects, i.e. groups (i) and (ii) of item III was considered *impracticable* owing to the *absence of laboratories.*[80] Earlier, the Hon'ble

[80] Ibid.

Mr Sivaswami Ayyar, in his demi-official of 29 July 1913, had observed that 'it would be desirable at the outset *not to make any provision for the scientific groups as they would inolve much expenditure in the way of laboratories, equipments*, etc.', which immediately found favour with the authorities.[81] It was also felt that the college for women would attract many women students since such students 'will *rather prefer* to take up group (iii)—literary subjects—than either group (i) or group (ii) *which will probably be more difficult for them*' (emphasis added). Within two years the Secretary of State allowed the college to be placed on a permanent footing. In 1917, with Her Majesty the Queen's permission the name of the college was changed to 'Queen Mary's College for Women.'[82]

At the Conference of Women Officers, the development of Queen Mary's College was one of the subjects discussed.[83] The suggestions made with regard to the expansion of Queen Mary's College were that provisions were to be made for a wider choice of Intermediate subjects, the development of science courses above the Intermediate and the provision of honours courses in some subjects. Geography and music had since been included among the Intermediate courses while the science block was in the process of being erected.[84]

It was urged that it was often difficult for women to get admission to the Honours' course in the Presidency College and that a certain number of students who were

[81] Notes connected with Educational G.O. no. 125, 29 January 1914.

[82] See University of Madras, *History of Higher Education in South India*, vol, II: 1857–1957, Madras: Associated Printers, 1957, p. 26.

[83] Educational G.O. no. 578, 23 March 1929.

[84] Ibid.

capable of doing Honours' work chose a pass course at Queen Marys' college in preference to attending a men's college. It was therefore urged, that, 'it was not good for the status of women's colleges and for the standard of work in them to have no Honours' courses'.[85] Further, it was observed that both in English and in History, the staff at Queen Mary's College were qualified to conduct Honours' courses and that the institution of these courses at an early date was possible and strongly recommended.[86]

In addition to Queen Mary's College, there were in existence at the beginning of the 1030s, four arts colleges under private management.[87] The strength of these colleges as on 31 March 1926 were as follows:

First Grade	*Strength*
1. Queen Mary's College	173
2. Madras Christian College for Women	129
3. St. Agnes College, Mangalore	65
Second Grade	
4. Teppakulam Holy Cross College, Trichy	7
5. Sarah Tucker College, Palamcottah	16
Total	390

Besides, there were also 72 women students studying in men's colleges due to the fact that none of the women's colleges provided instruction for the Honours' course.[88]

[85] Ibid.
[86] Ibid.
[87] Educational G.O. no. 888, 28 April 1928 (Ms).
[88] Ibid.

Perspectives on 'Suitable' Curricula for Girls

In 1913 the GOI Resolution on Educational Policy considered the immediate problem in the education of girls as one of *social development*.[89] While hesitating to lay down general lines of policy which would hamper local governments and administrations (because 'the existing customs and ideas opposed to the education of girls will require different handling in different parts of India') the GOI, nevertheless, commended the following principles for general consideration:

a. The education of girls should be practical with reference to the position which they will fill in social life;
b. It should not seek to imitate the education suitable for boys nor should it be dominated by examiniations;
c. Special attention should be paid to hygiene and the surroundings of school life;
d. The services of women should be more freely enlisted for instruction and inspection; and
e. Continuity in inspection and control should be specially aimed at.[90]

There had been a growing demand for alternative courses for girls and an expression of public opinion with reference to this point was made at the first 'All-India Women's Conference on Educational Reform' held in Poona in January 1927 which passed a resolution that 'alternative courses should be established to suit the needs of girls who do not intend to take up college education'.[91] The idea was not a new one and attempts

[89] Education, Progs nos. 103–8, March 1913, National Archives of India.

[90] Ibid.

[91] Quoted in Educational G.O. no. 578, 23 March 1929.

had been made to develop alternative courses in the then existing high schools for girls.[92] These, however, had met with little response. Attempts had been made in mission boarding schools in the Presidency, but, according to the authorities, parents had not been convinced that the value of a course (which did not lead to the acquirement of a recognized certificate) justified the heavy expenditure entailed in the form of school and boarding fees.

The exact implication of the term 'alternative courses' was never elucidated. In general, it appeared to convey the desire for a more general course of study than was possible under the then existing Secondary School Leaving Certificate scheme (this introduced specialization at a comparatively early stage), and for the inclusion of better and fuller courses in subjects such as drawing, music, practical hygiene, and domestic science *on the lines of the courses included in the curriculum of practically all secondary schools for girls in England* in addition to the subjects ordinarily included in the curriculum of secondary schools for Indian girls (emphasis added).[93]

In their Resolution on Female Education in 1919, the GOI alluded to the public criticism of the curricula hitherto followed: first, on the ground that the courses did not allow sufficient variety, and, second, that they were not properly adopted for the special use of girls. As regards the curriculum, the production of special textbooks suitable for girls in the higher classes of

[92] See, for example, the memorial of Mrs Sumant Mehta (who had earlier presided over a public meeting in Bombay) addressed to the Viceroy and Governor-General-General-in-Council, on Female Education in India, Education, Progs nos. 55–9, March 1916, National Archives of India.

[93] Educational G.O. no. 578, 23 March 1929.

primary schools was deemed a matter for consideration. Further, it was pointed out that

> there is a growing feeling against the exclusion of religious teaching and observances from school life, *and the feeling is more accentuated in the case of girls than in that of boys* . . . The Government of India are of opinion that it would not be advisable to lay down any uniform system to be followed in all localities in respect of religious teaching either for boys or for girls *but they feel that in the case of girls a rather greater degree of elasticity can be given to the curriculum in this respect and local bodies should do what they reasonably can to meet genuine local sentiment in the matter* (emphasis added).[94]

The character of the secondary education to be imparted to girls brought forth very divergent views. Broadly, there were two main schools of thought. One school wanted girls to be brought up on lines as similar as possible to those laid down for boys and prepare them for a university career. The other opinion wanted girls to be prepared primarily for home life and held that women were to be educated in all that concerned enlightened mothering, a good standard of maternal physique, better care of infancy, appropriate feeding, care and management of children, effective attention to children's diseases and generally to their physical condition, good sanitary environment, and other matters of domestic concern.[95]

The Calcutta Univesity Commission dealt with this subject at some length, and, among other things, suggested that

> in future schools should be so organised as to meet, on the one hand, the needs of the majority who will spend their lives

[94] Home (Education) G.O. no. 1334, 31 October 1919 (Press).
[95] Ibid.

in the *zenana* and whose education will cease at an early age, and, on the other hand, those of the *small but important minority* who will take to professional service or play a part in the *progressive section of Indian society*.[96] The government accepted fully the two principles underlying the proposals of the commission, namely the modification of the curriculum to suit the needs of girls and women of *different classes*, and secondly the utilization of the advice of ladies in formulating a suitable system of instruction' (emphasis added).[97]

The Conference of Women Officers in Madras expressed the need for the total revision of the Secondary School Leaving Certificate course and also laid down that:

a. No distinction was to be made between the courses for boys and girls insofar as the compulsory subjects were concerned;
b. It was decided that the compulsory subjects should include vernaculars, English, mathematics, history and citizenship geography and general science;
c. The possibility of including a good course of hygiene and domestic science among compulsory subjects was discussed but since it was felt that the high school course, as far as compulsory subjects were concerned, would be the same for boys as well as for girls, this subject could not be included among the compulsory subjects.[98]

It was agreed that there was no need for the development of alternative courses for women at the university stage, and, that the number of students who wished for courses

[96] Quoted in Home (Education) G.O. no. 1334, 31 October 1919 (Press)

[97] Ibid.

[98] Educational G.O. no. 578, 23 March 1929.

beyond the high school stage but who were provided for would be few, if any. It was thought that there were some girls who wished to study further than the SSLC but who would not wish to follow a full university course, and it was decided that these students could be provided for in the then existing Government College for Women (later named Queen Mary's College). It was not considered necessary to institute any special courses for them since it was agreed that courses in some of the subjects then included in the Intermediate course would be provided at Queen Mary's college for the benefit of ordinary students and that, with these, sufficient facilities would be afforded to these special students.[99]

The deliberations of a resolution moved in the Legislative Council (recommending the setting up of a committee of officials and non-officials for the purpose of revising the curricula of studies and for devising suitable methods to be followed for the improvement and greater diffusion of education among girls in the Presidency) is a telling commentary on the (gendered) ideology of the times.[100] K.R.V. Rao, mover of the resolution, wanted an enquiry into all matters touching the education of girls and women in all its aspects, domestic, intellectual, moral, artistic, physical and religious. 'Women in India are not supposed to compete with men in appointments and the education which girls have to be given from the beginning will have to be such as would be of use to them in after life, in order to make them good housewives and useful members of society', he concluded.[101]

[99] Ibid.

[100] Extract from the Proceedings of an Adjourned Meeting of the Council of the Governor of Fort St. George held on 25 November 1915, Educational G.O. no. 112, 4 February 1916.

[101] Ibid.

An androcentric approach to curricula framing was, thus, one part of the story: the primacy of this approach, however, led to (a) very minimal facilities being afforded to girl students in general as compared to those provided for boys; (b) very few options for diversification as far as higher education was concerned; and (c) a definite class-biased agenda for growth. Shades of this 'biological determinist'[102] argument to curricula framing was apparent in the reasoning put forth by Mayhew to institute a 'lighter' course for girls.

> What gives cause for alarm in the present situation is not the close resemblance of the girls' curriculum to that of boys nor the absence of special vacational training which must be premature until general education has been fairly established, but the excessive physical strain imposed on girls by requiring of them the same number of subjects and the same standard in those subjects as is required for boys. This is particularly disastrous under the climatic and physiological conditions that obtain in India. . . . It is certain, for instance, that the compulsory courses in English and Mathematics could, without domestic or national loss, be made far lighter for girls.[103]

The exact manner in which the colonizer's perspectives on education for women got incorporated into the curriculum designed for the colonized is yet to be explored concretely and in depth. It would not be out of place, however, to refer to studies that outline the

[102] In an excellent Introduction to a discussion on biological politics, Janet Sayers traces historically the appeal to biology to justify exclusion of women specially from higher education. See Janet Sayers, *Biological Politics: Feminist and Anti-feminist Perspectives*, London and New York: Tavistock, 1982.

[103] Mayhew and James, *Education and Politics in India*, pp. 233–4.

manner in which women's education was perceived in nineteenth-century England, which found its echo in the deliberations on educational policy for women in India which we have outlined above.

Sara Delamont's study of nineteenth-century women in England brings out very succintly the cultural and physical world that defined women's existence during that period.[104] According to Delamont, throughout the nineteenth century the debate about the proper education and life-work for women was conducted along class lines. Here, three strata were distinguished: the upper class (which in Britain meant the old aristocracy and landed gentry plus the richest families thrown up by the Industrial Revolution; and in America the long-established wealthy families); the newly-emerging middle classes, made up of professional and managerial workers rather than owners of land and capital; and the mass of the workers (including the skilled artisans and the unskilled labourers which in the USA meant the new immigrants). The role and status of women was quite different in the three spheres, and controversies over education and work were based on very different premises.[105]

'Double-conformity' is the term used by Delamont to define education for middle and upper-class girls and women who had to adhere to two sets of rigid standards: 'those of ladylike behaviour at all times *and* those of the dominant male cultural and education system'. Delamont has divided the campaigners of women's education into two groups: the *uncompromising*, 'who were determined that

[104] Sara Delamont, 'The Contradiction in Ladies' Education' and 'The Domestic Ideology and Women's Education', in *The Nineteenth Century Women*, ed. Sara Delamont and Lorna Duffin, London: Croom Helm, 1978.

[105] Delamont, 'The Contradiction in Ladies' Education', p. 134.

women should do what men did, warts and all'; and the separatists, 'who favoured modified courses for women'.[106]

The uncompromising group argued that a special curricula for girls would have no recognized standard or status, and would allow employers to discriminate and support the claim that women were mentally inferior to men. While not fully supporting the traditional curriculum, this group, however, pointed out that new subjects would only succeed as worthwhile when elite men took up such courses. The separatists, on the other hand, wanted courses for women which were

> particularly suited to their future as teachers, nurses and mothers. They were certainly genuine in their beliefs, but played into the hands of men who did not want women to have any education at all. These men were keen to educate women in separate courses, give them separate examinations and generally to confine them to a cultural ghetto.[107]

In retrospect, Delamont points out that the pioneers who held out for equal eductaional standards and curricula were correct to do so since a 'special women's course' would have led to women being confined forever in an intellectual and spiritual *purdah*. 'They recognized a simple truth—that separate *never* means equal—which has escaped many subsequent commentators.'[108]

Another very important aspect stressed by Delamont is the total reversal of the relations between sex and curriculum content in the working class versus the middle and upper classes.

> In the middle of the nineteenth century the *content* of working class education in both Britain and America was hardly differentiated by sex while the education of the upper, and the

[106] Ibid., p. 140.
[107] Ibid., p. 154.
[108] Ibid., p. 159.

emerging middle classes was highly sex-specific, with distinct curricula for boys and girls. By about 1920, however, a complete change had occurred, with the working classes receiving sex-specific instruction while the middle and upper classes were offered a curriculum relatively undifferentiated by sex.[109]

The deliberations in India at the official level (which is what we have covered in this chapter) on 'suitable' curricula for girls broadly corresponds to the arguments put forth by Delamont's two groups, namely the uncompromising and the separatists. But, as Delamont lays down, these were elitist solutions to the dilemmas of the times. Neither pattern was of any immediate use to working-class women. A detailed examination of the contents of what passed for women's education from a *class* standpoint is as important and needs to be tackled simultaneously with a study unravelling the androcentricity of the issue. Besides, various actors in this unfolding drama need to be examined, particularly the various women's groups (autonomous and those belonging to particular political parties) who made up the 'women's movement' then.

By Way of Conclusion

To recapitulate the main burden of our argument thus far:

a) The impetus for the development of the formal education of girls had more to do with the notion of imparting 'a far greater impulse to the educational and moral tone of the people in general and of men's education in particular'[110]

[109] Delamont, 'The Domestic Ideology and Women's Education', p. 164.

[110] An official documentation of this view point can be traced to the Educational Despatch of 1854 (Woods Despatch). See J.A. Richey, ed., *Selections from Educational Records*, part II: 1840-1859, Calcutta: Superintendent, Government Printing, 1922, p. 388.

than in any 'equal rights liberal reformist' espousal of equality of educational opportunities for girls;

b) Official data documents the disparity in the education of girls at various levels with the degree of disparity increasing as one went up the educational ladder. Educational 'backwardness' was also seen to be greater in the case of the more orthodox communities. The depressing (numerical) development of female education was sought to be explained as facts indicating

> *an indifference to the education of their girls on the part of the bulk of the community* much greater than was suggested by the mere percentage of girls in schools, small as that is, because it is a fair inference— that of all the girls born in the Presidency in any year only about 20,000 will receive even an elementary education as against as many as 15,000 ten years ago . . . *The cause of this indifference so far as they lie in the mental and social characteristics of the people are well known* (emphasis added).[111]

c) Throughout the period under study woman had been encouraged to attend schools only to face a curriculum that had been designed to perpetuate a culture of femininity and motherhood. A restricted curriculum and a low level of academic-achievement expectation from girls (conseqent upon a role that emphasized for women the fulfilment of her 'natural' destiny as wife and mother) had severe implications, most important being total exclusion of women from areas and careers traditionally defined as male domains.

[111] See, for example, the note by J.H. Stone, from the Office of the DPI, Madras, dated 17 March 1916, Notes to Educational G.O. no. 504, 9 May 1916.

d) The limited discussion surrounding the establishment of Queen Mary's College and the courses envisaged for the women students of the college document, among other things, 'the inferior quality' of the education imparted to women. The larger implication of this phenomenon needs to be spelt out. Even granting the advantages of an interventionist programme and a positive discrimination approach on behalf of girls and women to break what Nava refers to as the 'causal cycle of deprivation',[112] so long as schools/colleges impart different messages to their male and female students, development of female education could result only in numerical expansion over a period of time. Limited accessibility to higher education and, within this, the limited choice of courses of instruction could not but lead to a phenomenon that has been widely documented in feminist literature as that 'women tend to work in women's work'.
e) The service conditions envisaged for women teachers and administrators and the pay scales fixed for them, document on the surface the implicit recognition of a structural position of subordination and economic dependency on the part of women. Underlying most of the so-called progressive legislations was the need to keep intact relations of domination and subordination between the sexes, which would otherwise have suffered disruption, had women gained equality in the real sense of the term.
f) The usual features of a colonial relationship in the field of education in general, manifested itself in various ways. But in the field of women's education

[112] Nava, 'Gender and Education', pp. 69–78.

> it worked its way through the reproduction in the colony of some of the partriarchal relations of the colonizer. Colonial superiority for example, found expression in the assumed inability of the Indian women to work beyond the age of 50.

The problem of the expansion of women's education was compounded by a whole host of other issues, each of which needs to be explored further to get a picture of the complexity of the subject:

(i) In the first place the repeated emphasis on the moral education of females depicted shades of the evangelical emphasis, which Banks has shown to have characterized the education of British women.[113] When the need to increase the employment opportunities of women was stressed, then it was only the field of nursing and teaching that found a mention.

(ii) An in-depth community-wise analysis of educational opportunities that was provided and availed of is essential in the light of the fact, that, the scheme for the imposition of compulsory education in the first place was leniently applied in the case of non-Muslim girls, while Muslim girls were excluded altogether. What needs to be addressed is not just the role of the colonial state, but, more important, the role of the orthodox males of each community and their patriarchal domination which determined *how much* and *what kind* of education was imparted to the females of their respective communities.

[113] Olive Banks, *Faces of Feminism: A Study of Feminism as a Social Movement*, UK: Basil Blackwell, 1988, especially Chapter 2.

(iii) An aspect that was recorded in passing but not really elaborated nor studied in-depth thus far (to the best of our knowledge) was the shifting of the Widows' Home at Egmore to Triplicane in Madras (the latter a suburb in Madras that housed mainly orthodox brahmans) so that widows could be trained as teachers. Not only does this call for an examination of the magnitude of this social problem but also a probe into the question as to why the the government considered it 'an established fact that we must look to the class of widows for our chief supply of caste women teachers'.[114] There is also the need to explore this phenomenon from the angle expressed that 'unattached' ladies from different communities to make up the teaching staff.[115] Oram has shown in her study that during the 1920s and 1930s most women teachers in England and Wales were spinsters.[116] This was due to the regulations requiring women teachers to resign on marriage. In the Indian social context, it was argued that the 'universality of marriage and the wide prevalence of very early marriage make it almost impossible to employ unmarried women for the work'.[117] It was therefore felt that the 'vast array of Hindu widows, deprived of the right of second marriage and occupying domestic prositions of degrading inferiority, ought to supply the required service in schools'.[118]

[114] Letter from Sir Alfred Bourne, DPI Madras to the Secretary to Government, Educational Dept., dated 5 March 1913, Educational G.O. no. 586, 21 June 1913 (Press).

[115] Mayhew and James, *Education and Politics in India*, p. 226.

[116] Oram, 'Embittered, Sexless or Homosexual'.

[117] Mayhew and James, *Education and Politics in India*, p. 226.

[118] Ibid.

(iv) Another passing statement with tremendous political implications that needs to be studied was the explicit pandering to middle-class values and the primacy given to this class over all others. In the discussion on co-education, the Conference of Women Officers made it clear that 'there was a strong feeling against it (co-education) among this (middle) class and that, as it was amongst this class that most rapid progress could be made at present, co-education on any considerable scale could not be introduced effectively now'.[119]

In the West, the contested terrain for the main 'feminist' battle was the field of higher education. It was here that the different 'faces of feminism' manifested itself inasmuch as women themselves as individuals and as members of particular groups differed radically in their analysis of the subject of women's education and consequently came up with solutions that were diametrically opposed.[120]

An examination of the circumstances that brought in higher education for women in this country in general, and in the Presidency in particular, is long overdue. We hope to have made a beginning by concentrating in particular on the historical development of Queen Mary's College, the first Government College for women. This institution-based study, we hope, will not only throw light on many of the observations that we have made above, but more important, it is our contention that the manner in which these and other issues were *resolved* had important implications for the subsequent course of women's higher education.

[119] Reproduced in Educational G.O. no. 578, 23 March 1929.

[120] Banks, *Faces of Feminism*, especially the concluding chapter.

PART IV

Economic Development

Why Gender Matters

CHAPTER 11

Outside the Realm of Protective Labour Legislation

The Saga of Unpaid Labour in India

A remarkable 'achievement' of economic 'development' in post-Independence India has been not just the growth of the informal sector and of those being employed informally, but also the phenomenon of 'informalization of the formal sector'.[1] What is also truly remarkable is the consistent manner in which disproportionately larger numbers of women and their 'work' either become invisible in data systems or get captured in categories that fall outside the purview of protective legislation.

This chapter traces the trajectory of simultaneous exclusion and (peripheral) inclusion of women by going back to some of the seminal documents that were the outcomes of officially constituted commissions and

[*] Previously published in *Economic and Political Weekly*, October 2009.

[1] NCEUS, *Report on Conditions of Work and Promotion of Livelihoods in the Unorganised Sector*, New Delhi: Academic Foundation, 2008.

committees. These documents not only engaged with the broad theme of exclusion/inclusion extensively and holistically, but also strongly recommended, among other things, the enactment of new laws, modification and expansion of coverage of existing laws, and stringent implementation of all laws in the spirit of enhancing the status of the marginalized, women included, from second-class citizens to full citizenship. An avowed purpose of this exercise is to comprehend what accounts for the continued denial of 'worker' status to large numbers of women, whose presence as 'informally employed' and as 'unpaid family workers' is otherwise recognized. Through a critical reading of these documents, we revisit some of the arguments and recommendations of these bodies.

The main documents that we have examined include: Towards Equality: Report of the Committee on the Status of Women in India;[2] Shramshakti: Report of the National Commission on Self-Employed Women and Women in the Informal Sector;[3] Report of the Committees Constituted to Study the Problems and Issues of Unorganized Labour in Tamil Nadu;[4] Report of the Time Use Survey;[5] Report of the Second National

[2] GoI, *Towards Equality: Report of the Committee on the Status of Women in India*, New Delhi: Ministry of Education and Social Welfare, Department of Social Welfare, Government of India, December 1974.

[3] GoI, *Shramshakti: Report of the National Commission on Self-Employed Women and Women in the Informal Sector*, New Delhi: Department of Women and Child Development, Ministry of Human Resource Development, 1988.

[4] GoTN, *Report of the Committees Constituted to Study the Problems and Issues of Unorganised Labour in Tamil Nadu*, Chennai: Office of the Commissioner of Labour, 1998.

[5] GoI, *Report of the Time Use Survey*, New Delhi: Ministry of Statistics and Programme Implementation, Central Statistical Organisation, April 2000.

Commission on Labour;[6] Report on Conditions of Work and Promotion of Livelihoods in the Unorganized Sector;[7] and The Challenge of Employment in India: An Informal Economy Perspective.[8]

The chapter is organized as follows: in Section 1[9] we provide an overview of the dimensions of the problem of low-level and poor quality of employment in the country, with a specific emphasis on the categories that capture women's work. In terms of data we begin with the most recent available statistics and trace the situation of women's employment to the early decades of post-Independence India as captured and documented by the different reports mentioned above. In Section 2 we engage with specific aspects of ineffectiveness of protective labour laws as far as women are concerned. In Section 3 we reflect on the larger implications of the continued expansion in the numbers of, and time involved in, 'unpaid labour', as well as the continued denial of worker status to women.

Women Work but How and in What Capacity?

All the reports mentioned above, in different ways, lament the fact that the system has no credible data on the unorganized economy, where bulk of women work. More significant, official recognitions of double-burden

[6] GoI, *Report of the Second National Commission on Labour*, New Delhi: Ministry of Labour, 2002.

[7] NCEUS, *Report on Conditions of Work and Promotion of Livelihoods in the Unorganised Sector*.

[8] NCEUS, *The Challenge of Employment in India: An Informal Economy Perspective*, vol. 1, Main Report, New Delhi: Academic Foundation, April 2009.

[9] This section is based on NCEUS, *Report on Conditions of Work and Promotion of Livelihoods in the Unorganised Sector*, and NCEUS, *The Challenge of Employment in India: An Informal Economy Perspective*.

or even 'triple overlaps' (of gender stratification, economy, and family),[10] when it comes to women's work, have not translated into adequate quantity and quality of support services to relieve women of such double-burden and/or triple overlaps. What we, therefore, have are estimates of the different kinds of unpaid work that women are forced to undertake for their own survival and for the survival of the households into which they are either born or get married into. Over the years, the number and percentage of women in the unpaid category has increased, not decreased, even in periods when the economy has returned significantly high growth rates and has been characterized as 'shining'.

In this section, using data provided by the most recent of the above documents, namely, the Reports of the National Commission for Unorganized Sector (NCEUS 2008 and NCEUS 2009), first, we provide a glimpse of the dimensions of the nature, category, and quality of employment generated by the economy (as on 2004–5) to be able to situate and contextualize women's employment. Two, taking each of the reports mentioned above, we trace the observations that each have recorded on the twin issues of non-collection/non-availability of data relating to the unorganized economy in general, and women's work in particular, and on the theme of unpaid work.

As per the estimates of the NCEUS 2008, the total numbers employed (principal plus subsidiary) in the Indian economy, computed from the 61st round of the National Sample Survey 2004–5, was 458 million, of which the unorganized sector accounted for 395 million,

[10] R.L. Blumberg, ed., *Gender, Family and Economy: The Triple Overlap*, California: Sage, 1991.

accounting for 86 per cent of total workers in 2004–5. The commission has made a distinction between sectors of employment (organized and unorganized) and formal and informal employment in order to highlight the important fact that not all those employed in the organized sector are formally employed. Thus, for example, the commission finds that, while the total employment in the economy has increased between two NSS rounds (that is between 1999–2000 and 2004–5), the increase in total employment has been of the informal kind, even if, sectorally, employment increased by 8.5 million in the organized sector.[11] In other words, what this denotes, according to the commission, is 'informalization of the formal sector'.[12] A point that needs to be flagged right at the beginning is the following: it was only as late as 2004, when the NCEUS was constituted (which determinedly as a body grappled with the contentious issue of what constitutes the organized/unorganized sector and formal/informal economy and came up with definitions and estimates of the same), that the dimensions and ramifications of unorganized economy have become clearer and starker. Thus far, every other report mentioned above, and the system in general, has been content to merely describe the unorganized economy in terms of its functioning characteristics, even while admitting that the unorganized economy was where the bulk of Indian labour (upwards of 90 per cent) actually worked.

[11] The NCEUS has engaged extensively with the terms, formal/organized sector, informal/unorganized sector, formal/informal economy, and formal/informal workers (NCEUS, *The Challenge of Employment in India: An Informal Economy Perspective*, pp. 12–14).

[12] NCEUS, 'Report on Conditions of Work and Promotion of Livelihoods in the Unorganised Sector', p. 4.

In 2004–5, of the 148 million women workers in the Indian economy, 142 million or almost 96 per cent were unorganized workers (against 91 per cent unorganized male workers). This included 91 per cent of women workers in the unorganized sector plus those working informally in the organized sector. In terms of status of employment, the bulk of unorganized sector employment was self-employment, followed by casual employment. For the country as a whole, a great majority of the workers (males and females) were either self-employed (56.6 per cent) or casual workers (28 per cent). Only 15.3 per cent of the workers were regular salaried/wage workers. The self-employed category consists of own account workers, employers, and unpaid family workers. Data reveal a decline in the proportion of own account workers and employers for women from 24 per cent in 1983 to 17 per cent in 2004–5. On the other hand, the share of unpaid family workers had increased from 36 per cent to 44 per cent during this period. Within this, the rural female workers constituted the most disadvantaged in terms of workforce characteristics. Not only was the share of unpaid family workers among rural females the highest, it also had increased by 10 percentage points from 38 per cent in 1983 to 48 per cent in 2004–5.[13]

In 2004–5, the bulk of women workers overwhelmingly belonged to the self-employed category and also dominated the 'unpaid family workers' section within the category of self-employed. This comment is telling of how 'India Shining' has not only bypassed, but is actually overburdening without compensating, the bulk of women and women's work in this country. That the

[13] NCEUS, *The Challenge of Employment in India: An Informal Economy Perspective*, p. 59, see also Table 11.1.

Table 11.1: Percentage Distribution of Workers by Activity Status

Population Segment	Year	*Self-Employed*			Regular Salaried/ Wage Workers	Casual Workers	Total
		Own Account and Employers	*Unpaid Family Workers*	*Sub-Total*			
Rural male	1983	45.85	14.66	60.52	9.76	29.73	100
	1993–4	40.39	17.36	57.74	8.53	33.73	100
	2004–5	41.9	16.59	58.48	8.93	32.59	100
Rural female	1983	23.91	38.01	61.92	2.77	35.31	100
	1993–4	16.35	42.75	59.1	2.67	38.24	100
	2004–5	15.94	47.98	63.92	3.68	32.41	100
Urban male	1983	33.27	7.59	40.86	43.74	15.4	100
	1993–4	33.35	8.27	41.62	42.28	16.1	100
	2004–5	36.2	8.42	44.62	40.84	14.54	100
Urban female	1983	26.43	19.04	45.47	26.27	28.26	100
	1993–4	24.16	20.46	44.62	29.51	25.87	100
	2004–5	24.14	23.05	47.19	35.97	16.84	100

(Table 11.1 continued)

(Table 11.1 continued)

		Self-Employed					
Population Segment	*Year*	*Own Account and Employers*	*Unpaid Family Workers*	*Sub-Total*	*Regular Salaried/ Wage Workers*	*Casual Workers*	*Total*
Total male	1983	42.92	13.01	55.93	17.69	26.38	100
	1993–4	38.58	15.03	53.61	17.18	29.21	100
	2004–5	40.23	14.2	54.43	18.26	27.31	100
Total female	1983	24.21	35.76	59.97	5.55	34.48	100
	1993–4	17.45	39.6	57.05	6.46	36.49	100
	2004–5	17.28	43.91	61.18	8.95	29.86	100
Total persons	1983	36.6	20.69	57.29	13.59	29.11	100
	1993–4	31.74	22.88	54.72	13.71	31.57	100
	2004–5	32.83	23.77	56.61	15.26	28.13	100

Source: NCEUS, 2009, p. 59.

NCEUS is not the first body to officially highlight this phenomenon will become clear as we trace the official post-Independence history of unpaid work and the different facets of the unpaid work of Indian women beginning with the Report of the Committee on Status of Women.[14]

We quote in some detail the observations of the different committees and commissions on the theme of unpaid work only to underscore the following point: despite these observations and despite the fact that these bodies backed their observations with strong legal recommendations to rectify the disadvantages that women in particular suffered because of their overwhelming presence in the category of unpaid workers, the system continues to function in the 'business as usual' mode.

The 1974 Committee was constituted almost twenty-five years after Independence and its report entitled 'Towards Equality' could be regarded as the first comprehensive account of the status of women in India using a range of social, economic, political, and legal parameters to contextualize women's position within the polity and economy of independent India. The 1974 Committee immediately realized the almost complete non-existence of meaningful data on the unorganized sector, where the bulk of women worked and continue to work till date. Its observations on the difficulty of arriving at credible numbers of those employed are reproduced below:

> Next to agriculture the largest numbers of women are employed in various industries, trades and services in the unorganised sector both in rural and urban areas. The statistics relating to women workers in these unorganised and regulated industries and services are highly inadequate and unreliable.

[14] GoI, *Towards Equality*.

At present there is no agency responsible for the collection of employment statistics in the unorganised sector. The National Commission on Labour, confessing its difficulties in identifying unorganised labour by any exact definition, took recourse to describing some of their characteristics and constraints... While the Census of 1961 and 1971 give us some estimate of women in household industries, we regret to find that no clear estimate is available regarding the actual number of women engaged in the vast unorganised non-agricultural sector.[15]

On the theme of unpaid work, the 1974 Committee recorded thus:

The gradual commercialisation and modernisation of the economy and the efforts made by government to replace traditional by modern institutions of credit and marketing, to stabilise ownership of land, and to maintain minimum wages, have by no means succeeded in 'organising' the production relations to control the degree of exploitation of the weaker section . . . Traditional modes of production relations which defy modern classifications into employers and employees, labour and capital, rent and interest, still prevail in most industries in this sector. The impact of this intermixture has been greater on women . . . Many of them are unpaid family workers, both in family enterprises, and in wage employment where their contribution to the family earnings as helpers of the men earners is not always realised or admitted. These unpaid family workers are predominantly women and children. Most of them fulfil dual roles by engaging in economic and household activity. More than half of the women who enter the labour force before the age of 15 are unpaid family workers, as compared to one-third of the men in the same category . . . Despite the variations in the concepts and the timings of the survey, the proportion of unpaid family workers shows a remarkable steadiness in the various rounds... The proportion of unpaid family workers aged 10 and over, estimated from 1961 Census, was about

[15] GoI, *Towards Equality*, pp. 169–70.

14% for males and 41% for females . . . The distribution of the unpaid family workers by age-groups indicates that the proportion declines considerably in the case of males after the age of 24, but for females, who form a higher proportion in the age-group 10–19, the decline is marginal.[16]

Having noted the above, the 1974 Committee, however, did not *specifically* address the theme of unpaid work in its recommendations for action, which were otherwise very elaborate; much emphasis was placed on extending the coverage of existing legislation, strengthening the administrative infrastructure incharge of implementing labour policies and the like.

Fourteen years after the 1974 Committee, the rationale for the constitution of the National Commission on Self-Employed Women and Women in the Informal Sector (1988 Shramshakti Report) by the GOI was the following:

Despite the existence of various Constitutional and legal provisions safe-guarding women's employment a large number of women workers, particularly in the unorganised sector suffer from various disadvantages relating to their working lives as well as in their homes. The coverage of labour laws has not benefited these women workers in many crucial areas, especially health, maternal and social security . . . Government of India feel that it is necessary to conduct a comprehensive examination and study of self-employed women workers, as it is in this area that the lack of access to credit marketing, health and social security are most discernible. It has therefore been decided to constitute a Commission on Self-Employed women . . . the above terms of reference of the commission would also cover all unprotected women labour in the country and extend to women in the informal sector.[17]

[16] Ibid., pp. 157–9.
[17] GoI, *Shramshakti*, pp. 332–3.

It is interesting that the 1988 Shramshakti Report merely mentions in passing that the government had appointed a committee on the status of women which had 'made a comprehensive study of the problems of all women'[18] without engaging with crucial questions such as: did the government that had earlier appointed the 1974 Committee formally accept the committee's report? If yes, what, if any, were the actions initiated based on the recommendations of the 1974 Report? If not accepted, why not? In hindsight, reflecting on such questions is important for feminist praxis. While the 1988 Shramshakti Report has dwelt considerably on the theme of physically mobilizing and organizing the labouring women, no thought has gone into why, the simultaneous mobilization of academics/intellectuals to hold the government accountable for not engaging with reports of its own committees and commissions, could not have constituted an equally important mode of action. This is particularly so since a significant dimension of the problem earlier flagged by the 1974 Committee had to do with concepts, contexts, definitions, and estimates of the unorganized economy, where hardly any labour laws apply, but in which the bulk of the labour force ekes out a living. Nevertheless, in its own way, the 1988 Shramshakti Report also engaged with the dimensions of the category, self-employed, through an examination of NSSO data.

Self-employment, by and large, constitutes the dominant sector of employment in our economy... According to the 38th Round of the NSSO (1983) over 164.7 million workers (principal plus marginal workers by usual status in the age group 5 years and above), constituting 57.3% of the total

[18] Ibid., p. 7.

workforce, are absorbed in this sector. Out of a total of 98.4 million female workers, as many as 59.1 million (60.1%) are engaged as self-employed workers the percentage being somewhat higher than for males (55.9%). The proportion of females engaged as self-employed workers in the rural areas is much higher (61.9%) than in the urban areas (45.8%) . . . The total percentage of self-employed workers to total workers in the household enterprises in the case of males is 46.1% as against 18.7% in the case of females. On the other hand, the proportion of male workers working as helpers in household enterprises is 13.4% as against 36.1% in the case of females (emphasis added).[19]

A dimension of unpaid work covered by Shramshakti 1988 is the 'proportion of females engaged in domestic duties along with free collection of goods', (that is NSS Activity Code Status 93) and 'proportion of females attending domestic duties only' (that is NSS Activity Code Status 92) using NSS 38th Round data pertaining to 1983. Further, the report also provides information on the percentages of women (among those usually engaged in household duties) willing to accept work, part or full time, if the same is made available to them at their residence. Similar information is provided by NCEUS 2008 for 2004–5. What becomes immediately clear from comparing 1983 and 2004–5 data is that the percentages of women reporting domestic duties as principal status, and, further, the proportions of women combining domestic duties with a number of other activities that help their households save incomes, remains substantial between the two time periods. We illustrate with data relating to rural women: 53 per cent of rural women (age 15–59 years) in 2004–5 against 42 per cent of

[19] Ibid., pp. 33–5.

rural women (age 5 years and above) in 1983, reported being 'usually engaged in domestic duties'. Similarly, in 2004–5, of the rural women reporting domestic duties as their principal status, 72 per cent were willing to accept work at home on part-time basis, while 23 per cent were willing to accept work on full-time basis. In 1983, 61 per cent of the rural women (reporting domestic duties as principal status) were willing to accept work at home on part-time basis, 30 per cent on full-time basis, and 9 per cent wanted work occasionally. Both reports also give details of the type of work that women were willing to take up at home.

The chapter on recommendations in the 1988 Shramshakti Report begins thus:

> . . . Women's work as home-makers must be recognised as social/economic production. For, when women fetch water, gather fuel and fodder or tutor their children, they are performing services in the absence of which market services would have to be purchased. Only if this recognised, can other consequences flow from it such as broader definition of women's work. The National Commission recommends that all subsequent data collection efforts should enlarge the definition of women workers to include all such activities paid and unpaid performed within the home or outside as an employee or on own account.[20]

The report has a further section entitled, 'Support Services and Other Programmes', the preamble to which states:

> In line with our approach that all women are 'workers', the distinguishing feature of a woman worker is her responsibility for bearing and rearing children. In addition, the responsibility of doing all house-hold chores and looking after the aged and

[20] Ibid., pp. 249–50.

sick has traditionally been her responsibility . . . It is therefore necessary that social support services should be provided to women workers for assisting them to do their work at home and outside, better and with less worry.[21]

The 1988 Shramshakti Report no doubt carries forward the agenda of elaborating on the theme of unpaid work by women in terms of recognizing both women's unpaid work as family helpers, and domestic unpaid work. It also backs up the recognition of unpaid domestic work with recommendations aimed at reducing domestic drudgery. Nevertheless, the fact that large numbers of women employed as unpaid family labour continue to remain beyond the reach of any protective labour legislation, does not merit specific attention.

The decline in worker population ratios in the 1990s, particularly sharp among certain age categories of rural women, brought to the fore some interesting debates among economists anxious to interpret and explain the phenomenon.[22] While Sundaram attempted to attribute the declines to 'beneficial rise in student-population ratios', among others, Hirway's examination of the argument established the inadequacy of Sundaram's

[21] Ibid., p. 300.

[22] K. Sundaram, 'Employment-Unemployment Situation in the Nineties: Some Results from NSS 55th Round Survey', *Economic & Political Weekly*, vol. 36, no. 11, 17–23 March 2001a; K. Sundaram, 'Employment and Poverty in India in the Nineteen Nineties: Further Results from NSS 55th Round Employment-Unemployment Survey, 1999–2000', paper presented at the International Seminar on Understanding Socio-Economic Changes through National Surveys, National Sample Survey Organisation, New Delhi, 12–13 May 2001b; I. Hirway, 'Employment and Unemployment Situation in the 1990s: How Good Are NSS Data?', *Economic & Political Weekly*, vol. 37, no. 21, 25–31 May 2002, pp. 2027–36.

explanation. On the contrary, Hirway's probe brought out the limited ability of NSS surveys to capture the changing profile of work and workers in the economy. To quote Hirway:

> It seems to us that the concepts and methods used by NSSO to net work and workers are not able to capture the work of the poor, and particularly, of women satisfactorily . . . It is [therefore] possible that the decline in the Work participation Rates in the nineties is due to expansion of non-reported [by the NSSO] part of the workforce which is employed in what is known as 'difficult to measure sectors' [such as subsistence work, home-based work or informal work] of the economy.[23]

Time Use Surveys

To a large extent, this was rectified by the conduct of Time Use Survey (TUS) by the Central Statistical Organization of the GOI in 1999–2000. The report of the TUS[24] for the first time provides an official visibility to women's work burden through its data covering various household and non-household activities. The survey was conducted in 18,591 households and was spread over six selected states, namely Haryana, Madhya Pradesh, Orissa, Tamil Nadu, Gujarat, and Meghalaya. The report classifies activities using the 1993 System of National Accounts (SNA). It makes use of three categories: SNA, Extended SNA, and Non-SNA. The SNA activities consist of primary production activities, like crop farming, animal husbandry, fishing, forestry, processing and storage, mining, and quarrying;

[23] Hirway, 'Employment and Unemployment Situation in the 1990s', p. 2029,

[24] GoI, 'Report of the Time Use Survey'.

secondary activities like construction, manufacturing; and tertiary activities like trade, business, and services. Extended SNA activities include household maintenance, care for children, sick, and elderly. Non-SNA activities include learning, social and cultural activities, mass media, personal care, and self-maintenance. Table 11.2 compares work participation rates (WPRs) using NSSO and TUS methods, while Table 11.3 (p. 84) highlights, among other things, the time spent on paid/unpaid work.

1) Comparing data on WPRs based on the NSSO and the TUS, Hirway[25] draws some very crucial conclusions that have significant conceptual and policy implications: the WPRs based on the TUS are higher than those based on NSS for males as well as females.
2) The differences between the two sets are higher for women than for men.
3) The extent of underestimation of workforce under NSS rounds as well as the differences between male and female WPRs within a state, is not the same across all the states. Neither are these differences related to the level of economic growth of a state.
4) Dividing work into 'paid' and 'unpaid' categories (Table 11.3), Hirway finds that, while the share of unpaid SNA work is significant in India (for both men and women) in terms of the number of persons engaged in it as well as in terms of the time spent on such activities, however, uniformly across all states, the number of women engaged in unpaid activities as well as the time spent by

[25] Hirway, 'Employment and Unemployment Situation in the 1990s'.

Table 11.2: Comparing WPR between NSS and TUS (Per Cent)

	*NSSO 1993–4**		*NSSO 1999–2000*				*TUS 1998–9*		*Difference between TUS-WPR and NSS-WPR (1993–4)*		*Difference between TUS-WPRs and NSS-WPRs (1990–2000) Rural*	
			Rural		*Urban*							
States	*Male*	*Female*	*Male*	*Female*	*Male*	*Female*	*Male*	*Female*	*Male*	*Female*	*Male*	*Female*
Haryana	45.6	18.8	46.2	17.7	50.2	10	57.3	56.16	11.7	37.36	11.1	38.46
MP	52.5	27.17	51.2	30.7	47.3	12.1	60.5	49.43	7.96	22.26	9.27	18.73
Gujarat	54.6	26.39	57.1	35.5	52.9	12.5	60	44.17	5.42	17.78	2.92	8.67
Orissa	52.9	20.48	52.7	23.3	45.7	11.6	59.9	55.47	7	34.99	7.18	32.17
Tamil Nadu	56.6	34.2	56.6	38.1	55.2	20.1	66.1	50.25	9.47	16.05	9.5	12.15
Meghalaya	59.1	42.88	55.6	42	39.3	19.7	56.2	52.45	-2.83	9.57	0.62	10.45
Combined states/all India	52.6	23.41	51	25.3	50.9	12.8	61.3	50.32	8.73	26.91	10.32	25.02

* The data refer to weekly status of workers.
Source: Hirway, 2002, p. 2031.

Table 11.3: *State-wise Distribution of Time Spent (in Hours) in SNA Activities by Mode of Payment and Gender (Participants)*

States	*Male*			*Female*			*Total*		
	Paid	*Unpaid*	*Per Cent Time on Unpaid Activities*	*Paid*	*Unpaid*	*Per Cent Time on Unpaid Activities*	*Paid*	*Unpaid*	*Per Cent Time on Unpaid Activities*
Haryana	33.09 (1,152)	18.12 (1,347)	35.38	4.13 (215)	25.34 (1,494)	85.99	20.06 (1,387)	21.37 (2,841)	51.58
Madhya Pradesh	29.41 (5,247)	23.34 (6,311)	44.25	14.31 (3,072)	15.75 (4,391)	52.40	22.99 (8,319)	20.12 (10,702)	46.67
Gujarat	44.37 (3,959)	14.17 (3,897)	24.21	17.18 (1,747)	13.87 (2,541)	44.67	33.26 (5,706)	14.05 (6,438)	29.70
Orissa	31.25 (2,103)	22.42 (2,589)	41.77	8.00 (583)	18.18 (3,235)	69.44	20.55 (2,686)	20.47 (5,824)	49.90
Tamil Nadu	41.42 (5,633)	13.36 (4,863)	24.39	21.8 (,3034)	10.32 (4,280)	32.45	32.74 (8,667)	12.04 (9,143)	26.89
Meghalaya	17.34 (374)	35.39 (740)	67.12	7.83 (196)	25.34 (692)	78.39	12.65 (570)	30.44 (1,432)	70.64
Combined states	3654 (18,468)	18.12 (19,747)	33.15	14.87 (8,847)	15.18 (16,633)	50.52	27.16 (27,315)	16.85 (36,380)	38.29

Source: GoI, 2000; Quoted in Hirway, 2002, p. 2032.

women in such activities is higher than that on paid activities; women also spend more *time* on unpaid activities than men.

5) Hirway hypothesises (in the absence of time series data) that the decline in the NSS-based WPRs in the 1990s could be a result of the increased share of the unpaid component of the SNA in the 1990s, and hence, in a way is not really a decline but a shift, indicating deterioration in the quality of employment.

An increase in 'the difficult to measure' sectors of the SNA work as well as in extended SNA work does indicate deterioration in the quality of employment. The former indicates an increase in employment with low productivity and low wages, while the latter indicates an increased burden on women who are primarily responsible for carrying out unpaid domestic services.[26]

Taking SNA and extended SNA activities together, the GOI's own Report makes the following important observation:

> If we take SNA and extended SNA activities together . . . women were found to be working for longer hours than men. If we work out the average of women's work to the total work of male and female, it works out to 55%, which compares quite well with the figure of 53% quoted in the UNDP Human Development Report for 1995. Therefore, if extended SNA activities are included in economic activities, the contribution of women will be higher when compared to men (emphasis added).[27]

[26] Hirway, 'Employment and Unemployment Situation in the 1990s', p. 2035.

[27] GoI, *Report of the Time Use Survey*, p. 81.

As the NCEUS 2008 Report points out, recognition and inclusion of extended SNA activities as economic activities will not result in women getting higher incomes.

What it means is the absence of recognition of the kind of work, which although not in the realm of monetisation, is important to the sustenance of the family as well as the economy. *Recognition of women's contribution to extended SNA could and should lead to greater appreciation of public policies for the welfare of women*' (emphasis added).[28]

We will come back to this theme in Section 3.

Aspects of Ineffectiveness of Protective Labour Legislation

In Section 1, our effort was to trace the manner in which economic development has 'formalized' employment; worse, as far as women are concerned, the bulk of them as well the bulk of their time continues to be spent on 'unpaid activities' being it domestic or non-domestic. In this section we dwell on that minuscule percentage of women employed in the non-farm sector to whom, theoretically, protective labour legislation should apply, but, by and large, does not. There is no way we can provide an exhaustive account of the way in which the functioning of this sector makes women workers ineligible and/or excludes them from protective legislation, however 'ineffective' they may have been in the case of all labour. The emphasis here is more to highlight the official recognition of the non-applicability of existing protective labour legislation; further, the burden of our

[28] NCEUS, 'Report on Conditions of Work and Promotion of Livelihoods in the Unorganised Sector', p. 79.

argument is also that mere effective implementation alone will not suffice, since disabilities are built into the manner in which the legislations themselves have been framed and enacted.

The Report of the Second National Commission on Labour (SNCL 2002) and the Report of the Committees Constituted to Study the Problems and Issues of Unorganised Labour in Tamil Nadu (TN 1998) have recorded several examples of the blatant manner in which not only are provisions of the law violated on the ground, but, worse, very often, the machinery to administer the law remains either none-existent and/ or is yet to be made functional. Unlike the SNCL 2002, TN 1998 provides glimpses of how, administratively, protective legislation has been rendered dysfunctional. We, therefore, dwell at some length on the observations of TN 1998. In our opinion, the findings of the committee sum up what is by now well known, though it rarely gets officially endorsed. The committee identifies thirty-five occupations, some of which are covered by some labour welfare enactments, while others are not. The committee has found that the conditions of work do not vary much between protected or unprotected industries. Its overall findings are discussed with few illustrations under three broad heads: (a) Mode of recruitment of workers; (b) Conditions of work; and (c) Health and safety aspects of work.

Mode of Payment: A striking feature of most unorganized sector employment is that workers are employed largely through unregistered contractors or subcontractors.

The destinies of the workers are linked up with the machinations of a large number of contractors, on whose whims and fancies, likes and dislikes, depend the availability of work for this type of labour. These middlemen have the least regard for the health and welfare of the workers, and in fact, these middlemen exploit the workers by taking advantage of their economic dependence and ignorance.[29]

The larger implication of the contract system of employment is that large numbers of workers remain outside the purview of the Factories Act, since employers recognize and deal only with contractors and not directly with the labour that the contractors bring in. For example, the committee found that, in the saltpans of Vedaranyam, Tamil Nadu, barely fifty to sixty workers were on the payroll of the establishment out of a total strength of 600 workers. Similarly, in vessels manufacturing units, the committee notes that the most important characteristic of this employment is that workers are employed only indirectly on piece-rate basis or job-rate basis through a contractor who mediates between the actual employer and the workers. This particular employment has been included in the schedule of employment under the Minimum Wages Act of the Labour and Employment Department in 1978; besides, the minimum rates of wages have been fixed and revised periodically. Nevertheless, the committee notes as follows:

> Unfortunately, however, the benefits conferred by the minimum wages in law insofar as these workers are concerned, have not yet been translated into reality, strictly on account of the contract labour system carried on by the maistries [contractors] in such an ingenuous way that the number of workmen engaged in every such industrial establishment is always maintained below 10, with the result, neither the

[29] GoTN, *Report of the Committees Constituted to Study the Problems and Issues of Unorganised Labour in Tamil Nadu*, p. 22.

Contract Labour (Regulation and Abolition) Act, nor the provisions of the Factories' Act is made applicable to these unregulated factories.[30]

Conditions of Work: The committee found that working conditions in almost all the industries were deplorable. Further, it noted that employers used great ingenuity to keep their units outside the purview of the Factories Act. This allowed the employers to fix wages arbitrarily, often below the statutory provisions of the Minimum Wages Act for the concerned industry. A significant finding of the committee *is the active gender discrimination* practised by the industries covered by them. For example, commenting on the practices in the *appalam* (papad) manufacturing industry, the committee notes:

> Equal wage for equal work is something utopian and hitherto unheard of by the workers in this occupation. A female worker doing identical work in this occupation is denied 50% of the wages given to the male worker. A male worker earns around Rs 40 per day while a female worker is paid Rs.20 only per day.[31]

Similarly, in the coir industry, while a male worker earns, on average, about Rs.40 per day, a female worker is paid from Rs.25 to Rs.27 per day only.[32] Further the committee noted that the employees in the *appalam* industry were mostly girls who had been forced to drop out from schools and enter the industry to augment their family income.

A point stressed by the committee in the context of the match and fireworks industry was that large

[30] Ibid., p. 64.
[31] Ibid., p. 19.
[32] Ibid., p. 29.

numbers of women and children were engaged as home-based workers in processes that were delinked from other processes that required factory premises. In the latter processes only male workers were employed. Unfortunately, the committee does not proceed beyond recording this observation. To us, this fact has tremendous implications from a gender angle. Even if, eventually, the committee were to succeed in regulating the factories, this by itself was not sufficient to ensure regularization of those processes of the industry now carried on as home-based work by women and children.

Health and Safety Aspects of Work: In a refreshing departure, the committee commented extensively on safety and health aspects, even if at a general level. Its observations are based on what it encountered during field visits plus the perceptions of the workers whom it interviewed. It observed that the strain of working long hours in unhealthy and insanitary conditions and the low standard of living due to the meagre earnings, contributed to workers' poor state of health to a great extent.

In most industries, the workers are not provided with any protective equipment. In those units where such equipment is provided, the committee found them to be totally unsuitable. In bleaching and dyeing units, the committee found workers standing very close to the metal pot fixed over a furnace, and, without wearing any goggles. Workers were also exposed to risks from handling caustic soda, acids and other dangerous effluents emanating from the different processes. In the cashew nut industry (which is listed in the 'dangerous operation' category of the Tamil Nadu Factories Rules, 1950), the committee found that the scrubbing and shelling of cashew nut results in skin cancer. Contact with shell oil causes the peeling of outer skin though it does not result in permanent disablement. The committee found many workers afflicted by dermatitis. In industries, where the concentration of dust particles in workplaces was heavy and continuous, it found the workers prone to respiratory disorders.

In a nutshell, the committee recorded thus:

> Since government has not created any enforcement machinery to deal with these employments, even the maintenance of records and registers are not ensured. In this vicious-circled situation, the Committee would like to impress upon the government that creation of adequate infrastructure, with enough manpower and means of mobility is as important as that of scheduling of employment and a fixation of minimum wages. Unless there is enforcement, mere adding of the employments into the schedule and fixation of minimum wages would not do any good to the workers.[33]

Our purpose in discussing the committee's report is to highlight the *official* recognition, given, albeit belatedly, to not just the abysmal contractual and physical conditions of informally employed workers, but also the risks to their health associated with such employment. The committee believes that the creation of 'appropriate administrative and infrastructure machinery' to implement existing legislation will go a long way towards addressing the problems it highlights. On this point, we do not agree with the committee since, as the committee itself has documented, employers have been able to circumvent existing legislation and employ labour without formally recognizing them as such.

Below we highlight, thematically and through illustrative examples, certain observations made by the reports of the NCEUS 2008 and the SNCL 2002,

[33] Ibid., p. 84.

which, again, officially corroborates what have already been extensively documented independently by several independent researchers and by other official reports.

Denying the Presence of Women Workers and Devaluing the Work of Women

While discussing the mode of recruitment and nature of work in the brick and tiles industry, for example, the NCEUS 2008 notes that 'Only the male workers are registered as workers in the muster roll of the employer and the rest of the family remains invisible to statistics, policy and social protection provisions. Working hours for all workers are about 12–14 hours including for the women who are not on the muster roll.'[34]

The SNCL 2002, quoting, as illustration, a study conducted in Mumbai on 'Women Building Workers' notes as follows:

> Building workers are employed mostly on daily wages, and occasionally according to measurement of the work completed. However, names of women do not often appear on the wage register because their output gets added to that of their menfolk except in the case of single women workers. Wages are paid every ten days only to men, and these include the wages due to other members of the family. Often, maternity leave is not extended to women building workers, although it is a statutory obligation. This results in frequent miscarriages . . . In general, women building workers are deeply concerned about conditions of work. Pay inequalities, invisibility as producers and earners, blocked opportunities of advancement for want of skill, frequent relocation, lack of freedom to plan their work, hard and long working hours

[34] NCEUS, 'Report on Conditions of Work and Promotion of Livelihoods in the Unorganised Sector', p. 37.

and coping with multiple roles result in a high level of stress. It generates attitudes of passive acceptance of helplessness and misery and conformity, rather than reaction.[35]

This echoes the findings of several similar studies such as that of Meena Gopal[36] and Millie Nihila.[37] Gopal's study of the beedi industry in Tamil Nadu, describes in considerable detail, among other things, the manner in which the selective issuance of passbooks to women workers in the beedi industry enables the beedi contractors to exercise control over the work and time of the workers; worse, the anxiety that is deliberately allowed to build up before a passbook is issued (which quite often may not materialize) keeps women across households divided to the advantage of the contractors. The study provides an extremely nuanced account of how region, class, religion, gender, and organization of the industry combine to make this home-based activity extremely stressful for the women workers.

Nihila's study of the leather tanning industry, concentrated in the district of Dindigul in Tamil Nadu, centre stages the fact that the provision of the Factories Act, 1948 (according to which women and children are prohibited from being employed in tanning of leather because of the hazardous nature of operations involved in tanning) is used to deny worker status to women employed in the industry. According to her estimates, almost 30

[35] GoI, *Report of the Second National Commission on Labour*, pp. 637–8.

[36] Meena Gopal, 'Disempowered Despite Wage Work: Women Workers in Beedi Industry', *Economic & Political Weekly*, vol. 34, nos. 16 and 17, 17–24 April 1999.

[37] Millie Nihila, 'Marginalisation of Women Workers: Leather Tanning Industry in Tamil Nadu', *Economic & Political Weekly*, vol. 34, nos. 16 and 17, 17–24 April 1999.

per cent of the total tannery workforce is female. The manner in which this denial is achieved is by recruiting women through contractors; the latter are on the payrolls of the employers, not the actual women working. The combination of the provision of the Factories Act, 1948, and recruitment through contractors, has resulted in several adverse consequences for women workers. For example, separate toilets or restrooms for women do not exist; no demands for protective gear can be made by these women who have to bare-handedly skin dead animals, clean lime pits soaked with toxic chemicals and waste of skinned animals, among other arduous and unclean jobs.

Discrimination in Wage Structure and Wage Payment

The NCEUS 2008 finds that even in industries where gender stereotyping of tasks seemed to have broken down with men and women workers performing all tasks, the wage structure continued to remain gendered, with women uniformly receiving less wages than men. Further, literacy had no role to play in the determination of wages. In addition, the NCEUS 2008 also notes that there is a plethora of minimum wages set for different employments within a state and across states; uniformly these are differentially applied across gender. Worse, the NCEUS finds that:

> the share of wage workers securing wages below the National Minimum wage norm is significantly high across industries clearly indicating that the minimum wage regulations are hardly being followed and applied in most industries. In fact 85% of all casual workers in rural areas and 57% of them in urban areas get wage below the minimum wages.[38]

[38] NCEUS, 'Report on Conditions of Work and Promotion of Livelihoods in the Unorganised Sector', p. 48.

Overall, the official reports quoted above corroborate that lack of a clear-cut employer-employee relationship in the case of the self-employed and among the outworkers/ homeworkers, and lack of a designated place of work for the majority (particularly women) adds to the problem of invisibility of such enterprises. It is this invisibility at all levels and denial of status as worker that has enabled employers as well as the State to deny women their due, however minuscule the scale and poorly administered the statutory benefits admissible to legitimate workers may be. Worse, this invisibility also enables the employers and the State to deny the hazardous, inhuman, and exploitative conditions under which most women work.

What has received some attention in the Report of SNCL[39] and the Report of TN 1998 (but none

[39] The Second National Commission on Labour has examined extensively the functioning of institutions responsible for safety of workers in the mining industry, for example. Suffice it to note here the shocking findings of the commission relating to, among other things, the low priority accorded to recruitment and expansion of personnel needed to undertake the task even as the industry has grown by leaps and bounds. 'Recently, the Parliament's Standing Committee on Labour and Welfare (13th Lok Sabha) observed (para 2.64 of its report) that during the last 15 years, the size of the mining industry has increased fourfold, whereas the staff component of the DGMS has remained static, and this is grossly inadequate to meet safety operations in mines. The Committee further observed that out of 598 coalmines, the Dept has been able to make complete inspections in only 159 coalmines during the year 2000–1. The Dept has pleaded that due to inadequate staff, it could carry out inspection of all mines only once in four years. The shocking state of inadequacy of staff can be seen from the fact that at present, the Dept has only 130 inspecting officers against the sanctioned strength of 167 . . . It can be observed that the actual number of inspecting officers is about 22% lower than the sanctioned strength. We were informed that this was because of procedural delays in filling up

at all in the NCEUS Report 2008) is the theme of labour administration. For example, on the theme of occupational safety and health of workers, the SNCL Report 2002 makes it amply clear that occupational safety and health of labour has never been a priority item on the agenda of any government even going by simple indicators such as number of posts of safety inspectors created, number of vacancies that remain unfilled in these posts despite growth of such industries that mandatorily require monitoring, number of cases of violations filed, numbers disposed off, etc. The TN 1998 Report has more damaging observations: one, it points out how governments have desisted from using their powers of 'notification' of industries under Section 85 of the Factories Act, 1948, despite sizeable numbers of workers being employed in a range of industries not covered as yet by any labour laws. Two, the report also details how mindless, incomplete actions, such as the one undertaken in Tamil Nadu—namely, the bifurcation of labour department into a labour department and an inspectorate of factories—has resulted in a deadlock to the detriment of workers.[40] Three, the Report notes the

vacancies arising from retirement, etc. In fact, a shortage of 20–30% inspecting officers against the sanctioned strength normally exists in this organisation. In addition to this, there has hardly been any increase in the strength of inspecting officers since 1971 though the mining industry has increased several times during this period' (see GoI, *Report of the Second National Commission on Labour*, pp. 66 and 73).

[40] Subsequent to the bifurcation, the Tamil Nadu government issued a government order whereby the labour department was to recruit 60 assistant inspectors of labour (factories) to be deputed to the inspectorate of factories to oversee the implementation of the Factories Act. However, since the government has not created sixty posts of assistant inspectors of factories, the implementation of the

near impossibility of effective enforcement of any labour law given the present strength of the labour department.[41] Four, the report notes the paltry fines imposed on employers for violations of labour laws. To quote the report in some detail:

> The fine provided for the first offence under Tamil Nadu Shops and Establishment Act, 1947, Tamil Nadu Catering Establishment Act, 1958, Tamil Nadu Industrial Establishment [National and Festival Holidays] Act, 1958, respectively are Rs.25, extendable up to Rs.50 on certain counts. For the second offence, the fines respectively are Rs.250 on certain counts, while no enhancement of fine is provided for the second or subsequent offences on many other counts... Due to this, important benefits and privileges like minimum wages, service cards, leave, weekly rest and other benefits have not reached the workers. This also deprives them of important documents/evidences which are basically required even to prove their employment under the employer concerned... In fact, it is noticed that in many cases employers willingly violate the provisions and readily agree to pay the fine provided for such violations.[42]

What Do We Do with 'Unpaid Labour'?

In sum, the burden of our argument is the following: one, within the large, growing, amorphous segment called the unorganized economy, the dominant category is that of the self-employed, within which a significant percentage

---

Factories Act which includes the notification under Section 85 has not been possible.

[41] The TN 1998 Report records that an inspector in the labour department enforces twenty-one labour enactments. This is in addition to the regular administrative work, court work, apart from periodical special drives under Consumer Protection Acts.

[42] TN, *Report of the Committees Constituted to Study the Problems and Issues of Unorganised Labour in Tamil Nadu*, p. 91.

of women work as 'unpaid family workers'. Two, our data reveals that substantial numbers of women in the prime age group, 15–59 years, still return 'domestic duties' as their principal status. Three, those who reported domestic duties as their principal status were also involved in a number of activities aimed at helping their households save incomes if not to directly earn it. Four, more than one-third of the women reporting domestic duties as principal status were willing to accept work at home, part or full time. Five, the applicability of protective labour legislation to the vast numbers in the unorganized economy is abysmal, with effective coverage being even less. Six, labour law administration, as is currently constituted, is part of the problem of ineffective and non-coverage.

Read together, these reports, and their recommendations in particular, raise some disturbing questions relating to the resilience of the 'unpaid labour' category that no amount of effective coverage or even effective administration of protective labour legislation can resolve. This, in our opinion, has more to do with the nature and trajectory of economic development and the ensuing employment that this economic growth is generating. Otherwise, it is difficult to account for the sustained manner in which such large percentages of women continue to figure in the category of 'unpaid labour', be it 'unpaid family labour' or 'unpaid domestic labour'. While every one of these reports recognizes the category of unpaid labour, their recommendations have invariably addressed the existing set of laws that cater to *wage* labour.

At one level, the country as a whole, and feminists in particular, will need to think through the category of unpaid labour to arrive at a set of policies, which needs to operate simultaneously, if the disadvantages that go with being an unpaid labour need to be removed. At another level, taken individually, each of these reports seems to take as given the fact that the continued creation and expansion of the unorganized economy and also the condemnation of large numbers of women to the category of unpaid labour are an inevitable consequence of economic growth.

Further, as long as we continue to designate a number of routine household tasks as women's tasks, public policies will continue to remain gendered. To return to a quote earlier from the NCEUS 2008 Report: 'Recognition of women's contribution to extended SNA could, and should, lead to greater appreciation of public policies for the *welfare of women*'[43] (emphasis added). In other words, if the underlying assumptions of public policies are not questioned, the latter could contribute to essentializing and reinforcing domestic tasks as women's work, but in the name of enhancing women's welfare.

What does the above lead us to: one, the category of unpaid family labour currently has no protective labour legislation, since none are applicable to this category. The unpaid domestic labour category can be salvaged to a significant extent, if our gendered outlook on this category is replaced by household and citizenship-based protective legislation that enables every household and every household member to be relieved of such chores by effective provision through appropriate public policies, be it water, fuel, dependency care, etc.

Finally, we need to revisit and endorse the call for universal availability of maternal benefits and childcare facilities made by the Shramshakti Report 1988.

[43] NCEUS, 'Report on Conditions of Work and Promotion of Livelihoods in the Unorganised Sector', p. 79.

In short, this exercise has starkly brought out the fact that, while women's work and women as workers suffer exclusion from protective legislation, a disaggregated analysis of the nature and kind of exclusion calls for a nuanced and focused approach. It has also indicated that, at the moment, existing protective legislation has no solution to the category of unpaid family labour; at the same time, the unpaid domestic labour category will need a paradigm shift in policy conception if 'welfare of women' is truly of prime concern.

CHAPTER 12

The Formal Creation of Informality and Gender Injustice

Illustrations from India's Social Sector

The Context

While Western feminists have been continually engaging and interrogating the theme of 'doing/undoing/redoing' gender (to be discussed later), for countries such as India this framework needs to be supplemented and contextualized to accommodate and account for the nature and level of development; the latter still foregrounds much of the discussion on and about gender in our societies.

By superimposing the 'doing gender' framework onto the Indian state's agenda of 'doing development', we hope to demonstrate how the changing development

* Previously presented at the 56th Annual Conference of the Indian Society of Labour Economics (ISLE), held at Ranchi, 18–20 December 2014, and based on the author's J.P. Naik Memorial Lecture (instituted by the Centre for Women's Development Studies, Delhi), delivered on 13 August 2014 at Delhi University. Previously published in the *International Journal of Labour Economics*, 2015.

discourse, which today talks of, among other things, 'smart economics', has become a euphemism for using women and girls to 'fix the world'; of investing in women and girls so that they work *for* development as informal workers even if the name of the game is to achieve gender equality and empowerment of women.

Specific Concerns of the Chapter

After a brief discussion of the theoretical framework informing the argument of this chapter, we proceed to an examination of official reports and data; this part of the chapter attempts to demonstrate what development has meant to women and girl children, emphasizing in particular the point that the attempt to kill two birds (poverty reduction and gender inequality) with one stone (poverty alleviation/empowerment schemes) has ended up overshadowing commitments to change gender relations even as it has resulted in the 'feminization of responsibility and obligation'.[1]

The second part of this chapter, based on ethnographic studies, highlights how development programmes and welfare entitlements are understood and operationalized and get reworked on the ground with specific consequences for women and girl children.

The aim of the chapter is to bring home the message that juxtaposing the macro concerns of policies to address 'gender' with ground realities provides rich insights into how and why the GOI's manner of 'doing development' is actually contributing to the entrenchment of gender inequality, rather than working towards 'dismantling the gender system'. Informalization of work, with women

[1] S. Chant, 'The "Feminisation of Poverty" and the "Feminisation" of Anti-Poverty Programmes: Room for Revision?', *The Journal of Development Studies*, vol. 44, no. 2, 2008, pp. 165–97.

occupying a more central place in this informalization, is achieved through the formal mechanisms of the State; the latter, by 'doing development through gender' has moved further and further away from the feminist agenda of 'mainstreaming gender', understood in the sense of achieving a transformation of society that is premised on gender equality.

'Doing Development', 'Alleviating Poverty', 'Empowering Women': Framework for Analysis

In 1987, the journal *Gender and Society* carried several papers that began with a seminal piece on 'Doing Gender' by West and Zimmerman. Among other things, the latter article offered a critical assessment of the then existing perspectives on sex and gender, even as it introduced important distinctions among the terms 'sex', 'sex category', and 'gender'.[2] In 1995, in the same journal, West and Fenstermaker published the article 'Doing Difference' to make up for an earlier neglect of race and class, and, 'to extend our analysis to consider explicitly the relationships among gender, race and class, and to reconceptualize "difference" as an ongoing interactional accomplishment'.[3]

In 2009, *Gender and Society* revisited the theme in the form of a symposium that, in a sense, took stock of how 'Doing Gender' had been conceptualized and operationalized over the intervening period. Among the several contributions to this discussion, we highlight Barbara Risman's observations for the sharp manner in

[2] C. West and D.H. Zimmerman, 'Doing Gender', *Gender and Society*, vol. 1, no. 2, 1987, pp. 125–51.

[3] C. West and S. Fenstermaker, 'Doing Difference', *Gender and Society*, vol. 9, no. 1, February 1995, pp. 8–37.

which it captures the sanitized manner in which 'Doing Gender' has been operationalized. To quote Risman:

> First, the concept has been so integrated into the sociological lexicon that the implicit feminist critique embedded within it sometimes disappears entirely. Second, the feminist use of doing gender has become so diffuse that we have created a tautology: whatever groups of boys and girls, or men and women, do is a kind of gender.[4]

Several other scholars, including Deutsch,[5] for example, pointed out how, despite the revolutionary potential (of West and Zimmerman's 1987 article) for illuminating how to dismantle the gender system, 'doing gender' had, on the contrary, become a theory of gender persistence and the inevitability of inequality. Deutsch also points out (and this is important for the argument of this chapter) that, while the persistence of inequality cannot be ignored,

> one of the major contributions of the approach is to examine the limits of structural change... how the focus on the interactional level can also illuminate the possibility of change... (1) when and how social interactions become less gendered, not just differently gendered; (2) the conditions under which gender is irrelevant in social interactions; (3) whether all gendered interactions reinforce inequality; (4) how the structural (institutional) and interactional levels might work together to produce change . . . My plea is that we shift our inquiry about ongoing social interactions to focus on change. Although I do not have the answers, I believe we should change the questions.[6]

[4] B.J. Risman, 'From Doing to Undoing Gender: Gender as We Know It', *Gender and Society*, vol. 23, no. 1, February 2009, p. 81.

[5] F.M. Deutsch, 'Undoing Gender', *Gender and Society*, vol. 21, no. 1, February 2007, pp. 106–127.

[6] Ibid., p. 114.

Needless to add, much of the discussion on 'doing/undoing/redoing' gender and as documented in the pages of *Gender and Society* is in the context of Western societies. It is our contention that while the framework within which the 'doing of gender' is discussed remains relevant across time and space, what is conspicuous by its absence in the above discussion (whether in 1987 or 2009) is the context and level of 'development' of a country—political, economic, and social—a phenomenon that cannot be ignored and which still foregrounds much of the discussion on and about gender, in societies such as India.

In 1989, the journal *World Development*, in a special issue focusing on poverty, examined ways to improve the livelihoods of poor women through support for activities that could enhance their earnings. In this issue, based on field studies covering the sectors of dairying and silk production in India, Marty Chen spoke of the strategic significance of promoting women's work and earnings through a sectoral approach. Chen's rationale for advocating a sectoral approach stemmed from her following argument:

> In many developing countries, a distinction is made between mainstream development programs (directed at generating growth) and anti-poverty programs (directed at protecting the poor). The mainstream development programs are typically developed along sectoral lines. That is, critical activities of the economy are assigned, with significant budget appropriations, to specialized ministries or departments for support and development. Antipoverty programs on the other hand, are designed to deliver welfare services, productive assets, or employment to the poor, and are typically assigned to welfare ministries or departments. Women's programs—whether economic or social—are usually categorized and developed as antipoverty or welfare programs.[7]

[7] M. Chen, 'A Sectoral Approach to Promoting Women's Work: Lessons from India', *World Development*, vol. 17, no. 7, 1989, p. 1007.

It was Chen's hope that applying a sectoral frame to the analysis of women's work could provide a way to close the gap between

> the now well-documented economic roles of women and the as yet male-biased macroeconomic planning done by governments . . . because government programs are typically developed along sectoral lines, women can be linked to existing support systems and infrastructure. Finally, and perhaps most fundamentally, women's work and needs can be translated into broader policy issues relating to sectoral development.[8]

Further, Chen attributed a number of positives to the adoption of the sectoral approach:

> By working with women in the critical sectors of the economy, the approach serves not only to link women to sector-specific government programs but also, by so doing, to make their work in these sectors 'visible' to national policy makers. By conceptualizing women as an economic category (workers) rather than as social categories (mothers, wives, widows) the approach presents the case for women as economic agents and legitimate clients for the mainstream programs and policies of government. By tailoring interventions to meet the needs of specific sectoral groups, those interventions cover not just a given number of clients but potentially a whole sector of women workers. And, perhaps most importantly, by organizing women around common structural problems, the approach promotes empowerment as well as narrow economic goals.[9]

We have reproduced Chen's arguments in some detail to demonstrate how, almost twenty-five years on since Chen wrote the above, while women have indeed been inducted into several important development sectors

[8] Ibid., p. 1008.
[9] Ibid., p. 1015.

of the economy (such as healthcare and education), and while they and their work are not just 'visible' but constitute the backbone of some of these sectors, this visibility while nevertheless improving their *condition* (material state), has not necessarily contributed to improving their *position* (in society in terms of access to power and decision making).

Concretely, using 'paid employment' as a trope, we demonstrate how the Indian State attempts to kill several birds with one stone: (1) State-sponsored or State-executed women's empowerment programmes have become euphemisms to thrust responsibilities on women but which nomenclature enables governments to deny women the status of 'workers' even if, in some cases, women are gainfully employed; (2) increasingly, the expanding social sector welfare programmes of the State, at both the central and local levels, are being implemented through local women; the latter are, however, designated as volunteers and paid an honorarium—a 'smart economics' move that makes women work for development rather than development empowering women through the creation of formal employment. As illustrations of these attempts, we critically engage with the healthcare, education and social welfare sectors, wherein:

(a) The State continues to appoint large numbers of Accredited Social Health Activists (ASHAs) but who technically do not belong to the Health Ministry of either the local or the central government;
(b) The institution of *para*-teachers (contract teachers) has become the norm rather than the exception; and
(c) The conditions as well as the position of *anganwadi* and mid-day meal workers continues to remain

precarious even in states where the ostensibly 'well-administered' functioning of these schemes has earned kudos for the states concerned.

Empowering Women or Making Women Work for Development?

Chant and Sweetman's[10] trenchant critique, among other things, of the mission statements and goals for bringing about change laid down by development organizations (wherein investing in girls and women is seen as not only being fair but also a 'smart economic move'[11] to break intergenerational poverty and create a better world) forms the backdrop against which we assess the GoI's social welfare programmes that have an even longer history of being premised on the deployment of women as 'volunteers' and 'honorary' staff to fulfil the development agenda of the Indian State.

The discussion by Chant and Sweetman enables us to situate the Indian State's use of women and girls to 'fix the economy' in the global context; in a sense it also makes us realize that, at one level, the continuing devaluation of women's time, effort, and labour by the Indian State (a point to be elaborated below), and at another level, the entry of corporates into the social sector through the mandatory Corporate Social Responsibility (CSR) programmes, to a large extent, echoes the global agenda. The latter, as Chant and Sweetman record, works as follows: 'Development

[10] S. Chant and C. Sweetman, 'Fixing Women or Fixing the World? "Smart Economics", Efficiency Approaches and Gender Equality in Development', *Gender and Development*, vol. 20, no. 3, November 2012, pp. 517–29.

[11] Ibid., p. 520.

organizations and governments have been joined in the focus on the "business case" for gender equality and the empowerment of women, by businesses and enterprises which are interested in contributing to social good.'[12] However, Chant and Sweetman demonstrate how this smart economics move 'oversimplifies complexity and shifts responsibility';[13] more significant, they aver, 'smart economics is concerned with building women's capacities *in the interest of development rather than promoting women's rights for their own sake*' (emphasis added).[14]

The functioning of the healthcare and education sectors of the economy provides rich evidence of the manner in which the women of this country (poor, rural women in particular) contribute to development much more than what they benefit from development. For example, the National Rural Health Mission (NRHM) launched by the GoI in 2005 is a major flagship programme aimed at achieving several ambitious goals in the health sector, many of which are slated to be implemented, monitored, and fulfilled by the ASHAs, the cornerstone of the above mission. Using the ASHA programme as a case study, this chapter aims to demonstrate the stark disjuncture in the manner in which the GoI approaches the theme of recruitment, roles, responsibilities, and monetary compensation to ASHAs when juxtaposed against studies conducted on the ground, that, among other things, also capture the voices and perceptions of ASHAs themselves about the mission programme.

[12] Ibid., p. 520.
[13] Ibid., p. 525.
[14] Ibid., p. 527.

The GoI's take on the ASHA Programme

The Report of the Mid-Term Appraisal of the Eleventh Plan by the Planning Commission (PC, 2007–12)[15] is a good starting point to get an official appraisal of the status of healthcare and health infrastructure in the country. We concentrate on the section on human resources rather than physical infrastructure.

PC 2007–12, while acknowledging that the shortage of human resources in health is as pronounced as lack of physical infrastructure, interestingly also notes that the overall shortfall of female health workers and of Auxiliary Nurse Midwives (ANMs) was relatively low at 12.43 per cent in 2008 when compared to shortfalls of 54.3 per cent in the case of male health workers, 53.3 per cent in radiographers, 50.9 per cent in laboratory technicians, and 64.5 per cent in specialists. What is, therefore, eminently discernible is a concerted effort to recruit female health workers.

Several disturbing observations in terms of the nature and status of appointments of health personnel contained in PC 2007–12, include the following:

> It has been reported that due to contractual recruitments with NRHM funds, states have added 42,633 ANMs, 12,485 MBBS doctors, and 2,474 specialists. In the last 3 years under NRHM, 26,253 staff nurses, 7,399 AYUSH doctors, and 3,110 AYUSH paramedics were appointed. As contractual appointments are facilitated, the states tend to decrease their sanctioned posts. It must therefore be ensured by the states that they will, in the long run, bear the expenditure for such contractual appointments.[16]

[15] *Report of the Mid-Term Appraisal of the Eleventh Plan by the Planning Commission*, New Delhi: Planning Commission, 2007–12.

[16] Ibid., pp. 149, 151.

Specifically, on ASHAs, PC 2007–12 observes the following:

> The appointment of locally recruited women as ASHAs who would link potential beneficiaries with the health service system is an important element of NRHM. The good part is that 7.49 lakh ASHAs have been appointed; but several issues still need to be resolved. Not only is there a lack of transparency in the selection, ASHAs are often inadequately trained. Besides, their focus seems to be on facilitating institutional deliveries. The ASHA who accompanies the expectant mother faces considerable hardships because she has nowhere to stay for duration of confinement as institutional accommodation facilities are non-existent. They also often experience long delays in payment of incentives . . . the payments (under the Janani Suraksha Yojana) are delayed by three to four months [at times even a year in some states] and are often made only after repeated visits by claimants. There are complaints of unauthorized deductions by the disbursing functionaries. While cheque payments reduce leakages, they delay the process further. Due to lack of identity cards or proof of address, many women are unable to open bank accounts and therefore cannot avail of the benefits.[17]

The Scene on the Ground with Regard to the Institution of ASHAs

We fall back on a couple of fairly recent studies (one, an ethnographic sketch of a particular ASHA, and the other, a survey-based research study) that provide graphic details of the contexts, circumstances, and conditions under which ASHAs struggle to fulfil the State's expectations of them to become change agents apart from delivering on health goals.

[17] Ibid., p. 154.

We begin with Gjostein's[18] ethnographic study of an ASHA based in rural Rajasthan. This study is aimed at interrogating the Rajasthan state's depiction of the ASHAs in the following terms: 'She [the ASHA] is the link between the community and the health care provider[s]. [The] Department of Medical and Health at State and at Center is looking at ASHA *as a change agent who will bring the reforms* in improving the health status of [the] oppressed community of India'[19] (emphasis in original).

In the course of her exploration into the life and working experience of the ASHA, the author realizes and notes how complex is the terrain in which the ASHA is expected to fulfil the 'change agent' role:

> The ASHA . . . needs to deal with competing loyalties and conflicts of interest. The ASHAs must in practice manage and manoeuvre their many professional and personal roles: as a community member, as a government worker or 'lackey' under controlling superiors, and as a potential 'social activist'. Their position provides an interesting access point to examine the dynamics of changing gender roles and women's agency in contemporary rural India.[20]

An important detail captured in the study is the range of work that the ASHAs are expected to perform, as the author puts it, 'to promote the various pieces of "health advice" the Indian authorities have notoriously promoted to the population'.[21] These include: compliance with the

[18] D.K. Gjostein, 'A Veiled Change Agent: The "Accredited Social Health Activist" in Rural Rajasthan', in *Women, Gender and Everyday Social Transformation in India*, ed. K.B. Nielsen and A. Waldrop, UK and USA: Anthem Press, 2014, pp. 139–56.

[19] Ibid., p. 139.

[20] Ibid., p. 140.

[21] Ibid., p. 141.

small-family norm; vaccination of children; seeking out health check-ups during pregnancy; giving birth in a hospital; exclusively breastfeeding children for the first 6 months; using contraceptives and opting for sterilization after the birth of two children; construction of toilets; and so on.[22]

The ethnographic and participant observation methodologies deployed by the author enabled her to gain first-hand knowledge of the day-to-day functioning of the ASHA. She recounts her experience as follows:

> When I asked ASHAs about their position and work, none of them described themselves as 'activists' or 'change agents'. Rather, they explained their role by listing their various tasks . . . The ASHA's various responsibilities and tasks are . . . quite comprehensive, only for some of which they are compensated . . . In Rajasthan, the ASHAs have an additional role as a sahyogini (associate), an outreach person employed at the anganwadi centres. This means that in Rajasthan, ASHAs work for, are compensated by and report to superiors in two departments: the Department of Medical, Health and Family Welfare and the Department of Women and Child Development . . . *ASHAs are not defined as permanent government employees. Rather, they are compensated as 'honorary volunteers...* superiors often expected certain results from the ASHAs under them and held them accountable for achieving set monthly and yearly targets of, for example, hospital delivery, vaccination and sterilization. They enforced these expectations with different methods of pressure'[23] (emphasis added).

[22] Ibid.

[23] D.K. Gjostein, 'A Veiled Change Agent: The "Accredited Social Health Activist" in Rural Rajasthan', in *Women, Gender and Everyday Social Transformation in India*, ed. K.B. Nielsen and A. Waldrop, UK and USA: Anthem Press, 2014, p. 149

While at one level, as recorded above, superiors exerted pressure on ASHAs to produce results/achieve targets, the operation of some of the tasks expected of them brought them into direct confrontation with other functionaries, government as well as non-government. For example, the author speaks of being witness to frequent quarrels at the maternity wards between the nurses and ASHAs. The context for the quarrels arises from the manner in which the ASHA programme pits the ASHAs against nurses in hospitals. Underlying this antagonism is the monetary compensation that the ASHA is expected to receive for encouraging women to choose institutional delivery rather than deliver at home; the latter is aimed at achieving the State's agenda of reducing infant mortality, which is premised on the notion that non-institutional deliveries constitute the major cause of infant mortality in the country.

The author provides details of the specific manner in which the compensation scheme works and why the particular manner in which the compensation is to be availed of brings the ASHA into confrontation with hospital staff:

Since 2005 women had been paid Rs.1,400 under the NRHM's Janani Suraksha Yojana (JSY)—the safe motherhood scheme—to give birth at a hospital instead of at home. Additionally, the JSY schemes pay Rs.400 for transportation. If an ASHA accompanies a woman to the hospital, the transportation money is paid to her in addition to Rs.200 for herself. The latter amount is to compensate the ASHA not only for accompanying the woman to deliver at the hospital, but also for counselling and bringing her to three check-ups during the pregnancy. Some of the nurses would encourage families to come without an ASHA, by reasoning that they did not really need her there, and that they (the families) would be paid

Rs.400 more if they came alone. Nurses would frequently not authorize the ASHA's involvement in a delivery case unless she was present in the labour room at the time of the delivery. And without this authorization the ASHAs would not receive their compensation of Rs.200.[24]

The reason for reproducing the above in some detail is to underscore the following:

- The nature and number of tasks expected of the ASHA, which is one part of the story;
- That ASHAs are not considered government employees but 'honorary volunteers' so that it becomes convenient to compensate them for some tasks while leaving several others uncompensated, which is the second part of the story;
- That ASHAs, are expected to deliver the hitherto unachievable and not-so-easy development agendas of the GoI (such as bringing about an increase in institutional deliveries, and reduction in infant mortality, among other things), but under circumstances that expose them to confrontation and abuse, a scenario that has not been captured and recorded by any official document on the subject.

Hence, while there are 'official' reasons for delay in payment to ASHAs as recorded and reproduced from PC 2007–12 above, the actual reasons, such as those that involve the non-registration of the ASHA's name in cases brought to hospital for delivery, finds no mention anywhere and therefore merits no resolution. The concept of 'development', here understood in terms of health indicators and to be achieved through ASHAs, does

[24] Ibid., p. 151.

not simply exploit women. Doing development through gender is bad enough, but making it a humiliating experience is unpardonable.

Bhatia's[25] survey of the ASHA scheme in Maharashtra is the second study that we have found extremely useful for highlighting the theme of how the Indian State does development through gender. Bhatia's study, conducted in the Shahapur *taluka* in Maharashtra, was aimed at capturing the stakeholders' perspectives on the system of remuneration characterizing the ASHA scheme. The findings of Bhatia's study, in our opinion, complement the observations reproduced above from Gjostein's piece on Rajasthan.

Among the important points recorded by Bhatia is the role that the families of ASHAs play, particularly in a context wherein ASHAs receive their remuneration long after completion of tasks and submission of relevant documents. Under such circumstances, it is the families that have to provide an advance to the ASHAs to enable them to even begin their tasks. This, along with the fact that ASHAs were required to be away from their homes (even if within the vicinity of the village), had tremendous social repercussions that required supportive families—with the support being both social and economic, and which support was neither freely available nor could be taken for granted.

An important finding from the in-depth interviews was that the family of the ASHA was a key stakeholder in the ASHAs' understanding of their work. The ASHAs shared that the foremost challenge after joining was to step out of their

[25] K. Bhatia, 'Performance-based Incentives of the ASHA Scheme: Stakeholders' Perspectives', *Economic and Political Weekly*, vol. XLIX, no. 22, 31 May 2014, pp. 145–51.

homes for a purpose that was not related to their domestic requirements. They had to negotiate with their families to join and to continue and the family's perceptions of their remuneration were crucial in these negotiations. A perception of the task-incentive balance being a one-on-one equation made the post less worthwhile for their families because most of the incentives were seen as being low.[26]

The ASHAs in the area said that they were escorting pregnant women who were not from Below the Poverty Line (BPL) families and seriously ill persons without incentives. They were told to make daily rounds of their villages and anganwadis. Such gratis tasks were considered as 'free tasks'. The ASHAs said they were facing pressures from their families to discontinue because of the difficulties with the remuneration.

In this study, as part of the survey, both the ASHAs and the ASHA facilitators did a free listing of the responsibilities of the ASHA. 'The 244 ASHAs (covered by the survey) collectively listed 20 responsibilities. Just five tasks were paid incentives as per the task-incentive entitlements, the rest were gratis. The 29 ASHA facilitators had collectively mentioned 24 responsibilities with the same five paid tasks. Several unpaid sub-tasks were mentioned in these free listings.'[27]

The following observation by the author on the reluctance of the system to affiliate and acknowledge ASHAs as health workers of the Health Ministry reinforces our point of how this flagship programme of the GoI does development through gender and in the process exploits the very women whom the programme was meant to empower.

A point of consideration with regard to the ASHA scheme is that every aspect of the ASHAs' functioning from

[26] Ibid., p. 148.
[27] Ibid., p. 149.

selection to payment is through the health services, leading to an identification of the ASHAs with the health services and a sense of entitlement. All the mandated tasks of the ASHA are towards accomplishing the goals of the national health programmes. This is in common with all the health functionaries within the health services. Yet, none of the others involved in the national health programmes receive their payment according to their performance that month (unlike the ASHAs). The reluctance of the health services to take full ownership of the ASHAs while extending her functions revealed a gender hierarchical bias. Ironically, the ASHA scheme has selected these women due to the advantages of their gender and location within the community.[28]

The Institution of Para-Teachers

The education sector, like that of healthcare, employs large numbers of women, particularly in the elementary education sector, as teachers. Various factors over the years have led to unprecedented levels of attention and growth in this sector, necessitating the appointment of teachers. While it is well known that the demand for additional physical and human educational infrastructure is not uniform across different states of the country, what is, however, common right across the country is the increasing recruitment of teachers on a contractual basis. These teachers are also referred to as 'para-teachers'. Across the country, in order to meet the surge in demand for teachers, consequent to the explosion in enrolment, and at a time when states were and still are facing fiscal deficits, the contractual appointment of teachers was facilitated by the Centre to minimize the permanent recurring liability of teacher salaries in state budgets. Studies (such as those referred to below) mention that

[28] Ibid., p. 150.

several states have discontinued the hiring of regular teachers altogether in government schools; the new recruits are only para-teachers.

In order to illustrate how the institution of para-teachers, like the ASHA programme, uses women (and also men) to fulfil the State's need to meet its educational target (whether national or international), we refer to two studies that have explored this institution in some depth. Both studies cover similar ground, and hence we discuss them together. One is an exhaustive review of the institution of para-teachers by Govinda and Josephine published by UNESCO in 2004;[29] the second is a literature review of available studies covering the theme of para-teachers in India by Kingdon and Sipahimalani-Rao, published in 2010, in the *Economic and Political Weekly*.[30]

We begin with an important observation made by Govinda and Josephine, which, among other things, firmly establishes that the institution of para-teachers is not a passing phenomenon, rather one that is not only going to remain but also expand:

> Engagement of teachers on contract basis as opposed to employment on permanent tenures particularly in government schools is a recent phenomenon. The term 'para-teachers' is a generic term applied to characterize all teachers appointed on contract basis often under varying service conditions in terms of emoluments and qualification requirements. Some documents also refer to them as 'contract teachers'. In fact, official documents of state governments refer to them in

[29] R. Govinda and Y. Josephine, *Para Teachers in India: A Review*, Paris: International Institute of Educational Planning, UNESCO, October 2004.

[30] Geeta Gandhi Kingdon and Vandana Sipahimalani-Rao, 'Para-Teachers in India: Status and Impact', *Economic and Political Weekly*, vol. XLV, no. 12, 20 March 2010, pp. 59–67.

vernacular terms as *shiksha karmi, shiksha mitra, guruji*, and so on, depending on the schemes under which teachers are being employed. In one sense there is no clarity on who is a para teacher or under what kind of contract do teachers get engaged if not on permanent tenures . . . This is probably due to the perception that it is only a passing phase in the development of the system and would soon disappear. This, however, is not likely to happen in the near future unless a drastic revision of thinking at the national level emerges among education policy makers. At present . . . it is an expanding phenomenon and the policy pronouncements clearly favour its continuance.[31]

A point to be noted right at the outset is that a large number of males also function as para-teachers and in that sense they are also working for 'development' rather than 'development' working for them. The studies explode several myths associated with the above institution: that para-teachers are less qualified, and that they bring down the quality of teaching because of the lack of professional training in teaching, among others. What is significant for the purpose of our discussion is the following observation: '. . . all states pay para-teachers a fraction of their regular counterparts; in West Bengal, para teachers were paid just 14% of the wages of regular teachers in 2007.'[32]

How do champions (read economists, largely) of para-teacher schemes push through this programme? By putting forth the following arguments:

- There is greater accountability of the para-teacher because she/he is drawn from the community.
- There are better linkages with the community since the community is involved in the recruitment

[31] Govinda and Josephine, *Para Teachers in India: A Review*, p. 8.

[32] Kingdon and Sipahimalani-Rao, 'Para-Teachers in India: Status and Impact', p. 61.

process and local bodies most often pay their salaries.

- The para-teachers are about twice or thrice as cost-effective as regular teachers given their 'effectiveness in imparting learning at a cost to the taxpayer of only one-third to one-half of the regular teachers'.[33]

Given the fact that the institution of para-teachers has come to stay, it is imperative to move away from seeing the issue only as one of exploitation or of pitting the institution of para-teachers against the body of regular teachers. The discussion instead needs to be placed in the larger context of how it all began, namely as a (development) solution, wherein states embarking on ambitious programmes of enrolling students also needed to recruit teachers but, given their poor fiscal status, had little or no resources to pay and maintain *regular* teachers.

The perennial anxiety to find 'cost-effective' solutions when it comes to hiring teachers as well as health workers needs to be placed in the larger context of the debate among fiscal economists on, among other things, two issues: one, the practice of classifying expenditures in government budgets under 'Plan and non- Plan'; and, two, inadequate fiscal space for states to fulfil the objectives of plans even as major responsibilities for Plan implementation are devolved on them. The point that needs to be emphasized here is that 'Plan' expenditure has come to symbolize 'development' expenditure and, therefore, there has been a tendency on the part of governments to go in for larger and larger 'Plans', neglecting to undertake expenditure required for the

[33] Ibid., p. 66.

maintenance and running of existing assets. The recurrent expenditure on the salaries of teachers (once appointed) falls under the non-Plan category. Requirements for meeting non-Plan revenue expenditures have to be met out of transfers recommended by the Finance Commission, which does not go far enough to bring about parity in the Plan/non-Plan expenditure requirements.

The discussion of the theme of Plan/non-Plan fiscal expenditure and its implications on the development performance of states of the country measured by, say, healthcare, education, and employment indicators, is outside the scope of this chapter; the issue, however, needed to be flagged for the reason that it lies at the root of the problem as to why the states of the country not only show differential economic performance but are increasingly resorting to the phenomenon of doing development through gender.

Personnel in Other Social Sectors: 'Employees' or 'Volunteers'?

The Mid-Term Appraisal of the Eleventh Five Year Plan[34] approvingly records the role of the Mid-Day Meal Scheme (MDMS) in having brought about a positive impact on the enrolment and attendance of children (particularly from the weaker sections), elimination of 'classroom hunger', retention of girls in schools, better learning achievements, and the aspect of a shared common meal contributing to gender and social equity. It also quotes the Comptroller and Auditor General's (CAG) 2009 note emphasizing public support for the continuation of MDMS, with a majority of the parents and teachers

[34] *Report of the Mid-Term Appraisal of the Eleventh Plan*, mentioned above.

reporting a positive perception of the impact.[35] The expenditure incurred on cook-cum-helpers is, however, considered as an honorarium.

Palriwala and Neetha,[36] in their study of *anganwadi* and paid domestic workers, point out that though these workers are part of the organized sector, namely the government sector, *anganwadi* workers and helpers are not classified as employees, but as social workers/volunteers receiving a stipend. They are not entitled to the leave and social security benefits enjoyed by permanent, full-time, government employees—an illustration of the State's ability to violate its own labour regulatory framework, particularly in an arena such as care, where women are predominant.

What are the numbers of such *volunteers/social workers* that we are talking of here? As per PC 2007–12 data, the MDMS engages 15.7 lakh cooks, of which 85 per cent are women; *anganwadi* workers number 9,61,975, while helpers number 9,53,483. What is interesting in the Planning Commission's otherwise fairly long list of areas of concern (pertaining to the functioning of the MDMS) is the complete silence relating to the demand of MDMS workers to regularize their appointment.

A lot has been written about how the Tamil Nadu MDMS is a model to be emulated by most states. And yet hardly any mention is made of the workers, the backbone of this programme, and their fight to get themselves regularized. In a study[37] conducted by us, we noted the

[35] Ibid., p. 124.

[36] R. Palriwala and N. Neetha, 'Care Arrangements and Bargains: Anganwadi and Paid Domestic Workers in India', *International Labour Review*, vol. 149, no. 4, 2010, pp. 511–27.

[37] P. Swaminathan et al., 'Tamil Nadu's Mid-day Meal Scheme: Where Assumed Benefits Score Over Hard Data', *Economic and Political Weekly*, vol. 39, no. 44, 30 October 2004, pp. 4811–21.

following on the specific issue of mid-day meal workers based on conversation with unionized workers:

> An aspect on which the organisers, union members in particular, dwelt at length was their employment 'status'; the noon-meal personnel are not treated on par with other government employees, they are not entitled to monetary and miscellaneous benefits to which the government employees are eligible. The eligibility norms based on which noon-meal functionaries are appointed are not made apparent, thereby making it difficult to decipher the basis on which appointments and remunerations are arrived at. The noon-meal personnel form a parallel bureaucracy, as it were, with no regular scale and with very little security. There has been very little engagement thus far by the government regarding how it intends to deal with these personnel. The financial implications of absorbing them as regular government employees could be huge; at the same time without their deployment the scheme cannot be run on a day-to-day basis.[38]

Promoting Investment in Girls: Ground-Level Realities

However limited, ill-designed, or poorly implemented may be the State programmes to address issues of the poor and the marginalized, women and girls in particular, it cannot be denied that since Independence, considerable investment has gone into several aspects that impinge on the lives and livelihoods of the poor and the marginalized in the country. While the discussion thus far has been to examine how development has used gender, it is equally important to explore the implications that the particular manner in which development has been operationalized in the country has had for gender. There is no attempt

[38] Ibid., p. 4820.

here to conduct an exhaustive exploration; rather, we refer to a couple of ethnographic studies that have explored the phenomenon of how education of girls is being interpreted and acted upon on the ground. While the findings of these studies cannot as yet be generalized for the country as a whole, they cannot be ignored either, in our opinion. Papers such as these have made us aware of the express need to conduct more and varied studies that capture the fallouts of macro-level development programmes rather than simply assuming that development indicates progress, or that the outputs of development programmes cannot but be positive.

Education and Status Production

Still,[39] in her paper, 'Spoiled Brides and the Fear of Education: Honour and Social Mobility among Dalits in South India', examines the issues of female education, marriage, and honour among upwardly mobile Dalits. Using data collected during fifteen months of ethnographic fieldwork (2004–5) in a Dalit community in rural Andhra Pradesh, the author describes how families who constitute the upper strata of Dalits are educating their daughters in order to marry them 'upwards' within their caste to a groom with prospects of employment. Education allows these Dalit girls to become *housewives*, with the latter term to be interpreted as indicating an escape from a life of demeaning agricultural labour that involves 'hard work in the hot sun'.[40]

[39] C. Still, 'Spoiled Brides and the Fear of Education: Honour and Social Mobility among Dalits in South India', *Modern Asian Studies*, vol. 45, no. 5, September 2011, pp. 1119–46.

[40] Ibid., p. 1119.

As educated wives married into salaried households, the anxiety was to acquire middle-class virtues that set them apart from their labouring counterparts: '. . . their language, dress, movement and manners must convey shame and modesty. As their responsibility for maintaining family honour increases, they are progressively more scrutinized and controlled'.[41]

The author explores this heightened emphasis on honour among what she refers to as 'traditionally egalitarian Dalits' and suggests reasons for the increasing concern about female sexuality. *Education for girls is seen as a particularly risky business*: on the one hand, the author notes, education provides opportunities for sexual encounters, but on the other hand, it holds the promise of hypergamy. Given their already precarious circumstance, many Dalits choose to cut short the education of their daughters, rather than take the risk. While received literature views the education of girls as a positive phenomenon, particularly due to its potential for employment, Still's ethnographic research shows how education can be a 'contradictory resource' (emphasis added).

The pulling out of hard work in the sun consequent to being educated and married into an economically upwardly mobile household, according to the author, marks a new trend among Dalits, who were either previously constrained by economics to enforce this typically upper-caste sexual morality, or, they had no interest in doing so. And this raises the question of whether or not the advent of changes occurring among a few Dalit families (in terms of girls' education, 'prestige marriage', and withdrawal from work) is a 'good thing'

[41] Ibid., pp. 1119, 1126.

for Dalit women themselves, and whether Dalit social progress translates into women's social progress.

One explanation proffered by the author for the heightened concern about honour is that it is the most accessible way of elevating one's social status. In light of their lack of resources and political power, the control of women is one way in which they can more easily achieve a status that fits in with their emergent self-image of respectability and dignity.[42]

From a feminist point of view, upwardly mobile Dalit women are converted from valuable workers into sedentary status producers. However, quoting Patricia Jeffery's ethnographic study of *pirzada* women who live in strict *purdah* near a Sufi shrine in Delhi, Still emphasizes the need to examine how women themselves logically assess their situation within a particular economic and social framework. Therefore she concludes,

> This reminds us to look at the values that underpin Dalit women's active participation in the pursuit of honour and strategies of upward mobility, even when they seem detrimental overall. And while Dalits may not be using education in the way that liberals, feminists and policymakers expect, they are eager to educate their daughters nonetheless.[43]

In a similar vein, Ciotti,[44] in her paper, 'The Bourgeois Woman and the Half-Naked One: Or the Indian Nation's Contradictions Personified', explores the interplay between development, identity politics, and middle-class aspirations amongst low-caste Chamar women in rural

[42] Ibid., p. 1144.

[43] Ibid., p. 1146.

[44] M. Ciotti, 'The Burgeois Woman and the Half-Naked One': Or the Indian Nation's Contradictions Personified', *Modern Asian Studies*, vol. 44, no. 4, July 2010, pp. 785–815.

north India. The paper brings these discourses together, and in the process demonstrates

> how the Chamar appropriation of the 'modernizing' agenda has initiated a dual process. On the one hand, a minority of women has embarked on an embourgeoisement trajectory predicated on education, 'modern motherhood' and aspirations to white collar employment, and on the other hand, underprivileged women (with their 'unfit' personas) have become increasingly vulnerable to stigmatisation as a result of being in 'menial labour'.[45]

Germane to our discussion is Ciotti's explanation of what education, a relatively new phenomenon, means to the small section of the upwardly mobile Chamar community. Quoting one of her respondents, Ciotti notes:

> According to a young woman from a household supported by government employment, 'marriage is parents' main concern when they provide their daughters with education as well as for the latter, when they pursue their degrees'. Education however is not perceived by women as something purely ornamental, even if it does not mean a college degree, and even if the overwhelming majority of educated women will never find employment outside their household.[46]

On the contrary, most respondents listed a series of benefits to self and family because of being educated, much of which had to do with the civilizing properties of education.

These narratives and the author's fieldwork with women informants also pointed to a transformation of motherhood roles.

[45] Ibid., p. 786,
[46] Ibid., pp. 808–9.

Many Chamar mothers evoke the category coined by Nita Kumar of 'non-mothers' insofar as 'their poverty and insecurity makes their mothering invisible, by implication deficient and unsuccessful' compared with the mothers of the Indian intelligentsia, examined in the same context, the product of colonial modernity. The 'inadequacy' of the Chamar labourer mother is substituted in public and private spaces by the educated mother, suitable for a 'proper' up-bringing of children—for instance, she is able to help them with their homework. Together with the new working woman model, modern motherhood as a result of women's education is an entirely novel gender role in this Chamar community: it does not have a precedent in local history precisely because of the earlier lack of education among women.[47]

What do we make of the two ethnographic studies discussed above? The two studies, though confined to a small section of upwardly mobile Dalits, nevertheless starkly reveal the inadequacy of our development agenda as also the naïve and simplistic belief of our developmental state (read development economists) that the mere provision of and access to education can empower our women and confer so much agency on our girls that they would not only be able to change altogether the context of their present existence, but that it would also be in the direction prescribed in conventional development discourse.

Additionally, no one can fault the communities studied by the above scholars for aiming to use education to make their daughters transit from a life of 'dishonourable labour' to one perceived as more honourable and status-giving, even if the latter is at the cost of giving up paid employment. However, what present development efforts as well as feminist discourse needs to grapple with is

[47] Ibid., p. 810.

how to read and make sense of what seems like women colluding in their own subordination through their notions of honour, motherhood, and modernization.

Education and Early Marriage

Ghosh's[48] 2011 paper evokes interest for its attempt to explain 'the enormous and escalating magnitude of child marriage in West Bengal in recent years'. Ghosh's study combines field exploration with macro data from the Census. According to him, as per the 2001 Census, 37.16 per cent of the girls in the state of West Bengal got married before the age of 18 years, while the corresponding figure for the country, as a whole, is only 32.10 per cent. Further, among the nineteen districts of West Bengal, Malda (the study area of the chapter) accounted for the second highest percentage of child marriage in the state after Murshidabad in 2001.

In Ghosh's view, the perceptions of daughters about the reasons for child marriages differ strikingly for those of parents and other elders:

> ... both fathers and elders have identified 'poverty' as the major reason for fixing marriage of girls early. But a close scrutiny of their behavior in real life reveals that patriarchal values and institutions influence this pattern greatly. This is because parents with sound economic condition in Malda also fixed their daughter's marriage before they were eighteen ... In peasant families across Malda, notions of a girl's virginity and chastity are strongly linked to honour and status of a family or clan. Hence, there is tremendous pressure to minimize the risk of any untoward incidence or improper sexual activity through early marriage. The conservative peasant society of Malda does not normally report harassment cases of girls to

[48] B. Ghosh, 'Early Marriage of Girls in Contemporary Bengal: A Field View', *Social Change*, vol. 41, no. 1, 2011, pp. 41–61.

the police, because such harassment may mean that she has lost her chastity. The community and religious leaders, who very often enjoy moral sanction to control life beyond religion, typically support such value structure and norms.[49]

In the Focus Group Discussions (FGDs) conducted and reported by Ghosh, school-going girls are keen to pursue their education and avoid getting married early: 'They have, therefore, urged on the need for reforming the parents first to initiate change. Subordination as well as undervaluation of the role of the girl child within and outside family, therefore appears to be the major reason for the continuance of the practice of child marriage even today.'[50]

Reading between the lines of the paper, we realize that the problem in Malda is far more complex and definitely not one that can be resolved simply by 'enforcing right to education for all children, especially girls, and prolonging academic career of adolescent girls',[51] as suggested by Ghosh towards the end of his chapter. In fact, Malda to us represents a microcosm of the enormous challenges that require to be understood and tackled *simultaneously* rather than assuming that uni-dimensional programmes—such as increasing the time spent by girls in educational institutions—alone would suffice. Several of these complex factors have been flagged by Ghosh in the text of his paper (such as the quote reproduced earlier) but there seems to be an almost naïve notion that education can overcome some or all of these complex issues.

As in the case of Clarinda Still and Manuela Ciotti's papers discussed earlier, Ghosh's study also emphasizes the aspect of family status and honour which parents and community members strongly

[49] Ibid., p. 50.
[50] Ibid., p. 54.
[51] Ibid., p. 58.

feel could be jeopardized because of girls having to step out for educational purposes. Second, while the expenses connected with the conduct of marriage are deemed as inevitable, regardless of the economic status of households, expending money on girls' higher education, in particular, is deemed as unnecessary and avoidable since it is not only seen as not benefiting the natal family but also as a huge social and economic risk that families, given their position and dependence on the community in their immediate vicinity, are not prepared to shoulder. Third, the earlier the marriage of a girl is settled, the lesser the dowry that parents perceive they need to pay for the same—a point flagged by all three authors. Families lower down the economic ladder argue that imparting higher education to their daughters would require them to look for even more highly educated grooms; the latter would translate into higher dowry demands that such parents can ill-afford. What is, however, interesting is the observation that Ghosh records about economically well-off parents:

> It is noticeably revealed through FGDs that due to the gendered nature of role classification in rural families, parents prefer to send their sons to schools and prepare their daughters for marriage. It has been pointed out in some FDGs by mothers that economically well-off parents do spend money to buy a mango orchard or invest in a business; but when it comes to educational expenses of their offspring and particularly daughters, they vacillate . . . It was due to such differences in perspectives that parents gave least preference to the issue of 'lack of educational infrastructure and communication' faced by their daughters.[52]

From a development perspective, the negative correlation between increasing literacy and age at marriage puts

[52] Ibid., p. 53.

paid to years of governmental efforts to promote girls' education, mainly to increase the age at marriage and thereby reduce fertility.

By Way of Conclusion

This chapter has attempted to underscore the point that the Indian State's attempt at 'doing gender through development' in a large measure has been an exercise of 'doing development through gender', meaning that the manner in which the State has attempted to do development has had, and continues to have, adverse consequences for the larger and professed agenda of gender justice. Our exercise has revealed the manner in which gender inequality is being created and perpetuated in the process of economic development.

Using the social sectors as a case study, we have demonstrated how the State has thrust on women the responsibility of meeting the State's various objectives in the fields of healthcare, education, and child nutrition, among others. However, in almost all these areas, the programmes are so designed and implemented that the women deployed to achieve these objectives are denied the status of workers (but are instead referred to as honorary volunteers), which would have, theoretically at least, entitled them to some legislative protection under the various labour laws of the land.

Further, the State gets away by designating some of the welfare programmes as having been instituted to empower women; in the absence of such programmes, the argument goes that the women currently employed would not have had access to the remuneration that they now receive. Most studies evaluating such programmes are generally caught up in measuring the manner in which the implementation of these programmes has/has not 'empowered' women. The fact that such programmes signify another facet of the ways in which Indian women subsidize the Indian economy is one part of the story. More significant for labour economic studies is the question as to how one should confront the Indian State, which is, at once the arbiter on issues concerning violation of labour laws as also the defaulter when it comes to hiring personnel for its own programmes.

For the women's movement in the country, continued material deprivation of large numbers of households combined with sub-optimal solutions (as represented by the ASHAs, para-teachers, and mid-day meal workers) can by no stretch of the imagination take us any closer to the lofty ideals espoused in the 1995 Beijing Platform for Action, which was to ensure that 'the concerns for women and gender issues should not remain marginal to the ideas and practices of development organizations, but should be central to them, and hence located in their "mainstream"'.

It is our contention that, the hope that through the interaction of 'development and gender' change could be produced, has not been belied; except that this is not necessarily the kind of change that we have been struggling for. Moreover, the continuing challenge for feminist scholars and activists on the ground is the perennial need to track the consequences of both the actions taken as well as those not taken. I do not believe that we have not periodically changed the questions that we have or should be asking. However, all our attempts thus far have failed to make development (read the State) accountable to the agenda of gender justice, without which the project of doing gender, which includes the phenomenon of making development work for women and children of this country, would remain unfinished and therefore ongoing.

CHAPTER 13

Employment and Maternity Protection

Understanding the Poor Coverage of Beneficial Legislation through Content Analysis of Some Judgements

Context of the Exercise

The Tata Institute of Social Sciences (TISS) along with the International Labour Organization (ILO), New Delhi office, and the Ministry of Labour, had undertaken a study to assess the coverage and effectiveness of national efforts to provide quality maternity protection for all. TISS was the nodal agency for the project.

Among the overall objectives listed in the Terms of Reference document of TISS, it was hoped that the study would 'bring to light incidences/signs of evasion tactics deployed by employers to avoid paying maternity protection [for example hiring less women, hiring women on casual and contract basis] under the MB and ESI Acts in particular and in other schemes, and assess whether the evasion was aggravated in the case of an employer liability scheme.'

* Previously published as MIDS Working Paper no. 211, 2010.

This, a small part of the above study, was conceptualized as follows: post-Independence, the country has put in place a number of measures ostensibly to ensure that workers are employed under just and humane conditions and that they are provided with maternity relief, among others. An important piece of legislation in post-Independence India is The Maternity Benefit [MB] Act, 1961. Over the years, the courts have had to deal with several cases from aggrieved women workers who have alleged denial of benefits under this Act despite, according to them, being eligible for the benefits. This study undertook a content analysis of a few cases filed for relief under this Act, to help comprehend, among other things:

- Categories of workers who have been denied, or, given less than entitled benefit
- Nature of establishments that deny such benefits
- Reasons cited by establishments for denying benefits
- Reasons for courts' acceptance or rejection of arguments by employers/petitioners

The larger issue on which, we hoped, this exercise would throw light, is the oft-repeated argument that this country has the necessary laws but the problem lies largely in their poor implementation [see Box 13.1]. Analyzing the arguments of employers (whether private or public) for example, for denying benefits, should, in our opinion, be able to explicate how 'rules of operation' drafted to operationalize benefits under this Act actually work towards rendering workers ineligible for benefits legally due to them. Put differently, the significance of this exercise lies in unravelling policy practices that shift the policy away (in this case the policy as espoused in the Maternity Benefit Act, 1961) from its stated objectives.

Box 13.1

'... the most common criticisms made by analysts commenting on different sets of policies are: [i] A weak nexus between policy and instruments; [ii] the large degree to which administrative discretion has been retained and used to dilute or defeat policy objectives... On a technical plane, critics of policy have dealt with such inconsistencies as faults or fissures in policy formation. But I would suggest, that the Freudian insight that traces lapses to intention may be highly relevant in understanding policy contradiction. The model of reference could be Freud's treatment of lapses or errors as symptoms of conflicts; that is, as results of the mutual interference of two different intentions, the intention interfered with and the interfering tendency'.[1]

Appendix 1 reproduces a Table from an official document that, among other things, indicates the 'effectiveness' of coverage of workers under different legislations. Specifically, as per this document, as of 1999–2000, the MB Act, 1961, was able to cover only 16 per cent of the total number of workers eligible for coverage under this Act.

We have referred to around twenty judgments among the cases filed under this Act (details in Appendix 2). Several of these cases also refer to other similar cases/judgments by way of precedent in the text of the judgment itself. Such cross-references are crucial since, among other things, they point to the following: notwithstanding the fact that a particular judgment may have dealt with an issue of interpretation of law/Constitutional provision/particular clause under the MB Act, 1961, this by itself does not preclude filing of similar cases using similar arguments necessitating the reinforcement of an earlier judgment.

[1] S. Guhan, 'Towards a Policy for Analysis', *Public Policy and Policy Analysis in India*, ed. R.S. Ganapathy et al., New Delhi: Sage, 1985, p. 259.

The cases have been thematically ordered to highlight different aspects as well as the many ways in which the beneficial purpose for which this Act was enacted has been less than what it should have been. A point that we have noted is: because of the very nature of the litigation process in this country (and which is not unique to cases filed under the Act under consideration) an enormous amount of time, patience, not to mention, financial resources, have to be expended in the quest for justice. Suffice it to mention, in this context, the fact that, even as it took the aggrieved woman worker almost a decade in getting justice, the interim period was one of unemployment, since, in a few cases the application of the worker for maternal leave with benefit was answered by employers with termination notices. The litigation process, all the way from a local labour court/industrial tribunal to the apex court of the country, namely the Supreme Court, has taken upwards of a decade in several cases. Since this exercise is confined to content analysis of judgments, there is no way of ascertaining whether the apex court's directives, be it reinstatement of retrenched workers with back wages or any other, have been complied with within the time stipulated.

Themes Covered in the Judgments Studied

Questioning of Constitutional Validity of Acts Enacted for the Benefit of Workers, a Recurring Example of an Act Constantly Under Litigation being the Beedi and Cigar Workers [Conditions of Employment] Act, 1966

Private, non-State bodies have time and again raised issues relating to the Constitutional validity of imposition of whole Acts and/or parts of Acts. As we have noted in a few cases, the apex court has had to come to the rescue of workers, however torturous and time-consuming the process of adjudicating on such issues has been. It is significant that in one of the important legislations in this country, namely the Beedi and Cigar Workers [Conditions of Employment] Act, 1966, the apex court not only upheld the Constitutional validity of the Act but also pleaded with the Legislature to amend the act suitably to make it workable.

Box 13.2

Additional noting by Justice Alagiriswami in the Supreme Court Judgment dated 31 January 1974 relating to Mangalore Ganesh Beedi Works vs. Union of India.

The Act is a compromise between the original intentions of the Government and the modifications they had to make in the proposed measure as a result of concessions intended to bring the home workers within the scope of the Act. The original intention was not to permit beedi rolling in private homes which will involve thousands of labourers in thousands of far-flung homes and the difficulty of applying the provisions of the measures to them. The result is an act that is likely to give rise to many difficulties in its actual working. It is obvious on a reading of the measure that its purpose is to rope in every possible person who could be brought in as an employer. But the result of the definitions of the Act is that everybody would be a principal employer, employer and contractor and every labour will be contract labour...

The difficulty of applying the provisions of the Maternity Benefits Act is... apparent. The very purpose of allowing the home workers to work in their homes being that the work of rolling beedis is light work, which men and women can do in their homes during their spare hours, the provision of the Maternity Benefits Act regarding women not being allowed to do arduous labour for a certain period before and after delivery is not apparent. And how can the provision be applied

to women who cannot be said to be, so to say, employed continuously for a certain period before the confinement.
I must make it clear that my objection is not to any of the provisions on the ground of their unreasonableness or constitutionality... But good intentions should not result in a legislation which would become ineffective and lead to a lot of fruitless litigation over the years... I think it would be good in the interest of all concerned if the Act is amended as early as possible to remove all the lacunae and the difficulties pointed out above. These difficulties have arisen because of an attempt blindly to apply the provisions, which would be quite workable if they are applied to conditions where the Factories Act would be applicable, where the labour is regular in its attendance - every day as well as over a period, to conditions of work which are vastly different as well as to people who work at home without a conscious attempt to mould them to suit those conditions. The sooner that is done the better for all concerned.

That the apprehensions expressed by Justice Alagiriswami way back in 1974 (see Box 13.2) are not unfounded is very evident from the subsequent and continuing cases being filed under the Beedi and Cigar Workers (Conditions of Employment) Act, 1966, by women beedi workers denied maternity benefits legitimately due to them under the Act. For example: in a judgment delivered on 24 March 1995 (on a case initially filed before a Labour Court in Maharashtra on 24 October 1986), the Constitutional validity of a particular section of the Beedi and Cigar Workers (Conditions of Employment) Act, 1966, was again called into question (See Appendix 3 for details). What needs to be underlined in such cases is that the employers, through their Counsel, did not address substantive issues such as non-recognition and/or termination of the women workers (consequent to their application for maternity leave with benefit) that the Asst. Labour Commissioner had pointed out to be bad in law; rather, by questioning the authority of the Asst. Labour Commissioner to pass an order, they attempted to convert the case into one of violation of Article 14 of the Constitution. Once again, the apex court was called upon to uphold the Constitutional validity of the Beedi Act, 1966, so that the women beedi workers could get their legitimate due.

Notwithstanding the above, the denial of maternity benefits for woman beedi workers under some clause or the other of the Beedi Act, 1966, continues unabated. We will refer to some of these other cases under appropriate heads.

Lack of Clarity Regarding How the Maternity Benefit Act, 1961, is Expected to Interface with other Acts and/or Service Rules of Different Establishments Governing Conditions of Employment

A general but important theme for resolution that emerges from this exercise is the insufficient attention that has been paid all along to the interface, or rather the lack of it, between the Maternity Benefit Act, 1961, and other laws, Acts, etc., governing conditions of employment in particular sectors, industries within sectors, specific establishments, specific modes of employment, etc. The larger question that this raises is the following: given the importance of the Maternity Benefit Act, should not the legislative bodies of this country have followed up the enactment of this Act with 'rules of operation' clearly specifying how the provisions of this Act needed to be incorporated, even if it required amendments to other laws/Acts? Unfortunately, while to some extent the apex court of this country has performed this task, this redressal has been achieved at great personal cost in terms of time and money to those few tenacious individuals who, along with those who supported them in this endeavour, have been able to withstand the ordeal that has taken upwards of a decade. Notwithstanding the landmark pronouncements by the apex court on many issues of law, interpretations of laws, etc., in the course of its examination of the cases and subsequent judgments, the reach of these pronouncements have been minimal given that these pronouncements by themselves have not led to changes/amendments in other Acts/laws governing conditions of employment as far as women workers' access to maternity benefits is concerned.

Quantum of Benefit: Definition of 'Week' and Should Sundays be Included in Calculation of Maternity Leave Wages

A theme that is linked to the issue of non-interface of the MB Act, 1961, with other Acts/laws in operation is the quantum of maternity benefit, be it number of days of leave, before and after delivery, and/or monetary compensation during the period of leave. Whether State or the private sector, the attempt always is to pay the woman employee a lesser (than would have been admissible under the Maternity Benefit Act, 1961) quantum of benefit, be it leave or money. The manner in which lesser quantum of benefit is justified by employers and subsequently dealt with by courts is revealing. Elaborate discussions relating to what constitutes a 'week', which service rules govern a particular employment, and what is admissible under those service rules (even if the latter goes contrary to the provisions of the MB Act, 1961), whether the establishment is covered by the Act, etc., are a few of the themes that have engaged the courts in deciding eligibility and quantum of benefit (see Box 13.3).

> Box 13.3
>
> The Apex Court judgment delivered on 12 October 1977 relating to 'week' and wageless holidays for calculation of maternity leave wages:
>
> *[Thus] we are of the opinion that computation of maternity benefit has to be made for all the days including Sundays and rest days which may be wageless holidays comprised in the actual period of absence of the woman extending up to six weeks preceding and including the day of delivery as also for all the days falling within the six weeks immediately following the day of delivery thereby ensuring that the woman worker gets for the said period not only the amount equaling 100% of the wages which she was previously earning in terms of section 3[n] of the Act but also the benefit of the wages for all the Sundays and rest days falling within the aforesaid two periods which would ultimately be conducive to the interests of both the woman worker and her employer.*[2]

Provisions of MB Act, 1961 Vis-à-Vis Service Rules of Establishments: How Many Births Qualify for Maternity Protection?

It is interesting to note that, while the MB Act, 1961, itself 'does not fix any ceiling on the number of deliveries made by a female worker'—as ruled by the learned Judge of the Madras High Court in a judgment delivered on 9 June 2008 (see Box 13.4)—there are several cases where Service Rules of Establishments, including those of certain state governments, explicitly deny maternity benefit beyond two living children, citing the GoI's population control policy.

[2] 1978 AIR 12 1978 SCR [1] 701.

Box 13.4

In writ petitions filed by two owners of beedi establishments, against the Deputy Commissioner of Labour [Inspection, Beedi and Cigar Establishments] Chief Inspector, Appellate Authority under the Maternity Benefit Act, 1961 [Respondent 1], Inspector of Labour [Women], Under Maternity Benefit Act, 1961, Tirunelveli, [Respondent 2], and Ms. Bhadrakali and Ms. Santhammal, both beedi workers and Respondents 3, '*the short question that arises in these two writ petitions is whether the third respondent in each of the writ petitions are entitled to get maternity benefit in respect of the maternity leave availed by them for delivering their third child*'.

Learned counsel for Bhadrakali and Santhammal, the third respondents in both the writ petitions submitted that... *the MB Act does not provide any restriction on the benefit to be received by a woman worker if she delivers more than two times. He also submitted that the policy of the Government in having a two-child norm cannot be read in to the Act and whatever applies to a government servant need not be made applicable to the Beedi workers, who are governed by the provisions of MB Act. To show the difference between government servants and other workers, he also submitted that in respect of government servants, no Maternity Leave will be given if marriage does not precede delivery but whereas in the case of workers governed by the MB Act, even an unmarried female worker is entitled for the maternity benefit if she delivers a child... The allegations made by the third respondents before the appellate authority that undertakings have been taken from female workers that they will not claim any maternity benefit beyond two deliveries, is a serious allegation, and if proved, the petitioners are liable for prosecution under the provisions of the MB Act, 1961, read with Beedi and Cigar Act 1996.* [Emphasis added]

What needs to be emphasized at this juncture is the following: in the absence of an apex court ruling on the important point—namely, whether provisions of the MB Act, 1961, overrule service conditions of establishments that may contradict or be at variance with the provisions of the Act—judgments of high courts dealing with similar issues have been contradictory, some upholding the supremacy of the provisions of the MB Act, 1961, over service rules of individual establishments (whether public or private), while a few judgments have ruled that as long as service rules have not been amended, the provisions of the MB Act, 1961 cannot be deemed to be automatically applicable.

For example, in the case of Parkasho Devi vs. Uttar Haryana Bijli Vitran Nigam Limited and Others delivered at the Punjab High Court on 9 May 2008, it was averred that, since the service rules of the establishment expressly denied provision of maternity benefits beyond two living children, the same was being upheld by the High Court of Punjab and Haryana.

What is not clear to us, however, is why the judgment in Box 13.4 did not also deal with the theme of allegation referred to above, wherein, the women beedi workers were made to give an undertaking that they would not claim any maternity benefit beyond two deliveries.

Status of Employment Impinging on Eligibility to Avail of Maternity Leave and Benefit

In a landmark judgment (delivered on 8 March 2000) that touched the core of the nature of employment of large numbers of women in this country, the Supreme Court ruled that the MB Act, 1961, was applicable to daily wage earners and women employed temporarily, casually, and/or on contract (See Box 13.5). Once again, while the process of achieving justice through this judgment was arduous and time consuming, this judgment—by no less a body than the apex court itself—has not put paid to further litigation arising out of linking woman's nature of employment to her being eligible for maternity leave/benefit.

Subsequent to the Supreme Court ruling in the Delhi Muster Roll case, several judgments thereafter reinforced the point that status of employment cannot be made the basis for denial of maternity benefit (see, for example, Anima Goel vs. Haryana State Marketing Board judgment delivered on 17 November 2006 by the Punjab and Haryana Court; Mrs. Bharti Gupta vs. Rail India Technical and Economical Services Ltd. [RITES] and Others judgment delivered on 9 August 2005, etc.).

Circumventing Application of Beneficiary Legislation through Enactment of Government Resolutions

The case of Bhartiben Babulal Joshi vs. Administrative Officer (judgment delivered on 23 December 2003) reveals how Government Resolutions aiding ad hoc and temporary appointments become handy for even government establishments to deny maternity benefit to personnel thus appointed. Bharatiben Joshi was appointed as Vidya Sahayak (Assistant Teacher) and it was contended by her employer that while she could take maternity leave it would be without pay. The Assistant Government Pleader appearing for the respondents submitted that according to the Government Resolution, Vidya Sahayaks who were not regularly appointed were not entitled to such benefits and therefore the respondents were right in not granting such benefits to the petitioner.

Box 13.5

Municipal Corporation of Delhi vs. Female Workers [Muster Roll]: Judgment delivered on 8 March 2000 [Summary of Case and Judgment]

Female workers [muster roll] engaged by the MCD [Corporation] raised a demand for grant of maternity leave which was made available only to regular female workers but was denied to them on the ground that their services were not regularized and, therefore they were not entitled to any maternity leave. Their case was espoused by the Delhi Municipal Workers Union and consequently the following question was referred by the Secretary [Labour] Delhi Administration to the Industrial Tribunal for adjudication: Whether the female workers working on Muster Roll should be given any maternity benefit? If so, what directions are necessary in this regard?

The Industrial Tribunal, which has given an award in favour of the women employees, has noticed that women employees have been engaged by the Corporation on muster roll, that is to say on daily wage basis for doing various works in projects like construction of buildings, digging of trenches, making of roads, etc., but have been denied the benefit of maternity leave. The Tribunal has found that though the women employees were on muster roll and had been working for the Corporation for more than 10 years, they were not regularized. The Tribunal, however came to the conclusion that the provisions of the Maternity Benefit Act had not been applied to the Corporation and, therefore, it felt that there was a lacuna in the Act. It further felt that having regard to the activities of the Corporation, which had employed more than a thousand women employees, it should have been brought within the purview of the Act so that the maternity benefits contemplated by the Act could be extended to the women employees of the Corporation. It felt that this lacuna could be removed by the State Government by issuing the necessary notification under the Proviso to Section 2 of the

Act... It consequently issued a direction to the management of the Municipal Corporation, Delhi to extend the benefits of the Maternity Benefit Act, 1961, to such muster roll female employees who were in continuous service of the management for three years or more and who fulfilled the conditions set out in Section 5 of the Act...

Learned Counsel for the Corporation contended that since the provisions of the Act have not been applied to the Corporation, such a direction could not have been issued by the Tribunal.

The Apex Court however felt that, 'This is a narrow way of looking at the problem which is human in nature and anyone acquainted with the working of the Constitution, which aims at providing social and economic justice to the citizens of this country, would out rightly reject the contention'...

Next, it was contended that therefore the benefits contemplated by the MB Act, 1961 can be extended only to workmen in an 'industry' and not to muster roll employees of the Corporation.

Again the Apex Court felt that 'This is too stale an argument to be heard. Learned Counsel also forgets that Municipal Corporation was treated to be an 'industry' and, therefore, a reference was made to the Industrial Tribunal, which answered the reference against the Corporation, and it is this matter which is being agitated before us... Now it is to be remembered that the Municipal Corporations or Boards have already been held to be 'industry' within the meaning of 'Industrial Disputes Act'...

We conclude our discussion by providing that the direction issued by the Industrial Tribunal shall be complied with by the MCD by approaching the State Govt. as also the Central Govt. for issuing necessary Notification under the Proviso to Sub-section [1] of Section 2 of the MB Act 1961, if it has not already been issued. In the meantime, the benefits under the Act shall be provided to the women [muster roll] employees of the Corporation who have been working with them on daily wages.

However, the judge ruled thus:

> Considering the provisions of the MB Act, 1961, and also considering the observations made by the Apex Court in the Delhi Muster Roll case and also considering the facts of the present petition, according to my opinion, the ratio of the decision of the apex court would also apply to the facts of the present case because here also, benefit of maternity leave has been in substance denied to the petitioner only on the ground that she is not regularly appointed on the post of Vidya Sahayak and therefore, she is not entitled for such benefit on the basis of the GR, though maternity leave has been sanctioned by the respondents but without wages . . . I am therefore of the opinion that the petitioner is entitled for the maternity leave . . .

Truncating Quantum of Maternity Leave and Terminating Service

In the case of Seema Gupta vs. Guru Nanak Institute of Management (judgment delivered on 20 November 2006), the judgment is interesting in that the judge, among other things, widened the scope of discussion on implications of denial of maternity leave by establishments on the plea of 'exigencies of service' (see Box 13.6).

Addressing Dismissal and Stigma along with Denial of Maternity Protection

The judgment in the case relating to Yamini J. Dave vs. The Director, IUCAA and Another, delivered on 6 April 2004, brings out the many connected issues that had to be dealt with along with securing justice on the issue of maternity benefits (See Appendix 4 for details).

The several interlinked issues raised by this case and judgment are worth recapitulating: one, the initial appointment on probation was arbitrarily closed after a year and the employee was placed on a year-by-year extension—a provision not indicated in advertisement for the post; two, despite the employee having given due notice and thereafter proceeding on maternity leave, she was issued with termination order; three, the termination order was premised on a committee's allegation of misconduct by employee; four, management accepted of the committee's recommendation of dismissal of employee with no chance for the employee to present her case; five, the dismissal order was issued during maternity leave period, which itself was illegal.

Above all, the tortuous process of litigation, which began in 1994 and ended in 2004, also brings to the fore a crucial legal aspect of the trajectory of the case; namely, the fact that Yamini Dave's initial petition challenging her termination was dismissed by a single judge, which forced her to approach the apex court. Before the apex court went into the merits of the case, it had to deal with 'preliminary objection' raised by the IUCAA, the respondents; the latter argued that Dave's petition was not maintainable since the IUCAA is not a State/other authority within the meaning of Article 12 of the Constitution. Only after taking a decision on the maintainability of the petition did the apex court go into the details of the case. These procedural aspects speak volumes about the near impossibility of accessing beneficial legislation even when employed by a State authority.

Using Mode of Payment of Salary as a Factor to Deny Maternity Benefits

In his judgment delivered on 29 January 2008 in the case of Dr Hemlata Saraswat vs. State of Rajasthan, the judge came down very heavily on the government of Rajasthan and its Department of Medical and Health Services in

Box 13.6

Summary of Case and Judgment, Seema Gupta vs. Guru Nanak, 20/11/2006

The petitioner [Seema Gupta] was appointed as commerce lecturer in response to an advertisement by the respondent college. She joined the College on 1st May 2001. The appointee was to be on probation for one year which could be extended for another year... The petitioner was blessed with a child on 28.12.2003 and was sanctioned maternity leave for 135 days w.e.f. 29.12.2003. She had requested for maternity leave of 180 days as per the Guru Nanak Dev University Rules [GNDU Rules] which, it is averred, allowed maternity leave for that period. The Petitioner was informed that as the Central Civil Service Rules were applicable to her service the provisions of GNDU were inapplicable... By letter dated 15.09.2004 Seema Gupta referred to Rule 43[4][b] of CCS Leave Rules whereby she was entitled to continuation of maternity leave up to a maximum period of one year and requested for extension of maternity leave. It is stated that despite the request, petitioner was terminated on the basis of unauthorized leave/absence, on 14th Oct 2004 that is within two months of the extended maternity leave.

It is alleged that undisputedly the CCS Leave Rules were applicable to the petitioner and those Rules clearly stipulate that maternity leave can be extended up to one year. In case of maternity leave even the requirement of producing medical certificate has been waived off...

According to the Judge: This is not a traditional case of an employee seeking enforcement of her contract of service, but her lament that in spite of protective provisions, relating to maternity, and in spite of her request for extended leave, which was permissible, the employer in disdain of those norms, terminated her from service. I am also not impressed with the submission that the petitioner was an employee with lesser rights, since she was on ad-hoc basis. As per the version of the respondent, she was entitled to benefits under Rule 43.

> *The respondent, in my considered opinion treated the request for extension of leave by five months as a normal request, without applying its mind to the peculiarities of the case. It has not furnished any reasons or justification as to why the right to claim the extended period of one years' leave, a valuable one at that, had to be rejected. Exigencies of service bind all employers; that reason would be available in all cases where a request for extended maternity leave is sought. If such reasons given in a routine manner are to be upheld, the right for extended maternity leave of up to one year, would be meaningless, as every employer can cite that as a ground for denial. The special nature of the right then would exist only on paper, in negation.*
>
> *For the foregoing reasons, the impugned termination letter cannot be sustained; it is illegal and is hereby quashed. The respondent is directed to reinstate the petitioner to her post; the petitioner shall also be entitled to full arrears of salary...*

particular on several counts, not least being the State's doublespeak on gender justice, where, on the one hand, as the judge put it,

The government at all forums is speaking about gender equality, gender justice and betterment of status of women' and, on the other hand, it is denying the benefit of maternity leave to its own employees under the guise that appointment is not under the regular rules, forgetting that appointment in the first place was given after due selection by following regular process of selection.

The annoyance of the judge was also very palpable in the directions it issued to the State to recover costs 'from person/persons responsible for this unnecessary litigation'. We reproduce in some detail the judgment on this case (see Box 13.7) to reveal the continued manner in which government bureaucracies collude to make such appointment orders that denial of benefits appears as legitimate and as per law!

By Way of Conclusion

This study of judgments relating to cases under the MB Act, 1961, has been an eye-opener in more ways than one. To some extent it throws light on why the coverage of the Act has been abysmal, including and even in the government sector; in fact, the latter has time and again proved itself to be the worst employer as far as record of women workers being able to access beneficial legislation is concerned. Each of the themes into which the cases have been grouped themselves highlight several inter-connected issues. Suffice it to reiterate some of the more important themes that this exercise has thrown up for the tremendous implications for policy that they contain.

Box 13.7

Dr Smt. Hemlata Saraswat vs. State of Rajasthan and Others on 29 January 2008:

'In her writ petition, Dr. Hemlata Saraswat has questioned a communication dated 27.04.2006 denying her maternity leave on the ground that she is working as Medical Officer on consolidated salary and there is no provision in the Rules for granting her maternity leave.

'The petitioner has averred that on the recommendations of the Selection Committee, she came to be appointed on the post of Medical 'Officer on a consolidated salary of Rs.8000/ per month with issuance of appointment order on 15.09.2003 putting her engagement on contract basis... According to the petitioner, she proceeded on medical leave on 29.08.2005 by submitting a leave application, and after delivering a male child, resumed duties on 11.01.2006 with fitness certificate.

'The petitioner's grievance is that, though entitled, she has been denied maternity leave by the impugned communication dated 27.04.2006 on the ground that under the service rules, there was no provision for allowing maternity leave to persons working on consolidated salary; and she has not been allowed maternity leave despite submitting a representation on 17.02.2006 and serving a notice through lawyer on 17.04.2006.

'The petitioner has referred to the decisions rendered in Neetu Choudhary vs. State of Rajasthan and others. 2005 [2] DNJ [Raj] 676; and Smt. Sumitra Choudhary and Others vs, State of Rajasthan and Others, SB Civil Writ Petition no. 3295/2005 decided on 19.09.2005 wherein this Court has directed grant of benefit of maternity leave to temporary workers. It is contended that there is no rationale behind refusal of maternity leave to some of the female employees while granting the same to the others. No reply to the writ petition has been filed; and the core and essential facts as stated by the petitioner in her writ petition have not been denied...

'Having heard learned Counsel for the parties and having perused the material placed on record with reference to the law applicable to the case, this court is clearly of opinion that the communication dated 27.04.2006 emanating from the Directorate of Medical and Health Services, Rajasthan denying maternity leave to the petitioner with cryptic observation that the rules do not mention about grant of such leave to the Medical Officer working on consolidated salary cannot be said to be justified nor appears bona fide, particularly for having been issued even after the decisions of this Court in the case of Neetu Chowdhary [decided on 19.04.2005] and Smt. Sumitra Chowdhary [decided on 19.09.2005]; and this writ petition deserves to be allowed with costs.

'The present one was clearly an avoidable litigation if the authorities concerned would have dealt with the matter with due regard to their constitutional duties and sadly enough they have chosen to proceed in utter disregard of their duties, without regard to the requirements of the rules and even in

disregard to the decisions rendered by this Court. The petition thus deserves to be allowed with costs.

'This petition for writ is therefore allowed and the impugned communication dated 27.04.2006 stands quashed. The respondents shall take up for consideration sanctioning of maternity leave to the petitioner as applied; and all consequential benefits thereto shall be accorded within a period of 30 days from today. The petitioner shall be accorded within a period of 30 days from today. The petitioner shall also be entitled to costs quantified at Rs.5,500. It shall be permissible for the respondents, if so desired, but only after making payment to the petitioner, to recover the amount of costs, strictly in accordance with law, from the person/persons responsible for this unnecessary litigation.'

What the judgments also bring out starkly is the poor record of the State as employer. The manner in which women employed by the State have been excluded from provisions of the MB Act, 1961, have been several and varied: one, contrary to all norms of justice, the State has employed women workers but used nomenclatures such as daily, ad hoc, casual, etc., and then justified denial of maternity benefit on the ground that even the amended MB Act, 1961, applies only to regular and temporary workers, not casual, daily or ad hoc. Two, while recruitments have followed a set procedure, appointment letters have been arbitrarily changed to render the woman employee ineligible for any benefit—maternity or otherwise. Three, when the apex court has come down heavily on state governments for denying maternity benefits to women employees kept for years on contract or daily basis, the bureaucracy has come up with other ways of making woman employees ineligible, namely, by citing, for example, that women employees on consolidated mode of payment of salary are not eligible for benefit under the MB Act, 1961. The government's own Resolutions have become handy for other establishments to deny maternity benefit altogether and/or allow maternity leave but without any monetary benefit. To top it all, in a few of the cases, application for maternity leave has been answered with termination notices, an aspect that the apex court has specifically underlined as being illegal and bad in law.

From a feminist perspective, this exercise has been a learning exercise in several ways. An important learning is the realization that mere enactments of more laws to address specific feminist demands need to be backed by 'rules of operation' that also specify how binding these provisions are and whether existing laws governing establishments need to be amended in the light of these new women-friendly laws. The few cases dealt with above relating to operation of the MB Act, 1961, has revealed how and why the coverage of the Act, even in the organized sector, remains abysmal. Hence, while struggle for extending the coverage of the Act to establishments and women workers outside the purview of the Act needs to be strengthened, equally important is the need to struggle to unravel ways and means by which women workers in the organized sector get excluded from provisions of such beneficial legislation. Further, despite feminist opposition to population control policies, service rules of organizations, including some state governments, deny maternity benefits to women who already have two living children. While the MB Act, 1961, itself does not state anything on the number of times a woman worker can avail of benefits under the rule, service rules of organizations incorporating the GoI's population control policies have taken precedence over the MB Act, 1961, to the detriment of women workers.

In short, this exercise, taking the operation of the MB Act 1961, has revealed how institutional arrangements have contributed to making the Act largely dysfunctional. Viewing the theme from a feminist perspective and 'Asking the Woman Question'[3] reveals how the position of women workers reflects the organization of workplaces rather than the inherent characteristics of women as workers. This exposition of the effects of laws, such as the MB Act, 1961, has enabled us to demonstrate how structures, social and legal, embody norms that inherently render women workers different so that legislations directly aimed at facilitating women worker's maternity role instead become instruments not only for their subordination but also for their dismissal from work.

Acknowledgements

I am extremely grateful to the Tata Institute of Social Sciences, its Director and in particular, Professor Lakshmi Lingam, for the opportunity to conduct the exercise

[3] À la Katherine T. Bartlett, 'Feminist Legal Methods', in *Feminist Legal Theory: Readings in Law and Gender*, ed. Ktherine T. Bartlett and Rosanne Kennedy, Boulder, CO: Westview Press, 1991, pp. 370–403. Explicating on what 'Asking the Woman Question' is all about, Bartlett states as follows: 'The woman question asks about the gender implications of a social practice or rule: have women been left out of consideration? If so, in what way: how might that omission be corrected? What difference would it make to do so? In law, asking the woman question means examining how the law fails to take into account the experiences and values that seem more typical of women than of men, for whatever reason, or how existing legal standards and concepts might disadvantage women. The question assumes that some features of the law may be not only non-neutral in a general sense, but also 'male' in a specific sense. The purpose of the woman question is to expose those features and how they operate and to suggest how they might be corrected' [p. 371].

that enabled this chapter. I would also like to record my profuse thanks to Professor Lingam for her comments on an earlier draft. This work has benefited immensely from comments received from Dr Kamala Sankaran and Ms Geeta Ramaseshan. Thanks are also due to Rahul Saptkal for all logistical help in enabling this study. The contents of this chapter were originally presented at a seminar held at the Madras Institute of Development Studies, Chennai, on 7 December 2010. The very interesting and thought-provoking questions raised at this seminar would require further and more intense research not addressed in this chapter. Needless to conclude, I alone am responsible for the contents of this chapter.

Notes

1. S. Guhan, 'Towards a Policy for Analysis', in R.S. Ganapathy, S.R. Ganesh, Rushikesh M. Maru, Samuel Paul and Ram Mohan Rao, eds. *Public Policy and Policy Analysis in India*, New Delhi, Sage, pp. 255–63.
2. Katherine T., Bartlett, 'Feminist Legal Methods', in Katherine T. Bartlett and Rosanne Kennedy, eds. *Feminist Legal Theory: Readings in Law and Gender*, Boulder, Colorado, Westview Press, pp. 370–403.

Appendix 1

Table 13.1: Estimate of Workers Actually Covered under Important Regulations in India, 1999–2000

Sl. no.	*Name of the Act*	*Workers Actually Covered by Law (lakhs)**	*Percentage Share of Workers Covered by Regulations*		*Effectiveness of Coverage (%)***
			Total Workforce	*Hired Workers*	
1	Factories Act	88.2#	2.2	4.9	73.5
2	Shops and Establishments Act	68.8#	1.7	3.8	44.7
3	Plantation Labour Act	9.7$	0.2	0.5	35.6
4	Mines Act	6.4@	0.2	0.4	87.4
5	Contract Labour Act	74.2@	6.9	15.1	n. a.
6	Minimum Wages Act	141.1&	3.6	7.8	9.3
7	Employees State Insurance Act	75.7##	1.9	4.2	87.5
8	Employees Provident Fund Act	263.0@@	6.6	14.5	179.5
9	Workmen's Compensation Act	26.7$	0.7	1.5	20.3

Sl. no.	*Name of the Act*	*Workers Actually Covered by Law (lakhs)**	*Percentage Share of Workers Covered by Regulations*		*Effectiveness of Coverage (%)***
			Total Workforce	*Hired Workers*	
10	Maternity Benefit Act	6.3[$]	0.2	0.3	16.1
11	Beedi Workers Act	32.1[@]	0.8	1.8	92.0
12	Trade Unions Act	59.1[@]	1.5	3.3	15.2

Source: National Commission for Enterprises in the Unorganized Sector. 2009. Challenge of Employment: An Informal Sector Perspective, Vol. 1, Main Report, p. 187.

Notes: ** is the ratio of workers actually covered by law to workers covered by definition. Estimated from different sources of the Ministry of Labour and generally pertain to the employment in enterprises that have submitted returns under the particular Act.

@Annual Reports Ministry of Labour

Indian Labour Statistics

$ Indian Labour Year Book

& Report on the Functioning of the Minimum Wages Act

ESI Newsletter

@@ EPF website: https://www.epfindia.gov.in/.

APPENDIX 2

Cases Covered in the Study

[Note: All cases listed below were downloaded from http://indiankanoon.org in January 2010]

1. Manager, Vidarbha Tobacco Products [P] Ltd. vs Fulwantabai Ishwardas Meshram [Smt.] and others. Judgment delivered by Justice R.M. Lodha on 24 March 1995. Equivalent citations: 1995 [4] BomCr 565 [1996] ILLJ 101 Bom.
2. Anima Goel, Ms. Vs. Haryana State Agricultural Marketing Board. Judgment delivered by Justice M.M. Kumar on 17 November 2006. Equivalent citations: [2007] IIILLJ 64 P H, 2008 [1] SLJ 121 P H.
3. Yamini J Dave vs. The Director, IUCAA and Another. Judgment delivered by Justice K. Rathod on 6 April 2004.
4. N. Mohammed Mohideen and Another, vs The Dy Commissioner of Labour, Inspector of Labour, Bhadrakali and Santhammal, Judgment delivered on 9 June 2008 by Justice K. Chandru in High Court of Madras.
5. Mangalore Ganesh Beedi Works and another, vs. Union of India. Judgment delivered on 31 January 1974 by Justice A.N. Ray. Equivalent citations: 1974 AIR 832, 1974 SCR [3].
6. Seema Gupta vs. Guru Nanak Institute of Management. Judgment delivered on 20 November 2006 by Justice S. Ravindra Bhat.
7. Municipal Corporation of Delhi vs. Female Workers [Muster Roll] and another. Judgment delivered on 08 March 2000 by Justice Saghir Ahmad.
8. Mrs. Bharti Gupta vs. Rail India Technical and Economical Services Ltd. [RITES] and others.

Judgment delivered on 9 August 2005 by Justice S. Ravindra Bhat.

9. Tata Tea Ltd. vs Inspector of Plantations. Judgment delivered on 11 December 1990 by Justice Radhakrishna Menon.
10. Mrs. Pramila Rawat vs. District Judge, Lucknow, and another. Judgment delivered on 10 May 2000 by Justice Pradeep Kant.
11. Bhartiben Babulal Joshi vs. Administrative Officer. Judgment delivered on 23 December 2003 by Justice H. K. Rathod.
12. B. Shah vs. Presiding Officer, Labour Court, Coimbatore and others. Date of Judgment, 12 October 1977. Bench: Jaswant Singh and V.R. Krishna Iyer. Equivalent citations: 1978 AIR 12 1978 SCR [1] 701.
13. Dr Hemlata Saraswat vs. State of Rajasthan and others. Judgment delivered on 29 January 2008 by Justice Dinesh Maheswari.
14. Durgesh Sharma vs. State of Rajasthan and others. Judgment delivered on 24 September 2007 by Justice P.S. Asopa.
15. Aruna S. Pardeshi [Dr] vs. Dean, Swami Ramanand Tirth Medical College and others. Judgment delivered on 22 January 1987 by Justice G.H. Guttal. Equivalent citations 1987 [2] BomCr 311.
16. Ram Bahadur Thakur [P] Ltd. vs. Chief Inspector of Plantations. Judgment delivered on 9 February 1989 by Justice Sreedharan. Equivalent citations: [1989] IILJ 20 Ker.
17. Dr Thomas Eapen vs. Asst. Labour Officer and others. Judgment delivered on 17 March 1993 by Justice P.K. Shamsuddin. Equivalent citations: [1993] IILJ 847 Ker.

18. Parkasho Devi vs. Uttar Haryana Bijli Vitran Nigam Ltd. and Others. Judgment delivered on 9 May 2008 by Justice Mohinder Pal. Equivalent citations: [2008] 3 PLR 248.
19. Chairman, Punjab National Bank vs. Astamija Dash, 2008 AIR [SC] 3182: 2008 [7] SCR 365: 2008 [7] SC Ale 726: 2008 [3] LLJ 584. Justices S. vs. Astamija Dash, 2008 AIR [SC] 3182: 2008 [7] SCR 365: 2008 [7] SC Ale 726: 2008 [3] LLJ 584. Justices S. B. Sinha and V.S. Sirpurkar.
20. Arulin Ajitha Rani vs. The Principal, Film and Television Institute, Chennai. Judgment delivered on 27 June 2008 by Justice P.K. Misra, writ appeal no. 875 of 2006 in the High Court of Judicature at Madras.

Appendix 3

Summary of Case and Judgment in Vidarbha Tobacco Products [P] Ltd. vs. Fulwantabai Ishwardas Meshram and Others; Judgment delivered on 24 March 1995; 1995[4] Bom Cr 565 [1996] ILLJ 101 Bom.

Smt. Fulwantabai, the worker, in the said writ petition filed an appeal under Section 31 [2] of the Beedi and Cigar Workers [Conditions of Employment] Act, 1966, before the Asst Commissioner of Labour, Gondia, on 24.10.1986. It was inter alia averred in the said appeal by her that she was beedi roller and working as such for the last 4-5 years for Vidarbha Tobacco Products, Ekodi [the petitioner employer] through Shri Chand Khan Mohamed Sheikh and Shri Khalil, the respondent - contractors. According to the worker, the petitioner-employer and the contractor did not provide log book/card to the worker and her correct name was not recorded in the register and for that an enquiry was made on spot by the Govt. Labour Officer on 25.9.1986. Due to this enquiry, the contractor terminated the services of the worker with effect from 29.6.1986 after receiving her beedis and despite repeated requests, the contractor did not give tobacco and leaves to her. On the basis of these facts, the worker prayed before the Asst Commissioner of Lab that she should be reinstated with back wages from the date of her termination. The contractor as well as petitioner-employer contested the appeal before the Asst Lab Commissioner by filing the reply on 26.3.1987. Though the reply was common by them, the contractor and employer set up the plea that he did not have any knowledge as to whether the worker had been in service with the contractor at any time. It was admitted by them that the Govt. lab officer, Gondia visited the site on 25.9.1986. However, in para 4 of the reply, the employment of worker was denied and it was for that reason that no requisite notice was required to be served on her...

The Asst Lab Commissioner after holding the enquiry and hearing the parties, held that the termination of the worker was bad in law and accordingly by the said judgment dated 6.6.1988, set aside the termination of the workman and directed the employer and the contractor to reinstate the worker with immediate effect. The worker was held entitled to guaranteed wages of 50 percent till her reinstatement. Dissatisfied with the judgment passed by the Asst Lab Commissioner allowing the appeal of worker, setting aside her termination and directing the petitioner-employer to reinstate her with 50 percent of guaranteed wages till reinstatement, has given rise to writ petition no. 15 of 1989 and similar other five writ petitions relating to different workers by different employers...

Mr. Qazi, the learned counselor the petitioner-employer first of all has challenged the vires of Section 31 [2] [a] of the Beedi Workers Act, 1966... has contended that the said Section is violative of Art 14 of the Constitution of India as it confers unguided and uncontrolled powers on the State Govt. to appoint any person or anybody as an appellate authority for hearing the appeal filed by the employee challenging his/her discharge, dismissal or retrenchment...

What needs to be noted here is that, the employers through their Counsel did not address the substantive issues relating to termination of the workers that the Asst. Labour Commissioner had pointed out to be bad in law; rather by questioning the authority of the Asst. Labour Commissioner to pass an order, they attempted to convert the case into one of violation of Article 14 of the Constitution.

Despite the fact that the entire Beedi Workers Act 1966 has been held to be constitutionally valid by the Supreme Court in the Mangalore Beedi Works' case, Mr. Qazi contended that the Supreme Court did not examine the constitutionality of Section 31 [2] [a] of the Beedi Workers Act, 1966 from the point of view that it did not provide any guidelines but rather conferred unbridled and uncontrolled powers on the State Govt. and therefore the said provision being unconstitutional should be struck down...

The High Court Judge however ruled that... *discretion under Section 44 of the Beedi Act has been given to the State Govt; the latter may, by notification in the Official Gazette... make rule providing for the authority to whom and the time within which an appeal may be filed by a dismissed, discharged or retrenched employee... I am of the clear view that the said provisions contained in Section 31 [2] [a] is constitutional and cannot be invalidated on the ground of contravention of Article 14 of the Const. of India...*

No documentary evidence was produced by the employer to show that the workers were not in the employment with the contractor of the employer. The contractor and employer under law are required to maintain registers, logbooks etc. and from the production of the said documents if the workers were not working with them, it could have been shown that these two workers were not working with them as beedi workers. The very fact that no documentary evidence has been produced by the contractor or employer leads to an adverse inference against the employer... Therefore there is no merit in the contention of the learned counsel for petitioner-employer in these two writ petitions and the order passed by the Asst Commissioner of Lab on

6.6.1988 does not deserve to be interfered with in the extraordinary jurisdiction of this Court...It must be grasped that judiciary is respected not on account of its power to legalise injustice on technical grounds but because it is capable of removing injustice and is expected to do so...In the result, there is no merit in these seven writ petitions and all the writ petitions are dismissed with no order as to costs.

Appendix 4

The judgment in the case relating to Yamini J. Dave vs The Director, IUCAA and Another delivered on 06.04.2004, is dealt with in some detail below to bring out the many connected issues that had to be dealt with along with securing justice on the issue of maternity benefits.

In this Letters Patent Appeal, the appellant, Yamini Dave, has challenged the judgment passed by Single Judge in Special Civil Application no. 11047 of 1994 dated January 10, 1996, whereby the petition filed by the appellant had been dismissed.

The facts giving rise to the present Letters Patent Appeal may be narrated thus: The appellant, Yamini Dave, was appointed clerk-cum-typist by the respondents vide appointment letter dated Sept 9, 1991 pursuant to advertisement dated May 11, 1991, in INFLIBNET programme with IUCAA, an autonomous registered society established by UGC. The candidates appointed to the posts advertised were to remain on probation for a period of one year from the date of appointment and subject to service conditions and conduct rules approved by the governing body of INFLIBNET/IUCAA. Yamini Dave joined the post of clerk-cum-typist on Sept 11, 1991. By Office Order dated Sept 15, 1992, she was informed that her probationary period stood closed from 10.09.1992. The appellant proceeded on 90 days of maternity leave from May 3, 1994 to July 31, 1994, sought through application dated May 2, 1994. She reminded respondents vide letter dated May 28, 1994, to sanction her leave. The respondents sanctioned the leave vide order dated June 2, 1994... Again, the appellant sought extension of maternity leave from Aug 1, 1994 to September 4, 1994 as per rules applicable to Central Govt. employees. By Memorandum dated Sept 9, 1994, her services were terminated. The appellant challenged her termination through Special Civil Application no. 11047 of 1994. However same was dismissed.

In the light of material referred to above, it is clear that according to the advertisement, appointment of appellant was on probation for one year and appointment was made initially for a period of two years with clarification that post was likely to continue indefinitely. One-year probationary period stood closed with effect from 10th Sept 1992, and therefore issuance/extension of the appointment on year to year basis, which is admittedly not provided in the advertisement, appears to be contrary to the letter of appointment dated 9th Sept 1991. Therefore, the decision taken on 17th Aug 1993, in Office Note extending the appointment of appellant on year to year basis is contrary to the principles of natural justice because initial appointment was for a period of two years. So after two years, the respondents were not authorized to convert her appointment on contractual basis. In advertisement no such condition was incorporated or made known to the appellant. Even UGC had not instructed thus while sanctioning the post, but even then, decision has been taken to continue the appellant on year to year basis. That decision is illegal and arbitrary and it is hit by Article 14 of the Constitution of India. It is nowhere discussed what would be the legal effect of closing of period of probation. Closing the period of probation without any adverse remarks and allowing the appellant to continue in service thereafter, in the opinion of the Court, means that the appellant is a confirmed employee of the respondents. Based on the observations of a Committee dated 19th Aug 1994, that made allegation of misconduct against the appellant... services of the appellant were terminated on 9th September, 1994. ...considering the total facts, termination is not a simpliciter but it is attached with stigma... without giving any opportunity and without holding any departmental inquiry, termination order has been passed by the respondents... Even temporary employees are entitled to minimum requirement, that is, an opportunity of hearing before passing any adverse order...

The moment probation period is not extended further or no order of termination is passed against an employee or where probationary period is closed after completion of one year, it means that there is positive decision taken by the authority to the effect that probationary period has been cleared with satisfactory work by the employee. Even it is also not the case of the respondent that during probation period of one year, the appellant remained inefficient and was not found suitable and was inefficient. Whatever observations that were made by the committee related to subsequent period of probation, that is to say, when the appellant became a permanent employee of the respondent.

No doubt, that appointment on contractual basis for a period of one year was accepted by the appellant but that may not be sufficient because looking to the unemployment ratio in the country, naturally, anyone may surrender to the terms of the employer. But merely acceptance of the order does not amount to acceptance on free will. The respondent being the employer was a State Authority and it ought to have acted in accordance with law and in all fairness as is naturally expected from the State Authority, which is not found from the action of the respondent authorities...

Appellant had applied for maternity leave in the year 1994 and also applied for medical bills. The leave has been rejected which has been considered as absent period in the year 1994. However, in fact, the appellant had never proceeded on unauthorized leave or remained absent unauthorizedly during her service period. The period the appellant had requested for maternity leave which was rejected subsequently by the respondent and that is how created a situation that in the year 1994 as if the appellant worked only for 29 days. This is factually incorrect and seems to have been taken into consideration by the Committee while taking the impugned decision to discontinue the appellant. In view of the observations made by the Apex Court in MCD vs. Female Workers [Muster Roll] and Another reported in 2000 3 SCC 224, the appellant is entitled to maternity leave under the provisions of the Maternity Benefit Act, 1961, as well as Service Rules of IUCAA...

It is also necessary to note that services of the appellant have been discontinued during the period of maternity leave, and even this act of respondents is illegal and arbitrary.

Based on the relevant observations of the recommendations of the committee, ultimately, the service of the appellant has been terminated on 10th Sept 1994. Therefore, the question is whether the observations made by the Committee as 'casual', 'careless' and 'no improvement during the extension period' and remaining 'absent' can be said to be stigma or not? In fact, the appellant was deemed to be a confirmed employee as observed by us, but termination is based on such recommendations which made allegations against the appellant about misconduct and even though no opportunity was given to the appellant and straightaway her services have been terminated by the respondent. In such circumstances, it is the duty of the Court to lift the veil to find out the real cause for termination. If real cause is an allegation or misconduct, then an opportunity has to be given following the principles of natural justice...

If for the determination of suitability of the probationer for the post in question or for his further retention in service or for confirmation, an enquiry is held and it is on this basis of that enquiry that a decision is taken to terminate his service, the order will not be punitive in nature. But if there are allegations of misconduct and an enquiry is held to find out the truth of that misconduct and an order terminating the service is passed on the basis of that enquiry, the order would be punitive in nature as the enquiry was held not for assessing the general suitability of the employee for the post in question, but to find out the truth of allegations of misconduct against the employee.

Therefore, after considering the law laid down by the Apex Court in respect of the issue, namely, whether the order of termination is stigmatic or not and regular departmental inquiry is necessary or not and principles of natural justice required to be observed or not, in our opinion, looking to the decision taken by the committee on 19th August 1994... are bad and unfortunately same became basis to terminate the service of the appellant... Therefore, it is clear case of termination based on allegation attached with stigma. In spite of that no opportunity was given to the appellant who is deemed to be confirmed and as such no departmental inquiry was held and therefore, in such circumstances, the order of termination is held to be illegal.

If the employer terminates the service illegally and the termination is motivated as in this case, namely to resist the workman's demand for revision of wages, the termination may well amount to unfair labour practice. In such circumstances, reinstatement being the normal rule, it should be followed with full back wages.

Bibliography

Adams, John, 'Memorandum on the Proposed Victoria Technical Institute', *Papers Relating to Technical Education in India 1886–1904*, Calcutta: Office of the Superintendent of Government Printing, India, 1906, pp. 91–100.

Altbach, P.G. and Gail P. Kelly, ed., *Education and Colonialism*, New York: Longman, 1978.

Ambani, M. and Birla Kumaramangalam, *A Policy Framework for Reforms in Education*, Report presented to the Prime Minister's Council on Trade and Industry, New Delhi, 2000.

Ambirajan, S., 'Steam Intellect and the Raj: Technical Education in South India in the Nineteenth Century', in *The Steam Intellect Societies—Essays on Culture, Education and Industry Circa 1820-1914*, ed. Ian Inkster, Nottingham: Department of Adult Education, University of Nottingham, 1985.

———, 'The Content of Science and Technology Education in South India During the Colonial Period', mimeo, Madras, n.d.

Amin, A. and K. Robins. 'These are Not Marshallian Times', in *Innovation Networks: Spatial Perspectives*, ed. Roberto Camagni, London: Belhaven, 1991.

Banks, Olive, *Faces of Feminism: A Study of Feminism as a Social Movement*, UK: Basil Blackwell, 1988.

Basu, Aparna, *The Growth of Education and Political Development in India, 1898–1920*, New Delhi: Oxford University Press, 1974.

Bearce, D.G., *British Attitudes Towards India, 1784–1858*, Oxford: Oxford University Press, 1961.

Becattini, G., 'The Marshallian Industrial District as a Socio-Economic Notion', in *Industrial Districts and Inter-Firm Cooperation in Italy*, ed. F. Pyke, G. Becattini and W. Sengenberger, Geneva: International Institute for Labour Studies, 1990.

Bell, Martin and Keith Pavitt, 'Accumulating Technologies Capability in Developing Countries', *Proceedings of the World*

Bank Annual Conference on Development Economies, USA: IBRD/World Bank, 1992.

Bennell, P. and J. Segerstrom, 'Vocational Education and Training in Developing Countries: Has the World Bank Got It Right?', *International Journal of Educational Development*, vol. 18, no. 4, 1998, pp. 271–87.

Bhargava, K.D., ed., *Selections from Educational Records*, vol. IV (Technical Education in India, 1886–1907), New Delhi: Government of India for the National Archives of India, 1968.

Bhatia, K., 'Performance-based Incentives of the ASHA Scheme: Stakeholders' Perspectives', *Economic and Political Weekly*, vol. XLIX, no. 22, 31 May 2014, pp. 145–51.

Bhattacharya, Sabyasachi, 'Laissez-faire in India', *The Indian Economic and Social History Review*, vol. II, no. 1, January 1965, pp. 1–22.

Blumberg, R.L., ed., *Gender, Family and Economy: The Triple Overlap*, California: Sage, 1991.

Blumenthal, T., 'A Note on Relationship between Domestic R and D Imports of Technology', *Economic Development and Cultural Change*, vol. 27, no. 2, January 1979, pp. 303–6.

Brusco, S., 'The Idea of the Industrial District: Its Genesis', in *Industrial Districts and Inter-Firm Cooperation in Italy*, ed. F. Pyke, G. Becattini and W. Sengenberger, Geneva: International Institute for Labour Studies, 1990, pp. 10–19.

———, 'Small Firms and the Provision of Real Services', in *Industrial Districts and Local Economic Regeneration*, ed. F. Pyke and W. Sengenberger, Geneva: International Institute for Labour Studies, 1992, pp. 177–96.

Buck, B., 'Qualification Concepts in Vocational Training in the Federal Republic of Germany', in *Challenges for Apprenticeship and Vocational Training in the 1990s: German and American Perspectives*, ed. D. Dettke and C. Weil, Germany: Friedrich-Ebert-Stiftung, 1992, pp. 23–8.

Carnoy. M., 'Higher Education in a Global Innovation Economy', Paper prepared for a Seminar co-hosted by CHET and the Human Sciences Research Council, 31 July 1998.

Castro, C.J., 'Sustainable Development: Mainstream and Critical Perspectives', *Organ Environ*, vol. 17, no. 2, 2004, pp. 195–225.

Cawthorne, Pamela, 'Amoebic Capitalism as a Form of Accumulation: The Case of the Cotton Knitwear Industry in a South Indian

Town', PhD dissertation, Milton Keynes, The Open University, UK, 1990.

———, 'Of Networks and Markets: The Rise and Rise of a South Indian Town: The Example of Tiruppur's Cotton Knitwear Industry', *World Development*, vol. 23, no. 1, January 1995, pp. 43–56.

Chanana, Karuna, 'Social Change or Social Reform: The Education of Women in Pre-Independence India', in *Socialization Education and Women: Explorations in Gender Identity*, ed. Karuna Chanana, New Delhi: Orient Longman, 1988, pp. 96–128.

Chandler Jr., Alfred D., *Scale and Scope: The Dynamics of Industrial Enterprise*, Cambridge, MA: Harvard University Press, 1990.

Chant, S., 'The "Feminisation of Poverty" and the "Feminisation" of Anti-Poverty Programmes: Room for Revision?', *The Journal of Development Studies*, vol. 44, no. 2, 2008, pp. 165–97.

Chant, S. and C. Sweetman, 'Fixing Women or Fixing the World? "Smart Economics", Efficiency Approaches and Gender Equality in Development', *Gender and Development*, vol. 20, no. 3, November 2012, pp. 517–29.

Chatterjee, S. and R. Mohan, 'India's Garment Exports', *Economic and Political Weekly* (Review of Industry and Management), vol. 28, no. 35, 1993.

Chatterton, A., *A Monograph on Tanning and Working in Leather in the Madras Presidency*, Madras: Printed by the Superintendent, Government Press, 1904.

———, 'Industrial Evolution in India', *The Hindu*, Madras, 1912.

———, *Industrial Evolution in India*, Madras: Hindu Office, 1912.

———, *Agricultural and Industrial Problems in India*, Madras: G.A. Natesan and Co., n.d.

Chen, M., 'A Sectoral Approach to Promoting Women's Work: Lessons from India', *World Development*, vol. 17, no. 7, 1989, pp. 1007–16.

Cho, Myung-Rae, 'Weaving Flexibility: Large-small Firm Relations, Flexibility, and Regional Clusters in South Korea', in *Flexible Specialisation: The Dynamics of Small-scale Industries in the South*, ed. Poul Paderson et al., London: Intermediate Technology Publications, 1994.

Christerson, B. and Richard P. Appelbaum, 'Global and Local Subcontracting: Space, Ethnicity and the Organization of

Apparel Production', *World Development*, vol. 23, no. 8, 1995, pp. 1363–74.

Ciotti, M., '"The Burgeois Woman and the Half-Naked One": Or the Indian Nation's Contradictions Personified', *Modern Asian Studies*, vol. 44, no. 4, July 2010, pp. 785–815.

Crane, Robert I., 'Technical Education and Economic Development in India before World War I', in *Education and Economic Development*, ed. C.A. Andeson, and M.J. Bowman, Chicago: Aldine Publishing Company, 1965, pp. 167–201.

Davidson, D.J. and S. Frickel, 'Understanding Environmental Governance: A Critical Review', *Organ Environ*, vol. 17, no. 4, 2004, pp. 471–92.

Delamont, Sara, 'The Contradiction in Ladies' Education' and 'The Domestic Ideology and Women's Education', in *The Nineteenth Century Women*, ed. Sara Delamont and Lorna Duffin, London: Croom Helm, 1978.

Deutsch, F.M., 'Undoing Gender', *Gender and Society*, vol. 21, no. 1, February 2007, pp. 106–27.

Ehrke, M., 'German Apprenticeship System: A Trade Union View', in *Challenges for Apprenticeship and Vocational Training in the 1990s: German and American Perspectives*, ed. D. Dettke and C. Weil, Germany: Friedrich-Ebert-Stiftung, 1992.

Evans, Peter, 'The State as Problem and Solution: Predation, Embedded Autonomy, and Structural Change', in *The Politics of Economic Adjustment*, ed. Stephan Haggard and Robert R. Kaufman, New Jersey: Princeton University Press, 1992.

Fransman, Martin, 'Conceptualising Technical Changes in the Third World in the 1980s: An Interpretive Survey', *The Journal of Development Studies*, vol. 21, no. 4, July 1985.

Franz. W. and D. Soskice, 'The German Apprenticeship System', *Discussion Paper FS/94-302*, Berlin: Wissenschaftszentrum Berlin fur Sozialforschung, 1994.

Freeman, Bonnie Cook, 'Female Education in Patriarchal Power Systems', in *Education and Colonialism*, ed. Philip G. Altback and Gail P. Kelly, New York: Longman Inc, 1978.

Georg, W. and K. Rutters, and Winifred Schneider-Deters, ed., *Vocational Education and Training, Employment and Labour Relations in the Republic of Korea*, Baden-Baden: Nomos Verlagsgesellschaft, 1991.

Gereffi, G., 'New Realities of Industrial Development in East Asia and Latin America: Global, Regional and National Trends', in *States and Development in the Asian Pacific Rim*, ed. Richard Appelbaum and Jeffrey Henderson, Newbury, Park, CA: Sage, 1992, pp. 85–112.

———, 'The Organisation of Buyer-Driven Global Commodity Chains: How U.S. Retailers Shape Overseas Production Networks', in *Commodity Chains and Global Capitalism*, ed. G. Gereffi and M. Korzeniewicz, Westport: Praeger, 1994, pp. 95–122.

Gerschenkron, A., *Economic Backwardness in Historical Perspective: A Book of Essays*, Cambridge, MA: Belknap Press of Harvard University Press, 1962.

Ghosh, B., 'Early Marriage of Girls in Contemporary Bengal: A Field View', *Social Change*, vol. 41, no. 1, 2001, pp. 41–61.

Gjostein, D.K., 'A Veiled Change Agent: The "Accredited Social Health Activist" in Rural Rajasthan', in *Women, Gender and Everyday Social Transformation in India*, ed. K.B. Nielsen and A. Waldrop, USA and UK: Anthem Press, 2014, pp. 139–56.

Gopal, Meena, 'Disempowered Despite Wage Work: Women Workers in Beedi Industry', *Economic & Political Weekly*, vol. 34, nos. 16 and 17, 17–24 April 1999.

Gould, K.A., D.N. Pellow and A. Schnaiberg, 'Interrogating the Treadmill of Production: Everything You Wanted to Know about the Treadmill, but were Afraid to Ask', Paper prepared for the symposium on environment and the treadmill of production, University of Wisconsin, Madison, 31 October–1 November 2003.

Government of India, *Progress of Education in India*, Quinquennial Review, vols. 1–2, Delhi: Manager of Publications, 1927–32.

———, 'Towards Equality: Report of the Committee on the Status of Women in India', New Delhi: Ministry of Education and Social Welfare, Department of Social Welfare, Government of India, December 1974.

———, *Shramshakti: Report of the National Commission on Self-Employed Women and Women in the Informal Sector*, New Delhi: Department of Women and Child Development, Ministry of Human Resource Development, 1988.

———, *Report of the Time Use Survey*, New Delhi: Ministry of Statistics and Programme Implementation, Central Statistical Organisation, April 2000.

———, *Report of Task Force on Employment Opportunities*, New Delhi: Planning Commission, Government of India, 2001.

———, *Report of the Second National Commission on Labour*, New Delhi: Ministry of Labour, 2002.

———, *Special Group on Targeting Ten Million Employment Opportunities Per Year*, New Delhi: Planning Commission, Government of India, 2002.

———, *Revitalizing Technical Education: Report of the Review Committee on AICTE*, New Delhi: Ministry of Human Resource Development, September 2003.

Government of Tamil Nadu, *Report of the Committees Constituted to Study the Problems and Issues of Unorganised Labour in Tamil Nadu*, Chennai: Office of the Commissioner of Labour, 1998.

Govinda, R. and Y. Josephine, *Para Teachers in India: A Review*, Paris: International Institute of Educational Planning, UNESCO, October 2004.

Grabher, G., 'The Weakness of Strong Ties: The 'Lock-in' of Regional Development in the Ruhr Area', in *The Embedded Firm: On the Socio-Economics of Industrial Networks*, ed. G. Grabher, London: Routledge, 1993.

Granovetter, Mark, 'Economic Action and Social Structure: The Problem of Embeddedness', *American Journal of Sociology*, vol. 91, no. 3, November 1985.

Grigg, H.B., *Scheme for the Development of Scientific and Technical Education in Madras*, Madras: Department of Home Affairs, 1891.

Handmer, J.W. and R.S. Dovers, 'A Typology of Resilience: Rethinking Institutions for Sustainable Development', *Organ Environ*, vol. 9, no. 4, 1996, pp. 482–511.

Hirschman, Albert, *The Strategy of Economic Development*, New Haven, CT: Yale University Press, 1958.

Hirway, I., 'Employment and Unemployment Situation in the 1990s: How Good Are NSS Data?', *Economic & Political Weekly*, vol. 37, no. 21, 25–31 May 2002, pp. 2027–36.

Jacobson, Staffan, 'Government Policy and Performance of the Indian Engineering Industry', *Research Policy*, vol. 20, 1991.

Jenson, Jane, 'Lost in Translation: The Social Investment Perspective and Gender Equality', *Social Politics: International Studies in Gender, State and Society*, vol. 16, no. 4, December 2009, pp. 446–83.

Kalaiyarasan, A., 'A Gender Paradox in Tamil Nadu', *The Hindu*, Chennai, 31 July 2023.

Kelly, Gail Paradise, 'Failures of Androcentric Studies of Women's Education in the Third World', in *For Alma Mater: Theory and Practice in Feminist Scholarship*, ed. Paul A. Treichler, Urbana and Chicago: University of Illinois Press, 1985, pp. 292–306.

Kingdon, G. and V. Sipahimalani-Rao, 'Para-Teachers in India: Status and Impact', *Economic and Political Weekly*, vol. XLV, no. 12, 20 March 2010, pp. 59–67.

Krishnaswami, C., 'Dynamics of Capitalist Labour Process: Knitting Industry in Tamil Nadu', *Economic and Political Weekly*, 17 June 1989, pp. 1359–69.

Kumar, Krishna, *Origins of India's Textbook Culture*, Occasional Papers on History and Society, vol. 47, New Delhi: Nehru Memorial Museum and Library, 1987.

———, *Colonial Citizen as an Educational Ideal*, Occasional Papers on History and Society, second series, no. XIII, New Delhi: Nehru Memorial Museum and Library, November 1988.

———, *Political Agenda of Education: A Study of Colonialist and Nationalist Ideas*, New Delhi: Sage, 1991.

Lazonick, William, 'Organizational Integration in Three Industrial Revolutions', in *Evolving Technology and Market Structure*, ed. Arnold Heerje and Mark Perlman, Ann Arbor: The University of Michigan Press, 1990.

Levy, D.L., 'Environmental Management as Political Sustainability', *Organ Environ*, vol. 10, no. 2, 1997, pp. 126–47.

Mandakini, B., 'History of Hosiery Industry in Tiruppur', MPhil thesis, Department of History, Bharathiar University, Coimbatore, 1984.

Mangan, J.A., ed., 'Introduction', to *Benefits Bestowed? Education and British Imperialism*, Manchester and New York: Manchester University Press, 1988, pp. 1–23.

Mayhew, Arthur and H.R. James, *Education and Politics in India*, New Delhi: Booklovers, 1986.

McCormick, K., 'Japanese Engineers, Lifetime Employment and In-company Training: Continuity and Change in the Management of Engineering Manpower Resources', in *International Comparisons of Vocational Education and Training for Intermediate Skills*, ed. P. Ryan, London: The Falmer Press, 1991, pp. 159–82.

'Memorandum on the Department of Industries in the Madras Presidency', Appendix J, *Indian Industrial Commission, 1916–18*, Main Report, Calcutta, 1918, pp. 402–24.

'Memorandum on the Department of Industries', *Industrial Conference Papers*, Madras: Superintendent, Government Press, 1908.

Millie, Nihila, 'Marginalisation of Women Workers: Leather Tanning Industry in Tamil Nadu', *Economic and Political Weekly*, vol. 34, nos. 16 and 17, 17–24 April 1999.

Morris, Morris D., 'Towards a Reinterpretation of Nineteenth Century Indian Economic History', *The Indian Economic and Social History Review*, vol. V, no. 1, March 1968.

Mosk, C. and Y.-F. Nataka, 'Education and Occupation: An Enquiry into the Relationship between College Specialisation and the Labour Market in Postwar Japan', *Pacific Affairs*, vol. 65, no. 1, Spring 1992, pp. 50–67.

Mowery, David C., 'Industrial Research, 1900–1950', in *The Decline of the British Economy*, B. Elbaum and W. Lazonick, Oxford: Clarendon Press, 1986, pp. 189–222.

Mukherji, Saugata, 'Some Aspects of the Policy on Technical and Industrial Education in India under Colonial Rule from Late Nineteenth Century to Independence', Occasional Paper no. 123, Calcutta: Centre for Studies in Social Sciences, June 1990.

Nadvi, K. and H. Schmitz, 'Industrial Clusters in Less Developed Countries: Review of Experiences and Research Agenda', Discussion Paper no. 399, Sussex: IDS, January 1993.

Nagaraj, R., Introduction to *Industrialization for Employment and Growth in India: Lessons from Small Firm Clusters and Beyond*, ed. R. Nagaraj, New Delhi: Cambridge University Press, 2021, pp. 1–23.

Nathan, Dev et al., *Reverse Subsidies in Global Monopsony Capitalism: Gender, Labour, and Environmental Injustice in Garment Value Chains*, New Delhi: Cambridge University Press, 2022.

Nava, Mica, 'Gender and Education: A Discussion of Two Recent Books', *Feminist Review*, vol. 5, 1980, pp. 69–78.

NCEUS, *Report on Conditions of Work and Promotion of Livelihoods in the Unorganised Sector*, New Dehi: National Commission for Enterprises in the Unorganised Sector, 2007.

———, *The Challenge of Employment in India: An Informal Economy Perspective*, vol. 1, Main Report, New Delhi: National Commission for Enterprises in the Unorganised Sector, April 2009.

Nishimizu, M. and S. Robinson, 'Trade Policies and Productivity Change in Semi-industrialized Countries', Report no. 52, Washington DC: World Bank, Development Research Department, 1983.

'Note on Technical Education in Madras', in *Papers Relating to the Industrial Conference held at Ootacamund in September 1905*, Madras: Superintendent, Government Press, 1908, pp. 7–20.

O'Connor, Julia S., 'The State and Gender Equality: From Patriarchal to Women Friendly State', in *The Oxford Handbook of Transformations of the State*, ed. Stephan Leibfried et al., Oxford: Oxford University Press, 2015, pp. 482–98.

Oram, Alison, '"Embittered, Sexless or Homosexual": Attacks on Spinster Teachers, 1918–39', in *Current Issues in Women's History*, ed. Arima Angerman, London: Routledge, 1989.

Palriwala, R. and N. Neetha, 'Care Arrangements and Bargains: Anganwadi and Paid Domestic Workers in India', *International Labour Review*, vol. 149, no. 4, 2010, pp. 511–27.

Panikkar, K., 'Whither Indian Education', Inaugural Address to the *National Convention Against Communalisation of Education in India*, organised by SAHMAT, New Delhi, 4–6 August 2001.

Parpart, Jane. L., 'Exploring the Transformative Potential of Gender Mainstreaming in International Development Institutions', *Journal of International Development*, vol. 26, no. 3, April 2014, pp. 382–95.

Pillai, Mohanan P., 'Technology Transfer, Adaptation and Assimilation', *Economic and Political Weekly*, vol. XIV, no. 47, 24 November 1979, M 121–6.

Planning Commission, *Report of Task Force on Employment Opportunities*, New Delhi: Planning Commission, 2001.

———, *Special Group on Targeting Ten Million Employment Opportunities per Year*, New Delhi: Planning Commission, 2002.

Preston, Jo Anne, 'Female Aspiration and Male Ideology: Schoolteaching in Nineteenth Century New England', in *Current Issues in Women's History*, ed. Arima Angerman, London: Routledge, 1989, pp. 171–82.

Ravi Kumar, T. and Vijender Sharma, 'Downsizing Higher Education: An Emergent Crisis', *Economic and Political Weekly*, vol. 38, no. 7, 15–21 February 2003, pp. 603–7.

Report of the Indian Industrial Commission, New Delhi: Agricole Publishing Academy, 1916–18; repr., 1980.

Report of the Indian Jails Committee, vol. I, New Delhi: Government of India, 1919–20.

Reports of the MRTP Commission and Orders Thereupon of the Central Government under Sections 21, 22 and 23 of the MRTP Act, 1969, vol. IV, New Delhi: Department of Company Affairs, Ministry of Law, Justice and Company Affairs, Government of India.

Rhee, Yung Whee, 'The Catalyst Model of Development: Lessons from Bangladesh's Success with Garment Exports', *World Development*, vol. 18, no. 2, 1990.

Richery, J.A., ed., *Selections from Educational Records*, part II: 1840–1859, Calcutta: Superintendent Government Printing, India, 1922.

Risman, B.J., 'From Doing to Undoing Gender: Gender as We Know It', *Gender and Society*, vol. 23, no. 1, February 2009, pp. 81–4.

Rodrik, Dani, 'Industrial Policy for the Twenty-First Century', draft Working Paper prepared for UNIDO, September 2004, see https://drodrik.scholar.harvard.edu/files/dani-rodrik/files/industrial-policy-twenty-first-century.pdf.

Sayers, Janet, *Biological Politics: Feminist and Anti-feminist Perspectives*, London and New York: Tavistock, 1982.

Schilling, E.G., 'Occupational Aspects of Higher Education', in *Vocational Education and Training, Employment and Labour Relations in the Republic of Korea*, ed. W. Georg and K. Rutters, Baden-Baden: Nomos Verlagsgesellschaft, 1991.

Schmitz, H., 'Small Firms and Flexible Specialization in Developing Countries', *Labour and Society*, vol. 15, no. 3, 1990.

Shanmugam, S., 'A Plan for Tiruppur Hosiery Town', PhD thesis, School of Architecture, Anna University, Chennai, 1988.

Sharma, Vijender, 'WTO, GATS, and Future of Higher Education', *People's Democracy* (Weekly Organ of the Communist Party of India, Marxist), vol. 26, nos. 6–8, 10, 17 and 24 February 2002.

Sharp, H., ed., *Selections from Educational Records*, part I: 1781–1839, Calcutta: Superintendent Government Printing, India, 1920.

Spinanger, Dean, 'The Impact on Employment and Income of Structural and Technological Changes in the Clothing Industry', in *Industry on the Move*, ed. Gijsbert Van Liemt, Geneva: International Labour Office, 1992.

Still, C., 'Spoiled Brides and the Fear of Education: Honour and Social Mobility among Dalits in South India', *Modern Asian Studies*, vol. 45, no. 5, September 2011, pp. 1119–46.

Streeck, W., 'Institutional Mechanisms and Structural Elements of Vocational Training in Germany and the United States', in in *Challenges for Apprenticeship and Vocational Training in the 1990s: German and American Perspectives*, ed. D. Dettke and C. Weil, Germany: Friedrich-Ebert-Stiftung, 1992.

Subrahmanian, K.K., 'Collaboration Agreements and their Impact on Assimilation and Diffusion of Know-how and Outgo of Resources', in *Science and Technology Policy in the 1980s and Beyond*, ed. M. Gibbons, P. Gummett, and B. Udgonkar, UK: Longman, 1984, pp. 246–69.

Sundaram, K., 'Employment and Poverty in India in the Nineteen Nineties: Further Results from NSS 55th Round Employment-Unemployment Survey, 1999–2000', paper presented at the International Seminar on 'Understanding Socio-Economic Changes through National Surveys', organized by the National Sample Survey Organisation, New Delhi, 12–13 May 2001.

Sundaram, K., 'Employment-Unemployment Situation in the Nineties: Some Results from NSS 55th Round Survey', *Economic & Political Weekly*, vol. 36, no. 11, 17–23 March 2001.

Swaminathan, Padmini, 'Business Houses in South India: A Case Study of the Structure and Functioning of the TVS Group', Working Paper no. 59, Madras: Madras Institute of Development Studies, 1985.

———, 'State Intervention in Industrialization: A Case Study of the Madras Presidency', Working Paper no. 99, Madras: Madras Institute of Development Studies, January 1991.

———, 'Bridging the Technology-Gap: How Farsighted and Dynamics is the Indian Corporate Sector', Report prepared for the Development Research Group, Bombay: Reserve Bank of India, 1993.

———, 'The Interface between Employment and Education: The Need for a Discourse', in *Education and Social Change in South Asia*, ed. Krishna Kumar and Joachim Oesterheld, New Delhi: Orient Longman, 2007.

———, 'Literacy and Levels of Formal Education of the Indian Population: A National Report Card', Zakir Husain Second

Memorial Lecture, New Delhi: National Council of Educational Research and Training, 2009.

———, 'Outside the Realm of Protective Labour Legislation: Saga of Unpaid Labour in India', *Economic and Political Weekly*, vol. XLIV, no. 44, 31 October 2009, pp. 80–7.

———, 'The Formal Creation of Informality, and, therefore, Gender Injustice: Illustrations from India's Social Sector', *The Indian Journal of Labour Economics*, vol. 58, 2015, pp. 23–4.

Swaminathan, Padmini and J. Jeyaranjan, 'The Knitwear Cluster in Tiruppur: An Indian Industrial District in the Making', in *Economy and Organization: Indian Institutions under the Neoliberal Regime*, ed. A Bagchi, New Delhi: Sage, 1999.

Swaminathan, Padmini et al., 'Tamil Nadu's Midday Meal Scheme: Where Assumed Benefits Score Over Hard Data', *Economic and Political Weekly*, vol. 39, no. 44, 30 October 2004, pp. 4811–21.

'Teachers' Panel Opposes Report', *The Tribune*, 2 March 2002.

Teece, David J., 'The Dynamics of Industrial Capitalism: Perspective on Alfred Chandler's Scale and Scope', *Journal of Economic Literature*, vol. XXXI, March 1993.

'Text of Industrial Policy Statement', *Economic Times*, 25 July 1991.

The Business Line, Chennai, 29 May 1997.

The Economic Times, Chennai, 29 May 1997.

The India-Japan Study Committee, 'Problems and Prospects of the Technology Transfer between Japanese and Indian Companies', January 1986.

The Industrial Conference Papers, Madras: Superintendent Government Press, 1908.

Unger, Kurt, 'Industrial Structure, Technical Change and Microeconomic Behaviour in LDCs', in *Technical Change and Economic Theory*, ed. Giovanni Dosi, London and New York: Pinter, 1988.

University of Madras, *History of Higher Education in South India*, vol, II: 1857–1957, Madras: Associated Printers, 1957.

Verma, M.C., 'Review of Skilled Manpower Forecasts and Changes in Occupational Structures of India', *International Journal of Educational Development*, vol. 4, no. 3, 1984, pp. 173–221.

Vijayakumar, C., 'A Study of Hosiery Entrepreneurs at Tiruppur, Tamil Nadu', PhD thesis, Kerala University, Kerala, 1986.

Viswanathan, Gauri, *Masks of Conquest: Literary Study and British Rule in India*, London: Faber and Faber, 1990.

Wagner, K., 'The German Apprenticeship System After Unification', *Discussion Paper FS/98-301*, Berlin: Wissenschaftszentrum Berlin fur Sozialforschung, 1998.

Walby, Sylvia, *Theorizing Patriarchy*, UK: Basil Blackwell, 1990.

Wallace, J., *Technical Education for the Workman in Madras*, Papers Relating to the Industrial Conference held at Ootacamund in September 1905, Chennai: Tamil Nadu Archives, 1908.

West, C. and D.H. Zimmerman, 'Doing Gender', *Gender and Society*, vol. 1, no. 2, 1987, pp. 125–51.

West, C. and S. Fenstermaker, 'Doing Difference', *Gender and Society*, vol. 9, no. 1, February 1995, pp. 8–37.

World Bank, *The East Asian Miracle*, New York: Oxford University Press, 1993.

———, *Skill Development in India: The Vocational Education and Training System*, New Delhi: Human Development Unit, South Asia Region, January 2008.

Index

www.ingramcontent.com/pod-product-compliance
Lightning Source LLC
Chambersburg PA
CBHW051358240926
51852CB00004B/89/J
* 9 7 8 9 3 7 0 3 3 1 4 8 8 *